KONG
modemo

TABLE OF CONTENTS

BASICS 4

MAIN STORY WALKTHROUGH 15

CHAPTER I: 16
- Penthouse 18
- Main Lobby 21
- Parking Garage 23

CHAPTER II: 26
- Club Moderno 28
- Sindri Restaurant 32
- Saving Giovanna: The Helicopter Sequence 34
- Hotel Rooftop 36

CHAPTER III: 38
- Estádio do Galatians 40
- Galatians Media Room 43
- Galatians Souvenir Shop 44
- Concession Hall & Joga TV Booth 46
- Lower Stands & Hall of Fame 47
- Upper Stands 50
- Sniper Post 52
- Stadium Light Tower 54

CHAPTER IV: 56
- Walton's Bar 58
- Parking Lot/Alley 60
- Max's Apartment Building 61
- Hoboken Rooftops 64
- Renovation Project 66
- Chop Shop 67
- Backyard Gauntlet 69

CHAPTER V: 70
- Harbor 72
- Slipway 74
- Storage Warehouse 75
- Container Yard/Repair Garage 77
- Boathouse/Dry Docks 79
- Dry Docks Warehouse & Yard 81
- Pier Walkways 84
- The River Chase 86

CHAPTER VI: 90
- Executive Offices/Boardroom 92
- Cubicles 95
- Atrium/Front Lobby 96
- Escape the Fire 98

CHAPTER VII: 100
- Street Party 102
- O Palacio Bar 104
- Lower Favela 106
- Party Warehouse 108
- Middle Favela 110
- Upper Favela (Molotov Ambush) 114

CHAPTER VIII: 116
- Michelle's Grave 118
- Memorial Wall/Monument Circle 120
- Delaware Mount (Small Rotunda) 122
- The Cupola Sniper (Large Rotunda) 123
- Morgue 125
- Chapel 126

CHAPTER IX: 128
- The Police Raid 130

CHAPTER X: 136
- Bus Junk Yard/Fuel Depot 138
- Paint Bay 141
- Repair Bay 142
- Wash Bay 143
- Offices 144
- The Bus Escape 146

CHAPTER XI: 148
- Aboard the Yacht 150
- Operations Building 156
- Visitor Center 158

CHAPTER XII: 160
- Basement 162
- Hotel: 2nd Floor 163
- Hotel: 3rd Floor 166
- Hotel: 4th Floor 167
- Demolition Areas: 4th & 5th Floors 169
- Hotel Roof 172

CHAPTER XIII: 174
- Holding Cells 176
- Precinct Parking Lot 178
- Gym/Cafeteria Atrium 180
- 2nd Floor Offices 183
- 3rd Floor 185
- Top Floors 188

CHAPTER XIV: 190
- Baggage Processing Area 192
- Back Offices/Employee Lockers/ Public Restrooms 194
- Departure Concourse 196
- Tram Station/Control Office 198
- Tram Battle 200
- Fábricas Branco Hangar 202
- Runway 204

CLUES 206

GOLDEN GUNS 222

UNLOCKABLES 238

MULTIPLAYER 252

GAME CONTOLS

You can choose from four different controller configurations in *Max Payne 3*. The difference between Type 1 and 2 is the button swapping of ShootDodge™ and Cover. Type 3 is similar to Type 1—the only difference is the button swapping of Bullet Time® and Reload. Type 4 is radically different from the default Type 1 configuration. But if you'd rather sprint by pressing down the left control stick, this is the setting for you.

XBOX BUTTON	PS3 BUTTON	COMMAND
Left Trigger	L2	Shoulder Aim
LB	L1	(Hold) Weapon Wheel / (Tap) Select Grenade in multiplayer
Right Trigger	R2	Fire / Melee (when close)
RB	R1	ShootDodge
Y	TRIANGLE	Interact / Melee or Taunt in multiplayer
B	CIRCLE	Reload / Loot in multiplayer
A	X	(Hold) Sprint / Vault / Climb / (Double Tap) Roll
X	SQUARE	Enter and Cover
START	START	Pause
BACK	SELECT	Weapon Attachments / Leaderboard in multiplayer
RIGHT STICK	RIGHT STICK	Camera
RIGHT STICK BUTTON	R3	Bullet Time / Trigger Burst in multiplayer
LEFT STICK	LEFT STICK	Move
LEFT STICK BUTTON	L3	(Tap) Crouch / (Hold) Prone
UP	UP	Use Painkillers
RIGHT	RIGHT	Move reticle over right shoulder
DOWN	DOWN	Quick Turn 180 degrees / Drop Weapon (when Weapon Wheel displayed)
LEFT	LEFT	Move reticle over left shoulder

DIFFICULTY

The difficulty level and the type of target-locking options are presented at the start of the game. The normal setting for most beginners should be medium difficulty with a Soft Lock. Playing with these settings (or harder) unlocks Achievements (or Trophies) and Arcade levels. With any difficulty settings below medium, or when choosing the medium setting with the easier target locking option, Hard Lock cancels most Achievement or Trophy and Arcade level unlocking opportunities.

EASY

All targeting assist options are on by default. Health and Bullet Time rewards come easier in this mode.

MEDIUM

Soft targeting assistance with balanced health and Bullet Time rewards.

HARD

No targeting assistance with low health and Bullet Time rewards.

HARDCORE

Realistic damage with no targeting assistance.

OLD SCHOOL

Brutal difficulty without Last Man Standing available to save you.

HARD LOCK VS SOFT LOCK

When aiming with Hard Lock selected, the reticle is strongly guided to focus on enemies. With Soft Lock, the reticle is slightly guided toward enemies. If you use either of these settings, Soft Lock is recommended. It's easier to pull the reticle away from enemies to target other enemies or explosive objects. You also have the choice to use no target lock whatsoever. This option is for a more advanced player and offers more realism and more difficulty.

HEALTH

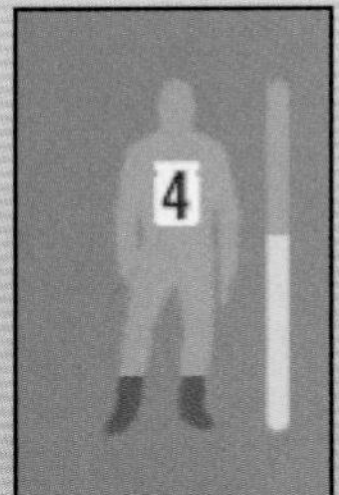

Max's health is illustrated with a human-shaped gauge located in the bottom right corner of the screen. When you take damage, the gauge fills red. Needless to say, a full red gauge equals death. You can recover health by collecting and using painkillers. These bottles are found scattered throughout the levels. The number of painkillers in a level is dependent on the difficulty setting. The number of painkillers you've collected appears in the middle of your health gauge. You can carry no more than nine painkillers at a time.

In multiplayer mode, health regenerates over time—you can also use painkillers that you've looted from dead opponents, but these are less available in multiplayer. So if you are taking a lot of damage, get to cover and stay there for a bit until you are healthy enough to get back to the battle.

LAST MAN STANDING

Last Man Standing uses one painkiller. If you have at least one painkiller bottle remaining, and you are fatally wounded, you have one last chance to redeem yourself. In the time allotted, if you can put a bullet through the opponent who fired the fatal shot, then you will return to your feet and recover some lost health. This feature is not available in multiplayer mode.

BULLET TIME

The Bullet Time gauge is the horizontal bar beside your health gauge in the lower right corner of the screen. This fills as enemies shoot at you or when you get kills. Well- placed body shots, headshots, and stringing kills together all earn you extra Bullet Time.

Bullet Time slows down time in the world around you, which allows you to move, walk, run, aim and fire slightly faster than everyone else, giving you an edge on your enemies. You can literally dodge bullets.

HEADSHOT TIME

One of the most effective uses of Bullet Time is to gain headshot after headshot while facing down a large group of enemies.

BULLET TIME CONSERVATION

Once Bullet Time is engaged you should only use the amount you need. As soon as your targets have been hit, turn Bullet Time off by pressing the Bullet Time button a second time. This allows you to conserve Bullet Time so you have some in reserve for your next confrontation.

BULLET TIME BONUSES

TARGETED BODY PART	% OF EXTRA BULLET TIME
Stomach	25%
Upper Arm	25%
Thigh	50%
Forearm	75%
Chest	100%
Hand	100%
Shin	150%
Groin	200%
Foot	200%
Headshot	200%

BULLET TIME BONUS WEAPON TIPS

SHOTGUNS give you the most Bullet Time, but it is difficult to earn multipliers with these weapons because there are more missed shots.

PISTOLS give you the second most amount of Bullet Time and are easiest weapons to keep multiplier bonuses going because of their accuracy.

RIFLES give a bit more than SMGs because they kill enemies faster.

SMGs give you the least amount of overall Bullet Time because of game balancing, since you can hit targets with more bullets in a shorter amount of time.

You can get up to a 4X multiplier on Bullet Time rewards if you can maintain an accuracy streak. For every four bullets that make contact without missing, you move into a higher multiplier bonus.

SHOOTDODGE

ShootDodge allows Bullet Time effects even if you do not have Bullet Time stored up. Activating ShootDodge in conjunction with any move direction on the left control stick initiates a spectacular ShootDodge maneuver. Max leaps into the air in the desired direction (forward, back, left or right, and points in-between). While in slow motion, you can target enemies anywhere around you. The direction you initially leaped from doesn't matter.

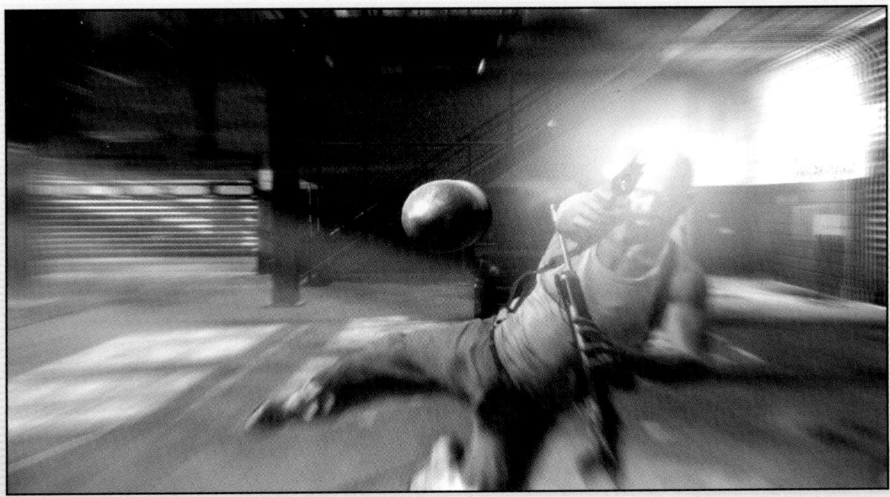

You always land in the prone position after using ShootDodge. From the prone position, you can continue shooting until you decide to get back to your feet. Simply press the left control stick in the direction you want to move again. ShootDodge is great for getting over or through objects that you could not otherwise overcome. Try using ShootDodge through glass and over counters, furniture, or short barriers.

PEEK-A-BOO, YOU'RE DEAD.

One of the most effective uses of ShootDodge is to defeat entrenched foes or enemies around corners.

FINAL KILL CAMERA

A spectacular, slow-motion camera with a unique angle automatically engages when you kill the final enemy. This lets you know that you've cleared the area. You can slow down the camera by holding the sprint button, or you can speed up the visual by holding the fire button. You can also use multiple combinations of each before the animation ends.

COVER

Using cover protects you from almost any attack unless a grenade is used or the enemy gets an advantageous angle on you. Press the cover button to hug walls and to crouch behind low objects such as furniture, vehicles, crates, etc. To leave cover, press the cover button again or tilt the left control stick in the opposite direction of cover to detach and return to free movement once again.

If you stay in cover too long, enemies use flanking and charge tactics to force you out of hiding. This often works to your advantage if you can pick them off as they advance.

Shooting from around or over cover is one of the best and safest offensive tactics. Pressing the Fire button without using the shoulder aim button is called "blind fire." You can slightly aim your shot, but it's not as accurate as an aimed shot around cover. However, it is very useful in certain situations.

MELEE

Pressing the Fire button in close quarters combat executes one of many brutal melee attacks. The move ends with a choice to pull the trigger and execute the enemy you subdued. If you are out of weapons or ammo during the melee maneuver, Max steals his foe's weapon and uses it instead.

WEAPON WHEEL

Max can only carry one two-handed weapon and two single-handed weapons at a time. You will notice he has two shoulder holsters. This allows him to manage this many weapons at once. He can holster two single-handed weapons while firing a two-handed weapon. He can double-wield (dual-wield) any single-handed weapons, but any equipped two-handed weapon will be dropped when this happens.

To customize which weapons are held and which will be double-wielded, you must first understand the weapon wheel. Press and hold the LB (Xbox 360) or L1 (PlayStation 3) to access the weapon wheel display. Use the right control stick to highlight the weapon you wish to use. You can choose single-handed weapons (mostly handguns or submachine guns), which are positioned to the left and right. Heavy, two-handed weapons are positioned at the bottom of the wheel.

DOUBLE-WIELDING WEAPONS

To double-wield weapons, display the weapon wheel, press up on the right control stick and select the top double weapon graphic. This graphic illustrates the weapons you are holding in your left and right hand. If you wish to mix or match the weapons you double-wield—and you have the means to do so—then you must first wield a single left-hand or right-hand weapon and swap that out for the weapon of your choice from the available ones lying around.

Once you have two of the weapons you desire for each hand, you can then use the weapon wheel to select the double- wielding option to hold both choice weapons at once. Again, you will drop any heavy weapon you carry when you hold two smaller weapons at once. To carry the maximum number of desired weapons, avoid double-wielding or be prepared to pick up your dropped heavy weapon before you leave an area.

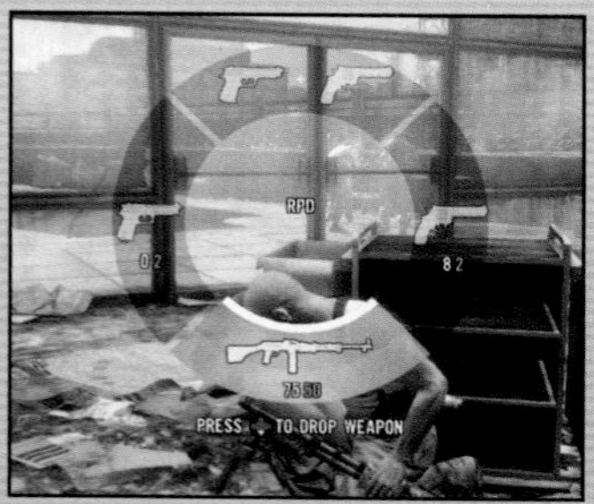

HEALTH: PAINKILLERS

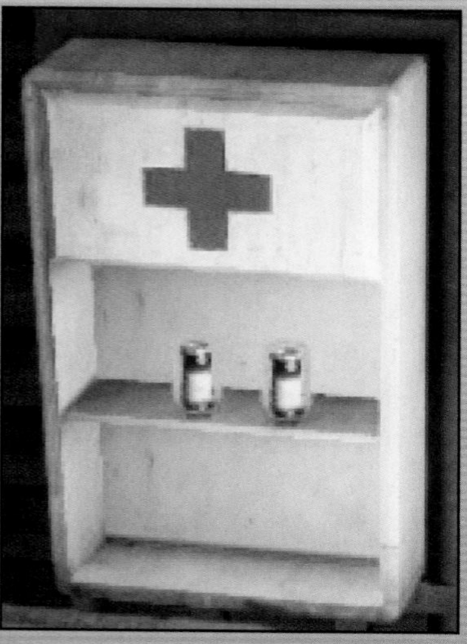

In the single player Story mode, Max only recovers from wounds using painkillers. Painkillers are health power-ups found throughout the various environments of the game. It could take as many as three painkiller bottles to fully recover from severe damage. In multiplayer mode, your character recovers lost health over time or by using looted painkillers.

AMMO

Walk, run, or roll over dropped weapons similar to the ones you carry to collect ammo. You can also steal weapons from enemies by performing a melee move when you are out of weapons or ammo. Take advantage of tactical weapon bags that max out your ammo capacity. Reload your current weapons when collecting ammo to make sure you pick up the maximum amount possible.

ARCADE MODE

Arcade mode levels are unlocked by beating them in the single player Story mode. You can play individual single player levels or play the entire story in Arcade mode. In Arcade mode, you have to race against the clock to complete levels quickly while causing as much destruction as possible along the way. You can unlock multiplayer avatar clothing by achieving platinum and you can gain multiplayer XP by reaching high scores in Arcade mode (Score Attack, New York Minute, and Hardcore New York Minute).

SCORE ATTACK

Score Attack levels are unlocked by beating them in Story mode. These levels can be played in any order. You can also collect and Clues in this mode, but not Golden Gun parts. Here you accumulate the highest score possible by achieving certain types of shots and kills. Points are awarded at various levels for body shots, headshots, kills, explosion kills, melee, and vehicle destruction. Multipliers are added to reward consecutive hits and using various game mechanics like ShootDodge, Bullet Time, or prone firing.

POINTS

LOCATION	POINTS
Body	10 points each
Head	100 points each
Kills	50 points each
Explosion kills	200 points each
Melee	100 points each
Vehicle destruction	250 points each

MULTIPLIERS

COMBOS	POINTS
3 Hits in a row	x 2
5 Hits in a row	x 3
10 Hits in a row	x 5
20 Hits in a row	x 10

Dying or missing ends these multipliers.

NEGATIVE POINTS

MOVE	NEGATIVE POINTS
You Get Shot	-10 points each
Take a painkiller	-10 points each
Enter Last Man Standing	-10 points
Kill innocent	-10 points each

FINAL KILL CAM BONUS

During the final kill cam, you'll notice that you can continue shooting the opponent even after he is dead. Doing this in Score Attack increases your hit points and can give you the largest multiplier in the session!

SCORE ATTACK CHAPTER II

LEVEL COMPLETE!

15881

NEW YORK MINUTE

New York Minute levels are unlocked by completing Story Mode once. This is a run-and-gun game against the clock. There are no targeting locks in this mode. Each level starts with only one minute on the clock. Take out enemies to add time: kills are worth 5 seconds, headshots are worth 6 seconds, melee kills are worth 10 seconds. Bullet Time will slow down the timer, and the timer pauses during cut scenes and final kill cams. If the clock reaches zero, you're dead.

If you choose to restart, you continue from the beginning of the level with the clock reset to 1 minute. An additional timer tracks how long each level takes. If you fail a checkpoint, the additional time it takes you to get to the checkpoint is added to your total playthrough clock.

The playthrough time is displayed at the end of the level. If the time is your best for that level, you receive a cup. After all level cups are displayed, the game displays a New York Minute leaderboard. This is similar to the Arcade Score mode's leaderboard but it shows times instead of scores. The end report shows your current level playthrough time, but the game only saves your shortest time.

HARDCORE NEW YORK MINUTE

Unlocked after playing through the Story mode, Hardcore New York Minute is the same as New York Minute but when you fail, instead of starting back at the beginning of the level, you start back at the beginning of the game. Yeah, that's hardcore.

COLLECTIBLES

There are two categories of Collectibles in the game: Golden Gun Parts and Clues. The collection of these items is tracked on the Pause menu, as well as the Scene Select screen. Clues are also displayed on the Arcade chapters section. Golden Guns cannot be collected in Arcade mode. This section of the guide provides descriptions of the Collectibles. For quick reference, be sure to check out our Collectibles section at the end of this guide. We've also included the Collectibles throughout the Story mode walkthrough so you can find them during normal progression through the game.

GOLDEN GUN PARTS

Every weapon in the game has a golden counterpart. Not only do Golden Guns look cool, but they also have enhanced stats that make them even more lethal. There are three Golden Gun Parts to find for each gun to make one complete Golden Gun. When all three parts have been collected, the next time you wield that weapon it will be gold. You can turn off the gold effect in the Options menu. Completing Golden Guns also unlocks Gold Tint in the multiplayer Arsenal Attachments menu.

CLUES

Clues are various items, bloodstains, pictures, scenes, and other oddities that catch Max's detective eye. These Clues hold secrets that unravel the mystery in the story. When they are examined, Max comments on what he sees so you too can be privy to his assessments. You can find Clues in both Story and Arcade mode.

WEAPONS

SINGLE-HANDED WEAPONS

.38 REVOLVER

This standard handgun packs quite a wallop at close range. It's a very damaging weapon but the tradeoff is a lesser rate of fire and lesser accuracy, ammo capacity, and range.

Rate of Fire	0.30
Damage	49
Clip Size	6
Effective Range	40
Impact Force	250
Reload Speed	Slow
Caliber	.38

PT92

This is a well-rounded semi-automatic with good range, accuracy, fire rate, and stopping power.

Rate of Fire	0.139
Damage	45
Clip Size	15
Effective Range	50
Impact Force	250
Reload Speed	Fast
Caliber	9mm

M10

The M10 is a compact machine pistol. Its lackluster power and accuracy are forgivable when you experience its increased fire rate and ammo capacity.

Rate of Fire	0.092
Damage	45
Clip Size	30
Effective Range	40
Impact Force	45
Reload Speed	Fast
Caliber	.45

1911

The M1911 pistol is a single-action, semi-auto handgun with .45 caliber rounds. It's very similar to the PT92 in stats, but has slightly better range.

Rate of Fire	0.1323
Damage	60
Clip Size	8
Effective Range	60
Impact Force	260
Reload Speed	Fast
Caliber	.45

M972

While the M10 has it beat on fire rate and accuracy, the M972 submachine gun has better range.

Rate of Fire	0.110
Damage	26
Clip Size	32
Effective Range	50
Impact Force	75
Reload Speed	Fast
Caliber	9mm

608 BULL

The 608 is a double-action revolver that chambers the .357 round. The long barrel gives it incredible accuracy and range. The rate of fire is low but is a good compromise for the other powerful features. Its damage is only surpassed by the .38 Revolver, but the Bull exceeds the .38 in all other stat categories.

Rate of Fire	0.22
Damage	85
Clip Size	8
Effective Range	50
Impact Force	320
Reload Speed	Slow
Caliber	.357

AUTO 9MM

Using this fully auto pistol is like firing a little submachine gun. The rate of fire is equal to the M10 but its damage, accuracy, ammo capacity, and range are not as strong. However, it is extremely exhilarating to operate this weapon.

Rate of Fire	0.095
Damage	25
Clip Size	33
Effective Range	50
Impact Force	60
Caliber	9mm

SAWN-OFF

The Sawn-Off shotgun is extremely powerful when used as a close-range weapon—as it's intended to be used. The damage is only matched by the M500, sniper rifles, and the RPG. Holster the weapon when fighting mid to long range.

Rate of Fire	0.7
Damage	101
Clip Size	2
Range	30
Impact Force	100
Reload Speed	Slow

MICRO 9MM

The Micro 9mm has the fastest rate of fire of all the weapons in the game. However, in comparison to other submachine guns, it has slightly less damage, range, and ammo capacity. It's more accurate than the M972 submachine gun, but the Micro 9mm is also much heavier.

Rate of Fire	0.086
Damage	25
Clip Size	32
Effective Range	45
Impact Force	60
Reload Speed	Fast
Caliber	9mm

DE .50

The DE is a gas-operated semi-automatic pistol with .50 caliber rounds that has an effective range of 50 meters. This is the third most powerful handgun in the arsenal and, like the 608 Bull, it has the best range. The DE's accuracy is fair and ammo capacity is average.

Rate of Fire	0.145
Damage	105
Clip Size	7
Effective Range	50
Impact Force	325
Reload Speed	Fast
Caliber	.50

TWO-HANDED WEAPONS

AK-47

The AK-47 is a great weapon due to its ease of use and durability. Stat-wise, it's a little heavy. But it's a well-balanced weapon and a great choice to take into any battle.

Rate of Fire	0.132
Damage	38
Clip Size	30
Range	65
Impact Force	70
Reload Speed	Med
Caliber	7.62

MINI-30

The Mini-30 is a well-rounded weapon that exceeds all of the AK-47's stats except for ammo capacity. It also is a little lighter than the AK, so you can move faster or pack more items in multiplayer mode.

Rate of Fire	0.101
Damage	60
Clip Size	10
Effective Range	150
Impact Force	275
Reload Speed	Med
Caliber	7.62

MPK

This assault rifle was designed for short-range battle by special services. The weapon offers more damage and accuracy in a lighter frame than the AK-47 but carries fewer rounds. This weapon has a superb rate of fire.

Rate of Fire	0.118
Damage	35
Clip Size	20
Effective Range	60
Impact Force	45
Reload Speed	Med
Caliber	9mm

M500

The M500 riot shotgun packs a monster punch at close range. The sniper rifle and the RPG are the only weapons that match its damage capabilities, neither of which are close- range weapons. It is more damaging but lighter than the M4 Super 90. The compromise is slightly less accuracy and slower rate of fire.

Rate of Fire	0.53
Damage	51
Clip Size	6
Range	30
Impact Force	110
Reload Speed	Slow
Caliber	12ga

SAF .40

This submachine has a magazine that holds 30 9mm rounds. It's very similar to the MPK, however the SAF .40 does slightly more damage, has a much faster rate of fire, and holds more ammo per magazine.

Rate of Fire	0.99
Damage	40
Clip Size	32
Effective Range	50
Impact Force	50
Reload Speed	Med
Caliber	5.56

M4 SUPER 90

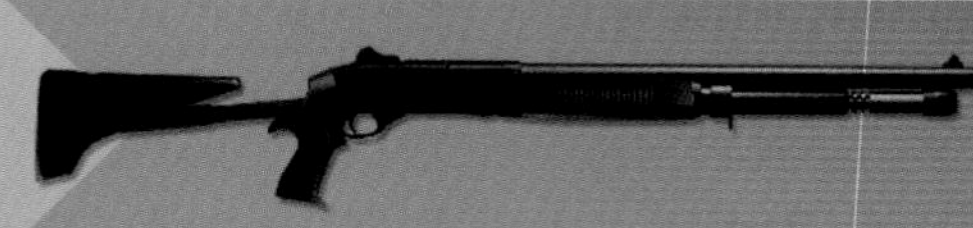

This combat shotgun weighs more than the M500, but the Super 90 makes up for it in all other stats except damage. It has better range, rate of fire, and ammo capacity—all slightly better than the M500.

Rate of Fire	0.4
Damage	60
Clip Size	7
Range	40
Impact Force	110
Reload Speed	Slow
Caliber	12ga

FAL

The FAL is a fine weapon, but the Mini-30 is lighter in weight and has it beat in most other stats. The FAL would be the next best choice.

Rate of Fire	0.142
Damage	52
Clip Size	20
Range	60
Impact Force	90
Reload Speed	Med
Caliber	7.62

RPD

The RPD is extremely damaging, but it will slow you down. It's one of the three heaviest weapons available. However, this is one of the best mid-range weapons in the game.

Rate of Fire	0.135
Damage	90
Clip Size	75
Range	50
Impact Force	250
Reload Speed	Med
Caliber	7.62

MD-97L

This weapon is a compact, semi-automatic version of the FAL. Where the FAL has a little more damage, this weapon offers a faster rate of fire and is more accurate. The range is equal to the FAL, but the MD-97L is a little heavier to tote.

Rate of Fire	0.101
Damage	30
Clip Size	30
Effective Range	75
Impact Force	95
Reload Speed	Med
Caliber	5.56

SPAS-15

This pump-action/semi-automatic combat shotgun is fed by a detachable box magazine holding 12-gauge 70mm rounds. It's heavier than the Super 90 and does less damage. Still, it more than makes up for this with a higher rate of fire. In the time it takes an opponent to fire one shot with the Super 90, you can deal twice the damage with two quick shots from the SPAS-15.

Rate of Fire	0.28
Damage	65
Clip Size	8
Range	40
Impact Force	115
Reload Speed	Med
Caliber	12ga

SUPER SPORT

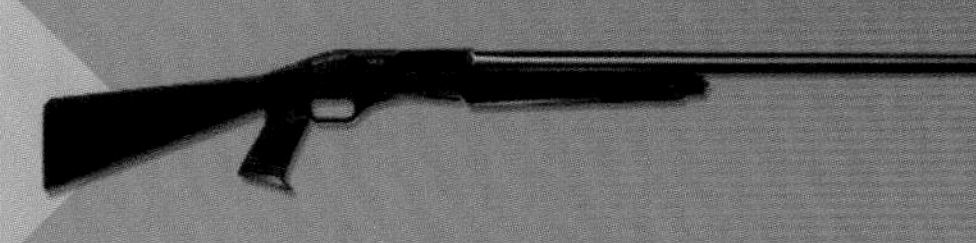

This semi-auto rifle does a lot of damage with a fast rate of fire. This is a very lethal weapon. It beats the SPAS-15 in all stats except damage, making it a great alternative shotgun choice.

Rate of Fire	0.19
Damage	40
Clip Size	5
Range	50
Impact Force	110
Reload Speed	Med
Caliber	12ga

G6 COMMANDO

This a well-rounded assault rifle has better damage and accuracy than the equally weighted MD-97L and holds more rounds per magazine. It is also more accurate and has a faster rate of fire than the slightly lighter and more damaging FAL. The AK-47, another mid-range weapon, has slightly more damage, but the Commando beats it in all other stats.

Rate of Fire	0.118
Damage	34
Clip Size	30
Range	75
Impact Force	50
Reload Speed	Med
Caliber	5.56

M82A1

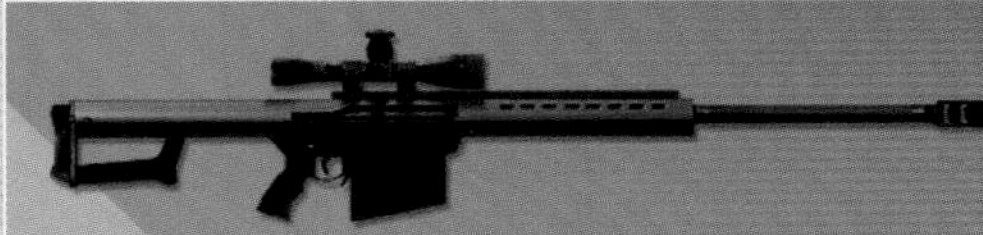

The M82A1 is a recoil-operated, semi-automatic anti-materiel scoped sniper rifle. The effective range of this weapon is 7.450 yards. No other weapon in the game matches its damage, accuracy, and range. This is not a run-and-gun weapon: make sure to have a decent mid-range weapon with you for protection as well.

Rate of Fire	0.45
Damage	120
Clip Size	10
Range	400
Impact Force	350
Reload Speed	Med
Caliber	.50

LMG .30

This recoil-operated light machine gun (LMG) is an extremely heavy weapon and will slow your movement considerably. It is one of the three heaviest weapons available. Use cover tactics to play it safe. Use cover while hunting for enemies and use this weapon to tear your opponents to shreds. It has outstanding ammo capacity, range, fire rate, and accuracy.

Rate of Fire	0.115
Damage	60
Clip Size	100
Range	50
Impact Force	220
Reload Speed	Med
Caliber	7.62

ROTARY GRENADE LAUNCHER

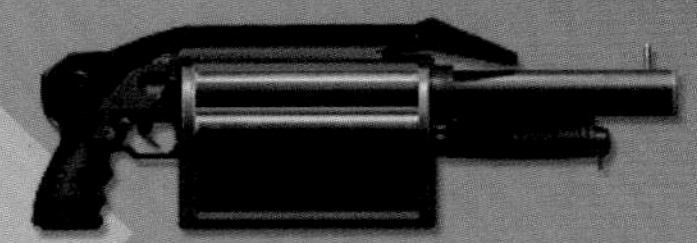

This shoulder-fired grenade launcher is not a very practical weapon and requires time to aim your shots in the correct arch to hit targets. It is a mid-range and very damaging weapon and is useful for targets that huddle together (i.e. enemies defending a base). Be sure to have a good mid-range option in your holster and use this for special occasions. This is one of the three heaviest weapons available and does a considerable amount of damage.

Rate of Fire	0.8
Damage	500 (to 5 meters)
Clip Size	6
Range	20
Impact Force	400
Reload Speed	Slow

LAW

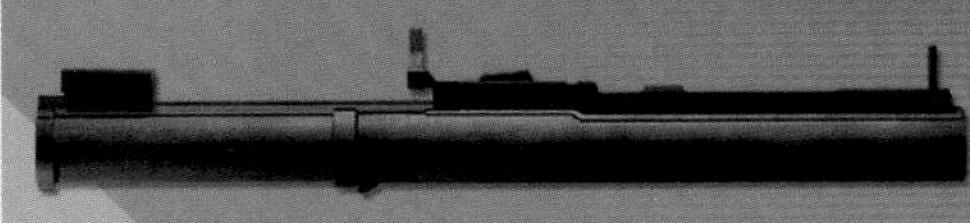

The Light Anti-Tank Weapon is a portable single shot anti-tank system that fires 66 mm unguided rockets. The warhead can inflict serious damage to heavy duty vehicles and structures.

Rate of Fire	0 (single shot)
Damage	500 (to 8 meters)
Clip Size	1
Range	100
Impact Force	500
Reload Speed	N/A

MAIN STORY
WALK THROUGH

It is always a good idea to let artists introduce their own stories. The following introduction is from Rockstar's internal design synopsis for *Max Payne 3*. Like Max himself, it tells you exactly what you need to know:

Max Payne 3 is the third game in a series of level-based, third-person shooters with a strong focus on firearm combat, detailed environments, and strong neo-noir storytelling. Several years have passed since the events of *Max Payne 2*, and Max Payne is no longer a Detective for the NYPD. A violent series of events has led Max out of the country to a job with an old acquaintance, this time as a private security contractor for a wealthy family in São Paulo, Brazil.

Of course, it doesn't take long for trouble to find Max once again, as the dangers of living in São Paulo soon threaten his employer and the few good people he has left in his life. The world of Max Payne has always been one steeped in both classic and neo-noir elements—stark contrasts, doomed characters, internal monologues, use of shadows, and a dark storyline. Max will soon find that every character he meets has hidden motives... and that trust is hard to come by.

The game spans 14 chapters that take the player through the seedy back alleys of Hoboken, New Jersey, all the way to the gleaming high-rises and sprawling favelas of São Paulo.

PROLOGUE: *THE END*

As our story begins, Max Payne—blood-spattered, head shaved—steps out of an aircraft hangar onto the tarmac of the São Paulo airport. Not far away lies a burned, mutilated man in a Special Operations uniform, sprawled on the ground. Max stands over the man... and points his pistol at the victim's head.

I SOMETHING ROTTEN IN THE AIR

SÃO PAULO, BRAZIL
10:05 PM, THURSDAY

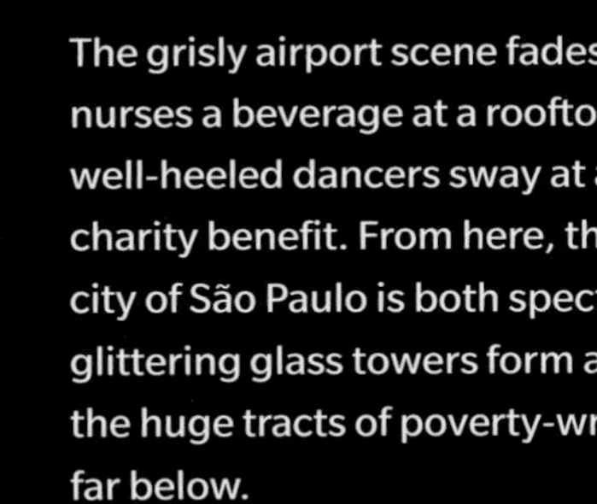

The grisly airport scene fades to a flashback: Max nurses a beverage at a rooftop railing. Behind him, well-heeled dancers sway at a gala cocktail party, a charity benefit. From here, the view of the sprawling city of São Paulo is both spectacular and ironic—glittering glass towers form a ring of affluence around the huge tracts of poverty-wracked *favelas* (slums) far below.

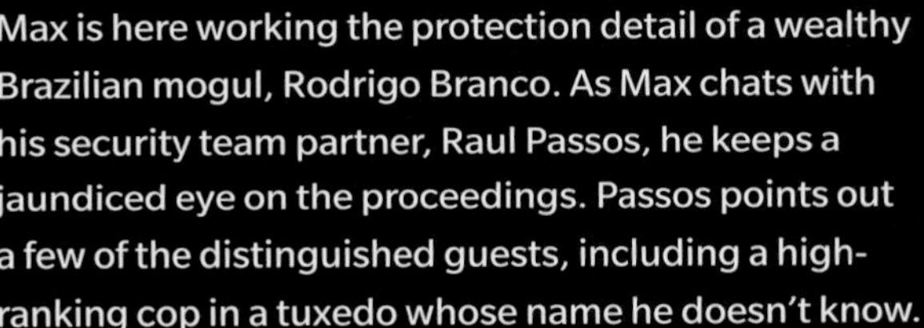

Max is here working the protection detail of a wealthy Brazilian mogul, Rodrigo Branco. As Max chats with his security team partner, Raul Passos, he keeps a jaundiced eye on the proceedings. Passos points out a few of the distinguished guests, including a high-ranking cop in a tuxedo whose name he doesn't know.

Max watches the Branco family work the crowd: Rodrigo, his wife Fabiana, and his youngest brother Marcelo. Soon the middle brother arrives: Victor Branco, a local politician—"smoother than an oil slick on an iceberg."

Suddenly, a crew of masked men brandishing weapons bursts from the elevator. The gunmen are members of Comando Sombra, one of the well-armed and highly organized drug gangs that rule the city's favelas. The group's specialties also include kidnapping high-profile targets.

Some of the thugs drag Fabiana Branco through a doorway while others haul her husband Rodrigo into the elevator. Max and Passos hustle to the nearby stairs; Max descends one flight, to the penthouse level, while Passos continues further downstairs.

YOUR FIRST OBJECTIVE:
RESCUE THE ABDUCTED BRANCOS.

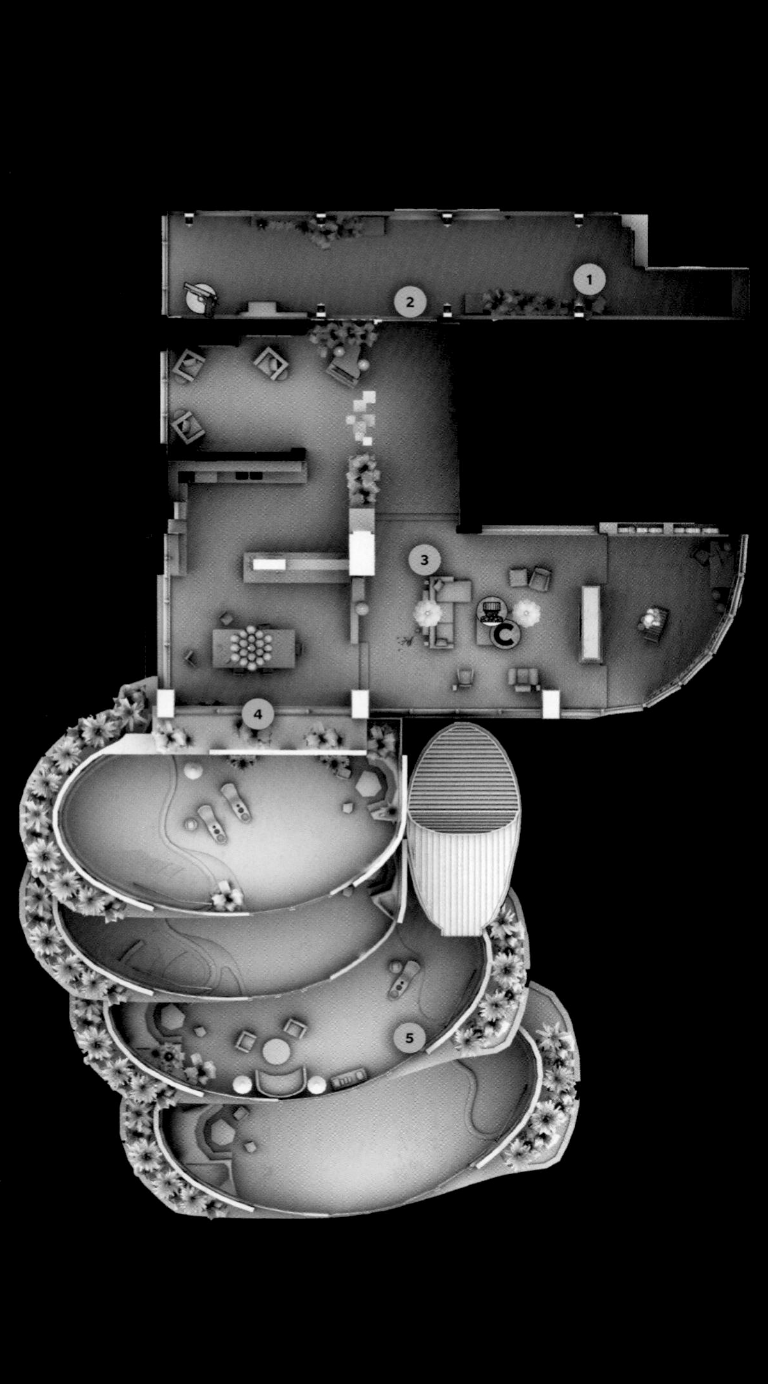

NEW WEAPONS

PT92 PISTOL

PAINKILLERS

MISSION

CLEAR THE ENTRY HALL.

Max exits the stairwell into the hallway **(1)** outside the tower's penthouse condominium. As the cinematic ends, a masked gunman steps through the condo's front doors **(2)** and points his weapon. You start the mission armed with a standard, Brazilian-made PT92 9mm pistol and four bottles of painkillers. You have a limited amount of time to find Fabiana before a kidnapper kills her.

The first confrontation begins with an onscreen prompt to enter Bullet Time. This lets you test out the brutally efficient feature and gives you a slow-motion chance to practice firing a weapon. Press the button indicated onscreen to enter Bullet Time then move the targeting reticule over the gunman up the hall. When the dot turns red, fire!

GET AHEAD

In Bullet Time, aim for your target's head if you can. Headshots give you one-shot kills and also fill up your Bullet Time meter faster.

After the first foe falls, move forward but keep your gun trained on the condo's doorway ahead on the left—two more masked gunmen emerge from it. Here you're prompted to use the controls indicated onscreen to make a classic Max Payne "ShootDodge" move—a nice defensive dive that also lets you target your foes in Bullet Time. As you dive, nail the thug on the right then quickly swivel your aim to the left to dispatch the third gunman in the doorway.

GOLDEN GUNS

Find the Golden PT92 pistol part at the end of the hall outside the condo. Look for Golden Gun Parts throughout the game. They combine to create upgraded weapons with enhanced stats. You can turn off Golden Gun effects in the Options Menu. For a full listing of all Golden Gun part locations, see our special section about Golden Gun parts elsewhere in this book.

PART 1/3 GOLDEN PT92

This Golden Gun Part is located at the end of the first hallway where you begin the game. After completing the ShootDodge training, head to the forward left corner of the hallway and pick up the first gun part.

As your targets fall, you can see more masked men inside the condo. Before you hunt them down, grab the weapons dropped by your first three victims. Pick up one PT92 pistol to give you two in your arsenal and then just walk over the other dropped pistols to acquire any extra ammo available. Open your weapon wheel and select the "dual wield" option with your pistols if you prefer. Then move through the condo's entry doors.

CLEAR THE GREAT ROOM.

Hurry! You don't have much time until one of the kidnappers executes Fabiana. Enter the condo's plush, high-ceilinged great room. Two more Comando Sombra gangsters lurk up ahead—one in plain sight down the entry hall and the other one just around the corner to the left by the liquor cabinet. Pick off the first gunman, then drive past the corner **(3)** in ShootDodge mode and swiveling to pick off the second thug.

Grab the painkillers on the coffee tables in the living room. If you clear the condo quickly, you have time to go back to the grand piano by the entry door. Approach its keys and press the button indicated onscreen to see what happens.

PAYNEFUL PIANO

Walk Max up to any piano you find in the game. Just approach the keys and press the Play button indicated onscreen to hear him fiddle with the theme song. (He's not too good at first but improves with practice.)

CELEBRITY MAGAZINE

This magazine is next to a bottle of painkillers located on the large coffee table in the middle of the penthouse living room.

FINAL KILL CAMERA

If one of your gunshots triggers a slow-motion vignette of the target's demise, then you just eliminated the last enemy in the current room or area. Known as the "final kill camera," this dramatic cinematic effect usually lets you relax and explore the current area before moving on. In some cases, the last kill triggers a cutscene that moves the story forward.

Remember that you're on a timer; don't dally long in the condo. Hustle through the glass double-doors **(4)** behind the dining table that lead out onto the balcony to trigger a cutscene.

Max spots a kidnapper holding Fabiana at gunpoint near the hot tub two balconies below **(5)**. Passos and other security personnel burst onto the scene, and a tense standoff ensues. For Max, the only way down is a nearby section of sloped roof. As he vaults over the railing and begins sliding down, the action automatically slows to Bullet Time.

PICK OFF THE KIDNAPPER IN BULLET TIME.

Target the kidnapper precisely—if you hit Fabiana, you fail the mission. If you successfully nail the kidnapper, your kill shot triggers a "final kill camera" sequence. Watch as your bullet pierces the gunman in slow motion.

As Marcelo Branco and the tuxedoed police official try to calm Fabiana, Max leaves in search of his boss, Rodrigo Branco. He rides the elevator down to the building's main floor lobby.

MISSION

CLEAR THE MAIN LOBBY

When the elevator arrives **(6)**, step out to see a masked gunman lurking near the lobby reception desk **(7)**. If you miss him, he runs off to the left... but be careful chasing him down because more gang members deploy as you round the desk. One is armed with an M500 shotgun. Here the game graciously introduces cover tactics.

You are lead to duck behind one of the big columns **(8)** near the reception desk where you are prompted to press your controller's Enter Cover button (indicated onscreen); Max "sticks" to the column. Now you can slide to either side of the column then hold in your Shoulder Aim control (also indicated onscreen) to lean out and target enemies.

Keep popping in and out of cover until you shoot down the last gunman in the lobby. Once again, the slow-motion "final kill camera" lets you know you've taken out the area's last gunman. Be sure to scoop up the new shotgun weapon dropped by your slain foe.

NEW WEAPONS

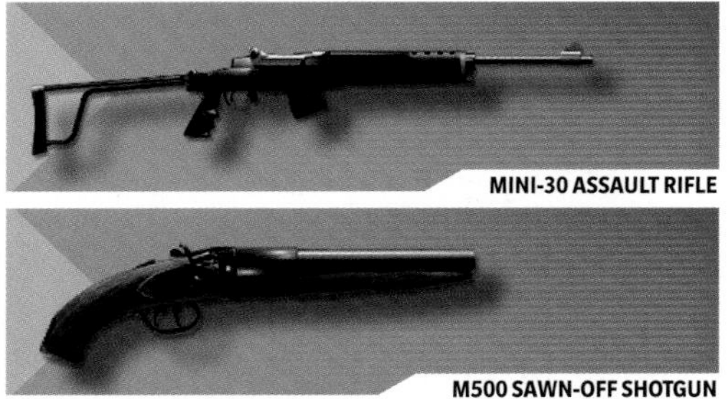

MINI-30 ASSAULT RIFLE

M500 SAWN-OFF SHOTGUN

PAINKILLERS

GET THE RED OUT

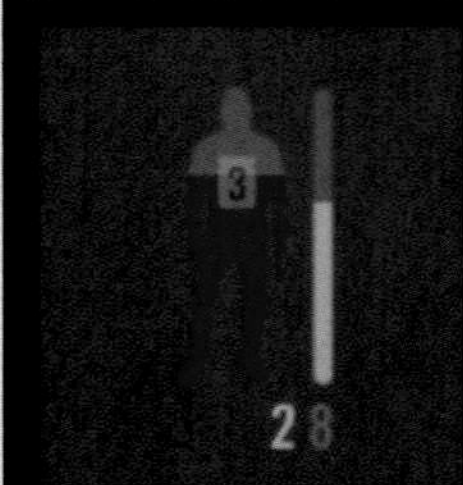

Keep a sharp eye on your health meter! Remember that as the meter fills up with red, it means Max's health is fading. Pop some painkillers if the damage level is high.

PART 2/3 GOLDEN PT92

After "Cover" training and the enemies are dead, turn around and retrieve this weapon part from in front of the first wooden planter in the room.

Continue through the lobby around the corner to the back hallway. Carefully approach the exit door **(9)** with your weapon aimed at it. When you get close, another masked killer pops out firing a Mini-30 assault rifle. Take him out fast! Then follow the tutorial on how you can manipulate the bullet cam when you trigger the final kill camera—you can slow it down even more, or even continue firing.

Go through the doorway past the restrooms—the doors marked "Masculino" (men) and "Feminino" (women)—and enter the stairwell **(10)**. Descend the stairs to "Nivel B" (Level B) and go through the doors into the parking garage beyond.

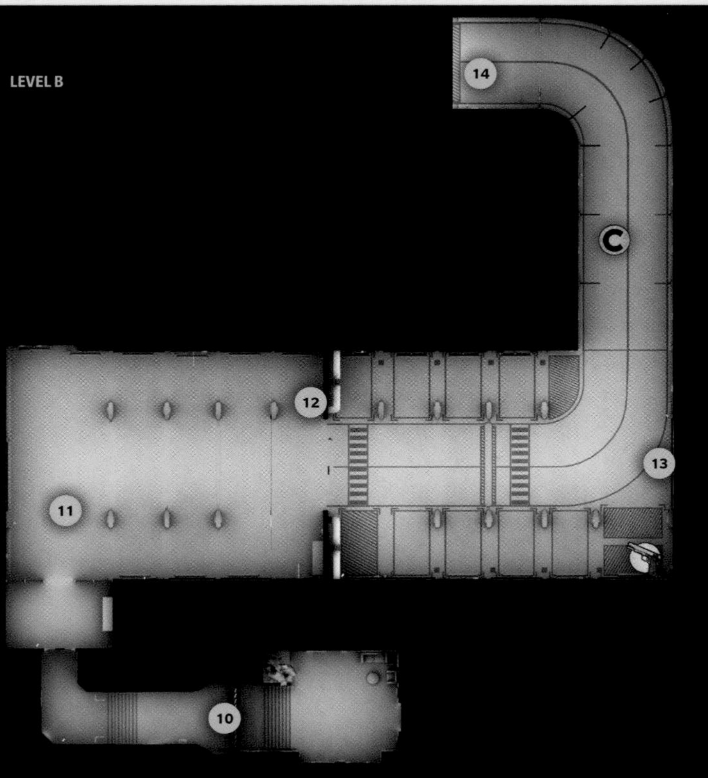

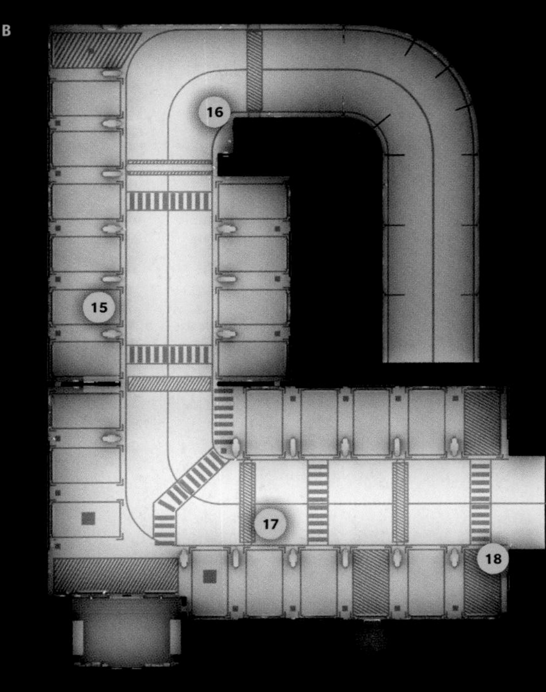

NEW WEAPONS

NONE

MISSION

CLEAR NIVEL B.

As Max enters the garage **(11)**, he spots seven masked kidnappers pushing Rodrigo across the B garage, proclaiming (in Portuguese) their intent to kill him. The group moves toward a ramp that leads up to the Nivel A (Level A) lot. When they spot Max, four of the gunmen spread out across the B lot to attack while the others drag Rodrigo ahead, dropping a heavy garage gate behind them to cut off pursuit.

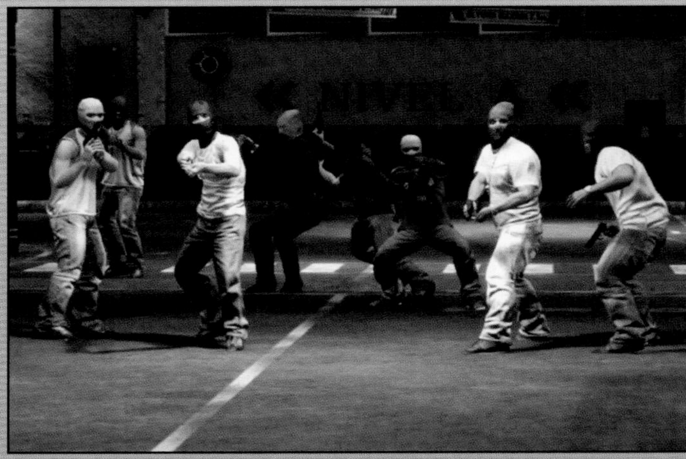

Use the garage pillars for cover as you pick off the four masked gunmen near the gate. When you drop the fourth thug and the final kill camera indicates the area is clear, pick up the guns and ammo from fallen kidnappers.

Approach the control panel with the flashing button **(12)** to the left of the gate and press the "Open garage door" button indicated onscreen. When the door opens, move across the lot toward the "Nivel A" sign **(13)** on the far wall and turn left to see an ascending ramp.

PART 3/3 GOLDEN PT92

This part is located in the parking lot in parking bay B01. This is just through the roll-up door that is triggered with a switch and in the forward right corner.

FIND A CLUE.

Start climbing the ramp to the top parking level, Nivel A. On the way up, approach the dropped photo on the ground and press the "Examine picture" button indicated onscreen: Rodrigo and Fabiana Branco are circled in red, clearly the two targets of this brazen raid. Continue up the ramp to the top **(14)**.

DROPPED PHOTO

The photo is on the sloped drive between parking garage levels.

CLEAR OUT NIVEL A.

You encounter four more masked gunmen in the A lot, but they have their backs to you as they exchange gunfire through the next gate with policemen in khaki uniforms. Take cover against the left wall **(15)** and concentrate on the right side of the garage first. If you have plenty of ammo, try shooting the white automobile parked in the A12 stall **(16)** until it explodes. The blast eliminates enemy shooters posted nearby.

CAR BOMBS

Every car in *Max Payne 3* is a potential explosive device. You can shoot vehicles until they detonate and take out nearby foes. It takes a number of bullets, so don't shoot cars if your ammo is low. Shooting the gas tank area or the engine through the grill will destroy the vehicle quickly.

Two more gunmen are posted on the garage's left side, just around the corner. Sprint across to the far side for cover or, better yet, try a diving ShootDodge attack. Start from the left wall, run forward a few steps, then dive to the right and swivel left to nail the two kidnappers in the A16 and A13 parking stalls.

When the last hostile gunman falls in slow motion, you trigger another short cutscene: Max punches the gate button and it slides open as the remaining kidnappers hustle Rodrigo into their getaway van **(17)**. Max reaches the van just as it roars away, tires squealing.

SHOOT OUT THE VAN'S TIRE.

In Bullet Time, shoot the van's left rear tire. With its tire punctured, the big Rucker van slaloms out of control and slams into a wall **(18)**. Three gunmen leap out for one last desperate attack.

RESCUE RODRIGO.

Here's another situation where Bullet Time is effective. Trigger it immediately while the gunmen are still near the van, which makes it easier to target all three before your meter runs out. When the last Comando Sombra gangster falls in slow motion, approach the rear of the van, where you hear Rodrigo pounding on the door. This triggers a quick cutscene: Rodrigo bursts wildly from the back doors, knocking Max to the pavement.

Here's a tricky moment: While Max is still prone on the ground, aim across the garage just past Rodrigo at the last two members of the kidnapping gang, who attack with intent to kill your boss. Rodrigo, blinded by the hood, nearly staggers into your line of fire, so be careful not to hit him.

When the last thug falls, watch the chapter-ending cutscene—Max guides Rodrigo to safety as uniformed special operations units, São Paulo's feared UFE (Unidade de Forças Especiais), suddenly rush in to secure the area. This leads to an interesting interaction. The tuxedoed cop from the party—his name is Becker—joins the commandos and engages in a sharp exchange with a detective and a pair of police regulars who've arrived on the scene too. Sounds like a turf dispute...

NOTHING BUT THE SECOND BEST

FLYING OVER SÃO PAULO
11:33 PM, THE FOLLOWING TUESDAY

Not even armed kidnapping attempts can stand in the way of the Branco family's high life. Just five days later Max accompanies Fabiana, her sister Giovanna, and Marcelo as they travel via helicopter (piloted by Passos) to a posh new nightclub called Club Moderno in downtown São Paulo.

En route, Max learns that Giovanna is the "good sister"—she works in a favela outreach program. The sisters have a warm relationship, and Giovanna seems to bring out the best in her sibling. But she speaks of strange incidents in the favela: dead bodies showing up in the neighborhood and people simply disappearing. Upon arrival, Max escorts the trio into the club while Passos stays behind with the chopper.

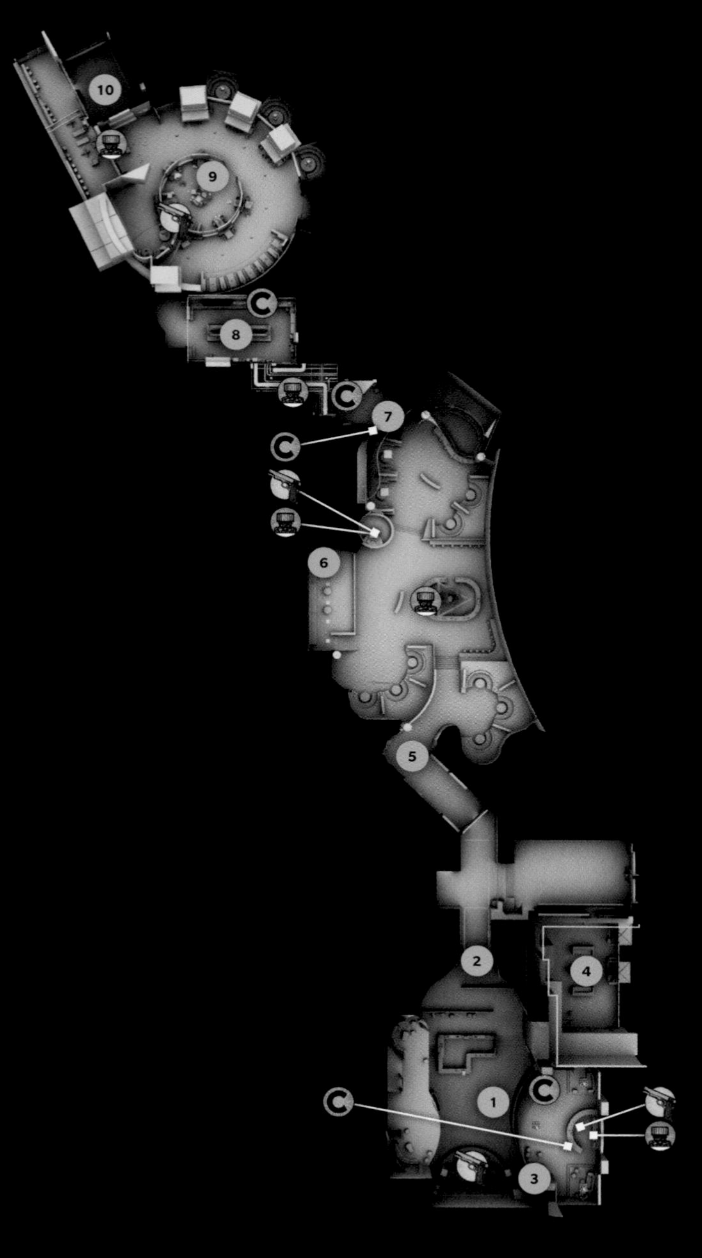

NEW WEAPONS

MISSION

CLEAR THE ENTRY HALL.

Club Moderno is a security contractor's nightmare. An artillery assault of house music underscores the disorienting chaos of strobe lights, sycophants, gyrating bodies, and close contact with characters of unknown intent. As the sisters hit the dance floor, Max follows Marcelo up a blue-lit staircase to the VIP Lounge, which overlooks the dancers though plate glass walls.

Unaware that another Comando Sombra hit team is moving into position in the club, Max drinks and listens to Marcelo whine about the preferential treatment given to Claudio, the local soccer star. Suddenly, on their leader's signal, gunmen seize control of the club and haul away both sisters, Fabiana and Giovanna.

CLEAR THE MAIN FLOOR.

Back up in the VIP Lounge, a gangster guns down the unfortunate Claudio. When the thug turns his attention to Marcelo, Max body-slams the intruder right through the window glass. As the two fall toward the dance floor below **(1)**, control returns to you in Bullet Time as the cutscene transitions seamlessly into live gameplay.

Do not waste this *awesome* slow-motion dive. As Max falls, target and eliminate the four Comando Sobra members descending the staircase to the right of the main floor bar plus two more gangsters on the club's upper tier. Nail as many in the head as possible before you reach the floor.

MICRO 9MM

Don't miss the Micro 9mm machine pistols dropped by fallen gunmen in Club Moderno. These compact but deadly rapid-fire weapons are classic components in any Max Payne arsenal. Dual-wield a pair for extra punch!

When Bullet Time ends, pick off any remaining gunmen as you quickly work your way up the stairs to the club's top tier. If you take too long to reach the doors, you must restart the level at the window-breaking shooting challenge. Reaching the door **(2)** triggers a quick cutscene: the doors are chained shut. Max cracks them open enough to see the kidnappers dragging off Fabiana and Giovanna. One of them, clearly the gang leader, orders a crew of gunmen to cover the escape.

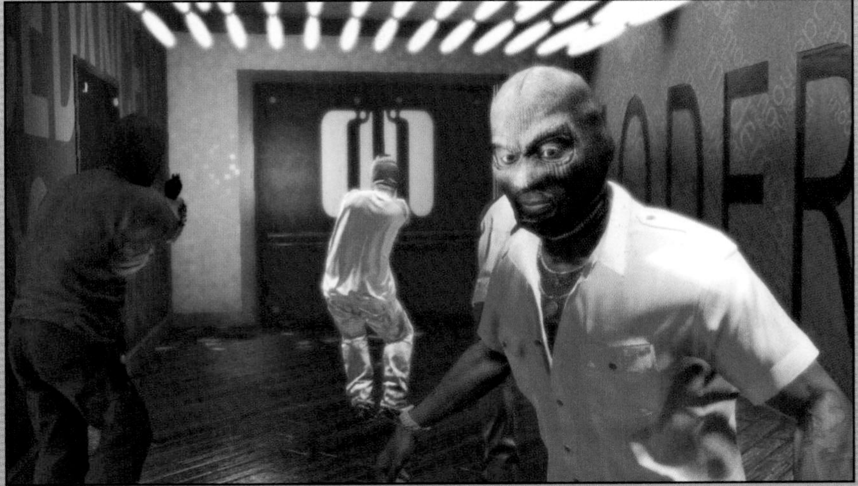

CLEAR THE VIP LOUNGE.

Now you must find a way to circumvent the chained exit. As you cross the dance floor toward the blue-lit staircase **(3)** winding up to the VIP Lounge, pick off the gunmen sent to halt your pursuit. Start with the one gunman on the floor near the VIP stairs. Shoot the others right through the curved glass as they scurry across the VIP Lounge above. Run upstairs into the lounge and nail any shooters you missed from below.

PART 1/3 GOLDEN .38 REVOLVER

You can find this weapon part on the floor of the DJ booth at the end of the dance floor. Get it on your way back to the VIP lounge after checking the barricaded exit.

BAR SNACKS

Don't miss the painkillers on the counter behind the bar in Club Moderno's VIP Lounge!

NIGHTCLUB FLYER

On the front edge of the bar, in the VIP room.

PART 1/3 GOLDEN MINI-30

Find this weapon part on the floor behind the VIP bar.

DEAD SOCCER STAR

On the floor of the VIP room found dead when you return to the VIP room. Claudio lies dead in front of the seat that Marcelo desired.

FIGHT YOUR WAY OUT OF CLUB MODERNO.

Cross the VIP Lounge and climb the winding staircase with red velvet walls to a lovely outdoor sitting area **(4)** overlooking the São Paulo skyline. Unfortunately, Comando Sombra gangsters are ruining the ambience by slaughtering the patrons here.

Clear the two gunmen out of the area then approach the transparent wall on the far end. Watch as the two gunmen you saw behind the glass run into the room through the next doorway. Gun them down before they know what hits them.

Turn left and enter the purple-lit corridor. When you reach the door, you trigger a cutscene: Max pushes open the door to find panicked patrons fleeing. The wounded Club Moderno owner reports that the killers went into the established next door—the Orbitas Lounge. Max enters to see two gangsters viciously execute one of the lounge patrons.

ORBITAS LOUNGE

SECURE THE ORBITAS LOUNGE.

You have no cover in this entry so sprint straight ahead then trigger a ShootDodge maneuver just as you reach the end of the lighted corridor **(5)**. Swivel to the right as you dive and pick off the gunmen immediately available as targets.

Sprint into the lounge and roll into cover in the booth immediately on the right. Nail the gunman in the circular bar up ahead then run toward it. Use Bullet Time to shoot the gangsters around the corner to the left...or if your meter is empty, just vault over the circular bar into the bartender area to cut off enemy shooting angles. Be sure to grab the green bottle of painkillers on the bar's interior shelf.

More gunmen lurk at the far end of the lounge and in the DJ balcony on the left. But instead of making a frontal assault, climb the nearby stairs up to the balcony and continue to the door **(6)** with the sign that reads "Somente Empregados" (Employees Only). This leads to the DJ's platform. Here you find a dead DJ, more painkillers, and a protected shooting perch for picking off the rest of the Comando Sombra gunmen across the lounge near the exit.

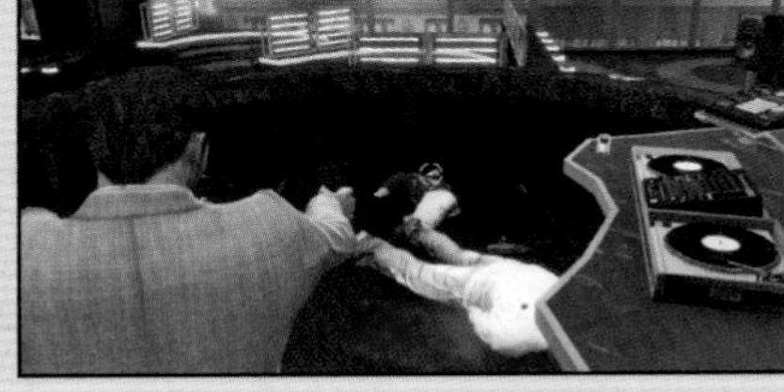

PART 2/3 GOLDEN .38 REVOLVER

You can find this weapon part on the floor in the DJ booth in the Orbitas Lounge. Follow the stairs on the left side of the room across a balcony seating area through a door and into the DJ booth/balcony. You can also find painkillers here.

When the Orbitas Lounge is finally secured, exit via the doors **(7)** by the auxiliary bar. Move past the restrooms and the big wall mural to doors marked with a "No Authorized Persons" sign. (The words are in Portuguese but the illustrated message is clear.) You enter a locker and storage area for a restaurant.

TORN DRESS PIECE

After leaving the lounge area you enter a bathroom hallway. Fabiana's *Torn Fabric* piece is on the edge of the counter near the kitchen doorway.

EX-COP

In the same bathroom area where you find Fabiana's *Torn Dress Piece*, push open the middle bathroom stall door on the left to meet retired police officer, Anders Detling from North Dakota.

MISSION

CLEAR THE KITCHEN.

Move across the locker room only slowing down to grab the two painkillers from inside the open locker. With your weapon aimed, push through the swinging door into the kitchen **(8)**. Gun down the two kidnappers at the far end. Unless you rush the exit door, two more thugs storm the kitchen through the restaurant door. Remain covered and gun them down. You can find and read the newspaper on the counter next to the sinks; Max comments on Victor Branco's political fortunes.

PORTUGUESE NEWSPAPER

This clue is found on the edge of the counter on the right side of the kitchen. Clear the room then read the paper about Victor Branco's political career.

Exit the kitchen via the far doors. This triggers a cutscene—Max pushes into the restaurant dining area. He sees Giovanna and Fabiana pushed through an exit door. The gang leader then directs more gunmen back into the dining room to cut off Max's pursuit.

CLEAR THE DINING ROOM.

Eliminate the Comando Sombra gunmen scattered across the dining room **(9)**. Start with shooting the gunman through the window on the left and continue round the restaurant using Bullet Time and headshots to conserve ammo; you could run low if you're not careful. When the last one falls, find the painkillers on the reception desk under the "Sindri Restaurante" sign and exit via its front door just to the right. Max steps into the lobby **(10)** just in time to see Fabiana and Giovanna ferried upward in a glass elevator to the helicopter pad on the roof.

GLOWING GOODNESS

Remember: Always watch for the glow of health-restoring painkiller bottles wherever you go.

PART 2/3 GOLDEN MINI-30

Find this weapon part in the circular restaurant seating area. The weapon is on the counter between booth seats.

Turn left and step toward the open doors to trigger a cutscene: Max steps onto an outdoor patio. He shoots through a plexiglass railing and climbs out onto a narrow ledge. Then he inches sideways until he can jump across to a motorized window-washer platform on the building.

WATCH THE COPTER SETUP.

The cinematic continues: Max uses the controls to raise the platform. He spots a helicopter carrying masked men—the gang's getaway craft, no doubt. Shooters from the copter sever the platform's cable, but Max scrambles onto the roof before the rig falls. Then he makes a death-defying leap to the landing strut of the Branco's helicopter piloted by Passos; Marcelo pulls Max aboard.

Max spots the Comando Sombra loading their two captives into the gang chopper on the helipad below. When the kidnappers are distracted by the Branco chopper, Giovanna manages to break free—the CS chopper departs with only Fabiana and a few captors aboard. Giovanna remains on the helipad surrounded by multiple gunmen. Max grabs a Mini-30 assault rifle with a laser sight and takes up a position at the open hatch.

MISSION

1: HELIPAD

Pick off the five gunmen on the helipad. Hurry! If you wait too long, they execute Giovanna. This can be a good place to use Bullet Time, but it's not necessary if your aim is good and you shoot fast. When the last thug drops, a cutscene plays: Giovanna takes off running down the ramp from the helipad. As she sprints across the rooftop structures, armed gangsters give chase.

2: STAIRS

After the cutscene, immediately target the lone gunman chasing Giovanna down the staircase. She trips on a coil of cable at the bottom, so nail the pursuer fast or he'll kill her. Halting the gunman triggers a quick cutscene: Giovanna scrambles to her feet and flees across the roof.

3: ROOFTOP

More Comando Sombra gang members join the pursuit of Giovanna, who hides behind a rooftop air conditioning unit (circled in our shot). A few gunmen emerge from behind the pipes on the left, while others descend the stairs or pop out from doorways. Gun them all down!

4: DOORWAY

Once you clear the roof, Giovanna stumbles off to the left and Passos pilots the helicopter along beside her. Suddenly she encounters a gunman who pops out of a doorway. Shoot him quickly to trigger another cutscene: as Giovanna hustles down the nearby stairs, a second masked killer (wearing a skulls t-shirt) emerges from the same door and pursues her onto a catwalk.

5: "THE LETTER RUN"

The catwalk runs in front of a series of huge red letters that spell "BOITATÁ," the Brazilian bank that owns the building. Pick off the pursuer behind Giovanna then watch for gunmen who pop out from ramps behind the second, fourth and last letter (from right to left) along the run.

If you nail the first two gunmen, Giovanna can run to the end of the catwalk, where one more thug waits around the corner of the "B" (the leftmost letter). Shoot him to trigger another quick scene: Giovanna finds a way through the towering letters onto the hotel rooftop behind them, but more gang members fall into pursuit. Passos swings the chopper around to follow her.

6: ROOFTOP EXIT

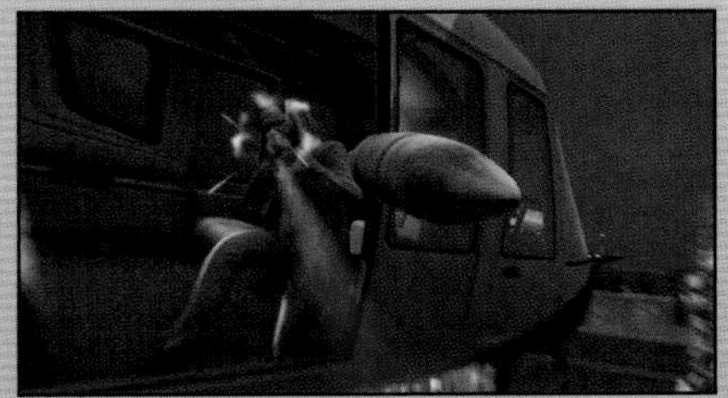

Shoot the multiple gunmen who weave through the antennae and air conditioning units, converging on the locked exit door where Giovanna is trapped. When all of these attackers are down, watch as the exit door bursts open and one last killer emerges from inside. Nail him quickly! His demise triggers the final kill camera—the roof is clear.

Watch as Giovanna enters the building and Passos pilots the copter back toward the hotel's rooftop helipad. Comando Sombra gangsters guard the pad, including one armed with a handheld RPG launcher. Passos swerves to miss a shot rocket. Max falls out of the craft's cabin but catches and dangles from a landing strut.

7: HELIPAD

When control returns, target the first rocket launched toward your helicopter and destroy it. Then quickly target the launcher-toting enemy standing on the "H" of the helipad. Once he's down, clear the helipad of the other gunmen to trigger a cutscene: a second RPG launcher arrives on the roof and fires!

QUICK SHOT

If you can hit the first RPG rocket quickly, before it leaves the helipad area, its explosion takes out all the bad guys on the pad.

Pick off the first rocket and nail the thug with the second RPG launcher. Be ready to pick off additional rockets if you don't hit the launcher guy right away. Don't let *any* rocket hit your copter or your craft will go down. Once you eliminate the RPG threat and the helipad is clear, Passos lowers the copter and Max drops onto the pad.

HOTEL ROOFTOP

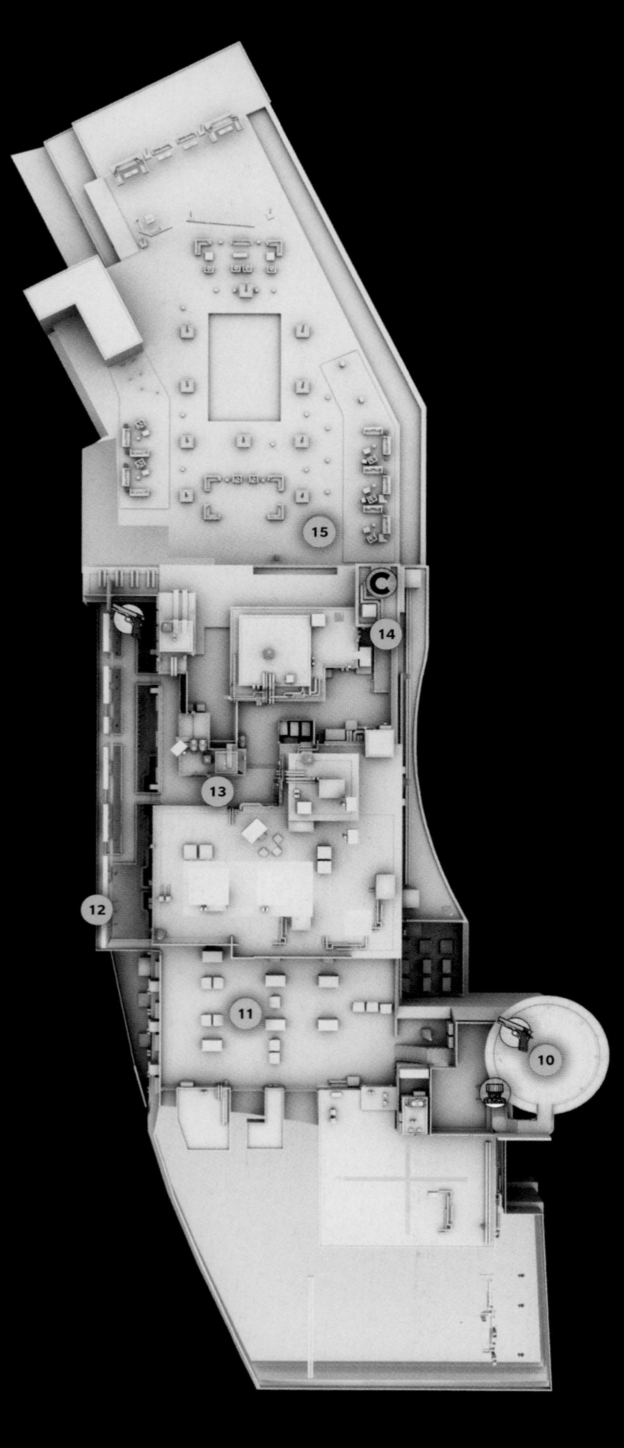

MISSION

FIND GIOVANNA.

Now you must retrace Giovanna's route across the rooftops and past the hotel letters. Collect dropped weapons from the helipad **(10)**. Move down the nearby staircase, grabbing the two painkillers in the first aid shelf near the bottom of the stairs. Watch for Comando Sombra gunmen rushing through the doorway in the vine-covered trellis that lines the roof.

PART 3/3 GOLDEN MINI-30
This gun part is in the glass-enclosed lounge beneath the helipad. Head down the stairs from the helipad, then turn right and push through the unlocked double doors. It's on the floor to the left, near a couch.

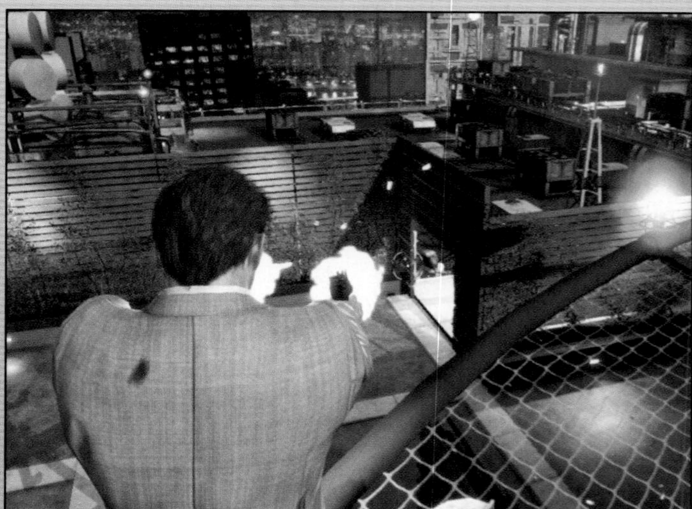

Take cover at this doorway: a big crew of thugs is posted on the rooftop beyond **(11)**. Try a ShootDodge dive down the stairs then roll into cover behind the cement barrier at the bottom right. You could also position yourself on the edge of the helipad before you descend and take out the first two gunmen on the rooftop and then rush for the cement barrier at the bottom of the second set of stairs to continue the fight with the rooftop gunmen. Fight your way across the roof, watching for gunmen who pop up suddenly from behind the fan housings.

NEW WEAPONS

NONE

PAINKILLERS

Once you clear the roof, proceed onto the catwalk that runs along the big hotel lettering **(12)**. Note that the catwalk runs both in front of and behind the letters. Fight down this walkway to the passage **(13)** behind the letters. Work your way across the next rooftop area killing the remaining six gunmen until you reach the same exit door **(14)** that Giovanna used earlier.

PART 3/3 GOLDEN .38 REVOLVER

The final part to the revolver is on the neon BOITATA billboard catwalk. It's at the far end where Giovanna reached, but turned around while you were sniping from the helicopter.

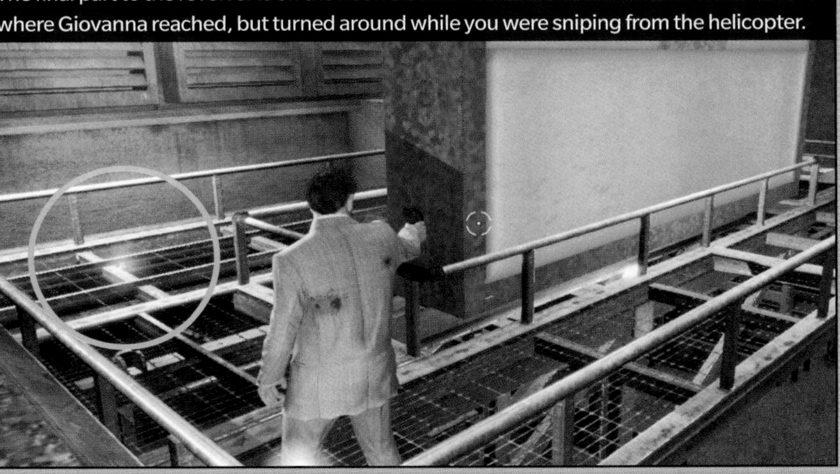

GIOVANNA'S NECKLACE

This clue is located on the third landing as you head down the stairwell leading away from the rooftop.

Go through the door and descend the staircase. Reaching the door at the bottom triggers a series of cutscenes that end this chapter and begin the next one. First, Max emerges onto an open patio **(15)** with a swimming pool. There he finds Giovanna alive and hiding. Passos and Marcelo join them, and Max observes an interesting intimacy between his partner and the boss's sister-in-law.

THE AFTERMATH

The scene shifts: a short time later, Max broods alone in his apartment...giving us another sordid glimpse into what his life has become.

III JUST ANOTHER DAY AT THE OFFICE

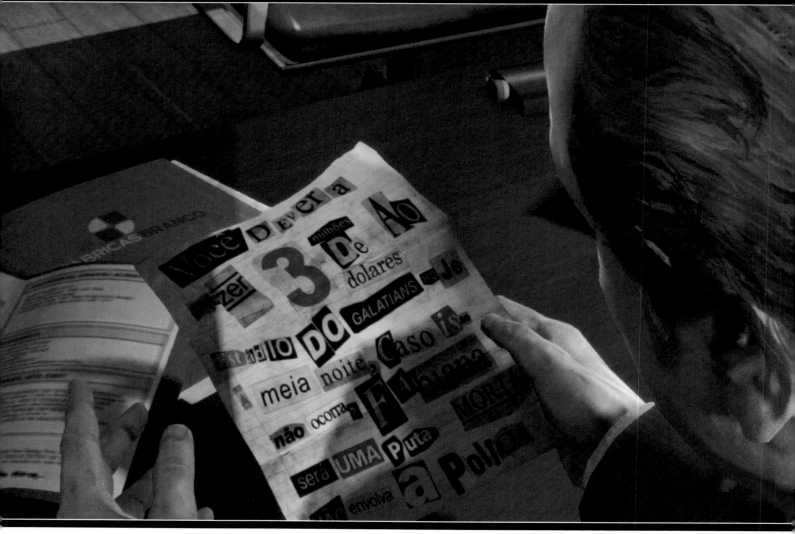

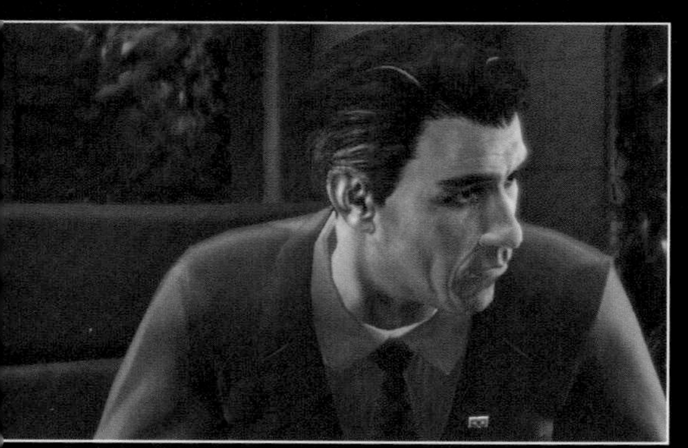

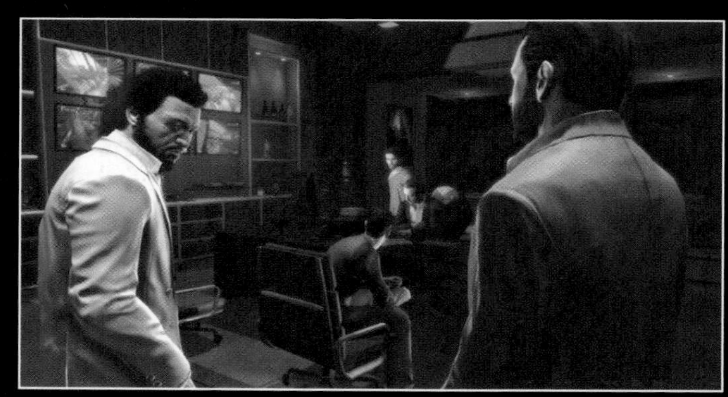

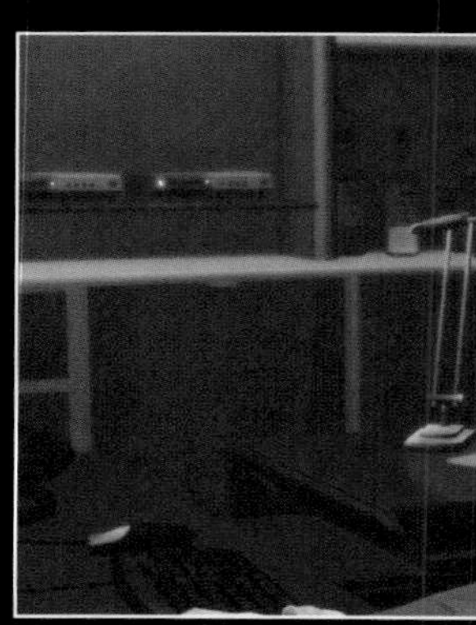

FÁBRICAS BRANCO GLOBAL HEADQUARTERS, SÃO PAULO

9:17 PM, WEDNESDAY

The next day at the offices of Branco's family company, the Branco brothers examine a ransom note in Rodrigo's office. Victor suggests that the kidnappers may be the Comando Sombra, the powerful gang from the favelas linked to the drug business. The note demands three million dollars for Fabiana's safe return. Max admits that he knows little about hostage negotiations but volunteers to deliver the ransom money with Passos.

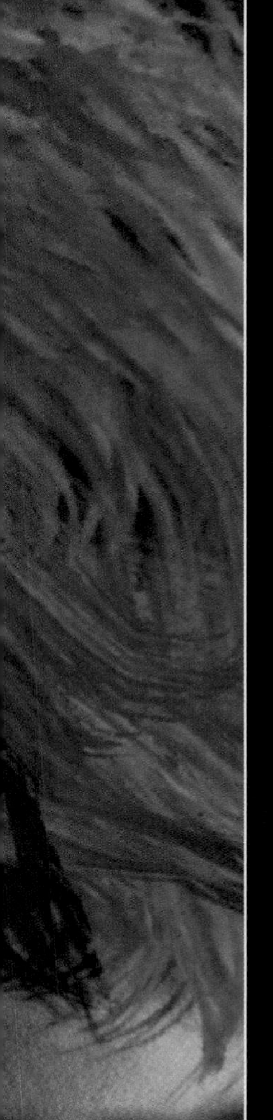

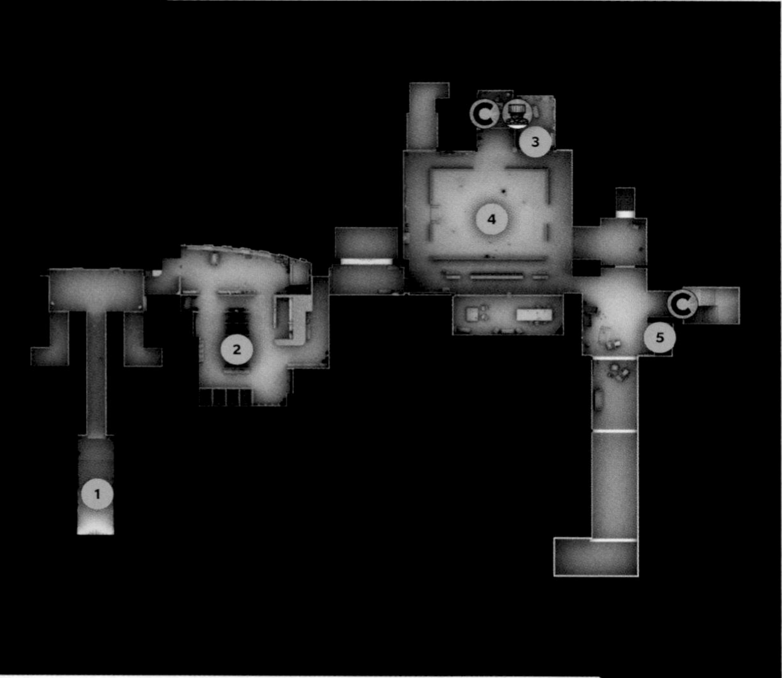

NEW WEAPONS

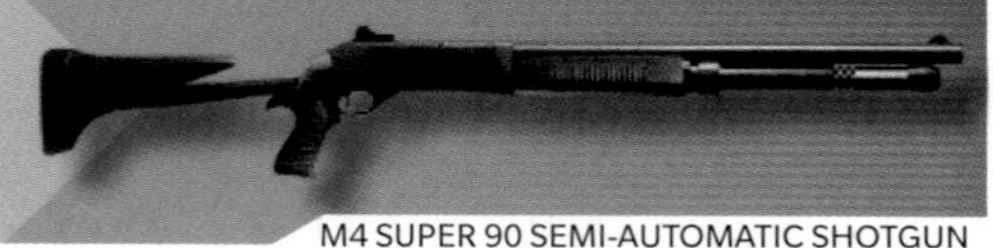

M4 SUPER 90 SEMI-AUTOMATIC SHOTGUN

PAINKILLERS

MISSION

11:55 PM, WEDNESDAY NIGHT

The scene shifts abruptly to the delivery site—the soccer stadium of the Galatians, a São Paulo club, where Passos has landed the Branco chopper. Hauling the money in a duffle bag, Max and Passos meet the Comando Sombra courier team in the center circle.

Just as the exchange is made, gunshots ring out—a sniper picks off several favela gangsters from a high perch in a skybox at the top of the stadium. Unfortunately, one of his bullets wings Max too. Two surviving thugs haul the moneybag to temporary safety under the bleachers. Passos calls for Max to join him in a passage leading under the stadium.

GET UNDER THE STADIUM!

Max and Passos do not have weapons, and Max is in bad shape, so the situation is dire. Stagger as fast as you can across the field toward Passos and enter the passage **(1)** to cut off the sniper's shooting angle. Follow Passos through the gate and downstairs into the stadium's basement level. At the corridor's end, your partner manages to surprise a guard and collect a weapon.

FIND FIRST AID.

Continue your painful progress into the next hall and turn right to trigger a scene. As Passos sneaks into the Galatian FC locker room **(2)**, Max notes the blood on the laundry hamper—looks like the bag man got hit. Follow Passos through the lockers to the far entrance.

As you approach the doors, Passos pushes through. He guns down two more thugs, grabs another pistol, and leads Max across the indoor practice field to the team training room **(3)** (under the sign "Centro Medico"). There he gives Max some pain medicine, bandages the wound, and hands over the new weapon.

The partners ponder the identity of the third party—someone with high-powered sniper rifles and, even more disturbing, with inside knowledge of the Brancos' secret cash-for-hostage transaction with Comando Sombra. After the discussion, Max and Passos slip out to the indoor practice field **(4)** and take cover against the field's barrier as more armed gangsters arrive.

HEALTH PICKUP

Medicine cabinets are always a good place to look for painkillers. You'll find some in the medical center ("Centro Medico").

BLOOD STAINED DOOR

Just as you leave the soccer and medical room area, Passos waits for you beside the elevator. The Blood Stained Door is adjacent to the elevator.

CLEAR THE INDOOR PRACTICE FIELD.

Three Comando Sombra gang members burst through the doorway across the field on the left. Take them all out and stay focused—another crew soon bursts through the doorway on the right wall as soon as two of the first group lie dead. Eliminate them from the same cover position, then pick up their dropped weapons and ammo, including the deadly M4 Super 90 semi-automatic shotgun. As Max points out after the gun battle: "The kidnappers seemed even more spooked than us." Before you move on, go back into the training room and score the painkillers from the medicine cabinet.

PICTURE OF VICTOR

Examine the large framed picture of Victor on the wall of the office beside the medical room where Passos patches up Max.

TAKE THE ELEVATOR.

Find and follow the red "Elevador" signs. Passos waits for you near the elevator **(5)**. Approach the green-lit panel on the wall and press the "Call Elevator" button indicated onscreen. Max and Passos automatically ride up from the basement to the next level of the stadium.

MISSION

CLEAR THE MEDIA ROOM.

Follow Passos through the doors into the Galatians FC media room. Passos starts some "enhanced interrogation" of a wounded Comando Sobra soldier. If you walk past his chair toward the back door **(7)** or if you shoot the hostage, you trigger the appearance of a squad of his compatriots who burst through that door. Take them out and then exit the room.

PART 1/3 GOLDEN M10

Discover this weapon part on the floor near a camera in the media room, which can safely be explored after defeating the attackers that storm the pressroom when the interrogation fails.

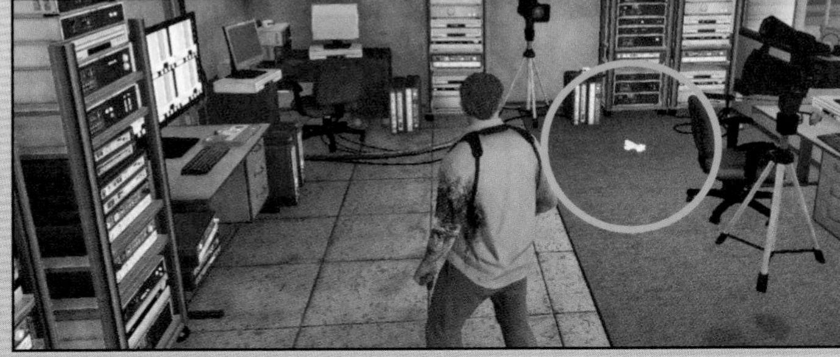

When you reach the hallway, aim your weapon at the second door **(8)** on the left wall. Move slowly forward until a last gunman bursts through the door. Gun him down—the area is clear now. Examine the room behind him to find more painkillers.

Follow Passos through the next doorway and climb the stairs **(9)** to the next stadium level to trigger another scene.

NEW WEAPONS

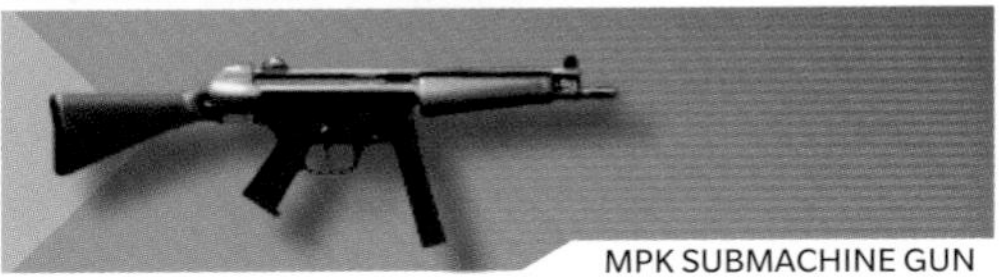

MPK SUBMACHINE GUN

PAINKILLERS

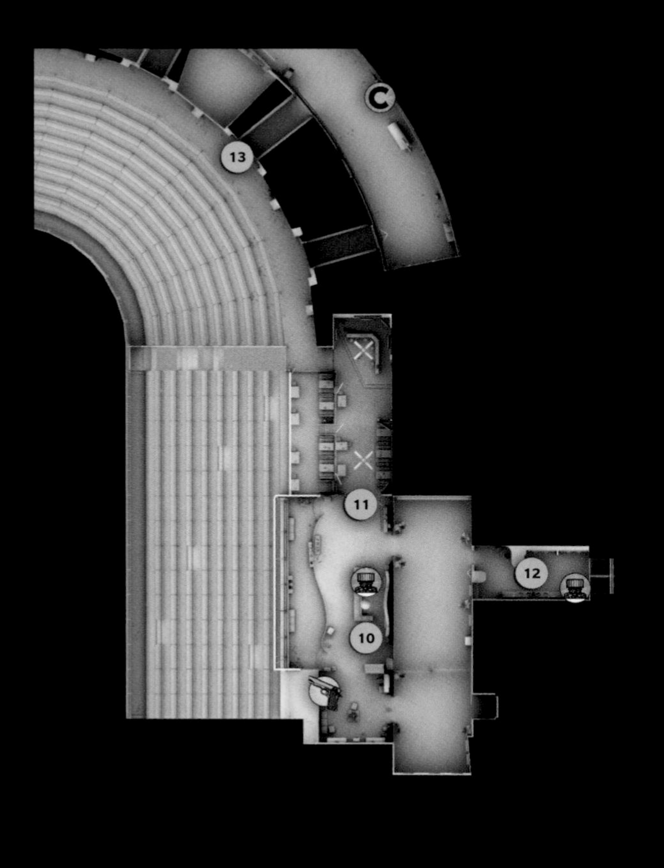

NEW WEAPONS

NONE

PAINKILLERS 

MISSION

CLEAR THE GALATIANS SOUVENIR SHOP.

Max and Passos arrive on the next level and enter the Galatians FC souvenir shop **(10)**. From cover, they spot the two Comando Sombra gangsters with the moneybag flee through the shop and pull down a metal shutter **(11)** behind them. A third gangster isn't so lucky—he gets caught by brutal paramilitary soldiers in flak jackets.

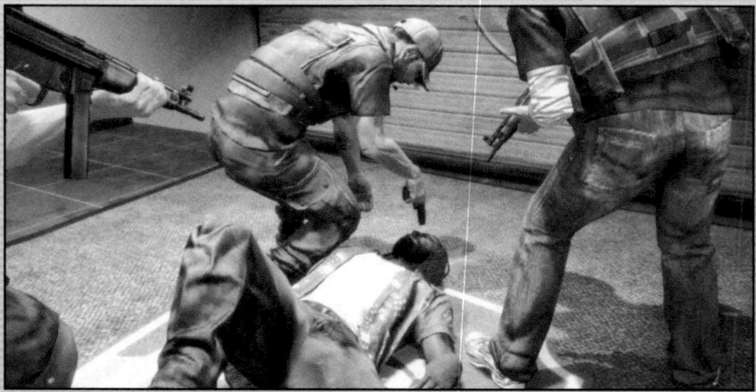

These new gunmen yank up the shutter to pursue the two bagmen who make a run for it into the stadium stands. The sniper is still active, however—a single high-powered rifle shot from his perch in the TV booth eliminates one Comando Sombra soldier, leaving only the fellow carrying the bag still alive.

Passos opens fire on the paramilitaries from behind. This is a tougher fight, since their body armor lets them absorb more punishment. These fighters are more aggressive too. You start in cover behind the checkout counter **(10)**, but one enemy quickly tries to flank your position, charging up the lower level to the left. Don't let him!

Once you thwart the flanking attempt, carefully pick off the remaining soldiers on the far side of the checkout counter. There's one behind the counter and two behind each side of the bar entrance ahead. Plunder their weapons (including a new submachine gun, the reliable MPK) then nab the painkillers behind the checkout counter and in the nearby restroom **(12)**. Make sure you've reloaded your weapons and collected all the ammo you can hold; the next challenge eats up a lot of rounds. Move forward into the next room, the bar, to trigger a scene—Passos inspects one of the fallen paramilitary soldiers. He marvels at their high-end gear and says, "These guys are *seriously* financed."

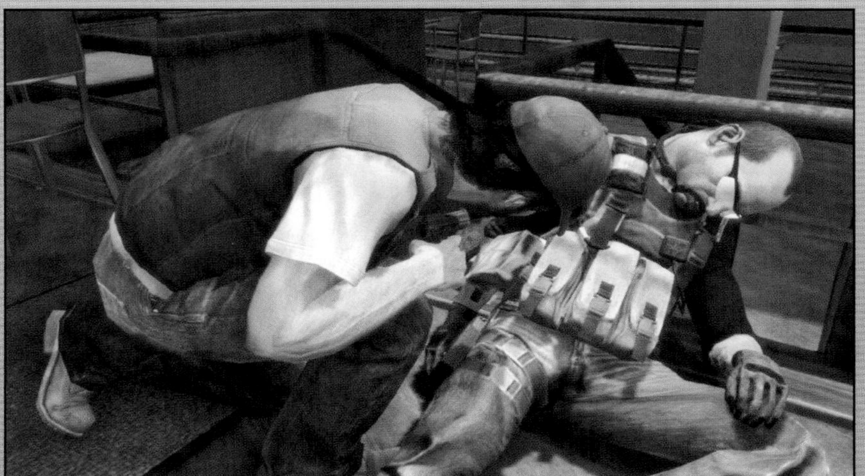

PART 1/3 GOLDEN M82A1

This gun part is on a low shelf on the left side of the room as you enter the gift shop. Turn around when you gain control of Max while covering behind the sales counter during the gunfight.

The scene ends with Passos impatiently rushing into the stadium's Level A stands—putting him back into the laser sight of the sniper. Sprint hard after Passos to the next entrance **(13)** marked "Entrada" (under the larger sign that reads "Inferior A"). Don't stop! If you hesitate, the sniper will nail you instantly.

CONCESSION HALL & JOGA TV BOOTH

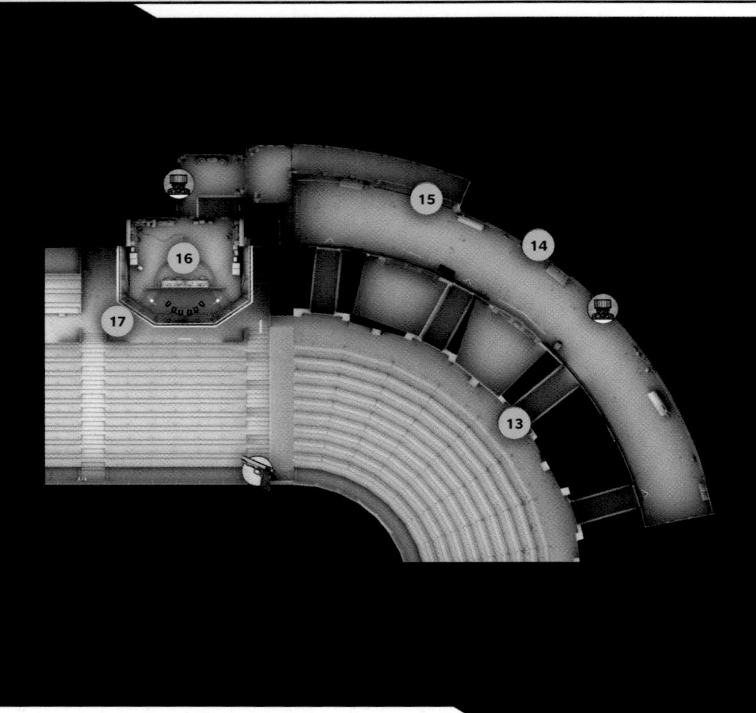

NEW WEAPONS

NONE

PAINKILLERS  

MISSION

CLEAR THE CONCESSION HALL.

The entrance leads into the stadium's concession area. As you reach the end of the connecting corridor, you see a "Bang!" soft drink sign on the wall directly across the concession hall. Numerous gunmen are deployed down the hall to the left. At the corner, lean out and aim first at the raised walkway on the hall's right side. Two shooters are posted up there **(14)**.

Once these first gunmen are eliminated, start plugging the other three paramilitary thugs in the hall. Two more advance on the raised walkway; another emerges from the open doorway on the right (across from the "Hippos Burger" sign) and charge aggressively down the hall. Fight your way forward through the concession stands. You can also nab painkillers from a medicine cabinet across from your entry hallway. Examine a bloodstain on a wall pillar on the right to hear comments from Max. Pick up weapons then move through the open doorway **(15)** under the "JOGA TV" sign where Passos waits for you.

BLOOD STAINED HALLWAY

After leaving the gift shop, Passos and Max clear a concessions hallway. After the battle, examine the bloody handprint on the column on the right wall.

TAKE OUT THE SNIPER IN THE TV BOOTH.

Fight your way to the JOGA TV booth **(16)** while gunning down the single enemy at the top of the ramp. Take the painkillers from the first aid cabinet beside the next doorway. There are two gunmen in the TV skybox; one behind the central console and another hiding behind a component rack to the far right. The guy behind the rack is last to attack, so seek out and kill the guy on the left first then aim at the component rack (circled in our shot) across the room—the guy in the hat who emerges is the sniper who shot Max and all the CS men on the field.

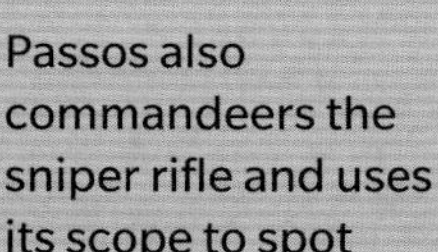

Sometimes, Passos will take this guy out for you depending on how long you take to deal with him. His demise triggers a cutscene: Passos digs a pair of headsets out of the sniper's bag. Now Max and Passos can split up yet stay in voice contact.

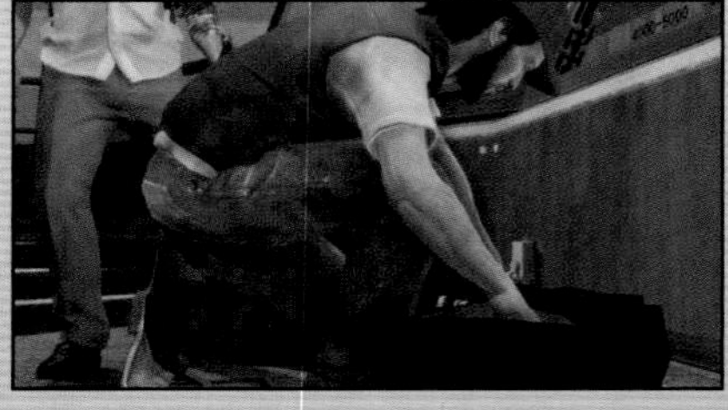

Passos also commandeers the sniper rifle and uses its scope to spot where the paramilitaries have cornered the gangster with the moneybag. As Max drops from the press box **(17)** to intervene, Passos takes up a position at the window to cover him.

LOWER STANDS & HALL OF FAME

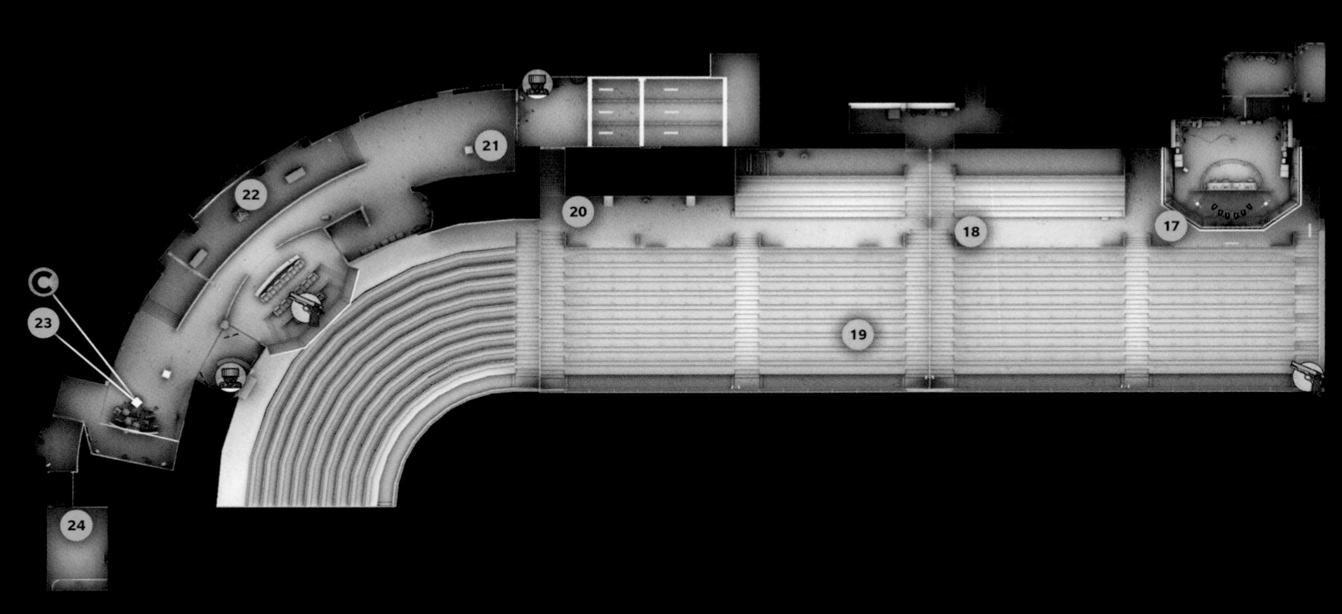

NEW WEAPONS NONE  PAINKILLERS 

MISSION

CLEAR THE LOWER BLEACHERS.

Four heavily armed paramilitary thugs are opening a gate directly ahead **(18)**. Dive into cover behind the bleacher base on the right (marked as section 2000-3000)...or, better yet, use a Bullet Time attack to eliminate the tightly grouped quartet in one glorious, slow-motion spray of bullets. When the last soldier falls, approach the gate to trigger a cutscene. The hunted Comando Sombra bagman hustles through a gate into a storage area.

PART 2/3 GOLDEN M10

When you leave the control room to enter the stands to try to retrieve the moneybag, continue down to the lowest level of the stands and find this weapon part in the lowest left corner.

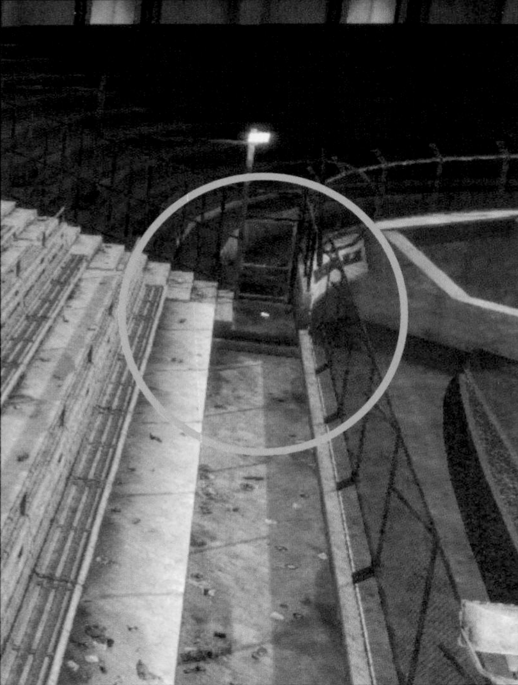

GRENADE WARNING

As Max and Passos discover, the Crachá Preto paramilitary group is well financed and heavily armed. Some carry grenades and do not hesitate to use them. When tossed, a live grenade glows red. You also see an onscreen icon (shown here) with an arrow that points toward the thrown grenade. Target and shoot grenades in the air if you can.

When a grenade lands, it starts flashing until it detonates just a few seconds later. (The flashing gets faster as the device gets closer to detonation.) If a grenade lands nearby, sprint away fast and/or dive behind very solid cover.

Before you can pursue the money-toting gangster, more paramilitary gunmen rush at you from the next bleacher section on the far side of the gate ahead. Two enemies also come creeping up on you from the lower bleachers to your left **(19)**. Tuck into the cover formed by the corner of the railing signs.

Start shooting but stay frosty—one of the attackers tosses grenades at you, so you may need to retreat quickly if one lands close. Take out the grenadier first then return your attention to other onrushing shooters on your level. As you advance, be on the lookout for a third and fourth gunman down in the bleachers to your left.

Continue to the top left corner of the bleacher section and find the stairwell marked "1000-2000." Two more foes are posted at the top of these stairs, so use the corner **(20)** for cover and swing out and shoot each enemy individually. When you drop both gunmen, the area is clear. Search through the carnage in the bleachers to load up on weapons and ammo then return to the staircase.

At the top of the stairs, find painkillers in a medicine cabinet. Approach the doors under the "Camarote Primcrédito" sign to trigger a cutscene: Max moves into cover in the club's "Hall of Fame" area as another crew of paramilitary soldiers enters.

CLEAR THE GALATIANS HALL OF FAME.

This is a nasty fight. You start in cover behind a support column **(21)** with the Galatians FC logo. Stay put! The hall is crawling with enemy troops, including some armed with grenades, and cover is scarce. Be patient and pick them off one by one from the cover of the initial location.

After you nail the first few foes, more gunmen stream into the area from the far end. Work your way along the lower level to the right, using the trophy cases and the big statue of star player Alfredo Davi **(22)** as cover.

HEALTH BOOST

A much-needed stash of painkillers sits behind the bar in the back corner of the Galatians FC Hall of Fame.

If you're low on health, find the bottles of painkillers behind the bar at the end of the hall, just beyond the luxury club seating area. When you reach the floral arrangements strewn around the memorial for the player Claudio **(23)**, one last enemy comes pushing through the exit doors. Nail him and then examine the memorial to hear Max's comments. Then turn right to exit the hall.

PART 3/3 GOLDEN M10

This part is located on the chair in the front row of the VIP lounge just before the soccer star memorial.

SOCCER STAR MEMORIAL

Claudio's memorial is located at the end of the VIP lounge where Max battles a large group of paramilitary.

TAKE THE ELEVATOR TO THE UPPER STANDS.

Speaking via radio to Passos, Max reports that he's found a maintenance elevator. Approach the green flashing button next to the shaft **(24)** and press the "Call elevator" button to ride up and trigger a cutscene: Passos uses his sniper scope to spot Max emerging into the upper stands—and he spots some "company" as well.

UPPER STANDS

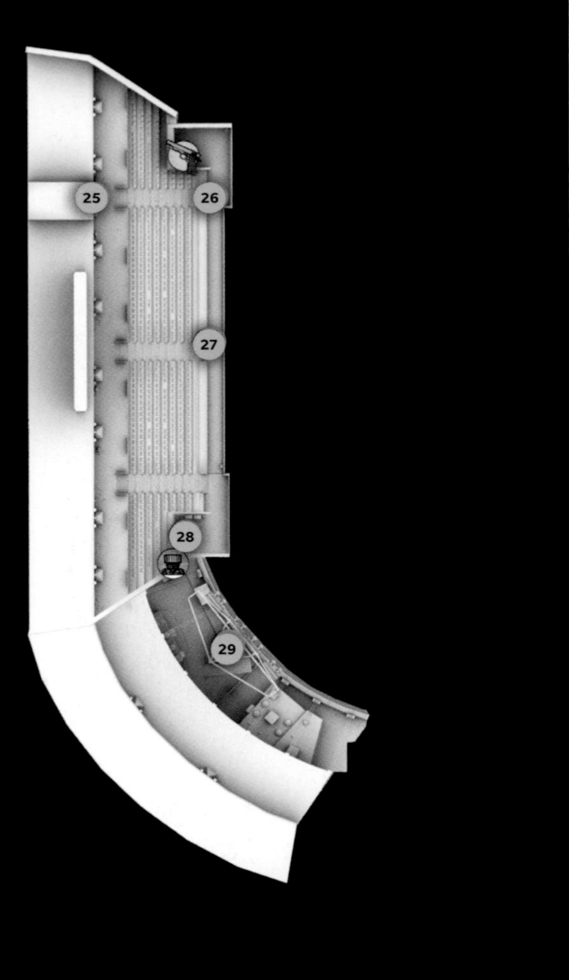

NEW WEAPONS

NONE

PAINKILLERS 

MISSION

CLEAR THE UPPER STANDS.

Max emerges at the top of a staircase **(25)**. The first two gunmen are at the bottom of the stairs **(26)**. Careful! One tosses a grenade right away. Try to pick it off just as he throws so the explosion KOs both foes. Be ready to sprint away if the grenade lands nearby!

As you descend the stairs, more attackers rush across the lower walkway **(27)**, including more grenade throwers. Others descend the stairs to the right, and one shooter follows you down the stairs you just descended. Don't let this last guy surprise you! Spin around and tag him as you back into the nook that is formed by the railing at the bottom of the first stairway. Then take cover and clear the stands. Watch closely for grenades flying your way.

GRIND: SLOW DIVE (8 SECOND SHOOTDODGE)

An advanced way to approach this battle is to run forward out of the elevator and ShootDodge forward over the descending stairs nailing the first two gunmen at the bottom of the stairs in the head. While still in the ShootDodge leap, pivot right and begin aiming for as many enemy heads as you can manage. When you land, run and take cover behind the large partition wall on the left on the lower bleacher walkway and take cover and shoot from around the corner to finish off the remaining enemies. There is a golden weapon part behind this wall.

PART 2/3 GOLDEN M82A1

When you exit the top floor of the stadium and look down on the enemies from the top row of bleachers, follow the stairs directly in front of you down to the bottom. Then turn left around the wall to find this weapon part. This wall is also great to use as cover from the remaining enemies in the area.

ELIMINATE THE SNIPER.

When the last gunman falls, a quick scene plays: a new sniper tries to target Max from a platform underneath the bank of lights directly under the "Estadio do Galatians" sign. But Passos uses his scoped rifle to force the shooter to stay low, keeping the heat off Max.

Sprint across the lower walkway (the one running along the bottom of the stands) to the exit gate at the far end **(28)**. Go through the gate, grab the painkillers from the medicine cabinet at the bottom of the next staircase, and climb the stairs on the left. Burst through the door at the top while firing up at the sniper posted just above the "Brasilia Esportes" sign **(29)** (circled in our screenshot). Take him out! If you don't nail him from below, you can get him on the stairs in a moment.

Another gunman is posted just ahead to the right, so move forward carefully after you nail the sniper. Dropping both of these foes triggers a scene: Max climbs to the sniper's post and appropriates the high-powered M82A1 rifle. When he hears that Passos is in trouble, he sets up to snipe his partner's pursuers.

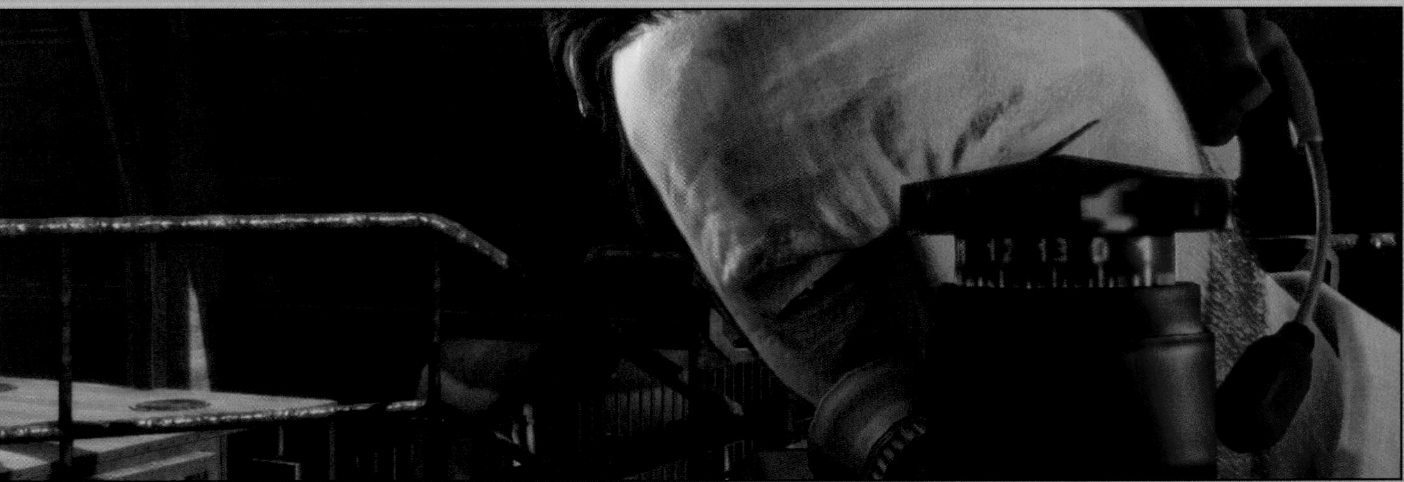

SNIPER POST

MISSION

PROTECT PASSOS.

Now you view section 2000-3000 of the far stands through the M82A1's telescopic scope as Passos ducks behind some seats at the bottom of a staircase. Target his pursuers in the following order:

Part 1: Swing your view up the stairs to the upper left and shoot the three gunmen descending the stairs. Hitting the third gunman triggers a final kill camera. Passos scrambles along the walkway to the left and hides at the bottom of the next staircase.

NEW WEAPONS

M82A1 SCOPED SEMI-AUTOMATIC RIFLE

SNIPER SCOPE

Tilt the left control stick up and down to zoom in and out in the sniper scope view. Zooming out allows you to spot the next enemy quickly. Once spotted, zoom in to make the kill. Use the right control stick to aim, and remember to use Bullet Time, too.

Part 2: Move your view up that staircase and shoot the lone gunman descending the stairs. Passos hustles farther to the left along the bleachers and then stops again at the gate for the next section (1000-2000).

Part 3: This next three-target sequence is tricky. Slide your view up the next staircase and shoot the single gunmen descending. (He moves down the far side of the iron bars that separate sections.) When he falls, quickly zoom out and scan over one staircase to the right. Zoom back in and nail the gunman trying to sneak around behind Passos. Then swing your view back left to the first staircase and nail the descending gunman on the near side of the iron bars.

Passos hustles through the gate into section 1000-2000 and climbs the stairs. But when he tries to exit via the doors at the top, he finds them locked! He descends to the middle walkway and hurries farther left across the stands.

Part 4: When Passos stops to take cover, swing your view left along the walkway and nail the three gunmen advancing toward him. Quickly swivel past Passos to the right and shoot the single soldier descending the stairs. Swivel back left past Passos to nail another gunman approaching along the walkway from the left. Finally, slide the view down the stairs below Passos to target the killer creeping upstairs to ambush your partner from below.

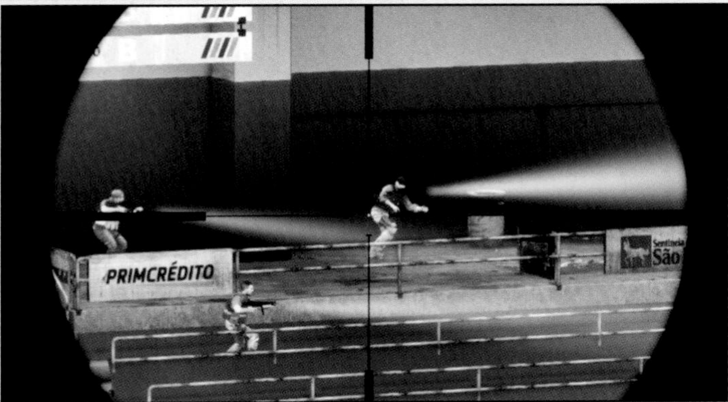

Part 5: When the last thug falls, Passos sprints left to the last staircase at the end of the section. Quickly scan up the stairs and nail the lone gunman descending. Shoot fast—he reaches Passos quickly. When he drops, your partner gives you the thumbs up and a long series of cutscenes play.

Another sniper targets Max from a lighting tower, and Passos starts working his way back to the helicopter. As Max moves through the stadium offices looking for a way to the sniper, he finds a control room with live feeds from the stadium security cameras. There he watches on a monitor as Passos spies a paramilitary squad that has cornered the Comando Sombra money carrier.

Passos overhears the captured gangster confess that Fabiana is being held at the old docks on the Tiete River, about 30 miles west of São Paulo. Then Max makes a run for the light rig to take out the last sniper.

STADIUM LIGHT TOWER

NEW WEAPONS NONE

PAINKILLERS 

MISSION

WORK YOUR WAY UP THE LIGHT TOWER.

You start in cover at the bottom of a staircase **(30)**. The lighting tower rises above you and, just below it, the sniper is perched in the tower's control platform. (Watch the sniper's red targeting laser to see where he's aiming.) While in cover at the corner, shoot the furthest gunman on the right. Move around the corner and pick off the remaining gunman posted at the top of the stairs **(31)**.

PART 3/3 GOLDEN M82A1

Immediately after the sniping challenge, find this weapon part behind a short column at the far right end of the top row of bleachers. The three enemies from the next area will advance when you retrieve this weapon part so prepare to fight them soon rather than later.

Now sprint upstairs until you get underneath the tower platform to cut off the sniper's view. Stop before you run through the open gate at the top—three more paramilitary thugs wait just around the corner. Lean through the doorway and gun them down. Then, climb the utility ladder **(32)** running up the light tower.

At the top, swivel left to target three gunmen down the metal catwalk. Using Bullet Time here is very useful. After you eliminate them, move down the catwalk and climb the next ladder **(33)** running up the tower. Three more gunmen wait for you on the upper catwalk that runs directly behind the lighting racks. Use Bullet Time as soon as you get to the top, nail the first enemy on the catwalk, then eliminate the two covering behind the short wall. Dropping the third one triggers the final kill camera, letting you know you've cleared the area.

TAKE OUT THE SNIPER.

Walk about halfway down the catwalk to the small platform **(34)** with a yellow and black striped railing. Simply walk to its end to trigger a spectacular "Max Payne Moment": Max leaps over the railing, slides down a slanted awning, grabs a collapsing strut, and whipsaws through the glass of the light platform, kicking the sniper across the room. When control returns, you are on the floor. Quickly target and shoot the sniper sprawled in front of you.

This triggers the mission-ending sequence of cutscenes: Max and Passos meet up and hustle down to the helicopter. As Passos fires up the chopper and they lift off, watch the curious reaction of the paramilitary commander. As the two partners fly off to lick their wounds, Max flashes back to their first meeting, five years ago...

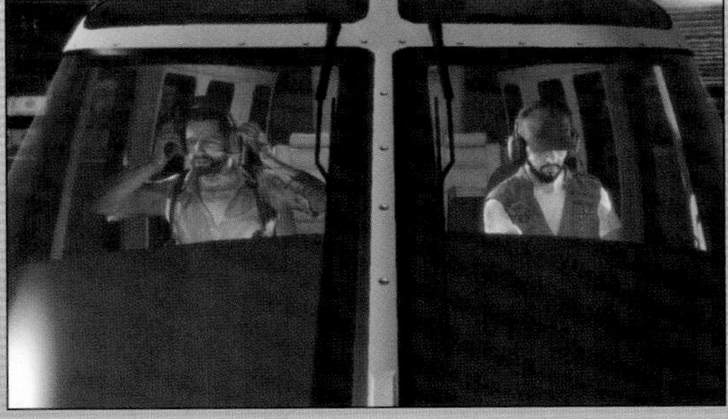

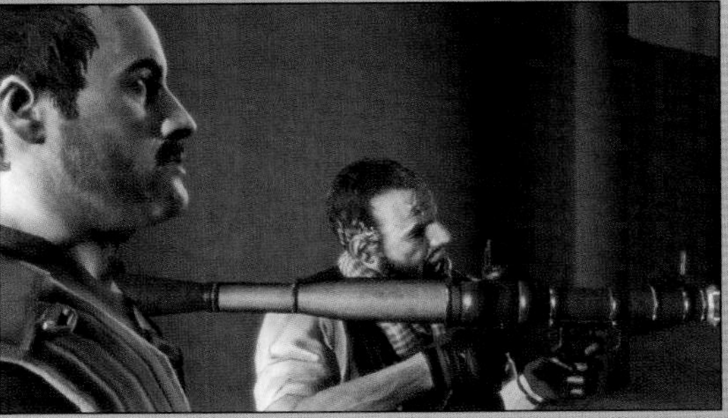

IV ANYONE CAN BUY ME A DRINK

HOBOKEN, NEW JERSEY

9:10 PM, MONDAY, A FEW MONTHS AGO

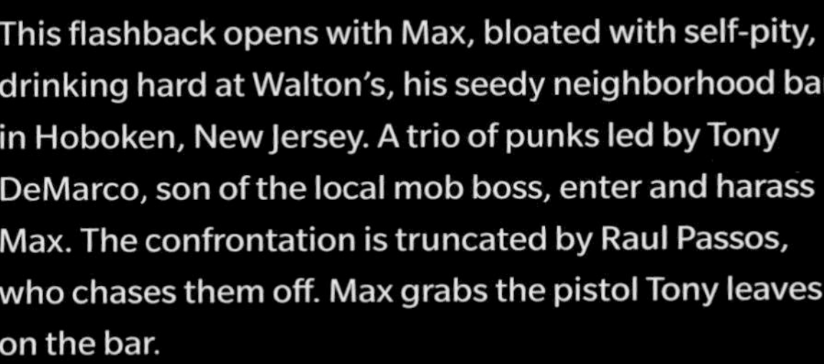

This flashback opens with Max, bloated with self-pity, drinking hard at Walton's, his seedy neighborhood bar in Hoboken, New Jersey. A trio of punks led by Tony DeMarco, son of the local mob boss, enter and harass Max. The confrontation is truncated by Raul Passos, who chases them off. Max grabs the pistol Tony leaves on the bar.

Passos claims he was Max's classmate at the Police Academy. After five years working the Homicide desk in the Bronx, Passos turned in his badge and began providing private security, working stints in both Central America and Brazil, his family's country of origin. He tells Max: "I take care of people."

After a few more drinks, Passos tries to recruit Max to work for his Brazilian "firm." But suddenly Tony and his crew return for some payback, and when he pistol-whips a mouthy female bar patron, the situation quickly spirals out of control...

WALTON'S BAR

BAR: MAIN LEVEL

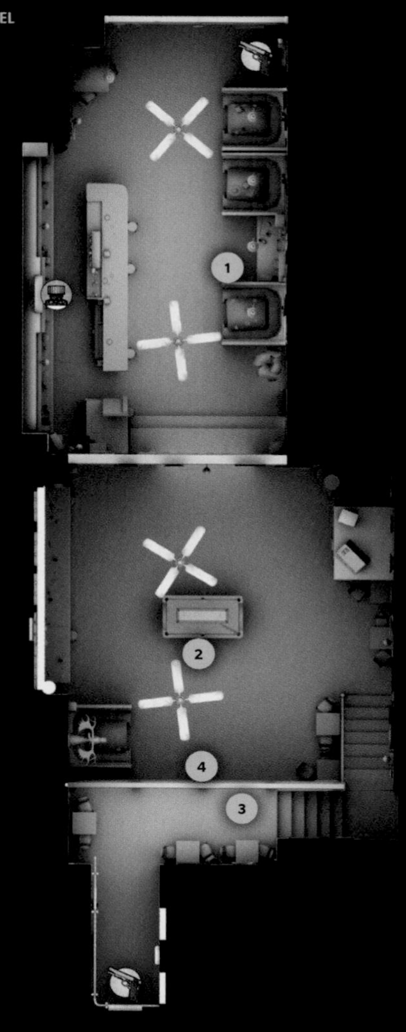

BAR: LOWER LEVEL

NEW WEAPONS

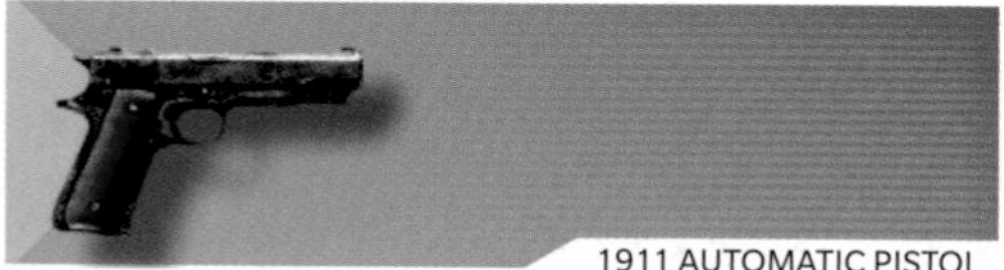

1911 AUTOMATIC PISTOL

PAINKILLERS

MISSION

CLEAR OUT THE BAR'S MAIN LEVEL.

After you gun down Tony DeMarco, you start in cover behind one of th bar booths **(1)**, armed with Max's 1911 automatic pistol and the 1911 that Tony left on the bar earlier. With help from Passos, pick off the goo in the bar area and behind the pool table **(2)** and then advance... but watch out for one more mobster firing an M4 Super 90 shotgun from t upper balcony in the back **(3)**. If you don't nail him early, he rushes do the left staircase as you step into the pool room. When you drop him, Passos pushes through a rear door **(4)** marked "Exit."

You can't exit via the barred front door, so you must follow Passos. But before you leave the bar's main level, nab the two painkiller bottles on the counter behind the bar. We recommend that you pick up the shotgun left by the fallen goon on the balcony—it's a good weapon for close quarters. Then trail Passos downstairs to the decrepit tavern's lower level.

PART 1/3 GOLDEN 1911

After clearing the bar and billiards room of enemies, turn around and find this weapon in the front right corner of the bar near the locked entrance.

PART 2/3 GOLDEN 1911

Clear the bar and the billiards room, head upstairs, and find this weapon part at the end of the upstairs hallway.

CLEAR THE BAR'S LOWER LEVEL.

The tavern's lower level features a bar with booths and an adjacent kitchen. When you arrive **(5)**, three more Jersey goons loiter across the room. So, go in strong with the shotgun that the balcony goon was carrying and use Bullet Time to blast the first three gunmen. Take cover behind the wall to the right or duck down behind the near end of the bar **(6)**.

More thugs open fire through the wall opening **(7)** from the adjacent kitchen or rush through the far doorway behind the bar. (More painkiller bottles sit on the counter behind this bar too.) Slide up beside the wall opening and lean out to pick off the kitchen shooters. You can also try a ShootDodge dive right through the kitchen opening!

Then proceed through the kitchen into the back room. Approach the exit door **(8)** to trigger a quick cutscene: Max and Passos climb the stairs up to the parking lot, where two more carloads of Tony's goons loiter.

PARKING LOT/ALLEY

NEW WEAPONS

NONE

MISSION

CLEAR THE PARKING LOT.

Open fire from your position behind a low brick wall **(10)** at the unsuspecting but heavily armed gunmen. (Reload *before* you open fire so your weapon has a full clip of bullets.) This is a good place to use a Bullet Time attack—you can take out many thugs with a single sweep. Shoot at targets right through the car windows.

PART 3/3 GOLDEN 1911

After eliminating the goons in the parking lot and before following Passos into the alleyway, return to the bottom of the stairs and find this weapon part beside the stairs.

Also remember that you can shoot any car's engine or gas tank and it will eventually explode like a bomb. You can easily eliminate any shooters who use their automobiles for cover. When the lot is clear, follow Passos to the gate at the head of the alley exit **(11)**.

CLEAR THE ALLEY.

When you enter the alley, another carload of armed punks arrives. Passos starts climbing a wall and calls for Max to cover him. Stay in cover at the corner **(12)** and pick off punks (or target their car until it explodes) as Passos works across the roof above you.

Soon two more carloads **(13)** of goons arrive. Once you eliminate them, a cutscene plays: Max and Passos meet up again, and Max leads the way to his apartment just around the corner.

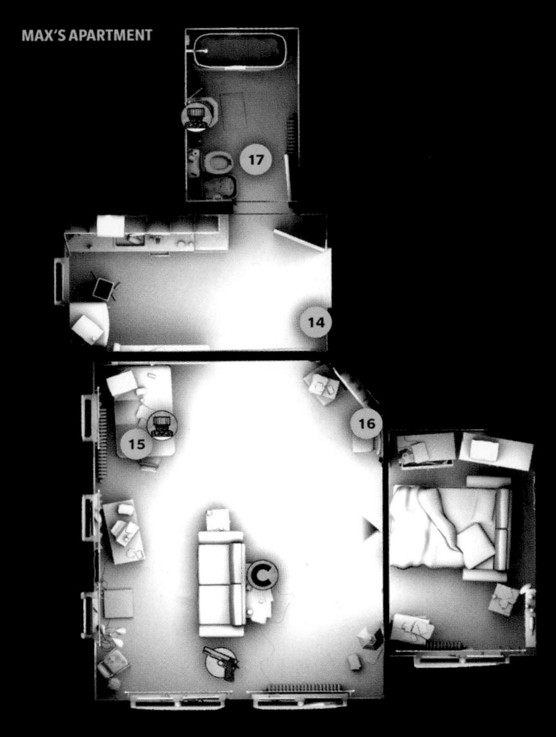

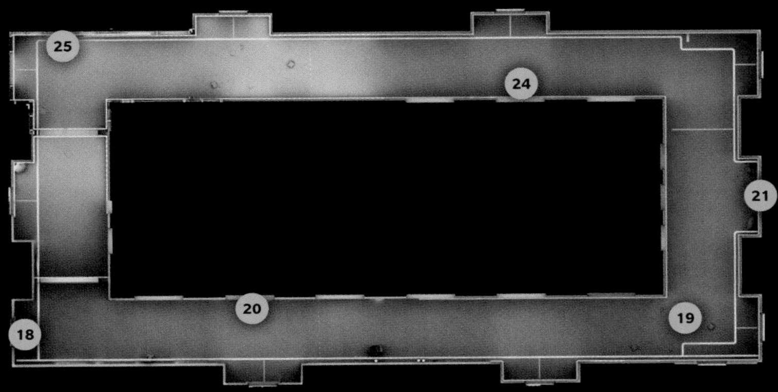

NEW WEAPONS

M10 MACHINE PISTOL

PAINKILLERS

MISSION

EXPLORE THE APARTMENT.

Watch as Passos "admires" the place and again offers Max a job in private security with a chance to make good money and start over. Max turns him down again but suddenly realizes he is the target of Anthony DeMarco, mob boss and the emotional, vengeful father of the newly deceased Tony. DeMarco deploys dozens of his goons around the building and vows to make Max pay for killing his son.

You start at Max's doorway **(14)** looking down a long hallway. Note the green targeting lasers beaming through the windows on the left side: mob shooters are set up on the rooftop across the building's open central courtyard. Before you run that gauntlet, find the extra 1911 pistol and the painkillers on Max's card table **(15)** in the living room, then grab the M4 Super 90 shotgun **(16)** leaning against the wall between the chair and bookshelf. You can also examine Max's old police badge: it sits on the low table behind his sofa. Finally, collect more painkillers from the medicine cabinet in the bathroom **(17)**.

PART 1/3 GOLDEN M500

This weapon part is inside Max's apartment on the floor between the window and the couch.

MAX'S NYPD BADGE

Find Max's NYPD Badge in his apartment on the edge of the table behind his living room couch.

RUN OR FIGHT DOWN THE HALL.

Go back to the door and walk a few steps from Max's apartment **(18)** down the hall while aiming at the far end. Three goons appear there **(19)**, so nail them quickly. One of them drops a new submachine gun, the compact but lethal M10. It has formidable stopping power for a dual-wield weapon.

Now you can take cover under the windows on the left side **(20)** and start picking off the rooftop shooters across the center courtyard to earn the "That Old Familiar Feeling" Achievement. Or you can ignore the shooters and make a full sprint down the hallway to the far end.

When you reach the far end of the corridor **(19)**, you trigger a cutscene: a mob gunman ambushes Max from behind, but Max's neighbor Mr. Brewer, a bearded American and Vietnam War vet, jumps in the fray. He also kindly "cleanses" the next corridor for you.

EXPLORE MR. BREWER'S APARTMENT.

MR. BREWER'S APARTMENT

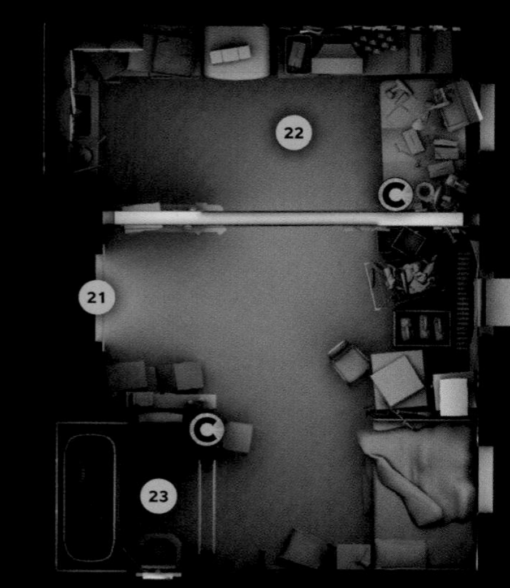

BURNED APARTMENT

NEW WEAPONS

NONE

After the explosion, you can explore Mr. Brewer's decrepit apartment **(21)**. Don't miss the painkillers in the kitchen **(22)**; there's nothing of interest the bathroom **(23)**. You can also watch his TV, examine his manifesto notebook, and view the wall of news clippings. Then exit the apartment, turn right, and follow the corridor around the corner.

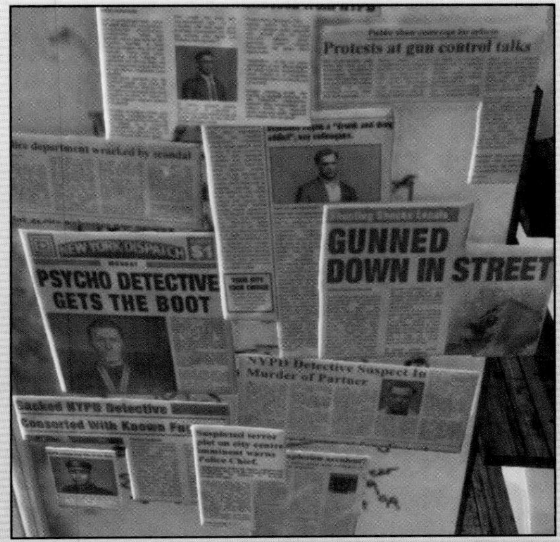

GET TO THE ROOF.

If you eliminated all of DeMarco's rooftop snipers back in the first hallway, you can proceed safely down this next hall. If you didn't eliminate them, they open fire on you again. You can either take cover beneath the windows on the left **(24)** and try to pick off the shooters, or you can just ignore them again and sprint the hall's full length. Step through the gruesome carnage wrought by Mr. Brewer's "cleansing" **(25)** and climb the stairs **(26)** to the roof access door.

BREWER'S JOURNAL

Mr. Brewer is Max's crazy hygiene-fanatic-human-bomb neighbor that blows himself up at the end of the second hallway. Enter his apartment and find the manifesto on the edge of his bomb-making table.

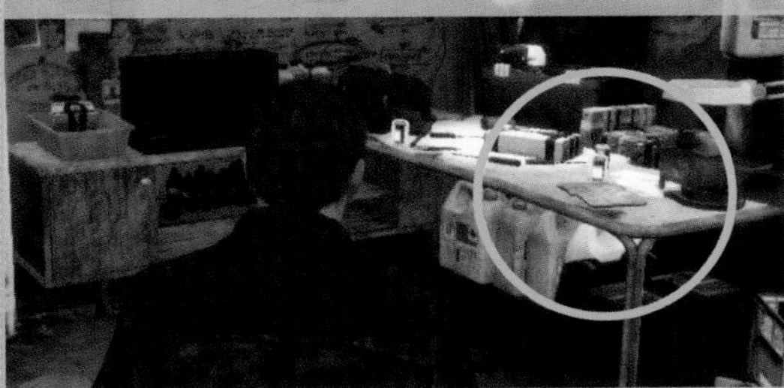

NEWSPAPER CLIPPINGS

Also in Mr. Brewer's apartment, near the doorway is a bunch of newspaper clippings stuck to the wall. Examine these.

PART 1/3 GOLDEN SAF 40 CAL

After watching Mr. Brewer blow himself up, find this weapon part on what's left of the burned apartment floor then head up the stairs to the rooftop.

ROOF OF MAX'S APARTMENT BUILDING

ADJOINING ROOFTOPS

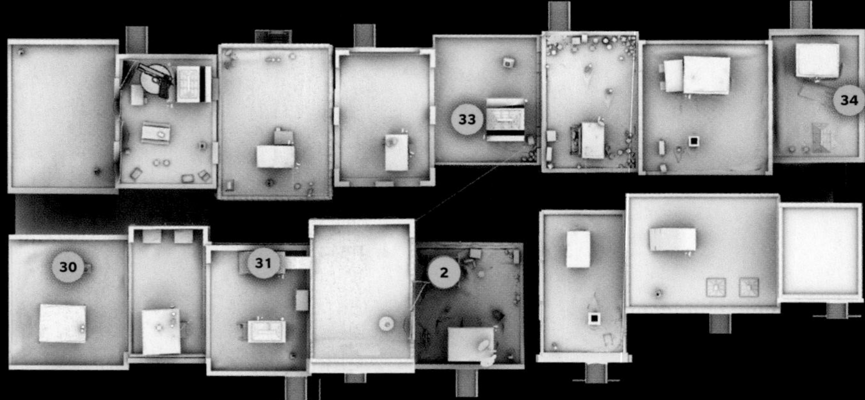

NEW WEAPONS NONE | PAINKILLERS 

MISSION

FIGHT ACROSS THE ROOFTOPS.

Now you must fight your way across a series of connecting rooftops against the backdrop of the New York City skyline across the river. You step out onto the roof of Max's apartment building **(27)** where three goons **(28)** confer across from the water tank. Use the roof structures for cover and watch out for gunmen trying to flank you.

PART 2/3 GOLDEN M500

Clear the first rooftop of danger, then double back and find this weapon part behind the stairs enclosure through which you accessed the roof.

PART 2/3 GOLDEN SAF 40 CAL

After the falling water tower Bullet Time challenge, traverse the rooftops to the left instead of following Passos to the right. You'll find this gun part on the last rooftop (the one with the fence). It's in the right corner beside a bird coop.

BLAST ON THE ROOF

Target the explosive yellow gas canister on the Hoboken rooftops when mob gunmen are near it.

Fight your way around the corner and nail two more mobsters then take cover at the brick wall **(29)** and target shooters on the next building's roof. Drop down onto that roof and take cover behind the narrow brick chimney **(30)** and clear the area. When the final kill camera indicates that you've gunned down the last mobster here, climb up the sloped ramp **(31).**

Cross the roof to trigger a cutscene: Max crawls atop an ancient water tank **(32)** as a crew of mobsters emerges from an access door on a roof across the alley **(33)**. Unfortunately, the goons hear him and open fire, shattering the tank's support struts. The structure, with Max still aboard, begins to collapse.

When control returns, Bullet Time is automatically activated. Use it to gun down all six of the mob gunmen before the tank falls. If you succeed, Max rides the collapsing tower then leaps across the alley gap. Passos emerges from the roof access door and admires Max's handiwork. Then he points out a nearby "wreck"—an abandoned building undergoing extensive renovation—and suggests it might provide a way down to the street.

Pick up an MPK submachine gun from the deceased thugs then follow Passos across the last two roofs. He leads you through another fallen water tank **(34)** into the renovation project.

RENOVATED BUILDING: LOWER FLOOR

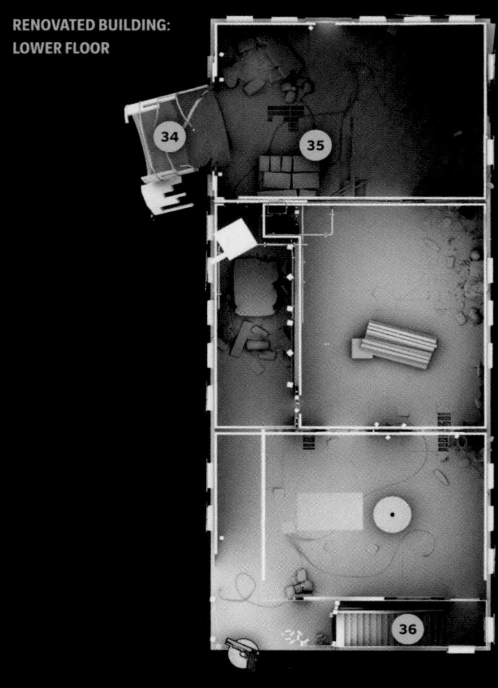

RENOVATED BUILDING: UPPER FLOOR

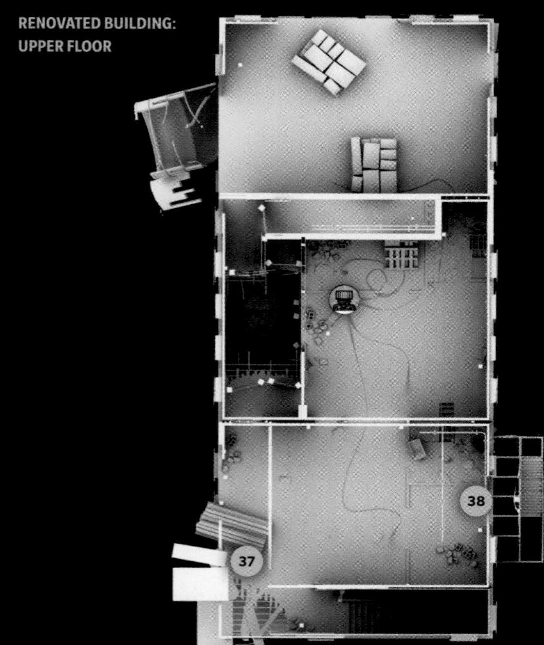

NEW WEAPONS

AK-47 ASSAULT RIFLE

PAINKILLERS

MISSION

CLEAR THE TWO FLOORS.

Join Passos behind the palette of boxes **(35)** and start blasting your way across the area. As you clear the first floor, find the AK-47 assault rifle dropped by a fallen goon. Then follow Passos to the staircase **(36)**, climb up to the next floor, and duck behind the stack of lumber **(37)**. From there, use your new weapon to repeat the process of clearing out the next floor.

DON'T ABANDON RAUL!

If you try to leave the abandoned building or go back downstairs after you reach the second level, a mob gunman will take out Passos.

PART 3/3 GOLDEN M500

After battling goons on the initial floor of the abandoned apartment building, head up the stairs to survive another ambush. The weapon part is outside and at the end of the scaffold. Get to it before you approach Passos on the fire escape or you'll miss the opportunity.

GET TO THE CHOP SHOP ROOF.

When that floor is cleared too, locate the painkillers on the portable generator near a corner light next to the bathroom. Then find Passos waiting at the fire escape **(38)**. Approach the exit to trigger a scene: Passos and Max descend the metal stairs to another roof below, one with glass skylights.

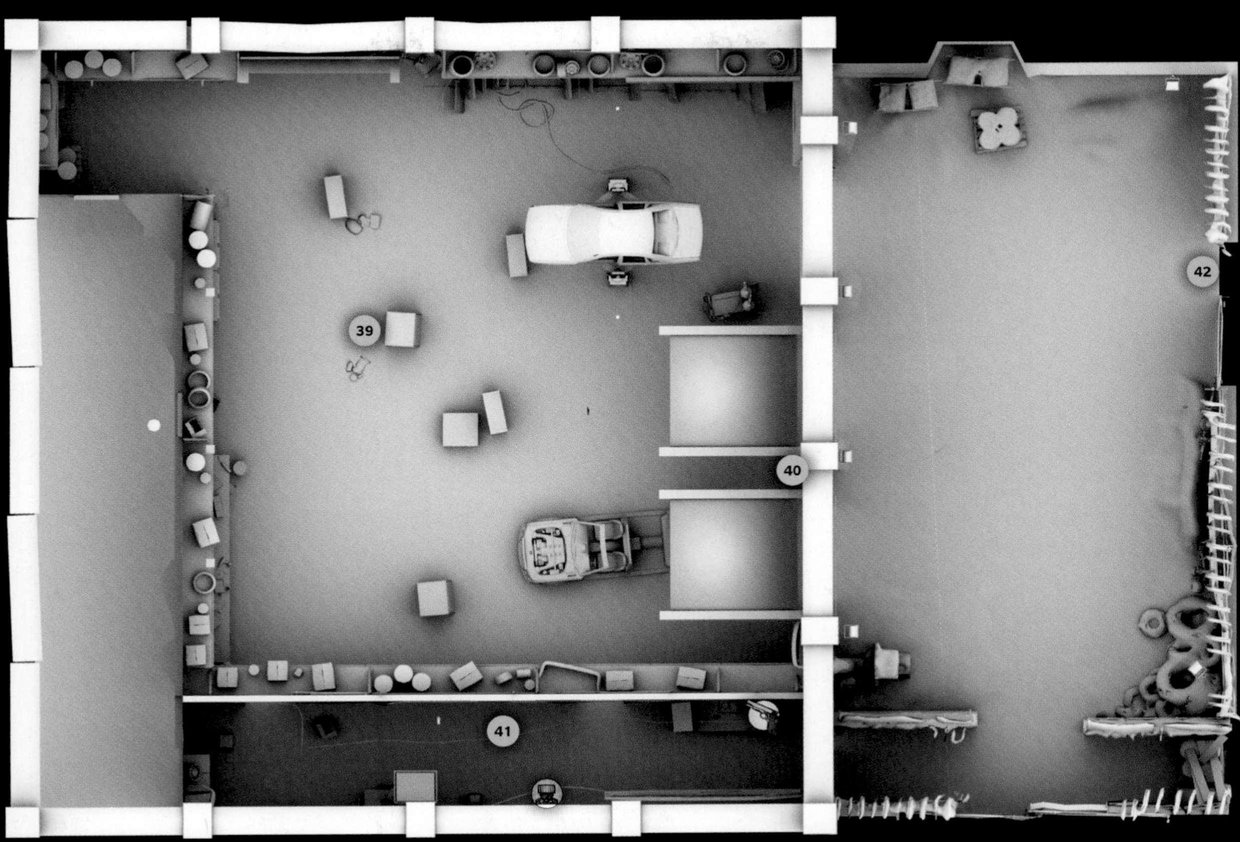

NEW WEAPONS

NONE

PAINKILLERS 

MISSION

FIGHT YOUR WAY INTO THE ALLEY.

Passos smashes a brick through one skylight and both men drop through the opening into an automobile chop shop. Surprise! How's it going, guys?

The chop shop guys flee just as a goon hit squad arrives in the open garage doorways. You start out in cover behind a small tool cabinet **(39)**. Here's a trick: to eliminate the first gunmen quickly, immediately target the large explosive canister (circled in our screenshot) sitting on a tool cabinet between open doors **(40)**.

You can shoot the hydraulic lift's control box (with the glowing red button) to drop the raised car onto any goons camping beneath it. Also be aware that some gunmen will try to flank you by moving through the office to the far right **(41)**. If things get desperate, you can rush the office and find painkillers in a medicine cabinet (between the fridge and file cabinets). Once the chop shop yard is cleared, follow Passos through the open gate **(42)** into the alley.

PART 3/3 GOLDEN SAF 40 CAL

After defeating the enemies in the chop shop, find this weapon part on a desk inside the shop's long office.

STAY WITH RAUL!

After you clear the chop shop yard, explore quickly to pick up painkillers, weapons, and ammo. If you wait too long to follow Passos after he pushes through the exit gate into the alley, a mobster will gun down your partner.

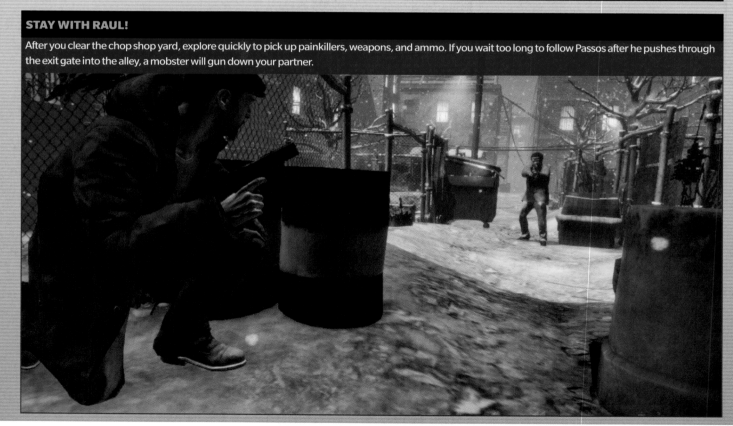

NEW WEAPONS

NONE

PAINKILLERS 

MISSION

FIGHT DOWN THE ALLEY.

From the gate **(42)**, fight your way down the alley lined with fenced backyards, which are filled with angry mob gunmen. Use the nearby dumpster **(43)** for cover and swing from side to side to get better shooting angles.

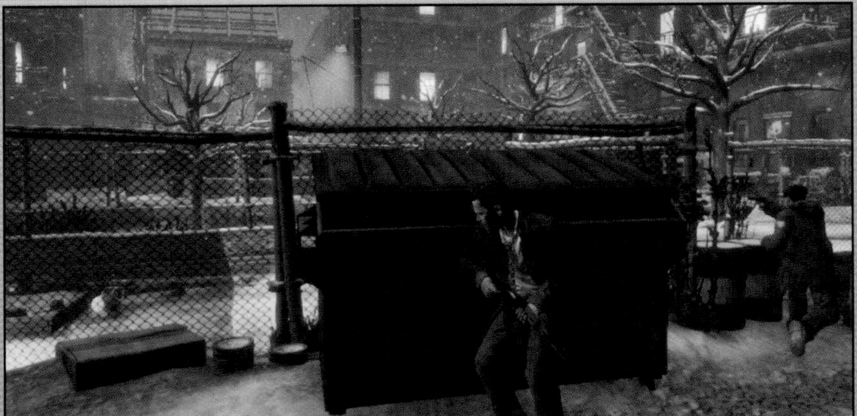

Once you take out the last goon, a cutscene plays: Max and Passos finally reach a safe back alley. Once again, Passos asks his newfound friend if he wants a job. A jump-cut moves a few months forward, returning to the search for Fabiana in Brazil.

V ALIVE IF NOT EXACTLY WELL

A FEW MILES UP THE TIETE RIVER

3:30 AM, FRIDAY

Barely more than a day after the debacle in the Galatians FC stadium, Max and Raul Passos troll the Tiete River in a sleek blue speedboat, searching for Fabiana Branco. Passos explains what he knows about Crachá Preto—the "Black Badge"—the right wing paramilitary group that now seems to be targeting Comando Sombra, the favela gang that abducted Fabiana. It's a complicated web of intrigue that doesn't make much sense yet, other than that big money is involved.

As they approach the old river harbor, Passos points out that it's a known Comando Sombra area. After a short conversation that careens between Max's self-loathing and Raul's self-absolution, Passos pilots the boat to a beach near the docks. Max wades ashore and spots a CS sentry on a balcony. Looks like this is the right place...

HARBOR

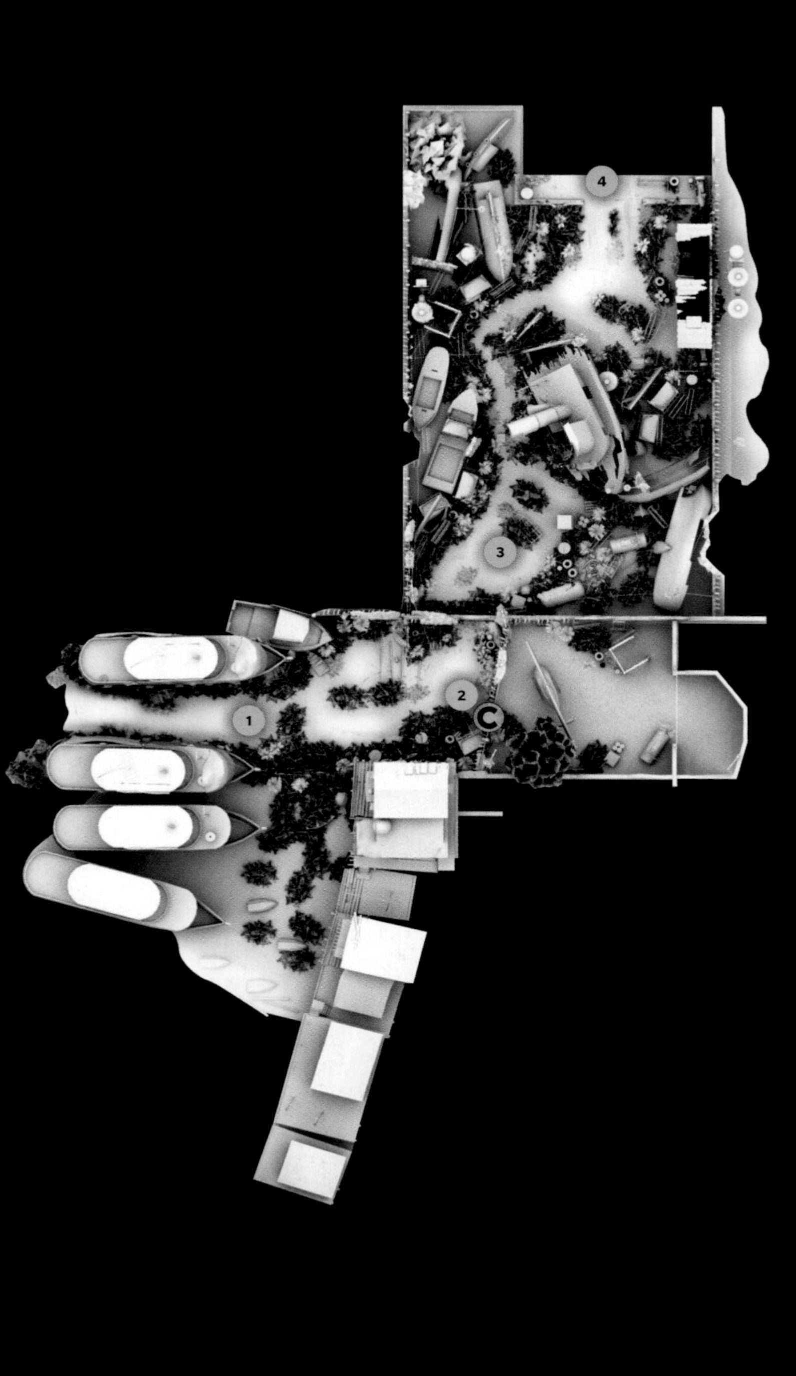

MISSION

FIND THE KIDNAPPERS' COPTER.

You start out on the shore **(1)** armed with a silenced PT92 pistol. Move forward to the fenced enclosure **(2)**. As you approach, press the "Inspect Helicopter" button indicated onscreen. Max verifies that it's the same chopper used by the Comando Sombra to escape the São Paulo nightclub with Fabiana.

PARKED HELICOPTER

This Clue is located in the beginning of the mission. At the end of the first area before you leap over the worn concrete wall, walk up to the fence and examine the nearby helicopter.

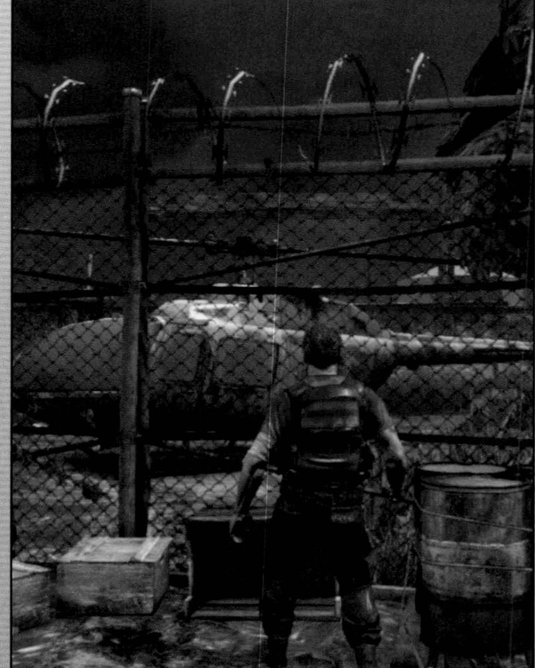

FIND THE SLIPWAY.

After the cinematic ends, walk straight ahead to the gap in the fence. Climb over the stone wall and drop down into an overgrown repair yard **(3)**.

NEW WEAPONS

NONE

PAINKILLERS 

Now move across the yard, veering to the left of the big rusted propeller. Veer back to the right around the wrecked, abandoned boat until you reach the doors etched with the number "1945" **(4)**. Shoot the padlock on the doors to open them.

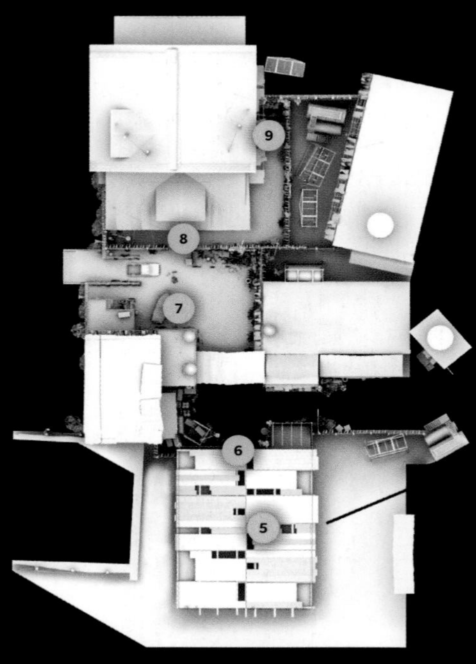

NEW WEAPONS

NONE

PAINKILLERS

MISSION

FIND THE SLIPWAY WAREHOUSE.

Go through the open doors, cross the yard **(5)**, and climb the stairs onto a platform **(6)** overlooking a slipway area where boats were once repaired but now lay scattered and abandoned. Ahead you should see a sign that reads "Portao 10" (which translates to "Gate 10"). Hop over the platform railing and approach the door just to the left of the sign.

WATCH SERRANO.

When you reach the door, a cutscene plays: Max sneaks to a covered boat **(7)** and observes a pair of Comando Sombra thugs who load boxes onto a pickup truck parked on a slipway ramp. The ramp slopes down to the water where a launch boat slowly motors past carrying the CS boss, Serrano—the same fellow you saw direct the kidnapping team's escape from Club Moderno.

FIGHT INTO THE WAREHOUSE.

Max says he wants to get "quietly" past these first thugs. Again, your pistol has a silencer, so wait until the two men finish loading boxes and walk together up the ramp alongside the truck. Then, pop up and shoot the first one in the head and then use that earned Bullet Time to nail the second thug before he can return fire. If either thug gets off a shot, the sound alerts other gangsters.

TRUCK TRICKS

Another way to silently dispatch the two truck loaders is tricky, but fun: When both guys have their heads down, pop up and shoot the yellow block under the right front tire. The truck takes them out! If either guy sees you, your stealth is blown.

If you can't get "quietly" past the first two gangsters, consider targeting their truck engine until it explodes. This takes out all nearby gunmen at once.

If you trigger the alarm, move down to the stern (rear) of the covered boat for safety: three more gangsters rush from the fenced warehouse enclosure **(8)** just to the right of the truck. Take them out and grab a second weapon. Enter the enclosure and find the entry doors **(9)** on the right side of the building.

MISSION

CLEAR THE FIRST STORAGE AREA.

Enter the warehouse to trigger a cutscene: Max steps into an office and spots a live camera feed playing on a desktop monitor **(10)**. It shows Fabiana—bound and gagged in a chair, and threatened roughly by her captors. The scene ends with Max hiding in cover at an interior window as a pair of CS thugs approaches the warehouse office.

NEW WEAPONS

608 BULL REVOLVER

PAINKILLERS

Using the office door and window **(11)** for cover, gun down the first two CS thugs and then clear the main floor **(12)** of the three others who appear. The last enemy to enter this room drops a 608 Bull revolver, described as "a veritable hand cannon" that features staggering firepower for a sidearm. Before you leave the area, collect two painkiller stashes back in the office: one in a medicine cabinet on the wall, the other sitting on a metal shelf next to the desk with the monitor.

Then examine the ransom note sitting on the desktop. It's in Portuguese, but you can probably decipher the main message: the kidnappers now want an additional $5 million for Fabiana, delivered to the Hotel Mona—no weapons, no police.

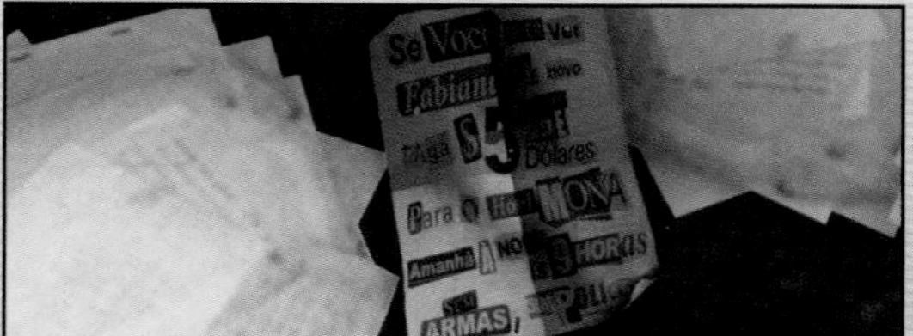

RANSOM NOTE

In the first warehouse—where you take cover by an office window to prepare for a shootout—the ransom note is on the same desk where the kidnap video is playing on the small monitor.

Proceed through the far doorway into the loading room. Don't miss the ammo case **(13)** on the floor; it provides ammo for all weapons. A Micro 9mm is also beside the ammo bag. This will come in handy for what's beyond the next door. Approach the roll-up door **(14)**: Max pulls it up to reveal a trio of thugs escaping the relentless rain in an alcove formed in the stack of shipping containers across the road.

CONTAINER YARD/REPAIR GARAGE

CONTAINER YARD

19
18
16
15
17
14

REPAIR GARAGE

MISSION

CLEAR THE CONTAINER YARD.

Quickly gun down the gangsters gathered at the table in the alcove **(15)**, then take down the two gunmen to your right. Two of the alcove thugs drop AK-47 assault rifles. Grab one to give your firepower a boost. When you get a chance, re-enter the warehouse and approach the ammo case to stock up on AK-47 ammo.

NEW WEAPONS NONE | PAINKILLERS 

Work your way across the yard. You can either move along the obvious path between truck cabs and stacked containers **(16)** or pull yourself up onto the containers and move through the gaps **(17)**. (We like the sneakier route because it leads you to a Golden weapon part.) Watch out for gangsters sneaking up behind you!

PART 1/3 GOLDEN MICRO 9MM

Open the roll-up door to exit the first warehouse and shoot the enemies. Once the area is clear, climb the shipping containers on the right to find this weapon part on top.

Three more gunmen are posted ahead in the last yard; one is tucked behind a forklift **(18)**. Shoot the explosive propane canister atop the forklift to take him out easily. Watch for one last gangster, who enters via the back gate. You eventually reach an alley that leads to a white security door **(19)** in the tin building on your right.

FIND THE HOSTAGE ROOM.

Approach the door to trigger a scene: Max enters a repair garage and finds the videocam setup where Fabiana was being held **(20)**. Unfortunately, the room is now abandoned: Max just missed them. Look for painkillers on the table near the camera and an ammo case **(21)** on the floor nearby which stocks up for all weapons. You should also watch the TV to get some illuminating background to the main story, and also examine the video camera.

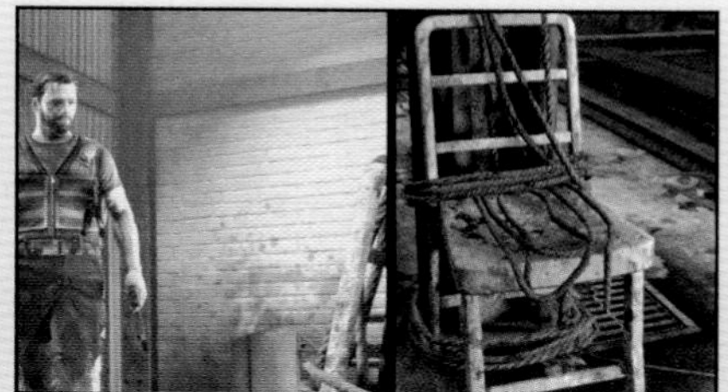

VIDEO CAMERA

When you reach the warehouse where Fabiana was being held captive, examine the video camera on the tripod. This is just before the boathouse shootout.

FIND THE BOATHOUSE.

Exit via the open garage door **(22)**, turn left, and climb the staircase to the next building **(23)**, the boathouse.

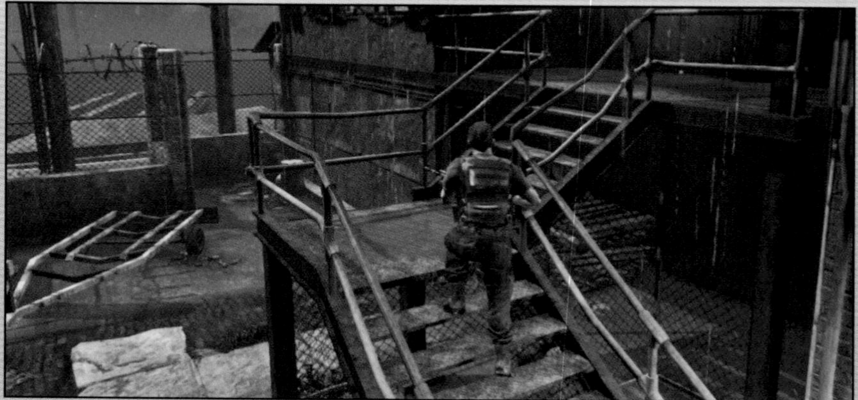

PART 2/3 GOLDEN MICRO 9MM

Exit the warehouse where Fabiana was being held and look for this weapon part in the nook between the building on the right and the fence.

DRY DOCKS OVERVIEW

33 28 27 23 22

BOATHOUSE

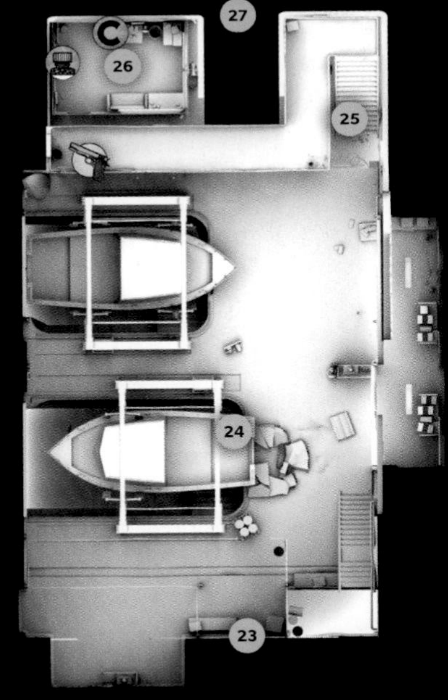

NEW WEAPONS

FAL BATTLE RIFLE

PAINKILLERS

MISSION

GO BULLET TIME IN THE BOATHOUSE.

Open the boathouse door **(23)** to trigger a scene: Max creeps across a platform and hops aboard a boat raised by a winch for hull repair. Crouched at the boat's gunwale **(24)** (upper edge of the boat's side), Max finally spots Fabiana as she's hauled out a far doorway by Serrano and friends.

When control returns, open fire at the big Comando Sombra crew on the boathouse floor below to trigger a spectacular sequence: one gangster targets the winch rope holding the boat and it snaps, sending Max off the stern in a slow-motion ShootDodge dive. You want to pick off as many gunmen as possible as you dive to the right, but start by nailing men from left to right and end with the explosive canister **(25)** on the stairs (circled in our screenshot). That should take out anyone you missed.

WICKED ACHIEVEMENT

To get the Achievement (or Trophy) named "Someting Wicked This Way Comes," you must take out all the thugs on the floor at the time of your jump using Free Aim mode. Your initial attack quickly triggers the challenge, so take out the two men carrying the crate directly below you and get the third guy welding the boat to their left. If you can get two or three before Max automatically jumps, then the challenge of shooting the rest of them is much easier.

CLEAR THE BOATHOUSE.

You hit the ground behind a crate. While still prone, immediately open fire to nail the two gunmen to the right. Stay in cover and get ready for two more men to rush down the stairs and spread out to either side of the room.

Once the boathouse is cleared, go into the office in the back left corner **(26)**. Nab the painkillers from the shelf then approach the table and press the "Examine picture" button indicated onscreen: Max discovers a photo that suggests the Comando Sombra ("Serrano's boys," as he calls them) is targeting *everyone* in the Branco family.

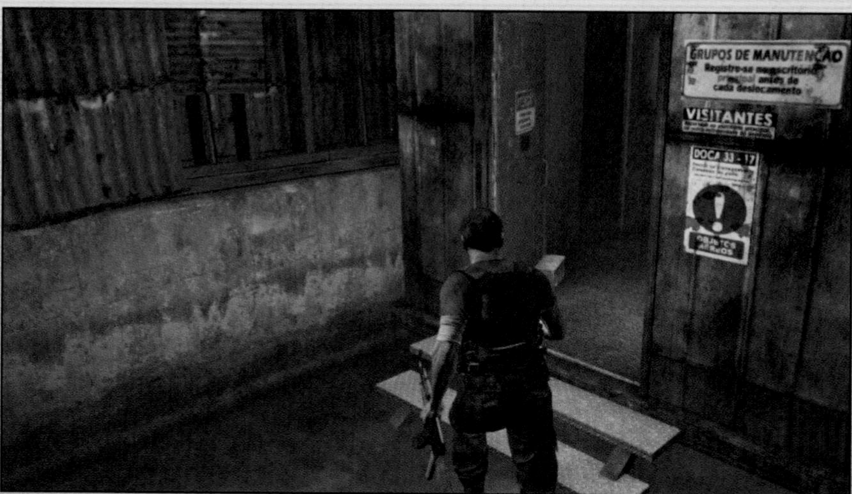

BRANCO FAMILY PHOTO

You must enter the small office inside the first boathouse to open the garage door. Inside this little office is a photo on the edge of the table. Examine it.

Approach the panel with the flashing button between the windows and press the "Open garage door" button indicated onscreen. Just outside the window, a metal door slides upward. Exit the office and go through this newly opened doorway **(27)**. It leads out into what Max calls "the next circle of this low-rent hell."

PART 3/3 GOLDEN MICRO 9MM

After the boathouse leaping shootout challenge and clearing all the enemies within, head to the second floor and find this weapon part at the end of the winding catwalk.

FIND THE DRY DOCKS WAREHOUSE.

Now you reach the dry docks area. Use the crates for cover and plug the gangsters who emerge from an open doorway **(28)** across the yard, next to the dumpster. Note that a Belgian-made FAL battle rifle and an M500 shotgun sit at the crates if you want a weapon change. A nearby ammo case provides ammo for all weapons in your possession.

DRY DOCKS WAREHOUSE (INTERIOR)

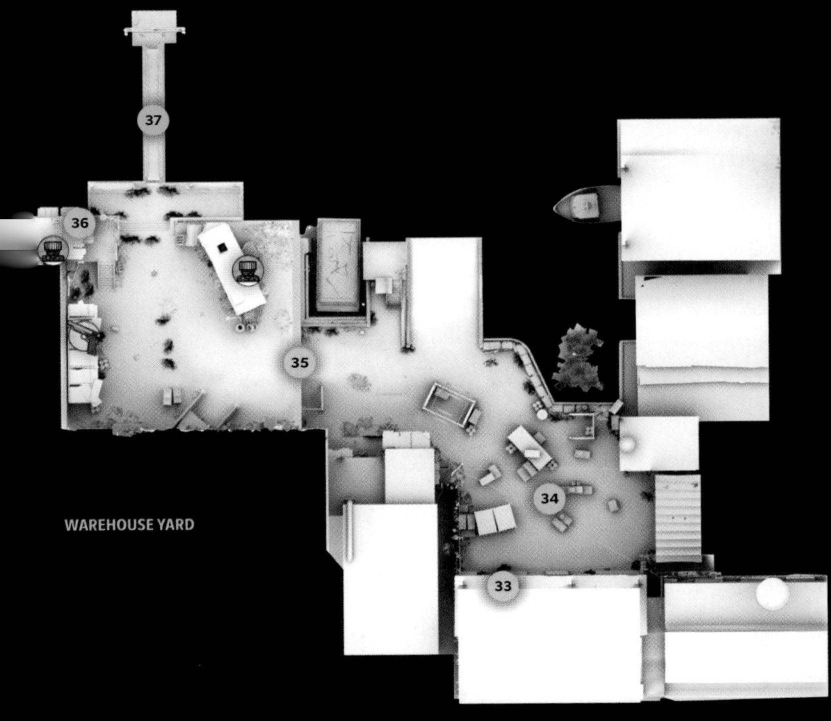

WAREHOUSE YARD

MISSION

CLEAR OUT THE WAREHOUSE INTERIOR.

Approach the open doorway, take cover to one side, and start picking off the gunmen inside the crate-strewn warehouse. After you eliminate the initial wave and push further inside the structure, a sliding door opens **(29)** to your left revealing two gunmen; another shooter appears up on the second-floor walkway. Dispatch the guy on the top floor first, and then take out the lower two using Bullet Time.

NEW WEAPONS

NONE | PAINKILLERS 

When the area is clear, find the alcove hung with girly pictures and approach the newspaper on the floor. Press the "Examine newspaper" button indicated onscreen for a close-up: the São Paulo rag features headlines about the Comando Sombra's failed kidnapping attempt at the luxury high-rise condo. As Max puts it, "Serrano was reading his reviews, the vain chump." Then enter the small corner office **(30)** to find some painkillers plus the blueprints for Club Moderno.

PART 1/3 GOLDEN LMG .30

Explore the area through the back doors of the dry docks warehouse to find this weapon part inside the trash-filled shipping container.

NIGHTCLUB FLOOR PLANS

Inside the dry docks warehouse is a small first floor office (across from the shack where you find the boathouse newspaper). The blueprints of the nightclub are on the edge of a table inside the office.

BOATHOUSE NEWSPAPER

Inside the dry docks warehouse is a small shack—below the catwalk in a corner across from the first floor office. On the floor of this shack is the newspaper.

Climb the stairs **(31)** inside the warehouse. They lead up to a raised catwalk. Follow this path through a metal door **(32)** to where the broken walkway ends. A CS gunman waits down below; kill him then drop down into the next area.

CLEAR OUT THE WAREHOUSE YARD.

Move to the windows on the right **(33)** that overlook an outdoor storage yard filled with crates, shipping containers, and more gunmen. Move back and forth along the row of windows to maintain cover. To take out attackers, target the explosive yellow gas canister (circled) sitting atop the nearby forklift **(34)**.

Gangsters toss grenades at you in this yard so be prepared to ditch your cover and to move to new cover. Bullet Time makes these moves much safer. Move toward the crates and hunt down any remaining thugs. Look for two other explosive canisters to target—one sits atop a rack of barrels just beyond the moving cart.

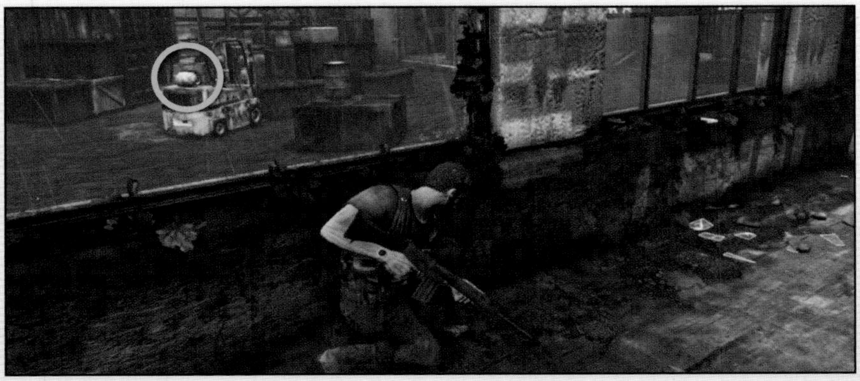

When the warehouse yard is finally clear, find the chain-link gate **(35)** with the red private property sign ("Propriedade Privada") and approach it to trigger a scene: Max slides the gate open and enters the slipway area.

ACTIVATE THE DOCKS WALKWAY.

Turn right and enter the dilapidated prefab office to find some painkillers in a wall cabinet. Exit and cross the yard to the control room with the white "Do Not Enter" sign above the door.

Grab more painkillers from the medicine cabinet, then approach the walkway control panel with the lever and flashing button **(36)**. Press the "Activate the walkway" control indicated onscreen. Max pulls the lever to extend the walkway **(37)**...and spots Fabiana with Serrano in another control shack down the docks.

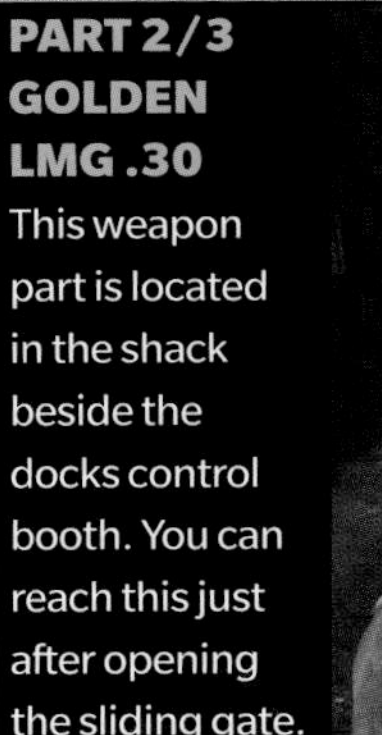

PART 2/3 GOLDEN LMG .30

This weapon part is located in the shack beside the docks control booth. You can reach this just after opening the sliding gate.

MISSION

FIGHT ALONG THE PIERS.

Exit the control shack and proceed across the walkway **(37)** you just activated. When you reach the next pier, be ready to exchange gunfire with thugs posted along the walkways ahead. The first team is near the shack where you just saw Fabiana with Serrano. A flare shoots up into the sky, illuminating the area.

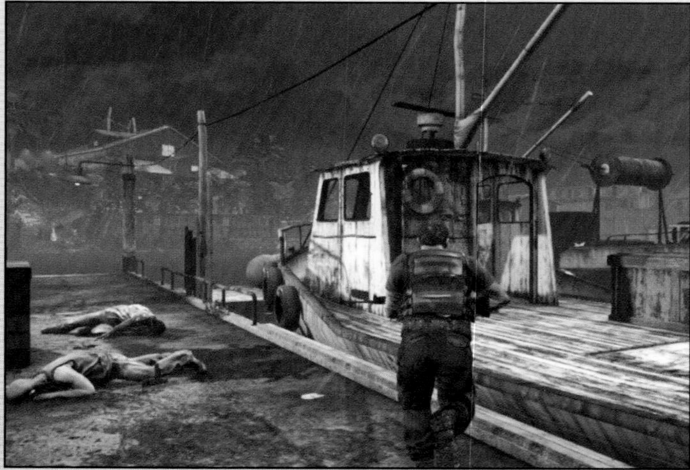

YELLOW CANISTERS

As always, look for yellow gas canisters strewn about the docks. Each one detonates like a bomb when you shoot it.

Careful! You can get caught in crossfire here because a patrol launch boat filled with shooters moves upstream to your left **(38)** as you battle the gunmen on the dock. Enter Bullet Time and fire from cover until the boat moves out of range. If you manage to drill every shooter on a launch boat, it slams into a pier in a fireball.

43

42

41

40

39

37

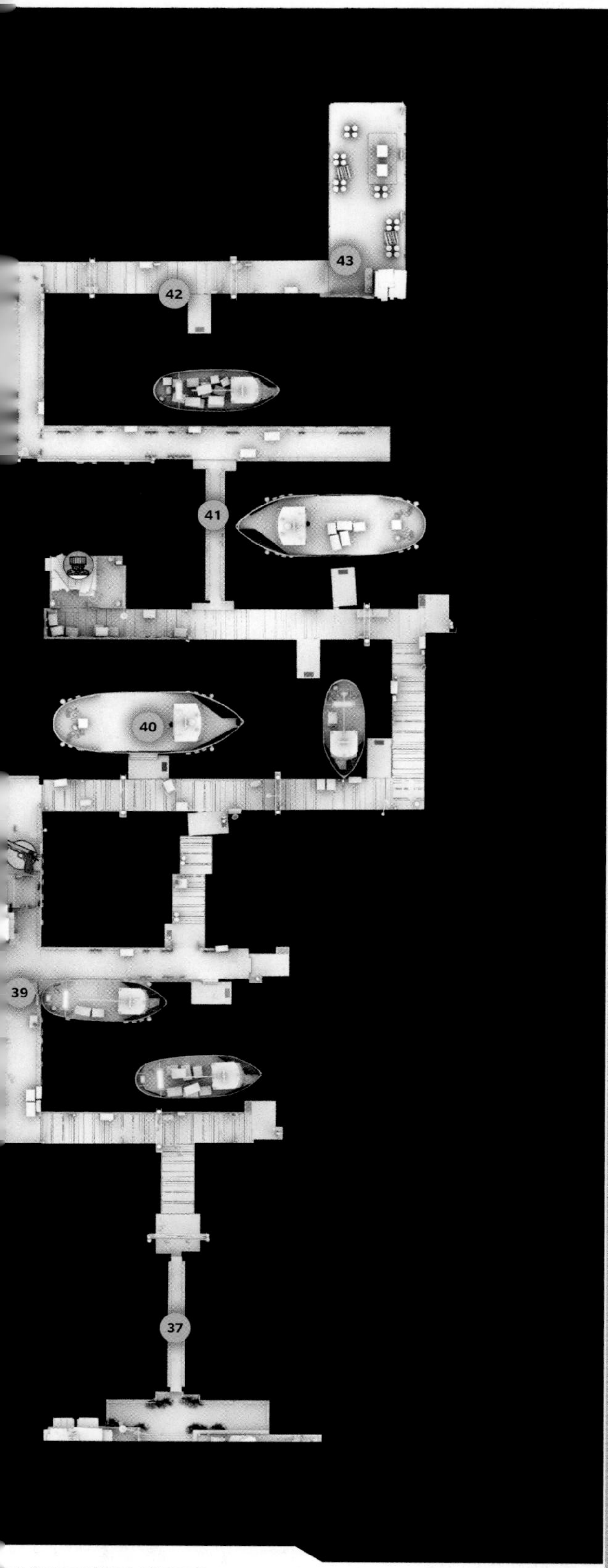

V WEAPONS

NONE

PAINKILLERS

Now start advancing along the narrow dock walkways that zigzag back and forth along the riverfront. Start with the tall crate stack **(39)** on the corner near the second docked boat. You can find a Red Dot Scoped FAL here. Use this weapon to plug enemies on the distant pier by shooting the yellow, explosive propane tanks in the distance to make short work of them. Look for one on the deck of the next boat **(40)** up ahead.

PART 3/3 GOLDEN LMG .30

This gun part is located on the opposite side of the first control shack you reach on the piers (near the scoped FAL). Follow the pier pathway to reach the back side of the shack; a fence keeps you from reaching it from the first side.

This is a long, brutal slog. Keep moving from crate to crate and use cover wisely. Be ready for aggressive charges by zealous gang members. Look for gunmen directly ahead as well as off to the side—some are on the docks, others are posted on moored boats.

Explore each control shack you reach to find more painkillers. Watch out for two more patrol launch boats making passes on the river with crews of shooters. When you cross another movable walkway **(41)** it swings away behind you, cutting off any retreat. Target one last explosive canister **(42)** across the water to clear your way. Eventually, you reach a dock with a red roof **(43)** and a "Petrol" sign.

TRIGGER THE BOAT CHASE.

Approach the petrol station gate to trigger a cutscene—Max reaches the last dock just as a Comando Sombra launch boat pulls away with Fabiana aboard. The gang's return fire hits a gas pump, triggering a dockside explosion that knocks Max into the water. Seconds later, Passos pulls up in the Brancos' blue speedboat and hauls Max aboard. Now the partners give chase to the escaping kidnappers.

MISSION

This is a classic "railshooter" sequence: Max takes up a powerful LMG .30 caliber light machine gun to fight off a variety of Comando Sombra attackers as Passos pilots the Branco boat full-speed down the river.

NEW WEAPONS

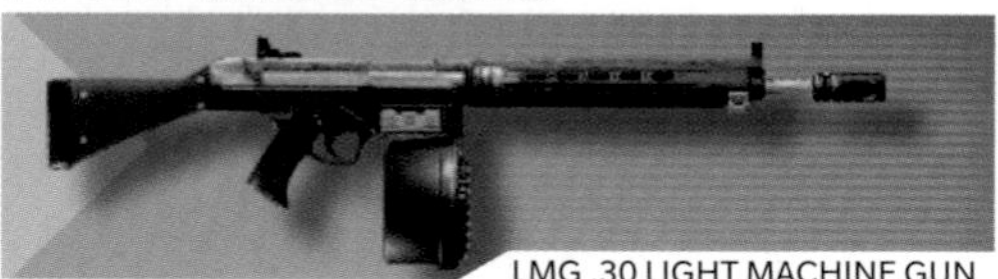

LMG .30 LIGHT MACHINE GUN

1: BOAT CHASERS

The battle starts with Max facing astern (to the rear) and two enemy speedboats on your tail, each carrying three shooters. Open fire! When you take out all three gunmen on a boat, the craft veers wildly and explodes.

SHORT BURSTS

Max's LMG .30 machine gun in the speedboat sequence can overheat if you unleash long, continuous bursts of fire. Fire the weapon in short bursts instead, readjusting your aim quickly between each burst.

When you get clear of the docks, a third speedboat careens across the river behind you then veers up a parallel channel on your starboard (right) side. Rely on your targeting reticule as you shoot through the foliage—it turns red whenever you get a bead on an enemy. Soon a cutscene plays: a speedboat tries to ram you on the port (left) side and ends up slamming through a riverside hut.

2: MOLOTOV THROWERS

Up ahead, Serrano and his crew restrain Fabiana on the Comando Sombra launch boat. A second launch boat swings in behind Serrano's boat to cut off your pursuit.

When control returns, you face forward as Passos pilots your speedboat behind the second launch down the narrow river channel. Some of its CS crewmen start tossing Molotov cocktails at you; others pop up and shoot at you. Each time you see one of the flaming projectiles, target and shoot it as quickly as you can! If a Molotov lands in or near your boat, you take significant damage. Watch out for gunmen on high bridges over the river, and be ready for a two-man speedboat team that overtakes you on your right, as well.

Keep picking off the flaming Molotovs until you veer around a bend near a riverfront village, which triggers another cutscene—a Comando Sombra gangster on a dock tosses a grenade that rocks Max's boat and damages the engine. Passos abandons the helm to examine the motor, leaving the boat on automatic pilot past the village docks.

3: THE VILLAGE

Protect Passos as he tinkers with the engine! Pick off the CS gunmen who rush to the riverside docks just downstream. Eventually Passos returns to the wheel just as another attacker tosses a grenade from the deck of a two-story house. If you shoot the grenade immediately, the explosion ignites a rack of gas canisters on the porch that soon detonates as well, turning the house into a fireball.

After the explosion, swivel to the right and pick off the CS gunmen who emerge on the opposite shore. Be sure to target the small gas canister sitting on the crate (circled in the screenshot) in front of the rightmost outhouse.

The next building downstream is surrounded with gunmen but note the sign overhead: "Gasoline, Alcohol, Kerosene." Spray the large tank inside with many rounds to send the place up in flames. The tower next to it collapses as well, but suddenly a pickup truck full of Comando Sombra marksmen speeds down the riverside road.

4: TRUCK CHASE

Open fire at the truck while it follows the road running parallel to your boat's course. Soon more vehicles, jeeps and trucks, join in the running gun battle. Keep picking off the shooters as you move downstream. Also keep in mind that vehicles explode when you target their engines. Be sure to swivel your view left occasionally to spot attacking vehicles that may be up ahead.

When the last vehicle is disabled, a cutscene plays: a collapsed bridge cuts off the river route up ahead as Serrano's patrol boats pull away. But Passos has an idea...

5: MANGROVE FOREST

As Passos takes a shortcut through the crisscrossing channels of a misty mangrove thicket, more CS-manned craft glide in to attack. Keep your view oriented to the rear and sides as hostile speedboats approach from side channels.

DAMAGE CUE

Visibility is poor in the mangroves so check your onscreen Damage indicator to determine the direction that attackers are shooting at you.

Once you eliminate these boats, another scene plays: Max identifies Serrano's boat again and spots Fabiana aboard. But the second launch boat is still deployed behind the lead boat.

6: UNDER THE PIER

Passos maneuvers beside the second launch boat but has to veer left and steer underneath a long pier to stay abreast. When control returns to you, start picking off the gunmen aboard. Soon another enemy speedboat pulls up behind the launch with the usual contingent of three gunmen. Pick them off too to trigger a spectacular final Bullet Time sequence.

7: SERRANO'S LAUNCH

Passos has no choice but to gun the motor and steer the boat up a collapsed section of the pier. This launches your boat into the air in slow-motion Bullet Time, flying side by side with Serrano's boat!

Fabiana is in the center of the deck (circled in our screenshot), surrounded by seven Comando Sombra gunmen. In Bullet Time, try to pick off all seven shooters without hitting Fabiana. If you shoot Fabiana, you fail the mission and return to the previous checkpoint.

When the sequence ends, Max and Passos watch helplessly as their boat engine dies and Serrano pilots his launch downstream.

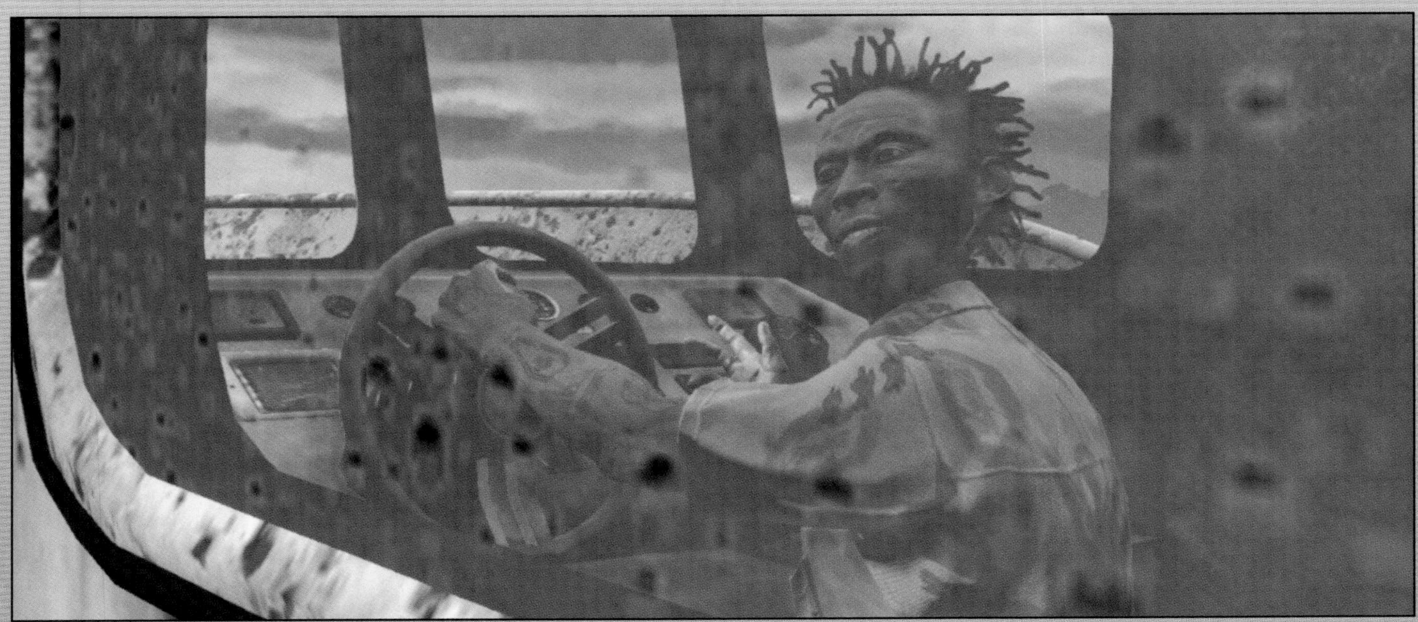

VI A DAME, A DORK, AND A DRUNK

FÁBRICAS BRANCO GLOBAL HEADQUARTERS, SÃO PAULO

11:35 AM, SUNDAY

Not long after the river escapade, Passos rousts Max from a deep, dark well of sleep for a meeting with "the boss" at company headquarters. The partners arrive at a pow-wow that includes all three Branco brothers plus the UFE commander, Colonel Becker, who assures Rodrigo that Fabiana will be returned safely and the kidnappers caught.

Max speaks alone with Rodrigo after Victor Branco leads the others to his helicopter. The eldest Branco questions the current state of his privileged life, but Max assures him he's at least a decent man. Suddenly, heavily armed men begin to invade the complex; Rodrigo spots them on his surveillance cameras.

The Fábricas Branco building has a multimillion-dollar security lockdown system...but unfortunately, the lockdown sequence fails to work. The company tech expert reports that he must get to the server room to reboot the system in order to get security systems back online. Max escorts the young man from the office and tells Rodrigo to lock himself in.

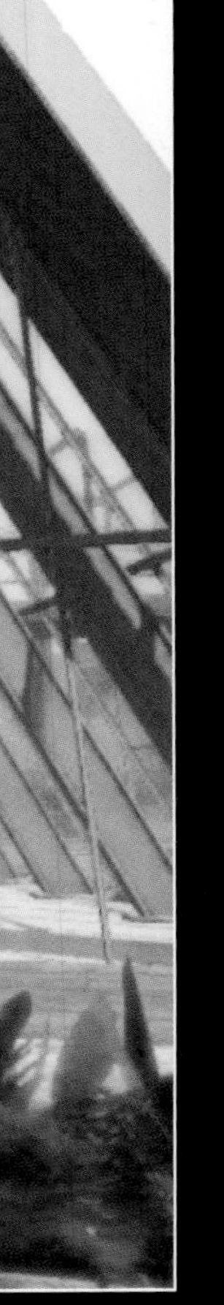

EXECUTIVE OFFICES/BOARDROOM

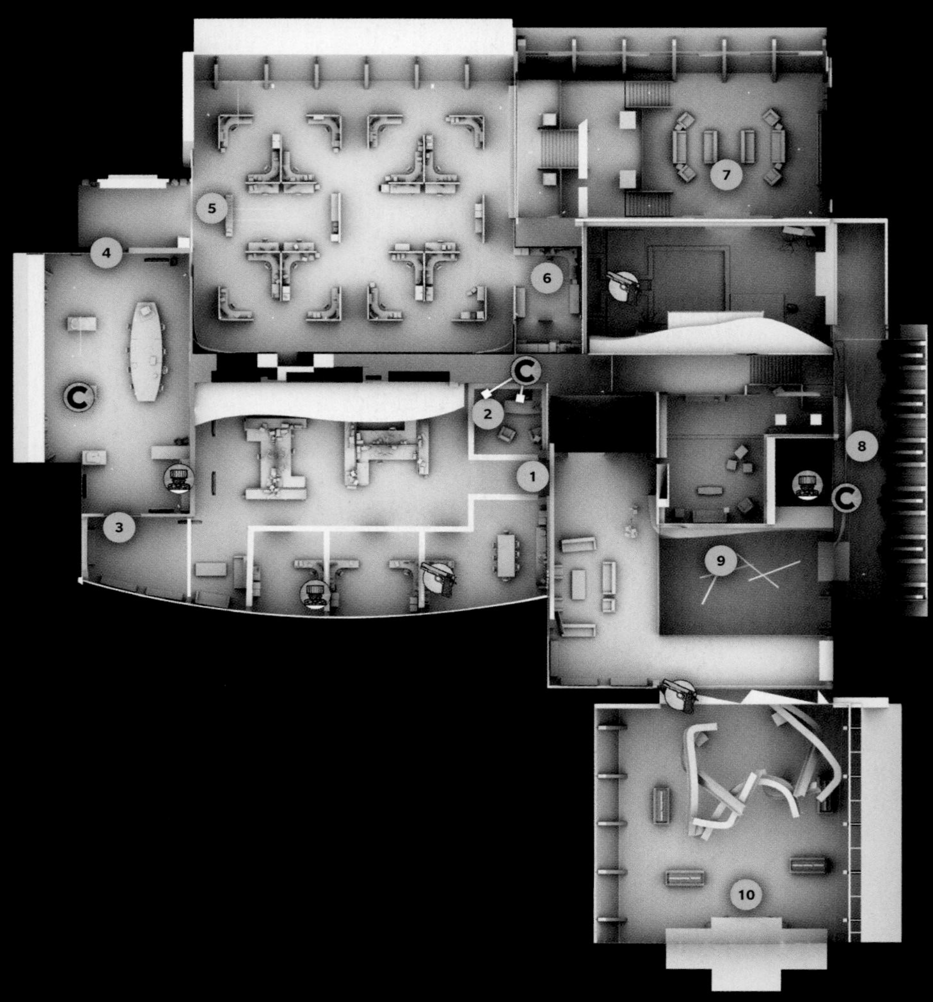

NEW WEAPONS

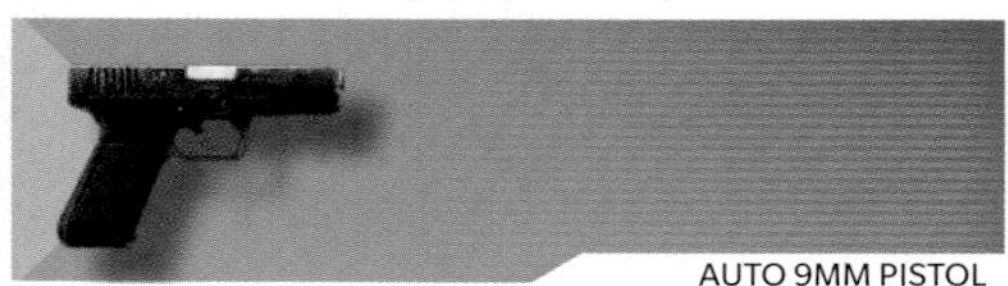

AUTO 9MM PISTOL

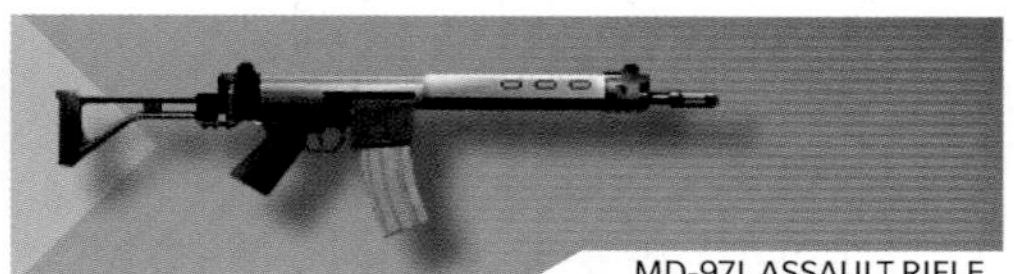

MD-97L ASSAULT RIFLE

PAINKILLERS 

MISSION

CLEAR THE DESIGNERS' AREA.

Max crosses the reception area outside Rodrigo's office and pushes through doors **(1)** into a room full of worktables surrounded by the glass walls of executive offices (including Victor Branco's office on the right) and conference rooms. The area is crawling with gunmen wearing body armor. Your Bullet Time begins to fill as you push through the doors. Activate Bullet Time and start aiming for heads—avoid wasting bullets on armor vests. Roll forward to the nearest table and use it for cover as you clear the area.

When you find cover, take out the two enemies on your extreme left and right. The one on the left is in the office: shoot him through the glass. Now finish off the remaining enemies in the back of the room. Once the room is safe, watch the cutscene: the IT tech enters and moves through the carnage. When control returns, pick up ammo and weapons, including the lethal MD-97L assault rifle. You can find painkillers on a desk in the office on the far-left; the one closest to the boardroom. Then enter Victor Branco's glass office **(2)**—the one in the corner next to the door with the "Saida" sign. Search his office for clues.

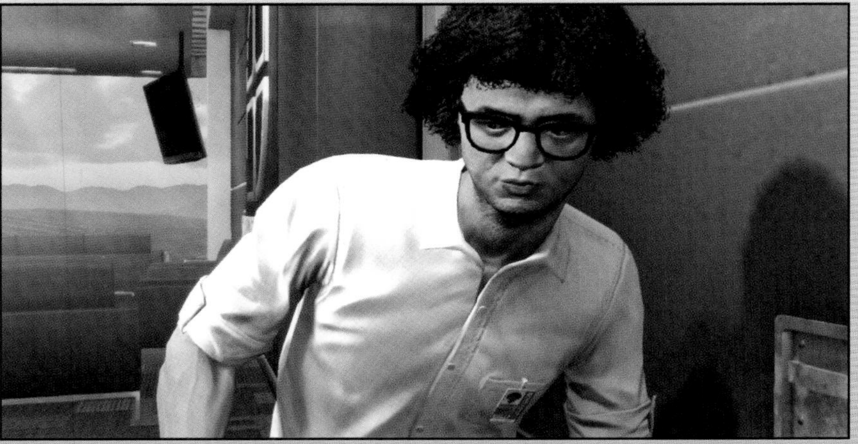

FILE ON FABIANA

The folder is on Victor Branco's desk inside his office. This is the first office on the right side of the first battle room.

RODRIGO'S EMAIL

After the first office shootout, turn back and enter Victor Branco's glass wall office and examine his computer on the filing cabinet beside his desk. The email shows that Victor is looking for campaign contributions since Rodrigo holds the purse strings rather tight.

ART 1 / 3 MD-97L

This weapon part is located on floor of the glass wall office, across from Victor Branco's office. This is the first battle area of the mission.

Reload then follow the IT guy to the next set of doors **(3)** where he punches in a code to the boardroom ("Sala de Reunides") and the door opens. As he enters, hostile soldiers burst into the room from the opposite entrance!

CLEAR THE BOARDROOM.

Immediately activate Bullet Time if you can. If you do so quickly, you can use just one deadly burst of your weapon to shoot all five of the attackers who rush through the far doorway. Otherwise, take cover behind the first desk on the left and begin using cover fire to take out the enemy. Use Bullet Time when you obtain it to make calculated head shots.

When the last gunmen falls, find the painkillers on the counter near the sink where you entered the room. You can also examine the model building in the center of the room.

ARCHITECTURAL MODELS

Examine the model in the middle of the second office battle scene.

Follow the IT guy past the big conference table and approach the far doorway **(4)** to trigger a scene: Max pushes through the doors and spots another squad of soldiers in an open area filled with office cubicles. The IT guy notes that the server room is just past the cubicles.

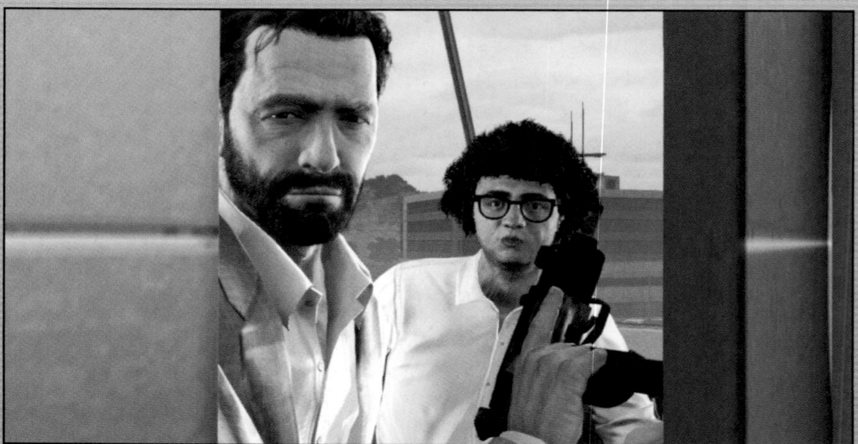

When you find cover, take out the two enemies on your extreme left and right. The one on the left is in the office: shoot him through the glass. Now finish off the remaining enemies in the back of the room. Once the room is safe, watch the cutscene: the IT tech enters and moves through the carnage. When control returns, pick up ammo and weapons, including the lethal MD-97L assault rifle. You can find painkillers on a desk in the office on the far-left; the one closest to the boardroom. Then enter Victor Branco's glass office **(2)**—the one in the corner next to the door with the "Saida" sign. Search his office for clues.

FILE ON FABIANA

The folder is on Victor Branco's desk inside his office. This is the first office on the right side of the first battle room.

RODRIGO'S EMAIL

After the first office shootout, turn back and enter Victor Branco's glass wall office and examine his computer on the filing cabinet beside his desk. The email shows that Victor is looking for campaign contributions since Rodrigo holds the purse strings rather tight.

ART 1/3 MD-97L

This weapon part is located on floor of the glass wall office, across from Victor Branco's office. This is the first battle area of the mission.

Reload then follow the IT guy to the next set of doors **(3)** where he punches in a code to the boardroom ("Sala de Reunides") and the door opens. As he enters, hostile soldiers burst into the room from the opposite entrance!

CLEAR THE BOARDROOM.

Immediately activate Bullet Time if you can. If you do so quickly, you can use just one deadly burst of your weapon to shoot all five of the attackers who rush through the far doorway. Otherwise, take cover behind the first desk on the left and begin using cover fire to take out the enemy. Use Bullet Time when you obtain it to make calculated head shots.

When the last gunmen falls, find the painkillers on the counter near the sink where you entered the room. You can also examine the model building in the center of the room.

ARCHITECTURAL MODELS

Examine the model in the middle of the second office battle scene.

Follow the IT guy past the big conference table and approach the far doorway **(4)** to trigger a scene: Max pushes through the doors and spots another squad of soldiers in an open area filled with office cubicles. The IT guy notes that the server room is just past the cubicles.

(See office overview map at beginning of chapter)

MISSION

CLEAR OUT THE CUBICLES.

Now Max realizes that these attackers are the same right- wing paramilitary guns-for-hire who jumped the ransom exchange in Galatians FC stadium—Crachá Preto, the "Black Badge." And there are a *lot* of them.

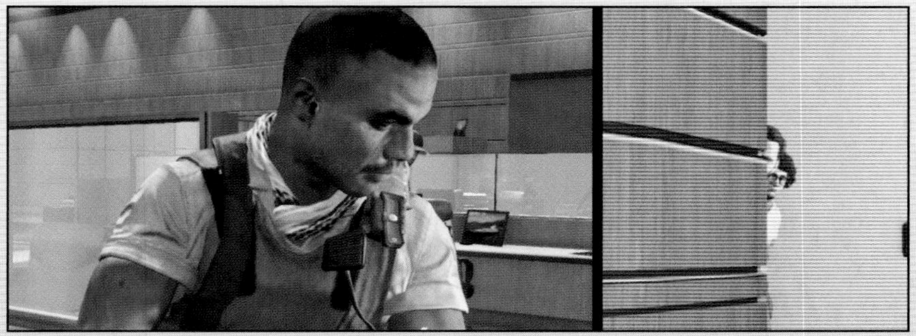

When control returns, you crouch in cover behind a stack of metal file cabinets **(5)**. Open fire at targets to your extreme left and right and then blast the ones across the room. Leave the last guy alive while you collect weapons or you may run out of ammo during the next attack. When you clear out the cubicles, Max and the IT guy proceed down the side aisle toward the server room.

FIGHT OFF THE SECOND WAVE.

Suddenly, more Crachá Preto soldiers smash through the ceiling skylights and zip-line into the area. Get into cover and start picking off attackers. Some of them toss grenades, so be ready to dive away if one lands near you. Again, watch for flanking attempts, especially to your left.

Use Bullet Time and ShootDodges as you move about the room eliminating this large assault force. If you have enough ammo, you don't need to move. If you are low, however, you need to seek out dropped weapons. Search the area for ammo/weapons once the second wave has been eliminated. When you're ready to move on, find the IT guy hiding in the little storage alcove to trigger a cutscene. He finally reaches the servers **(6)** and reboots the security system. Meanwhile, Max makes a sweep of the area, trying to get back to Rodrigo's office.

ATRIUM/FRONT LOBBY

(See office overview map at beginning of chapter)

MISSION

FIND THE FRONT LOBBY.

Move downstairs into the waiting area **(7)** to trigger a short scene—Rodrigo appears on his balcony, and Max reports on the situation. You regain control after Rodrigo retreats back into his office.

PART 3/3 MD-97L

Immediately after shouting up to Rodrigo Branco on the balcony above the waterfall courtyard, turn around and find this weapon part on the small bridge near the waterfall.

SCHOOL PICTURE

Find this clue (a series of three framed pictures) on the hallway wall just beyond the bathroom with the painkillers and before the lobby battle.

Step out of the lobby into the atrium with the pond and waterfall. Proceed to the glassed-in exterior passage **(8)**. Follow the passage to the small alcove on the right side and enter the restroom to find painkillers.

Continue down the passage to the exit ("Saida") sign then turn right. Approach the door to trigger another scene: Max enters the front lobby and finds mayhem at the reception desk **(9)**. Suddenly, a jeep carrying Crachá Preto gunmen smashes through the glass of the front entrance.

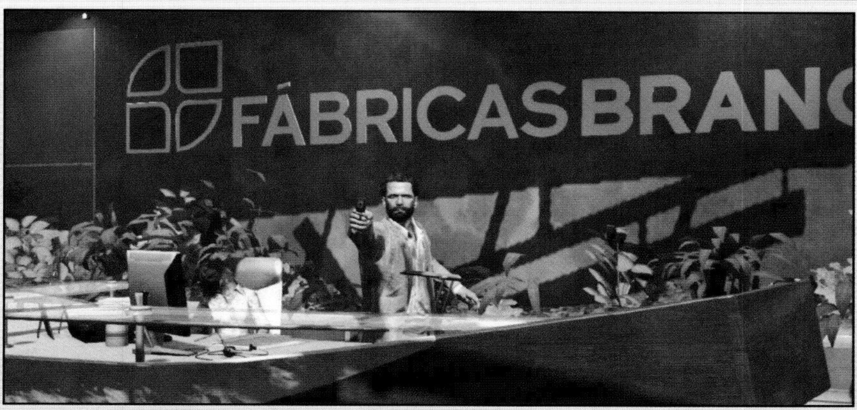

FEND OFF THE VEHICULAR ASSAULT.

You automatically go into Bullet Time, but even in slow motion this is a tricky challenge. In just a few seconds you must drill the jeep driver (circled) before the vehicle gets close or else it plows right through the reception desk...and crushes Max.

But the challenge doesn't end there. As the jeep passes, Max lunges forward in a ShootDodge dive as four more shooters rush through the doorway **(10)** ahead. Then a white van pulls up behind them and swiftly unloads four more Crachá Preto soldiers. If you can't take out all of them with your ShootDodge dive, hustle to the support column for cover and work carefully to clear the lobby.

TAKE OUT THE MACHINE GUNNER.

When the last gunman falls in the slow motion of the final kill camera, be ready for one last challenge. Two gunmen escort a soldier lugging a big LMG .30 machine gun from the van. If you're not in cover already, dive behind something immediately!

The machine gunner wears heavy body armor and can take a lot of hits, so lean around the cover and fire in short bursts. If you stay exposed even briefly, the machine gun takes you down. The task is complicated by the flanking attempts of the other two Crachá Preto gunmen.

Pick off these two wingmen first so you can concentrate your efforts on the machine gunner. The moment the second support gunman drops, ShootDodge to the nearest cover when the machine gunner reloads. While Shootdodging for new cover, aim and shoot at the gunner's head. Once you're in new cover, pop up to fire quick bursts. Shoot only in the very brief lulls between the machine gunner's own bursts. Remember, in Bullet Time you can see enemy bullets flying toward you and dodge them.

PART 3/3 MD-97L

After completing the difficult battle in the lobby, smash the architectural model display case on the right side of the room (near the reception desk) and take this gun part from inside.

RETURN TO RODRIGO'S OFFICE.

When the lobby is finally clear, walk behind the reception desk to trigger a series of cutscenes: Max returns to the reception area outside Rodrigo's office where his secretary reports no word from her boss since he locked himself in. Max knows of another entrance via the building's helipad, so he takes the elevator up to the roof.

Unfortunately, Max finds Rodrigo dead, shot cleanly through the head. Max picks up the framed photo of Fabiana from the desk. When he accidentally drops it, he discovers a bomb wired underneath Rodrigo's desk. Max manages to dive off the office balcony into the atrium just as the charge detonates.

ESCAPE THE FIRE

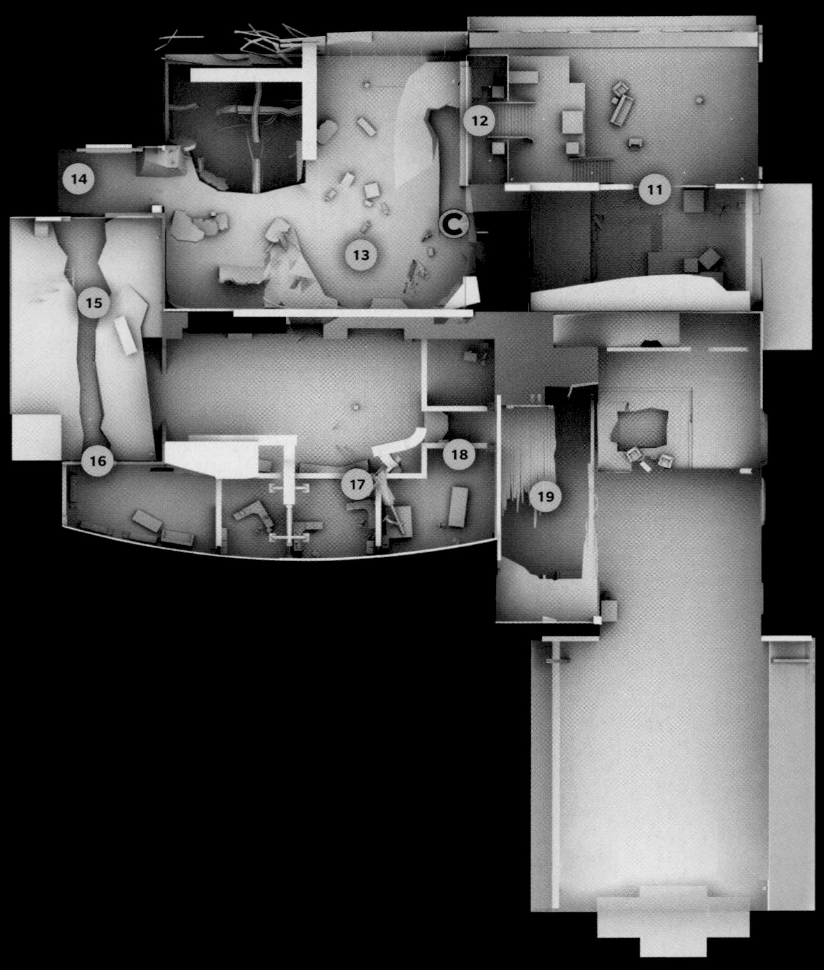

NEW WEAPONS NONE | PAINKILLERS 

MISSION

ESCAPE THE ATRIUM.

You start this escape sequence in the atrium, which appears to be completely surrounded by burning debris. It may seem counterintuitive, but the only escape route leads through the burning building. Stagger through the opening next to the red wall **(11)**.

GET UPSTAIRS TO THE CUBICLE AREA.

In the lobby, turn left and approach the stairs. After a brief cutscene of Max staggering upstairs, keep climbing until you reach a big metal security door **(12)**. Max manages to pull it open and stumble into the large cubicle-filled area you fought through earlier.

There, Max runs into a disoriented Crachá Preto soldier. Press the "Disarm" button indicated onscreen to punch him out, snag his weapon, and then shoot him. Then follow the aisle to examine the body of the unfortunate IT guy.

DEAD IT GUY

Examine your friendly IT guy's body after disarming the soldier in the beginning of the office fire challenge.

FLAMING FALLS

Maneuver carefully through the fiery office building. If you take a wrong step, Max can fall through burning gaps in the flooring and die. Avoid stepping on floorboards that are aflame or glowing.

Two more soldiers are waiting just around the corner **(13)**. Gun them down too. After an explosion rocks the building and collapses a section of floor, continue past the fallen gunmen into the corridor up ahead **(14)** where a bluish light flashes on and off—it leads into the boardroom. Avoid the burning hole in the floor to the right!

GET THROUGH THE BOARDROOM.

Raise your weapon as you step through the doors into the boardroom. Careful! A dying soldier sits on the floor directly ahead **(15)**—he's horribly burned, but he still opens fire when you arrive. Take him out quickly, collect his ammo, and continue down the center aisle to the far door **(16)**.

ESCAPE THE BURNING OFFICES.

Approaching the door triggers a cutscene—Max pushes into the office area to find a Crachá Preto squad of soldiers whose escape route is blocked by a tall metal file cabinet. From cover, pick off the gunmen using Bullet Time. Then walk up to the file cabinet **(17)**. Repeatedly press the "Push cabinet" button indicated onscreen until Max pushes over the cabinet.

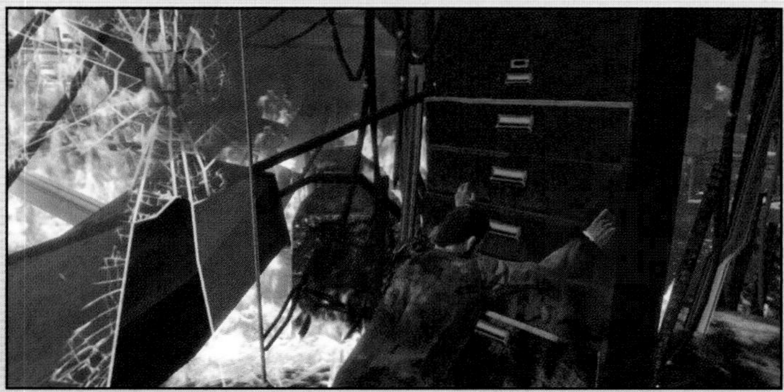

Climb over the cabinet into the next office. A glass wall **(18)** blocks your way out, but the heat shatters it as you approach. Simply push through the glass and step out into the hallway.

When you turn right at the corner, another explosion rocks the building. Walk carefully over the charred floorboards **(19)**, avoiding gaps in the burning floor, until you reach the raised walkway.

WATCH THE AFTERMATH.

The walkway collapses, but that's okay—Max ends up on the ground floor in the main lobby. There he finds a severely injured Crachá Preto soldier and manages to extract information. The Comando Sombra still has Fabiana. Where? The dying man says simply: "Up the hill." She's in the favela, where the gang holds sway.

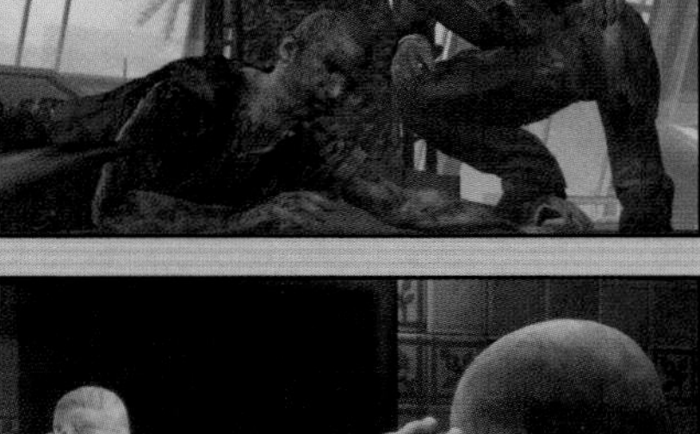

This chapter ends with a transformation: Max is back in his apartment after realizing he's been played for a fool. Seeing that he has "a liver like a French goose and skin like red leather," he decides to hunt down the truth, once and for all. And he chooses to do so both sober and bald.

VII A HANGOVER SENT DIRECT FROM MOTHER NATURE

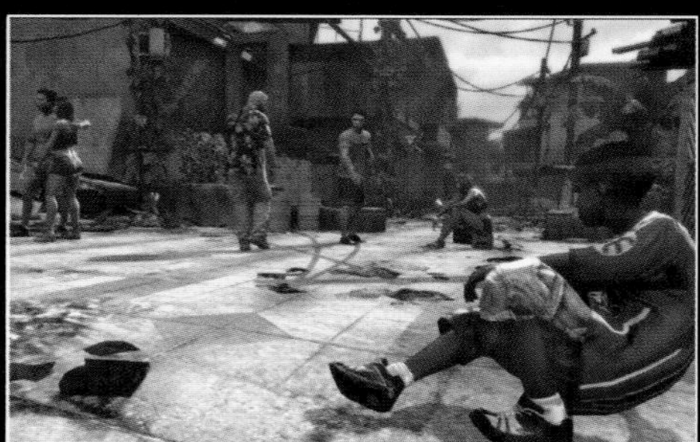

NOVA ESPERANÇA FAVELA, SÃO PAULO

1:15 PM, MONDAY

São Paulo is a booming metropolitan area, but a sizeable percentage of its 19 million residents live in crumbling slums and shantytowns called favelas. As the chapter opens, Max stands on the threshold of the notorious Nova Esperança ("New Hope") favela—home turf of many gangs, including the Comando Sombra. Before he starts heading "up the hill," Max phones in a report to the two surviving Branco brothers, Victor and Marcelo. He tells them he's going after Fabiana.

STREET PARTY

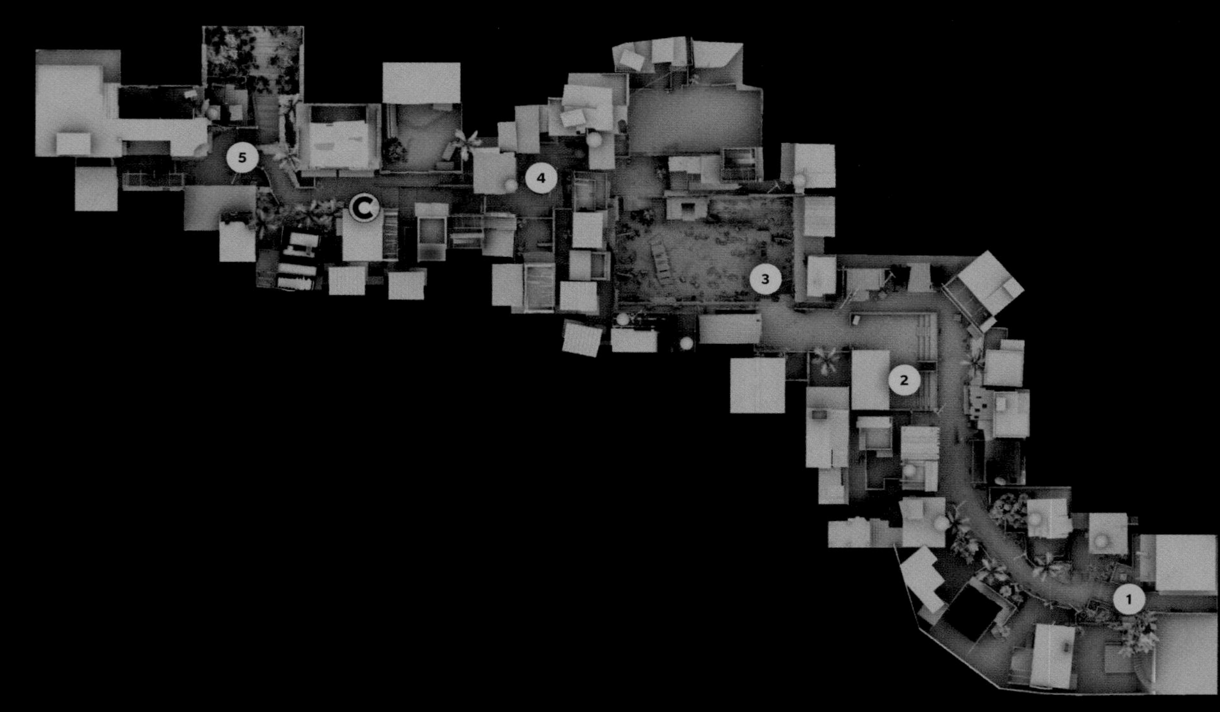

NEW WEAPONS NONE | PAINKILLERS 

MISSION

FIND THE STREET PARTY.

The cinematic sequence continues. As Max wanders the streets on the slum's tattered perimeter, he keeps his gun holstered but on display: this is no place to look like an innocent tourist. He picks up a "tour guide" after flashing a photo of Fabiana to a young boy. The kid leads Max deeper into the favela's labyrinth of back alleys.

When you gain control **(1)**, follow the young boy as he keeps calling back to you. The boy leads you down the curving road to a lively street party **(2)** where Max feels exposed "like a streetwalker in a monastery."

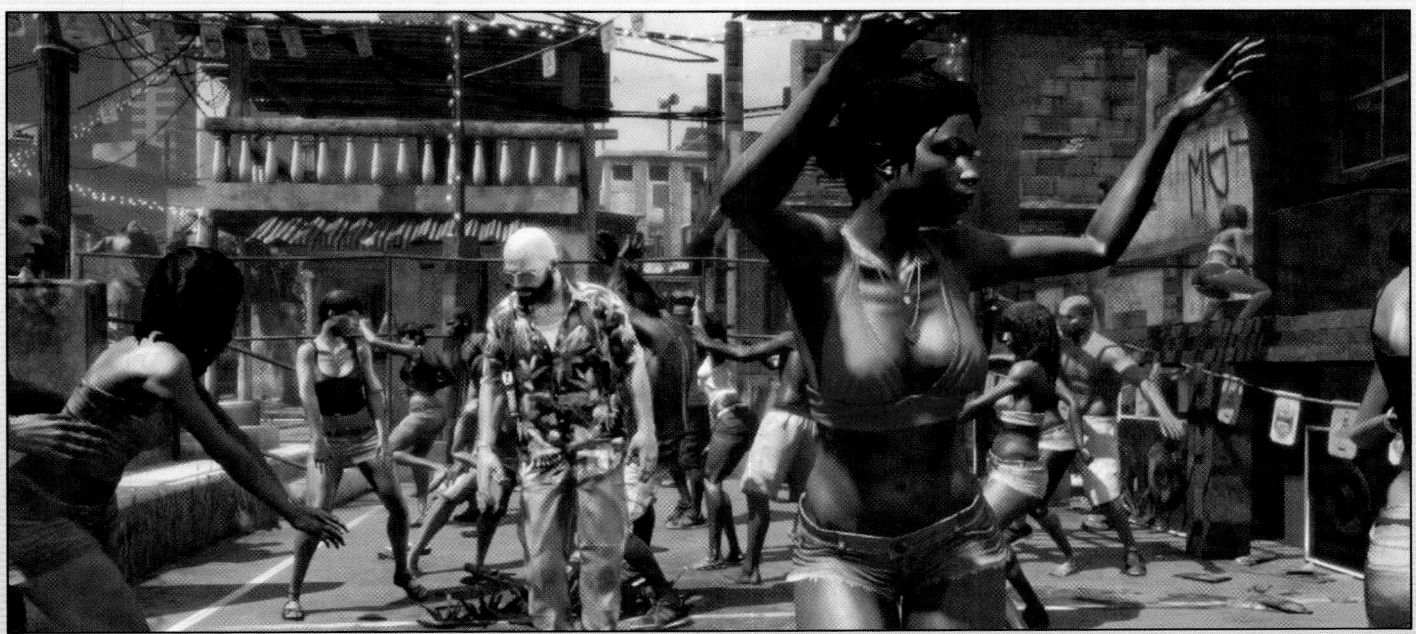

A trio of armed thugs forces Max into a deserted alley, robs him, and then kicks him into a sewer ditch **(3)**. When the scene ends, Max is alive but weaponless in the heart of gang territory.

FIND THE STRIP CLUB.

Climb the nearby wooden staircase past the kids playing street soccer until you reach the locals gathered around an outdoor table **(4)**. (Ironically, one of them wears a "Claudio" t-shirt.) Max doesn't get any help, and the group scatters.

EX-COP

Speak with Anders through an open window on the left just before you reach the strip club. Anjos de Morro (Angels of the Hill) is the charity business with which Giovanna works. You discover this when you find her flyer later.

Proceed along the narrow street. Soon you see a billboard up ahead for the "O Palacio Bar," with an arrow pointing off to the right. Continue along the walkway to the gate **(5)** and approach it to trigger another cutscene.

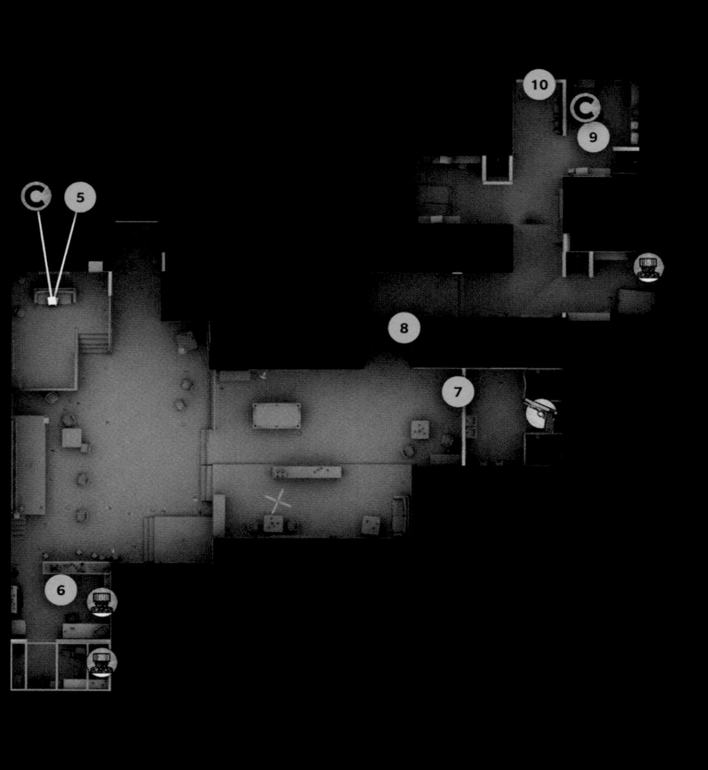

MISSION

MEET DA SILVA.

Max enters the sleazy strip club where a friendly police detective named Wilson Da Silva buys him a drink. Da Silva tells Max that the Branco situation was a setup, and Max is the fall guy. He opens a file and points out Serrano, the Comando Sombra leader. Then he shows Max the head of the Crachá Preto, a man named Neves, as well as the group's second in command, Milo Rego. They look familiar...

NEW WEAPONS

DE .50 SEMI-AUTOMATIC PISTOL

PAINKILLERS

Finally, Da Silva suggests that Victor Branco, Rodrigo's brother and a right-wing politician, is somehow involved in all of this, as is the elite UFE police division (the one commanded by Colonel Becker). But the detective doesn't understand how or why yet. He hands Max a 1911 pistol and tells him Fabiana Branco is "up the hill"—the same words used earlier by the dying Crachá Preta soldier. After Da Silva exits, a crew of local gang members approaches and starts some trouble.

CLEAR THE STRIP CLUB'S MAIN FLOOR.

When you gain control **(5)**, you automatically enter Bullet Time to clear the main floor of gangsters. Try to use the Bullet Time gift to nail all three of the nearest enemies in the head. Do not waste time on shooting civilians. Shoot one more enemy on the dance floor then finally the bartender **(6)** who wields a Sawn-Off Shotgun. Watch for more shooters emerging from a door behind the pool room to the left. One gunman bursts from the restroom door **(7)** behind the pool table as you approach.

Pick up dropped weapons and ammo, including an AK-47 and the new Sawn-Off Shotgun that you can double wield. You can also find painkillers in two places: behind the bar and in the storeroom behind the bar.

PHOTO OF SERRANO

After the initial shootout with the thugs in the strip club (including one guy in the connecting hallway), return to the area where you started and find Serrano's photo on the floor near the couch.

CLEAR THE STRIP CLUB'S BACK ROOMS.

Move down the hall beyond the pool table but take cover at the corner **(8)**—a thug rushes up the corridor here. Lean out and gun him down. A second gunman appears in the following hallway intersection. Lean out around the corner and plug him.

Slide around the next corner and nail the gunman who steps out of the last room **(9)** on the right to clear the area. Then nab the painkillers stashed in the first back room and exit the club via the pink back doors **(10)**.

PART 1/3 GOLDEN SAWN-OFF

Find this gun part in the strip club bathroom, on the floor in the middle stall.

TOURIST

In the last "bedroom" on the right before the exit; a young American man is hiding under the bed. Approach the bed and speak with the coward who's in the wrong place at the wrong time.

LOWER FAVELA

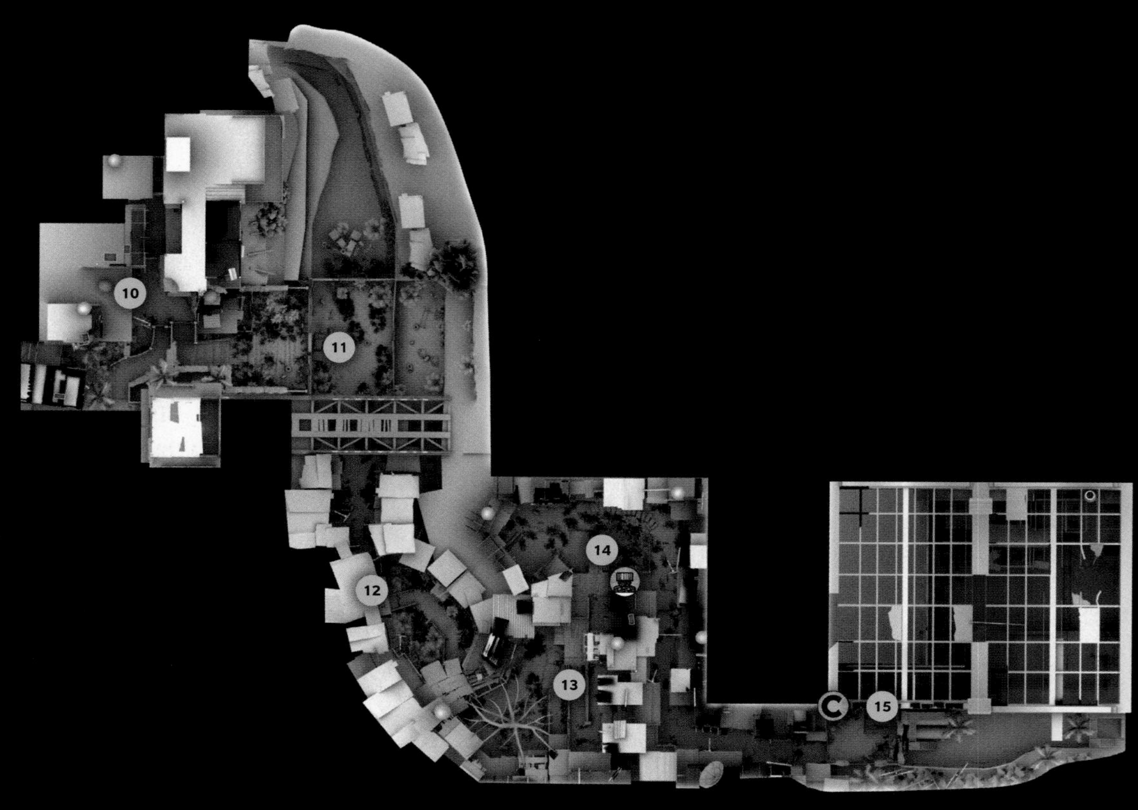

NEW WEAPONS NONE | PAINKILLERS 

MISSION

FIGHT THROUGH THE LOWER FAVELA.

Push through the chain-link gate, and descend the stairs. Approach the gap in the fence to trigger a quick cutscene: as two armed pursuers approach, Max drops to the favela's lower level **(11)** to avoid detection. Unfortunately, a fireworks display announces his presence to the neighborhood.

Follow the twisted pathways between shacks. When you reach the first staircase **(12)**, two gunmen appear up on the rooftops, one to the left and the other to your right. Shoot them and continue through the gate into the next neighborhood. Max notes that these gangsters don't appear to be Comando Sombra.

Three more gangsters attack from the ground, stairs, and balcony of the next courtyard. Pick off these attackers then climb the stairs **(13)** to unleash another wave. Gangsters pop out of doorways and scuttle across the upper balcony to attack.

After you terminate these threats, approach the drop-off and shoot the two gunmen on the rooftops across the gap. To your right you see some painkillers on a table behind a chain-link fence. To reach them you must drop off the awning to the ground **(14)** and then fight your way up the curving staircase. One rooftop gang member and two at the top of the stairs attack when you drop down into the courtyard. When you reach the top of the stairs, shoot the distant gunman in the second-floor window and the one on the pathway.

FIND THE WAREHOUSE DOORS.

After you nab the painkillers, fight down the narrow path between shacks and defeat the second-floor balcony shooter and then the two final gunmen on the pathway. When you dispatch the last gangster here (an event marked as always by the final kill camera) you can proceed unmolested to the padlocked blue doors **(15)**. Shoot the padlock to unlock it.

LOWER GANG SPRAY TAG

Examine the gang tag on the wall to the left of the padlocked door to the party warehouse.

NEW WEAPONS

NONE

PAINKILLERS 

MISSION

USE BULLET TIME TO CLEAR THE WAREHOUSE FLOOR.

Push through the blue doors to trigger a scene: Max crashes a "testosterone fest" and recognizes the same three gangsters who robbed him earlier. He ends up riding an industrial winch chain **(16)** upward as Bullet Time automatically kicks in.

Pick off the four gunmen below, then quickly swivel to the right and nail the two thugs on the first walkway as you rise. Shoot the single gunman at the end of the highest walkway **(17)**, target another with an AK-47 who rushes to join him, and finally aim left to nail one gunman running up the distant stairs. (Note: If you can dispatch all nine of these enemies while still hanging from the winch chain, you complete the "So Much for Being Subtle" Achievement.)

FIND THE OFFICE WITH THE SCOPED RIFLE.

Max automatically swings from the chain onto the walkway. Sprint to the corner and take cover behind the metal sheeting. Eliminate the other gang members on the walkway starting with the gunman covering behind the same rail around the corner. (If you completed the Achievement, then this walkway is clear of enemies.) Pick up the AK-47 then target other gangsters across the warehouse from your high vantage point. Descend the stairs **(18)** at the end of the walkway and enter the office on the next level down.

SNIPE THE WALKWAY GANGSTERS.

Collect the painkillers on the shelf and note the ammo case in the far corner that provides ammo for all weapons. Then pick up the Mini-30 rifle leaning against the office windows **(19)**. It has a red dot scope, so it functions well as a mid-range sniper rifle. Take cover under the windows and start picking off the shooters on the walkways across the warehouse.

WAREHOUSE CANISTERS

Use your scoped Mini-30 to target the explosive gas canisters on the opposite balcony to eliminate multiple foes quickly.

When you clear the far walkways, be ready for a gunman to burst through the other office doorway **(20)** behind you! Consider quickly switching back to a pistol or another weapon. It's not easy to find targets at close range with a sniper scope. Make a sideways Shootdodge dive across the doorway to nail this attacker and the one behind him by the stairs.

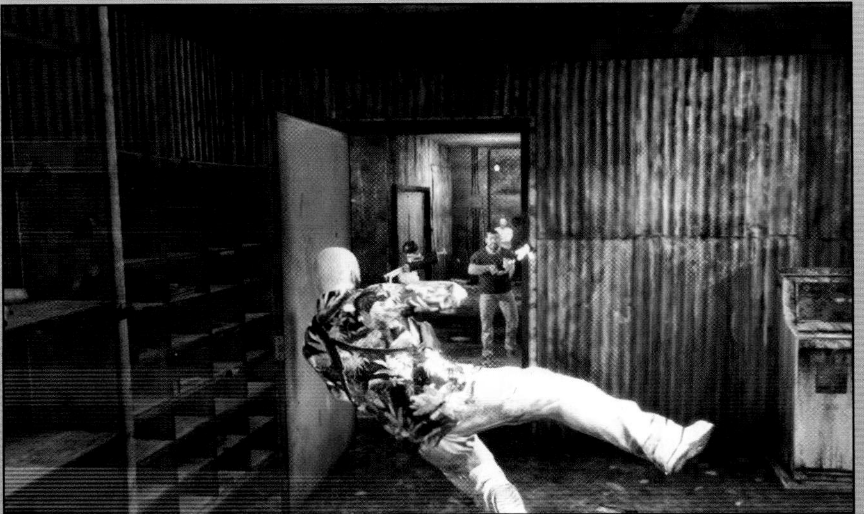

PART 2/3 GOLDEN SAWN-OFF

After sniping the enemies inside the party warehouse from the middle level room, exit through the next door and find this part on the ground in the nook on the left before you head downstairs.

GET TO THE RAILWAY LOADING DOCK.

Fight your way downstairs to the warehouse floor (where you started) then up the staircase in the opposite corner **(21)**. It leads up to the worktable area. Enter Bullet Time and blast the three gunmen that run out of the next hallway. Eliminate the last few gunmen in the corridor.

PART 1/3 GOLDEN SPAS-15

Find this gun part behind a pile of rubble on the second level as you are leaving the party warehouse. If you look back into the room from the hallway exit, you can clearly see this hidden item.

Go through that doorway to find painkillers on a table and two Sawn-Off Shotguns on a shelf in the "lounge" (the room with the sofa). Exit and climb the final staircase **(23)** to the blue exit doors. With your weapon aimed, push through the doors and gun down the last gangster in the area.

MIDDLE FAVELA

MIDDLE FAVELA OVERVIEW

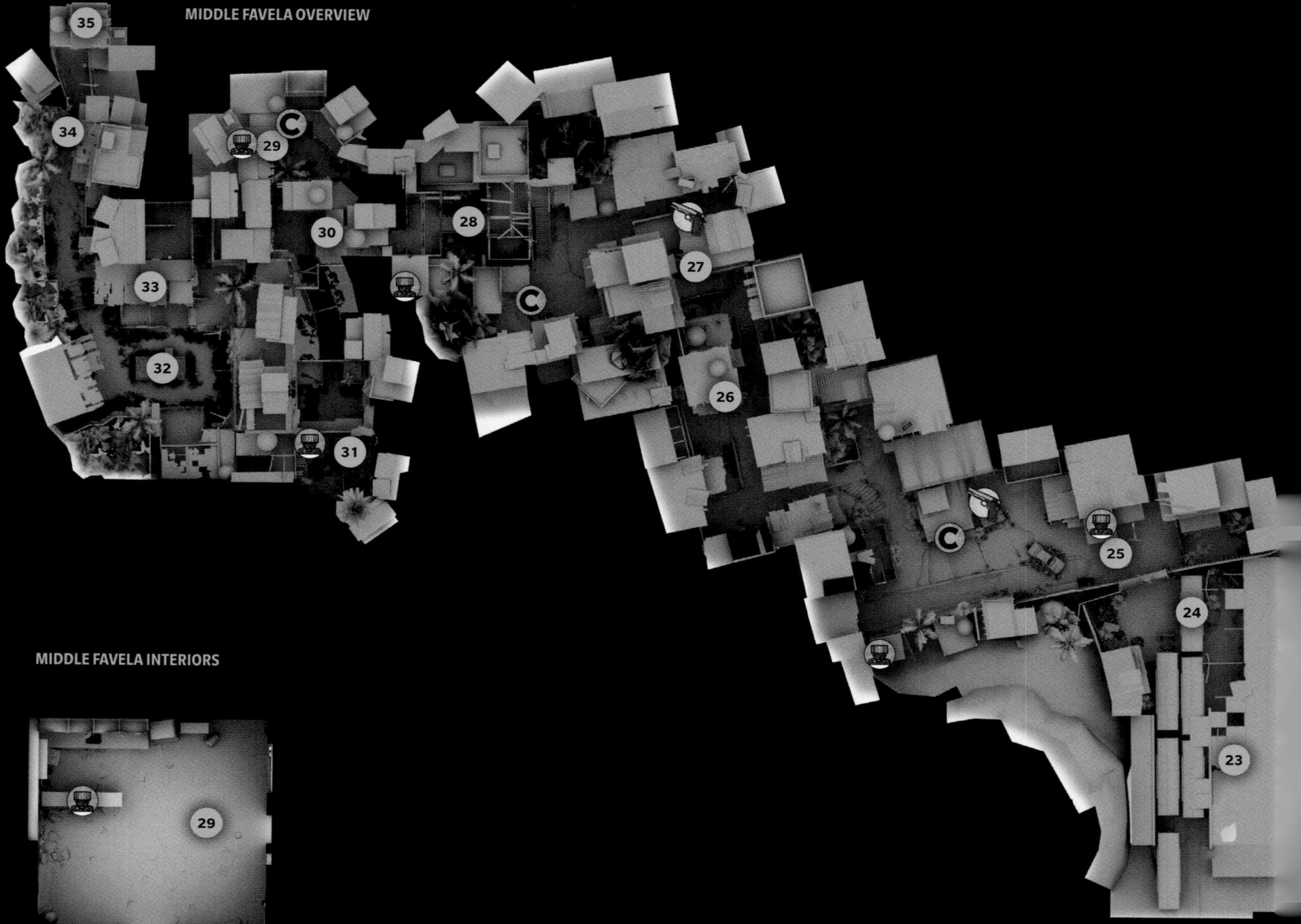

35 34 29 30 28 27 33 32 26 31 25 24 23

MIDDLE FAVELA INTERIORS

29 33 37 36 35

NEW WEAPONS NONE | PAINKILLERS 

MISSION

You find yourself on a decaying railway loading dock. Move through the opening in the rail car **(24)** and turn right to approach the big red metal gate. Your approach triggers a quick scene: Max pushes through the gate into a new area **(25)** and spots a new crew of gangsters—hooded, tougher looking, more capable, but still not Comando Sombra. As Max says, "I could tell I was moving up the food chain."

PART 2/3 GOLDEN SPAS-15

When you reach the middle of the Favela, a cinematic introduces the new gang. Before you exit this area through the back right alleyway, find this gun part behind a stack of wood on the right side of the same building with the middle favela gang tag.

FIGHT YOUR WAY TO THE BRIDGE.

Your task is to keep working your way "up the hill" toward the Comando Sombra home turf at the top. This middle-level favela is the turf of the Tropa Z (translates to "Troop Z")—you'll find their gang graffiti tag sprayed on a nearby wall. Grab the lovely gift of painkillers on the outdoor table just to your right—you'll need it. More painkillers are in a tiny room in the far left corner of the yard. If you fire your weapon, a gunman on the balcony above the gang spray tag will come out shooting, and fireworks will warn others in the area.

MIDDLE GANG SPRAY TAG

A hooded gang member is seen patrolling the rooftop in a cinematic after leaving the party warehouse and entering the new gang territory. Examine the gang tag below the balcony he was patrolling. If you fire your weapon in this area, this gang member will reenter the balcony and attack.

Follow the path through the neighborhood and shoot the rooftop gunman at the dead-end. Stop and cover at the corner before the stairs. Swing out and shoot the three gunmen in the second-floor window **(26)**. Patiently pick them off from cover. (Alternately, if you pass through this small section of the favela without shooting, the Tropa Z will not attack you first.) Continue up more stairs until you reach graffiti of a dead rabbit **(27)**. Shoot the hooded man on the rooftop around the corner before he shoots a flare.

Drop down the ledge and proceed to the wall mural of the late soccer star Claudio. Approach it and press the "Examine shrine" control indicated onscreen to get a close-up look.

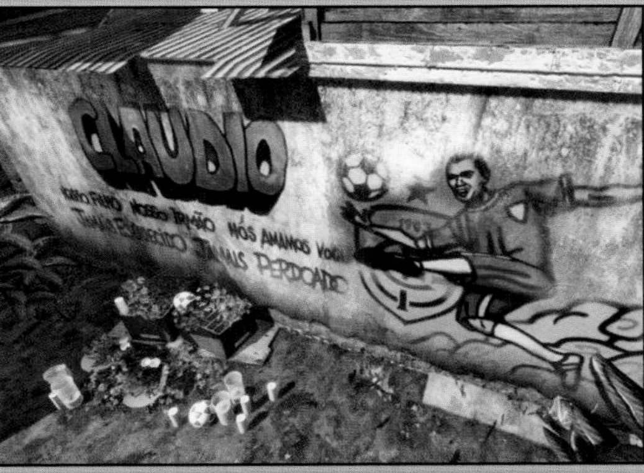

PART 3/3 GOLDEN SPAS-15

Just beyond the four consecutive flights of stairs, a hooded gang member is seen on an adjacent rooftop holding up the flare with which he'll announce your presence. Shoot him and drop off this staircase, and head to the dead-end on the right. Turn back and look at the base of the stair structure to find the weapon part.

As you fight to the other side, one more hooded gunman waits in a small room to your left. Make a Shootdodge dive and swivel left to blast. Enter the room to find more painkillers. Then drop down to the grassy alley and continue on.

SHRINE TO CLAUDIO

When you reach the middle gang territory and after spotting the flare-shooting thug, there is a clearing where you can find this shrine near a wooden staircase.

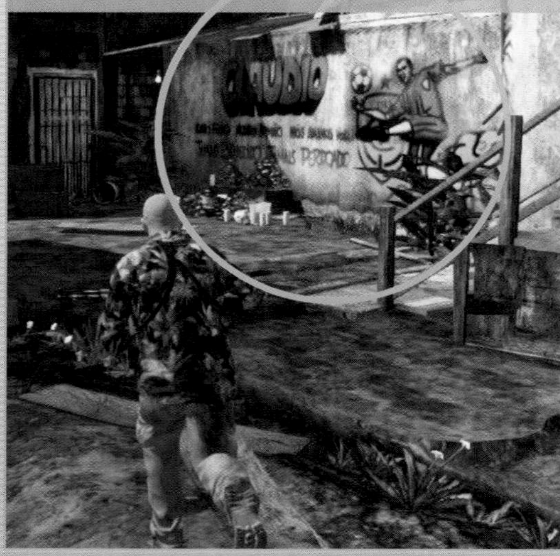

Work your way up the next staircase to the doorway. Around the corner, three gunmen guard a narrow walkbridge **(28)**. There's a yellow explosive canister to the right of the killers, but it's not easy to spot from your side of the bridge.

FLYER FOR GIOVANNA

Find Giovanna's Anjos do Morro charity flyer on the ground to the right of the graffiti-laden doorway that you must push through to enter the ramshackle apartment in mid favela.

WORK YOUR WAY TO THE FOUNTAIN.

Approach the wooden door at the end of the passage with your weapon aimed. The moment you enter **(29)**, a gunman pushes over a table and opens fire at you from behind it. The table is flimsy, however, so shoot right through it. Then swivel left to shoot two more hooded gunmen, including one hiding in the doorway. Be ready or else this first thug will knock you right to the floor! The kitchen counter holds a painkiller pickup and is also a good place to cover after killing the table pusher.

Before you exit via the back door, shoot through the window (the one over the "Macumba" graffiti) at the door directly across the small courtyard **(30)**. When that door swings open, another gangster opens fire from inside. Enter Bullet Time and dispatch him.

Fight down the back alleys and connecting structures that feature gangsters emerging from doorways and onto rooftop ledges. When you push through a wooden door into an open courtyard, watch for more rooftop shooters to your right **(31)**. When you finally reach a wooden fence, hop over and drop down into a courtyard with the ruins of a town fountain **(32)**.

CLEAR OUT THE FOUNTAIN SQUARE.

Take cover behind the stone rim of the fountain and start picking off the hooded and masked gangsters rushing at you from the blue brick house **(33)** directly ahead. Blast the biggest, highest threat next. Take out the gunmen in the small yard in the right corner and then blast the second-floor balcony gunner.

Note that you can make this assault much easier if you target the pair of explosive gas canisters near the building's entrance—one just to the left of the door and the other against the wall at the bottom of the front stairs.

Shoot the last man that appears inside the house as he pops up from cover behind the main windows. Head to the left side of the yard and destroy the enemy through the fence at the side of the house. When the attacks stop, enter the building.

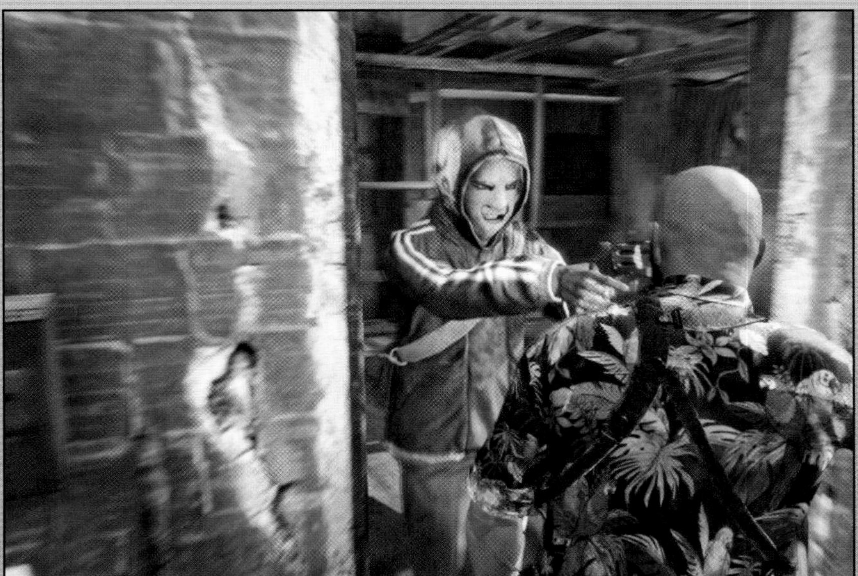

Inside you find painkillers on the Oxidado table. Grab the goods and exit via the back door. Turn right at the colorful wall mural and push through the next door **(34)** to trigger a scene: Max takes a peek into the next building, which appears to be the gang's main drug den.

LAY SIEGE TO THE DRUG DEN.

Gun down the poor fool who exits without seeing you at the window. Use both the doorway and the window for cover as you clear out the rest of the gang. Inside **(35)** you find quite an operation: drugs galore, including some painkillers. (You can examine the drugs.)

BAG OF OXIDADO

The Oxidado is in the drug house that Max eventually blows up. The drug is in the first room that you clear. Examine these drugs on the kitchen counter.

Exit via the door in the back **(36)** to trigger a scene: Max climbs upstairs **(37)** decides to do his bit for the drug trade and blows the place to splinters. As he gets clear of the explosion, he discovers that he's finally "up the hill" into Comando Sombra territory.

UPPER FAVELA (MOLOTOV AMBUSH)

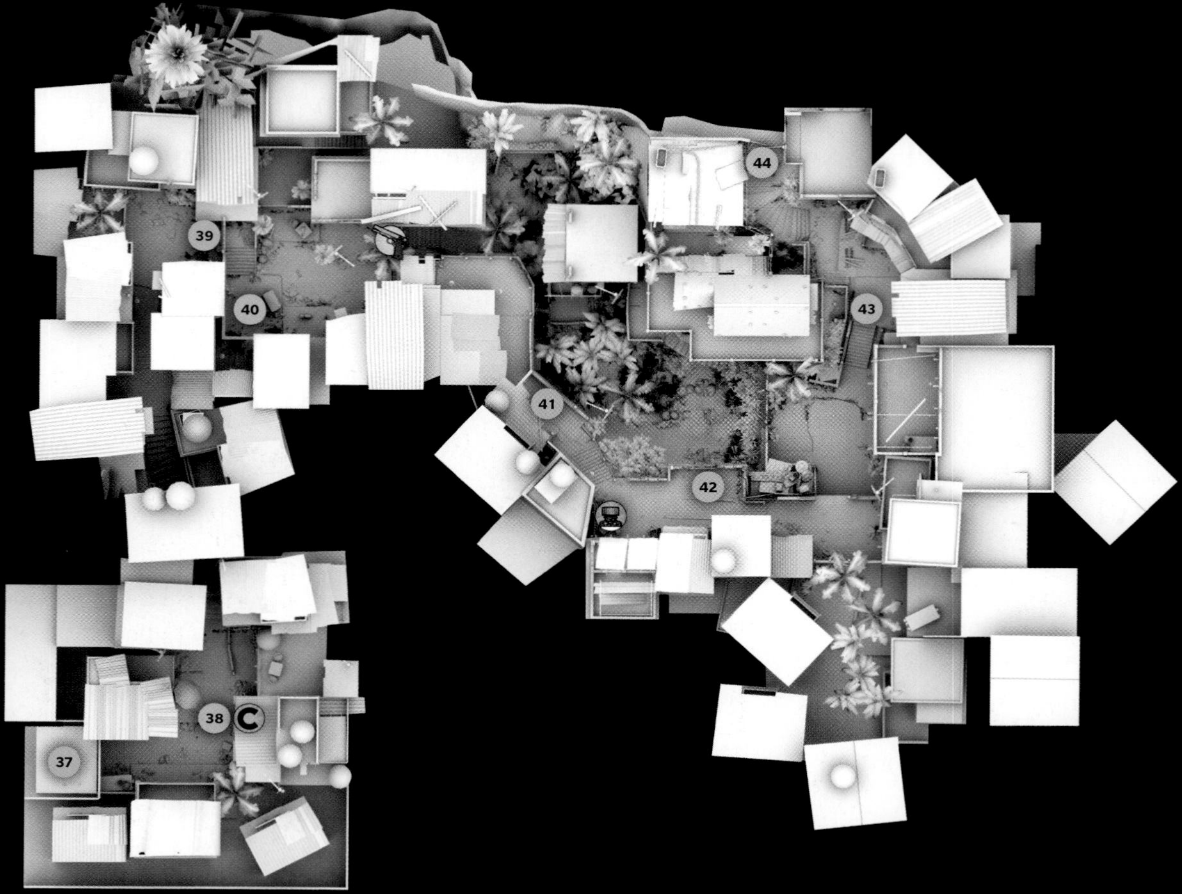

NEW WEAPONS NONE | PAINKILLERS 

MISSION

FIGHT OFF THE MOLOTOV AMBUSH.

After the explosion you stand in a small courtyard **(38)** where Comando Sobra graffiti is prominently displayed. Veer left and climb the series of staircases until you reach a barred metal gate **(39)**. Approach it for a cutscene: Max steps through the gate, but a Comando Sombra thug locks it behind him. Trapped!

UPPER GANG SPRAY TAG

You start in a new area facing this gang tag moments after blowing up the Oxidado drug lab. Examine the Comando Sombra gang tag.

Other gangsters emerge onto roofs and balconies ahead and start bombarding Max with fiery Molotov cocktails. Max ducks behind a box covered by a red tarp. Stay in cover behind the box. Focus first on targeting any thrown Molotovs. Don't let them reach your position! Between throws, kill the rooftop throwers, then the balcony shooters, and then finally the gunman entering the yard through your next exit.

PART 3/3 GOLDEN SAWN-OFF

This weapon part is in the Molotov battle area. Once you deal with the enemy, approach the gate to the left of the exit stairs. Be careful: someone will shoot at you from farther ahead. Eliminate those enemies through the gate and then pick up this weapon part near the gate.

After you clear the first neighborhood, continue working your way uphill. Climb the stairs and follow the walkways **(41)**, picking off rooftop or balcony shooters and watching carefully for thrown Molotovs. Look for painkillers sitting on outdoor tables en route.

Eventually you reach a section of railing with numerous exposed red bricks **(42)**. Here a particularly nasty wave of CS thugs opens fire from the houses across the ravine. They emerge in great numbers, so stay low and shoot in controlled bursts. Watch out for the occasional Molotov thrower as well.

TAKE OUT THE RPG LAUNCHER.

After you clear the area and push forward, you suddenly trigger the appearance of a Comando Sombra gangster toting an RPG launcher **(43)**. He shoots—aim for the rocket while in auto Bullet Time and fire *immediately* to detonate the rocket and take out the rocketeer. Then pick off any remaining shooters who appear on the balconies to the left.

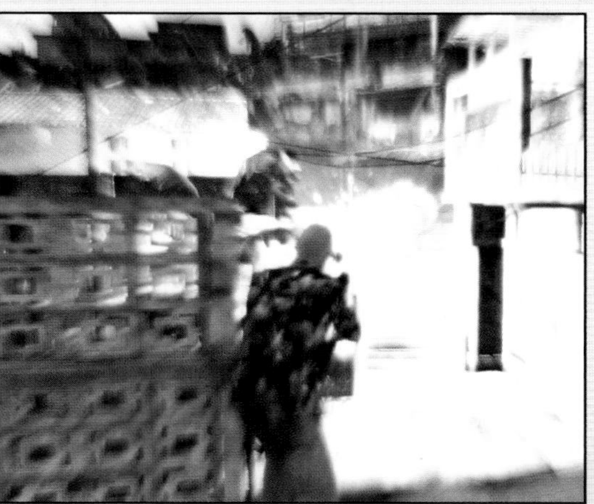

WATCH MAX CONFRONT THE KIDNAPPERS.

After you blow up the RPG, drop down the brick wall and continue pushing uphill to an iron gate **(44)**. Reaching it triggers a long cutscene: Max finally reaches Serrano's hilltop home base and finds Fabiana. Unfortunately, her sister Giovanna and Marcelo Branco have joined her in captivity. Watch as Max tries to intervene in the desperate situation...with unfortunate results.

Suddenly the building rocks from explosions outside, and Serrano starts yelling about the UFE. The Comando Sombra crew hauls off Marcelo and Giovanna in great haste. The aftermath leaves Max held at gunpoint and standing over another mistake. The situation triggers a new flashback to New Jersey, five years earlier...

VIII AIN'T NO REPRIEVEMENT GONNA BE FOUND OTHERWISE

GOLGOTHA CEMETERY, NORTH BERGEN, NEW JERSEY
4:00 PM, FRIDAY, A FEW MONTHS AGO

Max's flashback takes him to New Jersey, shortly after the first Hoboken encounter with Anthony DeMarco's goons. Max stands at the gravesite of his wife Michelle. She was brutally murdered along with their newborn daughter Rose years earlier (as seen in the original *Max Payne*) in a home invasion that Max could not prevent. Passos is with him but steps away from the gravesite to give Max a private moment.

In voiceover, Max speaks of "the Mona business"—a reference to Mona Sax, a contract assassin with whom he got involved in previous escapades. Like Michelle and now Fabiana, she was another woman he couldn't protect. But before he gets a chance to brood for very long, Max confronts some representatives of his more immediate past...

MICHELLE'S GRAVE

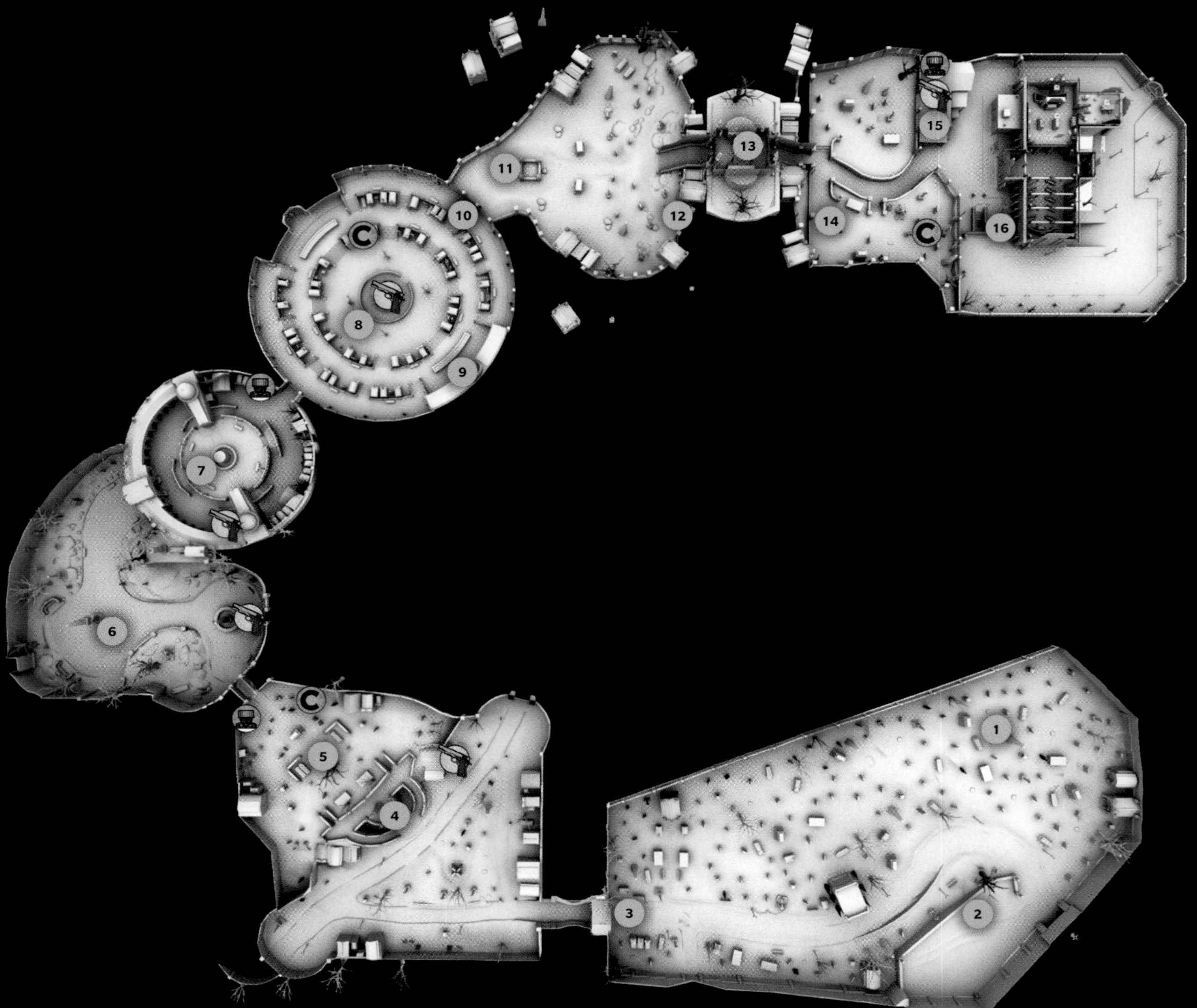

NEW WEAPONS NONE | PAINKILLERS 

MISSION

GET TO THE LOWER GATE.

You start out in cover behind Michelle Payne's gravestone **(1)**. Gun down the first trio and get ready to battle your way across a cemetery crawling with Anthony DeMarco's Jersey goons. Your first objective is to reach the lower cemetery gates at the bottom of the road. The simple method is to fight your way directly down the grave-studded slope toward the gates and use the tombs and stone markers as cover. But a good alternate tactic is to sprint uphill to the left toward the upper gates and then duck behind the low brick retaining wall **(2)** that lines the parking lot and overlooks the cemetery.

The parking lot's wall provides great cover from a high vantage point. It also forces attackers to cross the road in the open to reach you, making them easier targets. When the final kill camera indicates that you've cleared the area, watch as Max and Passos automatically slip through the lower gate **(3)**.

PART 1/3 GOLDEN AUTO 9MM

This gun part is found before the two-stair hill just after you shoot the van gate crasher. There are two small mausoleums to the right of the first set of stairs on the right (below the grenade launching mobster). The weapon part is on the ground before the second mausoleum.

PICK OFF THE VAN DRIVER.

As the two partners move down the road just beyond the gate, a mob van suddenly roars in from behind. Aim through the gate at the van's windshield and nail the driver before the vehicle can smash through the gates and run over Max.

(Refer to the cemetery overview map.)

MISSION

NAIL THE GRENADE LAUNCHER AT THE MEMORIAL WALL.

After the van crashes, a short scene plays: Max and Passos end up hiding behind tombs as mobsters open fire from a raised platform **(4)** at the top of two curving staircases. One goon at the base of the tall pillar in the platform's center (circled) starts peppering your position with a multi-chamber Grenade Launcher. Other shooters start descending the stairs on either side.

NEW WEAPONS

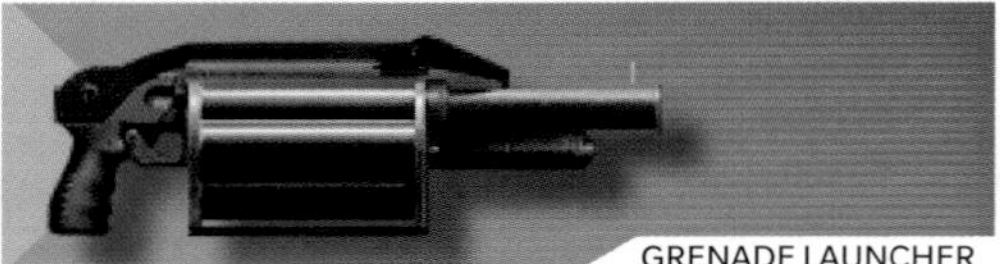

GRENADE LAUNCHER

Grenades are lethal if they explode near Max, even if you're in cover behind a gravestone. So target the guy with the Grenade Launcher *immediately* to end the threat—his first couple grenades fall short, but he finds the range by the third shot. Don't lose track of the onrushing shooters on the curving staircases! After you clear the platform, climb up to the wall of memorial plaques.

CLEAR THE UPPER CEMETERY.

We suggest you pick up the dropped Grenade Launcher near the tall pillar before moving up the next staircase. A big crew of mobsters awaits your arrival in the upper yard **(5)** beyond the memorial, and a quick grenade can thin their ranks. (You may have only one grenade left—the number remaining in the weapon depends on how quickly you dispatched the goon with the Grenade Launcher in the previous step.) Mop up with a shotgun or dual-wielded 1911 pistols. After you clear the yard, find the painkillers stashed in the old wooden shed near the gate where Passos waits for you.

VALERIE'S TOMBSTONE

After defeating the mobsters in the upper cemetery area behind the grenade-launching mobster on the balcony, find Detective Valerie Winterson's tombstone on the right side and before approaching Passos at the gate ahead. Max is the reason she is buried here (play Max Payne 2 to learn why).

Approach the exit gate to trigger a cutscene: Passos leads Max through the gate, and the two advance into a woodsy garden overlooking a paved circle **(6)**, where a veritable goon convention has gathered below.

CLEAR THE CIRCLE.

Passos pushes downhill to a position behind the mob van to draw their attention, and the fight begins. Passos nails one of the initial crew of seven. When you regain control, immediately trigger a Bullet Time attack and dispatch all six remaining goons. Five are clumped together near the cars, but one stands behind the monument and is hard to hit at first unless you make a Shootdodge dive to the left. Remember that gunfire can detonate an automobile too—the mobsters have three explosive vehicles down there! Three more goons rush up the cobblestone road, so finish them off, too.

PART 1/3 GOLDEN 608 BULL

This part is in a small area adjacent to the collection of parked vehicles where Passos leaves you. The gun part is on the ground, behind the circular planter.

CLEAR THE FOUNTAIN PLAZA.

After you clear the circle, follow the cobblestone road downhill as it curves to the next monumental gate. Be ready—as you approach, another gunman pops through the gate. He raises his hands and tries to retreat. Eliminate him before he can and proceed through the gate into a circular plaza **(7)** around a big fountain.

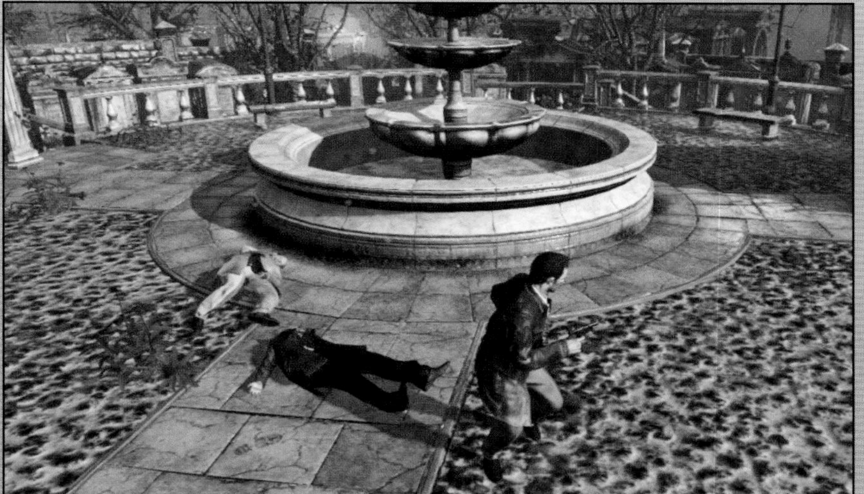

The place is crawling with killers, so find cover quickly. Slide from side to side along the lower level before you try climbing the stairs. If this area proves difficult for you, first shoot through the entryway at as many enemies that show themselves *before* you enter. Once the area is cleared, look for painkillers in a small wooden shed to the side. Then approach the iron gate with the "Delaware Mount" sign at the top.

PART 2/3 GOLDEN AUTO 9MM

This weapon part is on a shelf in the dead end to the right as you enter the rotunda. If you've crossed over the fountain platform, you've gone too far. Be sure to clear the area of enemies before attempting recovery.

(Refer to the cemetery overview map.)

MISSION

RESCUE PASSOS.

Reaching the Delaware Mount gate triggers a long cutscene. One of DeMarco's men holds Passos at gunpoint in front of a small rotunda **(8)** in the center of a circle of mausoleums. Other mob gunmen are moving into position around the rotunda as well. When control returns, immediately activate Bullet Time and target and shoot the goon holding Passos hostage.

CLEAR THE ROTUNDA AREA.

Passos nabs the dropped gun and ducks inside the rotunda as the other goons open fire at him. Start fighting your way around the upper circle. A good tactic is to sprint immediately to the right and follow the cobblestone path. Veer to the right of the low brick wall **(9)** that's planted with foliage. This lets you slip behind the shooters who are focusing their attention on Passos.

PART 2/3

GOLDEN 608 BULL

"You Max Payne?" This weapon part is beside the sarcophagus and behind the goon holding a gun to Passos' head.

NICOLE MAUSOLEUM

Nicole Horne's mausoleum is located in the same rotunda where you saved Passos from the guy with a gun to his head. This mausoleum is in the lower area—the most inner circular walkway. Nicole is the one who ordered the hit on Max's wife.

Keep circling and flanking the mobsters until you clear the rotunda circle. Then go to where Passos waits for you to trigger a cutscene: an unfortunate cemetery worker named Greg opens the next gate **(10)**. Greg immediately takes one for the team as a mob sniper opens fire from the cupola of a larger rotunda beyond the gate. Max and Passos scramble into cover **(11)** in the graveyard below the shooter.

(Refer to the cemetery overview map.)

MISSION

GET CLOSE ENOUGH TO TARGET THE SNIPER.

You must get closer to the cupola sniper (circled in our screenshot) in order to target him. Passos will give you cover but wait for his signal. When he cries "Move up, Max!" make a hard sprint to the big gravestone directly ahead on the right side of the cobblestone path. Passos lays down cover fire. *Go no farther than the big gravestone!* If you try to get farther, the sniper will nail you. Note that you can observe the shooter's green targeting laser to see where he's aiming.

When you reach the first stone, three goons pop out of the rotunda building and open fire from the top of the staircase. Stay in cover, enter Bullet Time, and lean around to pick them off as they descend the stairs to try to advance on your position. Don't lean out for long or the sniper's targeting laser (and subsequently, his bullet) will find you!

Eliminating the last gunman triggers a cutscene: Max and Passos climb the stairs and enter the rotunda structure **(13)** to hide. Unfortunately, a big crew of Anthony DeMarco's armed henchmen are waiting inside...

When all three goons are down, Passos reloads. Again, wait for his signal. When it comes, dash straight to the next grave marker, a tall cross, on the right side of the path. When you arrive there, three more goons emerge from the mausoleum doors. Enter Bullet Time and dispatch them *quickly* because their bullets and the sniper's fire can whittle away the marker you're using for cover.

ELIMINATE THE SNIPER.

When the three goons are down, wait for Passos to give the signal once again. This time you can sprint all the way to safety and out of the sniper's viewing angle on the right side of the mausoleum building **(12)**. Immediately target the sniper (circled) up in his cupola perch! Then dispatch two more goons who emerge from the rotunda door. (If you take too long to terminate the sniper, these last two goons can emerge before that job is done.)

Watch the long scene as the mobsters march Max and Passos down to meet the still-distraught Anthony DeMarco, who tosses Max a shovel and orders him to dig his own grave **(14)**.

ESCAPE THE GRAVEYARD.

As Max digs, control returns to you. Press the fire button to "Hit Thug" with the shovel. Max and Passos overcome the guards and gain weapons.

When full control returns, watch out for the shotgun-toting thug who ascends the steps just to the left. After you dispatch him, you can examine the tombstone of Vincent Gognitti just beyond the sitting angel statue. (Fans of previous *Max Payne* games will recognize Vinnie's name.)

VINNIE'S TOMBSTONE

After beating the goons with a shovel, move forward in the same graveyard just beyond an angel tombstone and you'll find "Vincent Gognitti's" tomb. It's easy to spot, as it is much darker than the others in the area.

Now move down the cobblestone road past the vine-covered sign for the office on the right. You see the stained-glass windows of the cemetery chapel up ahead. More gunmen emerge near the cemetery office (an open workshop) on the left **(15)** just past the "Office" sign. Another is hiding just past the sign on the right. Be ready for him.

FIND THE MORGUE EMPLOYEE ENTRANCE.

Clear out the cemetery office. Watch for a gunman who pops out as you move toward the back room. Don't overlook the painkillers sitting on the engraving worktable in the back corner.

PART 3/3 GOLDEN AUTO 9MM

Find this gun part on the small bathroom floor inside the marble shed outside the morgue. You reach this just after leaving the graveyard from your shovel-wielding escape.

Exit the office and fight down the long cobblestone walkway along the chapel. Note the sign that points out the steps to the morgue's "Employee Entrance," off to the right. Dispatch any remaining mobsters and proceed down the stairs **(16)** to the morgue.

MISSION

CLEAR THE MORGUE.

Enter the morgue's delivery garage **(17)** with gun raised. Immediately swivel left to target the goons through the glass in the embalming room **(18)**. (Your shots can ignite a number of flammable liquids in there.) After you nail the last gunman who rushes you from the far corridor, Passos automatically moves through the exit.

GET TO THE CHAPEL.

Scour the morgue's rooms for ammo and find the painkillers: in the small office adjacent to the delivery garage, next to the pizza box in the refrigerated body storage room, and on the corner counter in the back right area of the morgue embalming room. Then step into the hall **(19)** to follow Passos and trigger a quick scene: Max and Passos exit the morgue and step into the quiet, elegant vestibule **(20)** of the cemetery chapel. Max says, "This place looks about as good as any to make a stand." Then the partners enter the chapel's nave.

NEW WEAPONS

NONE

PAINKILLERS 

CHAPEL: MAIN FLOOR

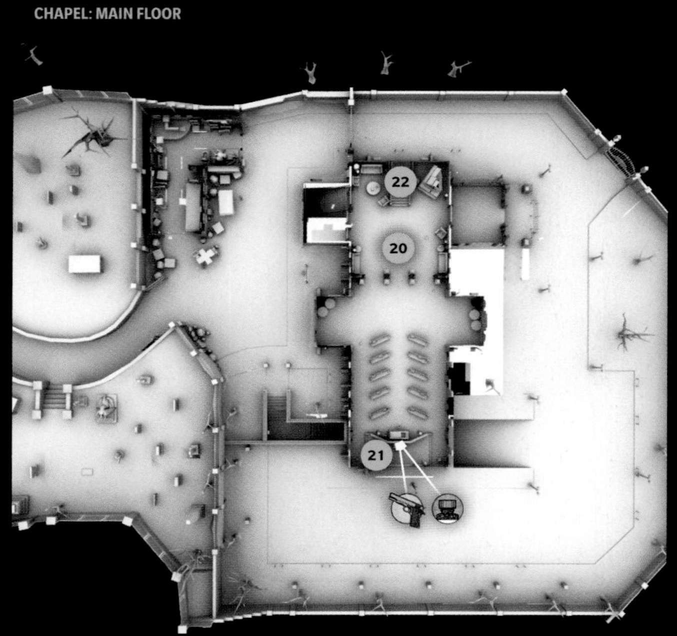

CHAPEL: BALCONY

MISSION

WIPE OUT THE FIRST GOON WAVE.

When Max and Passos cross the nave and reach the pulpit **(21)**, another goon squad bursts through the entrance and attacks. Focus on dispatching this swarm on the ground floor. Note that a bottle of painkillers sits on the edge of the pulpit.

PART 3/3 GOLDEN 608 BULL

Find this weapon part on the floor behind the pulpit inside the church. Pick it up after you clear the enemies from the first floor but before you head to the second floor to take out the balcony gunman.

TAKE OUT THE BALCONY SHOOTER.

When no attackers remain on the ground floor, a lone gunman (circled in our shot) up in the balcony opens fire with a semi-automatic shotgun. Every time you aim at him, he drops down behind the railing! Hustle across the nave into the vestibule, then head upstairs **(22)**. (Tip: If may seem frivolous, but you can stop and play the piano before you climb the stairs.) The balcony is a coffin display area, so nail the lone shooter before he dodges between coffins for cover. Now hurry to the railing **(23)**! Grab the fierce SPAS-15, a 12-gauge semi-automatic shotgun dropped by the shooter. Next to the shotgun sits an ammo case with refills for all weapons.

NEW WEAPONS

SPAS-15 COMBAT SHOTGUN

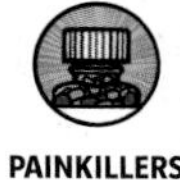

PAINKILLERS

STOP THE GOONS FROM KILLING PASSOS.

Below, a new wave of DeMarco's henchmen tries to rush the altar to kill Passos **(24)**. You don't have enough time to go back downstairs and save your partner, so blast the attackers from the balcony. Don't let them get close to your partner! Use Bullet Time to make this task much more manageable.

Once the last goon falls, watch as Max and Passos climb upstairs to the funeral director's office **(25)**. There, Passos makes a call to his connection in Queens...seeking a quiet place where Max Payne can finally escape the wrath of Anthony DeMarco, if not his inner demons.

IX HERE I WAS AGAIN, HALF WAY DOWN THE WORLD

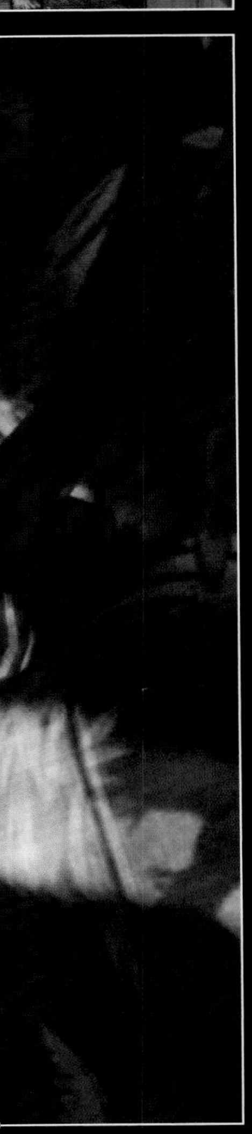

NOVA ESPERANÇA FAVELA

7:19 PM, MONDAY

This next chapter is short and brutal. Max's Jersey reveries end when a new reality transforms the present situation. The Comando Sombra thug assigned to guard him is losing his wits as gunfire erupts outside and is accompanied by the blare of loudspeakers. The distraction is enough for Max to disarm the poor fool and escape the room. He emerges onto a porch **(1)** to see uniformed men below and a police helicopter above.

THE POLICE RAID

MISSION

ESCAPE THE UPPER FAVELA.

Descend the stairs to the next landing, turn right, and enter the shabby courtyard. Pick up the painkillers and the PT92 pistol too, so you can double-wield. Continue down the debris-strewn path to another staircase. This one leads up into a ramshackle room **(2)** with dead occupants. Here you can score more painkillers on the bench in the back alcove and some pistol ammo from the dead body leaning on the wall. Exit via the open doorway.

DEAD GANG MEMBERS

Examine the body leaning up against the far wall in the first apartment you pass through in this level. Max will comment about São Paulo's finest and the Comando Sombra.

As you descend the next staircase, you can hear gunfire below on the street to the left: uniformed police are shooting favela residents! Pick off the cops or leave them alone then continue down. When the stairs end, double back on the balcony and find the G6 Commando assault rifle **(3)** in the shadowy nook under the stairs. Now return to the bottom of the stairs and drop into the shattered courtyard below. Comando Sombra gang members are just around the corner to the left **(4)**...but as you approach them, a huge explosion rocks the street. It tears apart the building across the road, kills the gangsters, and knocks Max down.

NEW WEAPONS

G6 COMMANDO ASSAULT RIFLE

M972 SUBMACHINE GUN

PAINKILLERS

This triggers a cutscene: Max scrambles behind a partition. The attacking cops have the UFE Special Operations patches on their shoulders. Max sneaks down the street and slips into a back alley. When control returns **(5)**, proceed downhill until you reach a housing courtyard where CS gangsters exchange fire with these police units.

Shoot the three UFE cops behind the raised, fenced yard on the left and continue through the narrow alleyway. There's more PT92 ammo at the top of a small flight of stairs opposite the chain link fencing that the UFE cops are behind. A pair of helicopters hover near one balcony **(6)**. Keep going until Max spots Marcelo and Giovanna below—now being herded along by the cops! What's going on?

Keep moving until a second scene plays: Max reaches a fenced balcony **(7)** and observes a vicious UFE raid on a residence. Police units kick in the door and slaughter an unarmed inhabitant.

INTERRUPT THE HOUSE RAIDS.

This is a tough battle here. The UFE wear heavy body armor, so they're hard to kill. Begin the battle by remaining crouched near the railing and pivot and shoot the cop coming up the stairs toward you. Shoot him directly in the head multiple times. Move cautiously to the stairs: another is right behind him. Obtain headshots and take their ammo. Turn your aim across the yard and nail the cop on the next balcony in the head. When you near the bottom of the stairs, two more cops enter the courtyard through the next alleyway. Take them out and be sure to pick up any weapons they drop, including lethal G6 Commando assault rifles and M972 submachine guns. (For an SMG, the M972 is a heavy hitter with good accuracy.)

PART 1/3 GOLDEN DE .50

This gun part is in the lower doorway dugout found during the first brutal alley firefight with the armored and helmeted UFE cops on your return to the Favela.

Once you clear the area, proceed down the next alley until you see an unarmed favela resident banging on a door and trying to escape—the police simply gun him down, showing no mercy whatsoever. Be ready for two UFE gunmen just around the corner to the left **(8)**. Use the corner for cover, swing around, and take them out. Examine the body of a third soldier fallen on the steps. Then continue down the narrow alley that leads through the next gate.

DEAD UFE MEMBERS

The dead UFE member is located around the corner from where you see a resident shot in an alley. This is just after the big alley shootout with the armored UFE and just before the old lady's house. Kill the two remaining UFE members around the corner then examine the body.

Continue up to the next apartment door **(9)** and enter. Inside this fairly cozy apartment (relatively speaking), you encounter a woman cooking and playing music. She flees into the bedroom upon your entrance, locking the door behind her. Find the painkillers in her bathroom medicine cabinet then exit her front door onto a stone patio.

PART 1/3 GOLDEN M972

This weapon part is in the old lady's apartment. She runs and hides in a backroom when she spots you. The gun part is on her bathroom shower floor.

The UFE helicopter hovers just beyond the raised patio but drifts off to the left as you arrive. Target the police forces across the alley. They're deployed along the opposite balconies and exchanging gunfire with Comando Sombra forces on your side of the alley.

Descend the staircase and push through the door on the left into the living room. Stay in cover beneath the broken windows **(10)** and start picking off the UFE cops across the way. One of them tosses grenades, so shoot the glowing projectiles in the air before they can reach you. You can also find an M972 on the table and a G6 Commando on the floor next to the dead favela resident.

TAKE OUT THE COPTER.

When the UFE infantry are eliminated, hop through the window, shoot the UFE cop on the rooftop on the right, and proceed along the balconies until you trigger a cutscene: Max finds himself targeted by sharpshooters up on an UFE police helicopter. Max leaps over a railing onto a sloping roof **(11)** and goes into Bullet Time as he slides down the shingles.

When the cutscene ends and control returns, target the two airborne riflemen. As they fall out of the craft, another UFE steps to the chopper's hatch and fires an RPG at you. Quickly nail the projectile so it explodes and takes out the helicopter. Max slides off the roof and ends up on the floor of a shack below.

DEAD RESIDENTS

After the old lady's house and the helicopter shooting challenge, you reach a spot where three UFE members are harassing a resident and end up killing him. Once the gun battle is over, examine the resident's body.

PART 2/3 GOLDEN M972

This gun part is at the bottom of the third consecutive set of stairs you reach after you fall through a ceiling after the helicopter shooting challenge.

PART 2/3 GOLDEN DE .50

Check the heavy vegetative corner along the metal gate just after seeing the round-up scene. Keep the camera positioned around your feet and you will find this gun part in the corner thick with bushes and overgrowth.

GET ACROSS THE LEDGE.

Descend the stairs **(12)** and follow the path to a clearing where three UFE soldiers are torturing a favela resident **(13)**. Enter Bullet Time and aim for heads only. Wipe them out and acquire the painkillers on the table behind them. Continue down to the street to trigger a scene: Max watches **(14)** as police units march a crew of favela residents down the street.

PART 3/3 GOLDEN M972

Just as the round-up cinematic ends, you find yourself in a heavily vegetated yard. On the other side of the forward left corner wall is a nook near a gate where you can find this gun part.

Continue up the next staircase to a gate. Here, Max must sneak along the ledge **(15)** directly over the street where more residents are rounded up and herded into a prison van. Push the movement controller to the left to make Max slide along the ledge.

FIND MARCELO AND GIOVANNA.

When Max finally reaches the end of the ledge, creep along the low brick wall, enter Bullet Time, and gun down the two UFE cops on the walkway bridge **(16)** up ahead. Two more are posted on the far side, so dispatch them before you cross. (Target the explosive canister under the window for quick kills.) One more cop is posted inside a barred porch at the end of the walkway bridge. Nail him in the head, cross the bridge, and turn left at the stack of tires.

PART 3/3 GOLDEN DE .50

The last gun part in this chapter is found in the area where you battle the last group of soldiers on a walkway bridge. After eliminating the enemies in the area and before you jump down to the lower sidewalk, push through an unlocked gate near the jump that leads into a barred porch. This is where you discover the last gun part for the Golden DE. 50.

Drop down over the ledge **(17)** near the barred porch and fight through one last UFE squad: three cops rushing up the stairs and one on a nearby balcony. Continue downstairs to the end of the path and push open the wooden door on the right. This triggers a scene: Max enters the grocery store **(18)** and gets disarmed by frightened favela residents. Then he finds the Crachá Preto vigilantes making a chilling exchange, sealed with a handshake, with the UFE "death squad cops."

Max decides to follow the Crachá Preto lieutenant, Milo Rego, and this leads him to Marcelo and Giovanna. The situation is not pleasant, especially for the Branco brother. Max cannot halt the grisly consequences, but he manages to face off with Rego.

DEFEAT MILO REGO.

When control returns, press the series of controller buttons indicated onscreen to win the fight, which proceeds in four phases. (Be quick—if you're not, Max is killed.) First, press the Shoulder Aim button to "Block" Rego's blow. Press the Fire button to "Disarm" and seize his machete. Press the Interact button to "Kick" and boot him backward, and then hit the Sprint button to "Strike" and finish the oily bastard.

After the fight, Max slides down the nearby drainage spillway with Giovanna to hide from Álvaro Neves, the Crachá Preto commander. Giovanna gives Max a plausible explanation for the brutality they just witnessed, and then the fugitive pair lays low for a couple of hours. When the coast is clear, Max leads Fabiana's sister out of the favela.

X IT'S DRIVE OR SHOOT SISTER

TERMINAL DA PAZ
4:51 AM, TUESDAY

Some time later, Max and Giovanna manage to escape the killing grounds of Nova Esperança and reach one of São Paulo's central bus depots, Terminal da Paz. After Giovanna calls Passos from a phone booth for pickup, they slip behind the bus yard to wait.

When Giovanna suffers stomach convulsions, Max assumes its just nerves after the horror of the past 24 hours. They scale a fence into a municipal junkyard—where old buses go to die—and find refuge in the shell of a city bus. Here, Max learns the real reason why Giovanna is losing her lunch. Unfortunately, someone has tipped off the Crachá Preto goons for hire, and soon paramilitary gunmen start combing the yard.

BUS JUNK YARD/FUEL DEPOT

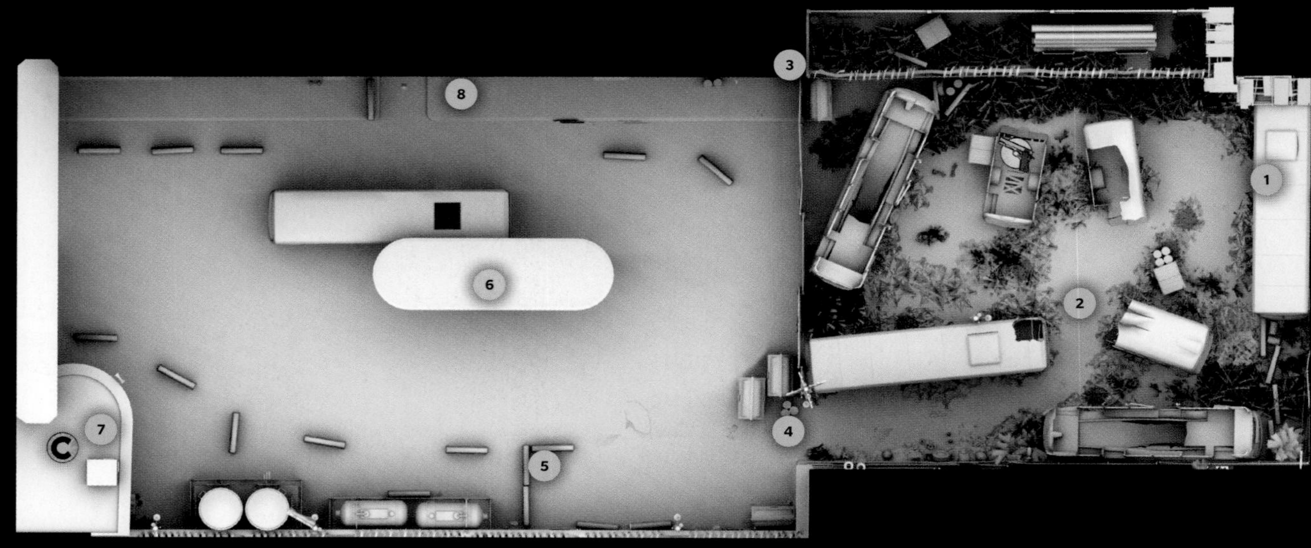

NEW WEAPONS NONE | PAINKILLERS 

MISSION

CLEAR THE JUNKYARD.

You start inside a junked city bus **(1)**. This is a good place to use Bullet Time, with several gunmen in plain sight **(2)** and more ready to rush in behind them. You start with an empty Bullet Time gauge, however, so try to achieve a headshot immediately and then engage Bullet Time from that accomplishment to obtain an easier headshot next. Repeat until all are dead. After you clear the yard, Giovanna panics and runs into the green targeting lasers of two snipers atop a building overlooking the junkyard.

DISPATCH THE TWO SNIPERS.

When control returns, lean around the bus section where Max is in cover. The snipers (circled in our screenshot) are both perched at the corner of the roof **(3)** closest to you, just to the left of the "São Paulo Fantastico!" sign. Use Bullet Time to riddle both shooters with lead.

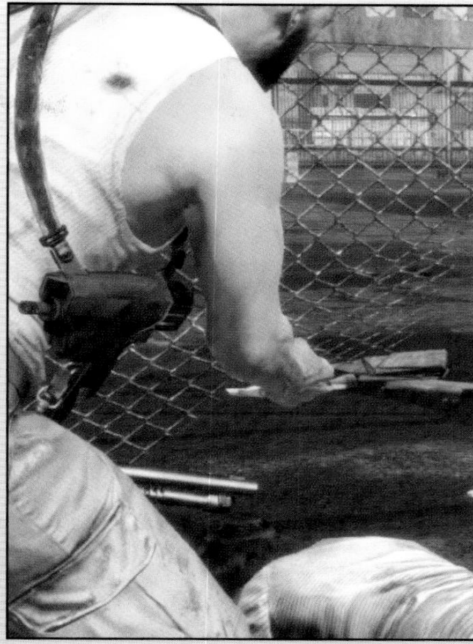

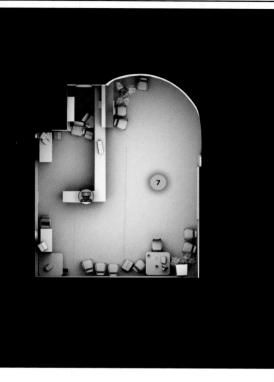

PART 1/3 GOLDEN FN FAL

This gun part is located in the bus graveyard where you begin the chapter. It's on the floor of the half-bus with the chopped rooftop.

CLEAR OUT THE FUEL DEPOT.

Now you're in the Terminal da Paz fuel depot. First, swivel right and take out another sniper (circled in our screenshot) who emerges on the catwalk of the Terminal da Paz sign.

Other Crachá Preto soldiers open fire at you from across the depot. One group emerges from the fuel depot office (under the "Segurança" sign) on the left, and another deploys from behind the bus parked at the fuel pumps to the right (including one grenade-throwing attacker). A good tactic is to hustle forward to duck behind the L-shaped group of concrete dividers **(5)** then start shooting the fuel pumps **(6)**. They catch fire and eventually explode, igniting the bus as well. This eliminates any gunmen nearby.

After you pick off the snipers, collect dropped weapons (9mm SMGs and M4 Super 90 shotguns) from the fallen Crachá Preto in the junkyard. Then follow Giovanna's voice until you find her across the yard at the gate **(4)**. Max helps her slide underneath the chain link fence, and she opens the gate from the other side.

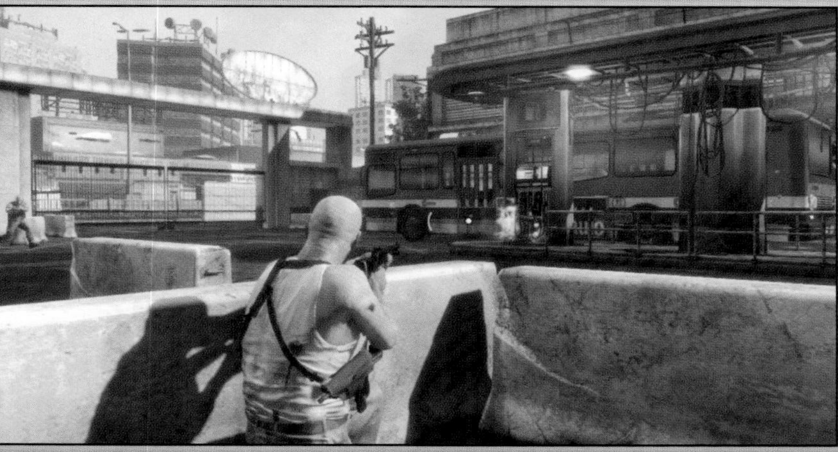

Turn your attention to the paramilitaries rushing you from the depot office **(7)**. Be wary—one of them tosses grenades, so target him first! If the thrower manages to drop a grenade behind the concrete dividers, make a ShootDodge dive over the top and pick off shooters at the same time that you're dodging the grenade. Stay away from Giovanna's hiding place during this fight—if a stray grenade kills her, you fail the mission.

When the depot is clear, search the office for painkillers. You can also examine a São Paulo newspaper on the counter. The front-page story features a photo of Rodrigo Branco plus a surveillance camera shot of Max with a headline that roughly translates to "Motive for the massacre in the city's center is unclear."

OFFICE NEWSPAPER

Examine the newspaper on the countertop inside the fuel depot office. This is the second battle area in the mission. Max is front-page news.

Return to the gate **(4)** where Giovanna waits. This triggers a cutscene: Giovanna shows some spunk in helping Max climb a fire escape **(8)** to reach an upper doorway into the terminal's main building. But more Crachá Preto gunmen spot them and rush to an open garage door on the far side of the structure.

NEW WEAPONS NONE | PAINKILLERS 

MISSION

CLEAR THE PAINT BAY.

Inside, Max automatically grabs a crane hook **(9)** and drops in Bullet Time as a large squad of eight hostile gunmen rush into the bay below, where buses are painted. You can try to dispatch them all before Max reaches the floor—this unlocks the Achievement named "The Only Choice Given" as long as you are using Free Aim. Another good tactic is to wait a few seconds until the full Crachá Preto crew is inside the garage then target the big gas tank (circled in our screenshot) on the forklift **(10)** to the right and retreat out of its blast radius. The explosion can eliminate most of the attackers. Mop up the rest on the floor.

When the paint bay is clear, Giovanna reports that there's no way down for her. Max sends her ahead to the next room while he tries to figure out a way to get there on the ground.

PART 1/3 GOLDEN M4 SUPER 90

After defeating the enemies in the paint bay where you completed the hoist aerial shooting challenge, you can find this gun part on the floor of the paint storage room.

Approach the flashing button **(11)** and press the "Open paint booth door" button indicated onscreen. Enter the booth when it opens and push through the plastic door-cover strips **(12)** on the right. Approach the blue doors beyond to trigger a cutscene: Max enters the next room, a repair garage with buses raised on hydraulic lifts.

REPAIR BAY

NEW WEAPONS

NONE

PAINKILLERS 

MISSION

CLEAR THE REPAIR BAY.

Giovanna sees no way down here either. Seconds later, another Crachá Preto hit squad bursts into the garage from the opposite side. Max takes cover behind a metal tool chest **(13)**. Dispatch the first squad. Note that you can target either one of the two hydraulic lift controls (circled in our shot) to drop a raised bus right on top of enemies.

GRENADE WARNING

Crachá Preto units often include soldiers with grenades. Watch for the grenade icon onscreen. Be ready to sprint away from your current position, no matter how cozy it seems, if a grenade lands nearby.

You can also target the forklift's gas tank **(14)** on the right side of the garage to take out a second Crachá Preto squad rushing out of the corner office. After all the enemies on the ground floor are dispatched, a cutscene is triggered: Two death squad goons chase Giovanna across the catwalks above! After she makes a daring escape, control returns to you. Quickly eliminate the two shooters on the catwalk above the center of the garage—you can do this by shooting at the catwalk floor where they stand and cause them to fall to their deaths!

Three more gunmen emerge from the door where you entered the bay. You can drop the other bus on them! After you thwart this last attack, Giovanna lowers a staircase **(15)** to the floor. Before you climb to join her, explore the garage to pick up ammo and weapons. Don't miss the painkillers in the corner office **(16)**.

PART 2/3 GOLDEN M4 SUPER 90

After clearing the repair bay of enemies, find this gun part on a corner workbench on the opposite side of the room from the stairs Giovanna lowers.

When you're done scouring the floor, climb the lowered staircase and explore the office at the top **(17)** to find more painkillers and watch some "Captain Baseball Bat Boy" on the TV. Exit and follow the corridor to the exit door. Go through and join Giovanna on a balcony overlooking the terminal's vehicle wash bay.

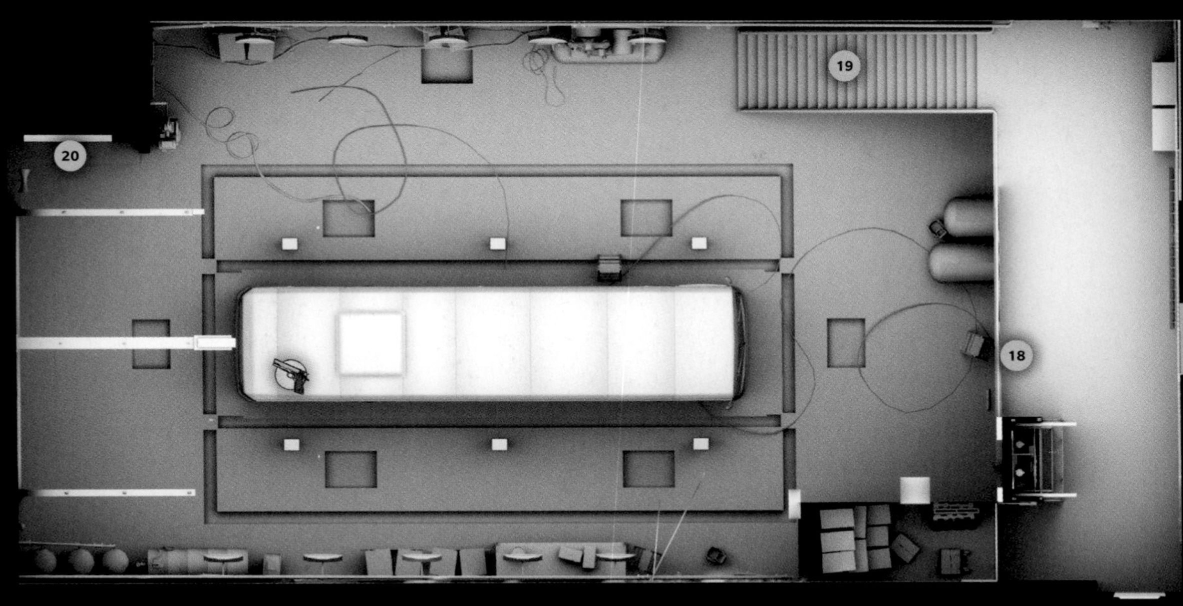

NEW WEAPONS

NONE

MISSION

CLEAR THE WASH BAY.

The balcony railing provides good cover, so just stay put **(18)** and systematically eliminate the paramilitary pursuers below. Several will try to rush up the stairs to the right **(19)**, but don't let them. When the area is clear, approach the blue exit door **(20)** to trigger a cutscene.

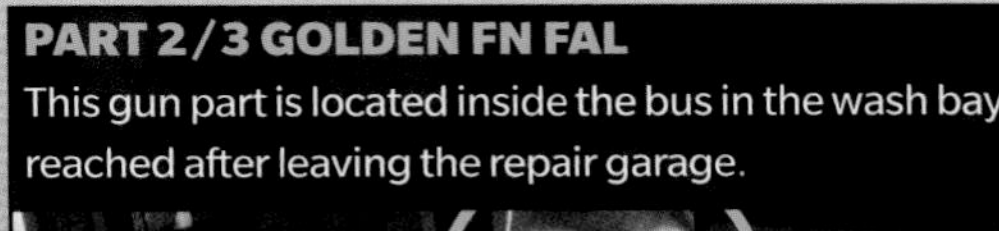

PART 2/3 GOLDEN FN FAL

This gun part is located inside the bus in the wash bay reached after leaving the repair garage.

Max and Giovanna cross an open-air patio with lunch tables. Then Max boosts Giovanna through a window and she unlocks the door leading into the terminal's administrative offices.

OFFICES

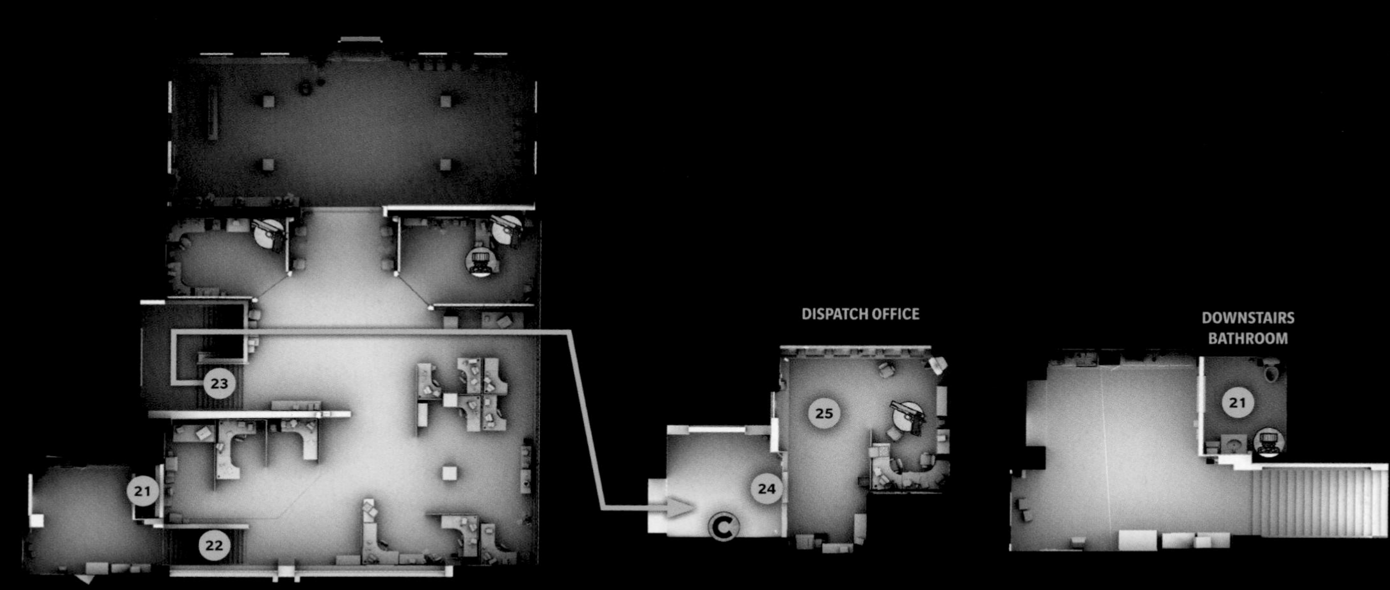

NEW WEAPONS NONE | PAINKILLERS 

MISSION

CLEAR THE UPSTAIRS OFFICES.

Before you climb the stairs up to the office level, enter the bathroom **(21)** on the other side of Giovanna (the door with the sign that reads "Banheiro"). Inside you find some painkillers in the medicine cabinet to the right.

Then climb carefully upstairs to the office... which is crawling with paramilitary thugs. As you near the top, stop **(22)** when your view is just above the level of the top stair and start firing. Watch for gunmen approaching from the left!

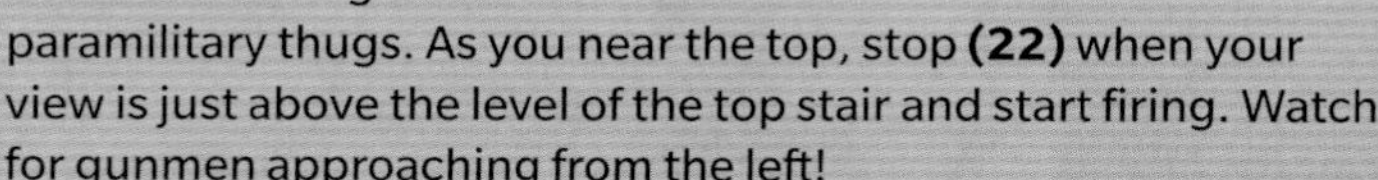

After you clear the office, find the painkillers on the desk in the right corner office. Then go down the next set of stairs **(23)** ahead of Giovanna.

PART 3/3 GOLDEN M4 SUPER 90

This gun part is located in the second floor of the office where a battle with many guards occurs. Find this gun part on the desk in the corner office on the right as you come up the stairs.

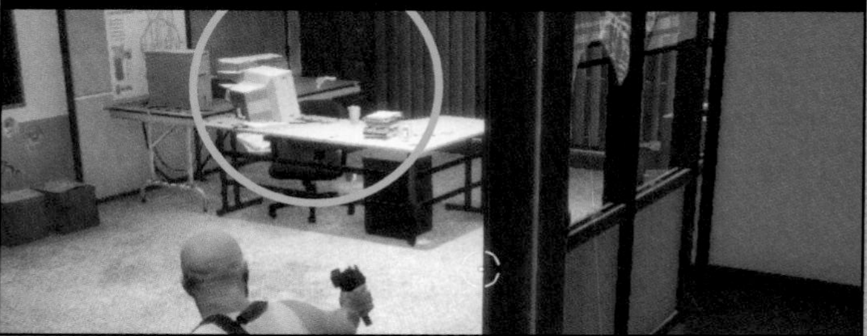

OPEN THE SECURITY DOOR.

Pick off the gunman in the doorway **(24)** directly across from the bottom of the stairs. Move along the right wall—you can examine the poster of Camila Machado next to the bus route map.

AD CAMPAIGN POSTER

When you leave Giovanna near the office bathroom to clear the floor above, and once you head down the next set of stairs, one more soldier attacks from a security room. A Camila Machado ad campaign poster is located in the hallway in-between. Examine it.

Continue into the dispatch office **(25)** and approach the control panel with the flashing button. Press the "Open security door" button indicated onscreen to trigger a cutscene.

PART 3/3 GOLDEN FN FAL

Find this gun part behind the desk in the office at the bottom of the stairs. It's in the same room with the security door button.

Giovanna walks through the newly opened doors but runs into a Crachá Preto gunman. When control returns, Max is rushing into the entry. In Bullet Time, immediately nail the gunman before he can execute Giovanna. A successful shot triggers a series of cutscenes.

Max leads Giovanna outside and across the terminal lot to a working bus. He puts her at the steering wheel then takes up a shooting position in the doorway.

MISSION

1: TERMINAL PLATFORM

The first sequence is just a short drive along the terminal arrival platform. Your onscreen Damage indicator is now a bus-shaped icon that fills slowly with red as the bus takes damage. If the indicator fills up completely, your bus is destroyed and you fail the mission. Eliminate as many attackers along the route as possible. At the end of the terminal, the bus reaches an open lot and a brief cutscene plays: Max urges Giovanna to keep steering straight.

2: FUEL DEPOT

Now the bus veers around the corner and across a lot where more hostile gunmen swarm. Target the fuel pump station to the right. If you can detonate it, the explosion takes out many of the Crachá Preto attackers.

3: TUNNEL WITH RPG

Next, Giovanna swerves into a tunnel, scraping the side of the bus along the wall. When control returns, pick off a few gunmen emerging from a side stairwell...but watch for a rocket-propelled grenade coming at you from up ahead. Pick it off! (Don't worry if you miss this first rocket—it misses the bus and hits a pillar.) Then nail the RPG launcher before he can fire again.

4: BUS STOP ISLAND

After you get past the RPG, Giovanna steers past a long, covered traffic island lined with loading stops for the various bus lines. Eliminate as many gunmen as possible to minimize the damage your bus takes.

Suddenly, a helicopter appears overhead—Passos to the rescue! But when another city bus sideswipes Giovanna, she loses control and slams through a wall into a building. When the dust settles, Max sends Giovanna rushing off to meet Passos on the building's roof while he turns to face a veritable army of paramilitary thugs.

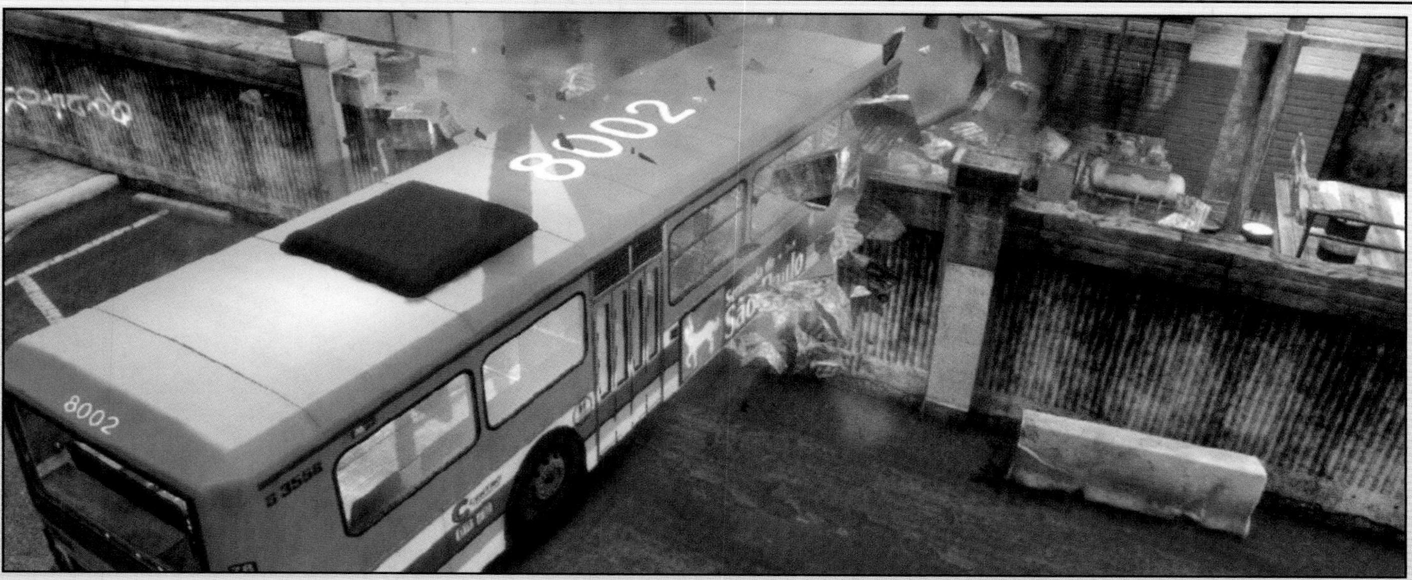

5: THE STANDOFF

Just before you regain control, you see a quick cinematic: a Crachá Preto soldier runs at your bus and tosses a grenade as more carloads of attackers arrive. Shoot the grenade quickly! Then shoot the thrower.

A lot of bullets are coming your way in this firefight, so don't stay exposed for long. Pop out of cover and squeeze off short bursts, targeting just one or two victims at a time, then quickly duck back down. Consider targeting automobile engines as well. Remember: when cars explode, they can eliminate multiple attackers.

WATCH THE AFTERMATH.

When you hit the last gunman and the final kill camera is activated, take a breath and view the long cutscene that ends the chapter: Max watches his rescue flight slice across the urban sky without him. Then Max's new friend, the helpful Detective Da Silva, offers a ride and provides some very interesting conversation topics.

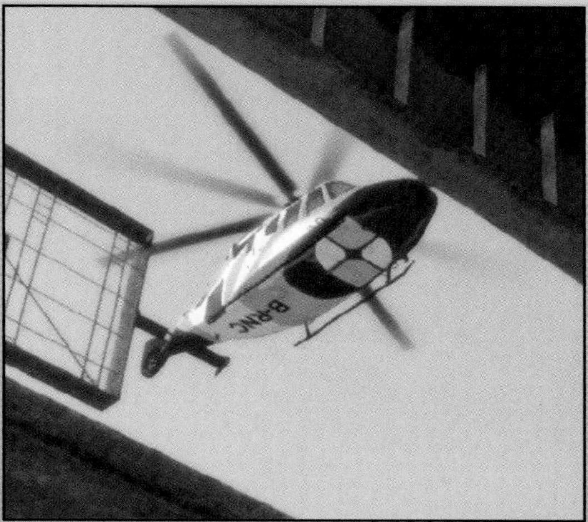

XI SUN TAN OIL, STALE MARGARITAS, AND GREED

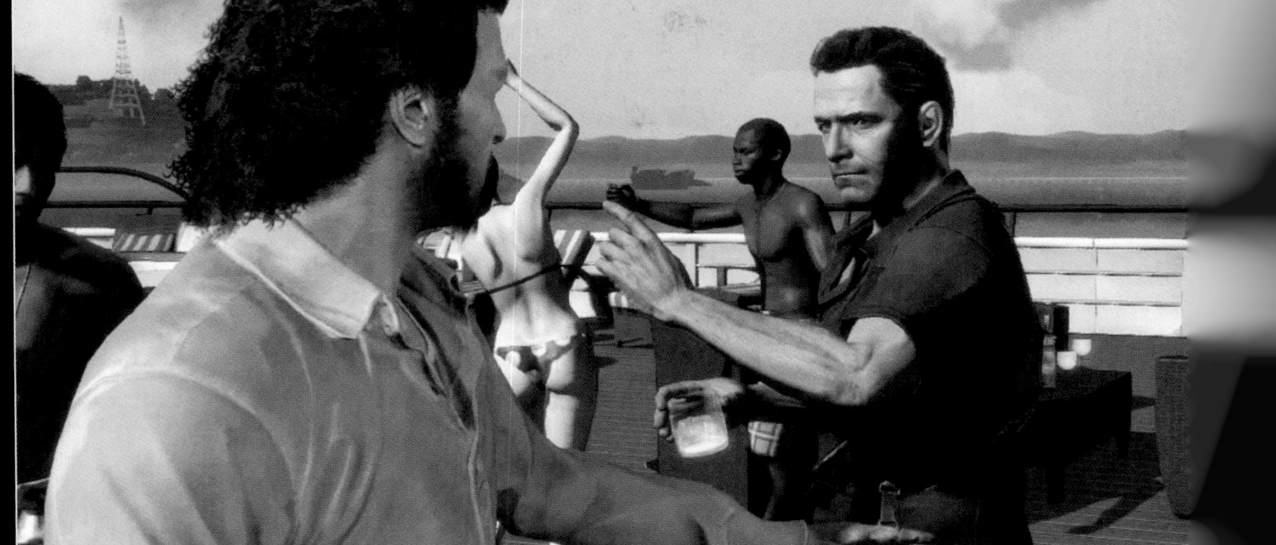

BASTIDAS LOCKS, PANAMA CANAL, PANAMA

5:18 PM, TUESDAY, A COUPLE OF MONTHS AGO

Detective Da Silva points out discrepancies in the way the Brancos are paying Raul Passos and reminds Max of a recent security gig in Panama. This triggers the memory: Max flashes back to getting loaded with Passos and Marcelo Branco on a massive yacht as coked-up socialites dance to house music on the open deck. The yacht is moored in the Bastidas Locks, near the Panama Canal Visitor's Center.

The luxury craft belongs to a friend of Marcelo's named Daphne Bernstein, wealthy ex-wife of a Wall Street tycoon. She tells him, "Marcelo, you're going to be the death of me!" Later, as Passos and Marcelo wander off to discuss the arrival of a truck, Max heads down to his private room on the lower deck for a drunken nap. But soon he awakens to sounds of vandalism in the corridor outside. Armed men in camouflage uniforms are kicking open doors of staterooms down the hall...

ABOARD THE YACHT

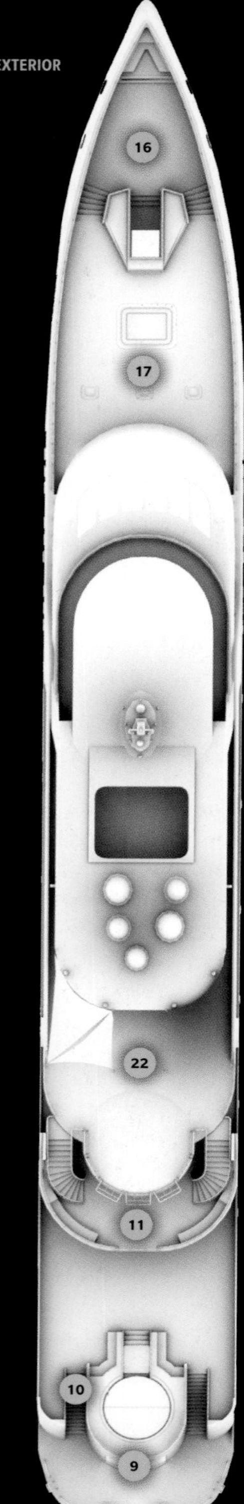

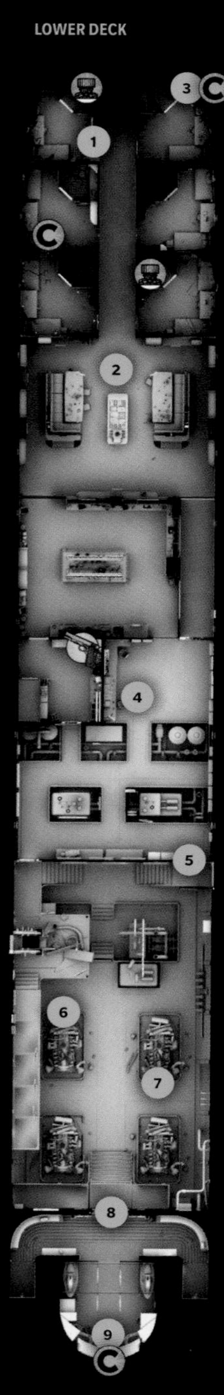

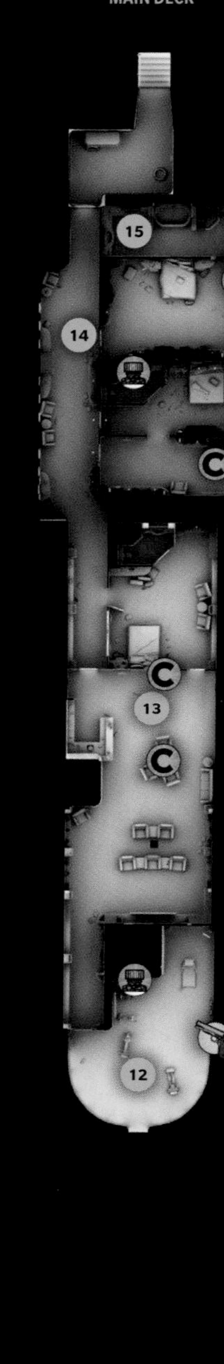

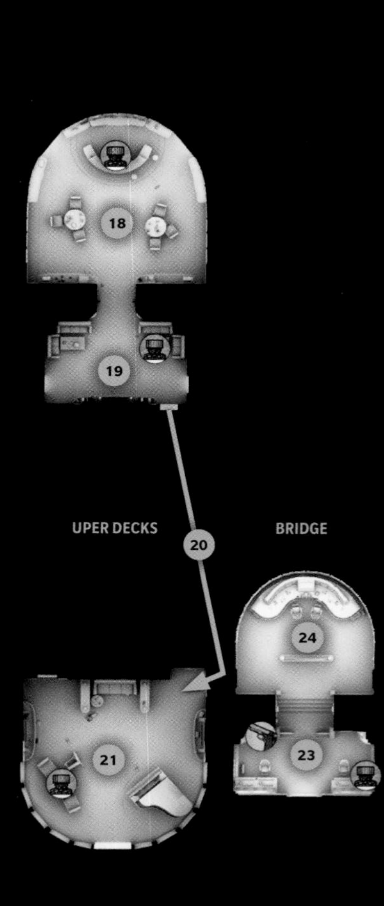

NEW WEAPONS NONE | PAINKILLERS 

MISSION: LOWER DECK

CLEAR THE LOWER DECK.

When you gain control, Max waits in cover at his room's door **(1)**, armed with an Auto 9mm pistol. Plug the hijacker in the hallway with a headshot then repeat with a second gunman who emerges through the doorway on the left. Move down the corridor toward the yacht's dining and galley area **(2)**, the big room with a black and white tiled floor. Use cabin doorways for cover and the Bullet Time you just added to your gauge to clear intruders.

Before you move farther to the back, pick up dropped M972 submachine guns and search the staterooms. First, nab the painkillers back in Max's bathroom. Enter the room directly across the hall **(3)** to find an interesting note on the dresser. It says "Max Payne, Walton's Bar, Hoboken"... which seems to indicate that the meeting with Passos in New Jersey wasn't just a lucky coincidence. You can also find painkillers in another cabin's bathroom.

NOTES ON MAX

Clear the hallway and kitchen of enemies in the beginning of the level. Then, explore the cabin directly across the hallway from Max's room to find this note on Max.

PASSOS' BED

From the beginning of the level, enter Passos' room, which is the second cabin on the right (first one after Max's cabin), and examine Passos' bed.

PART 1/3 GOLDEN SUPER SPORT

From your cabin, pass through the dining area and enter the kitchen through the door on the right. Once inside the kitchen, keep moving forward through the doorway with the plastic strips. Then, turn and look down into the left corner to find this gun part.

When you're finished exploring, return through the dining area and push farther down into the next room: a high-tech communications console. Approach the monitor-filled control panel **(4)** to trigger a quick cutscene: Max scans the readouts and spots more intruders back in the engine room. When control returns, continue farther astern to the engine room doorway **(5).**

Reaching the doorway triggers a cutscene: Max spots three gunmen in paramilitary-style army fatigues up ahead. Something's wrong—flashing emergency lights and sirens warn of impending engine overload, and then the entry door locks shut behind Max. He descends the stairs into the engine room and makes a rush at the hijackers. When control returns, use Bullet Time to gun them down, including the fourth enemy who enters the room from the next room. Gunning down the fourth intruder triggers a blinding explosion that rocks the room and knocks Max flat.

ESCAPE THE ENGINE ROOM!

As Max notes, the burning engines start consuming all the oxygen from the sealed engine compartment. You must hurry to both of the glowing red Emergency Fuel Shut-Off signs at **(6)** and **(7)**. Approach each one and press the "Shut off fuel feed" control indicated onscreen. When you do, Max turns the wheel that closes the fuel valve. Hurry! You don't have much time—your health meter is draining. When you shut off the second fuel feed, the exit door **(8)** slides open and two more enemies enter to attack. Gun them down.

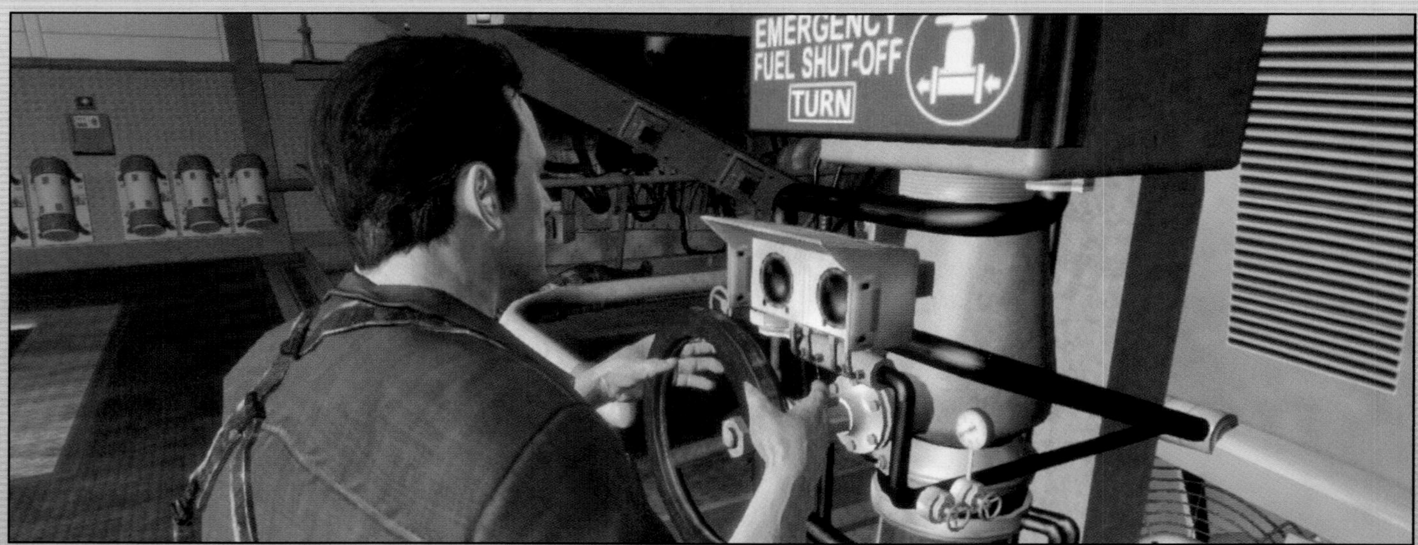

Exit straight through the equipment storage hold filled with scuba gear and jet skis. The back hatch **(9)** swings open when you approach so you can see the canal beyond the yacht's stern.

Step onto the exterior of the boat and examine the bloodstain on the deck floor. Then climb the stairs **(10)** to discover that hijackers are shooting indiscriminately from the upper deck at a bikini-clad passenger. The killers belong to the A.U.P., a Panamanian paramilitary death squad.

BLOOD TRAIL

When exiting the first floor stern of the ship, through the showers and scuba supply room, you can find a bloodstain on the floor as the back door opens.

Nail the four gunmen (circled in the screenshot) who appear on the yacht's upper decks **(11)**. Explore the deck to find golden weapon parts and carnage.

PART 2/3 GOLDEN SUPER SPORT

After surviving the engine room explosion, go outside to the back of the ship. After defeating the enemies on the upper deck, and before reentering the ship via the fitness room, find this gun part hidden at the dead-end walkway on the right side of the ship's fitness room.

MISSION: MAIN DECK

FIND MEDS IN THE EXERCISE ROOM.

Now you're on the yacht's main deck. Go through the open door into the fitness room **(12)** and take the painkillers from the medicine chest on the back wall. As you approach the partially opened door that leads to the main deck cabins, note the blood smear on the floor. This hijacking crew is brutal and merciless.

CLEAR THE MOVIE SCREENING ROOM.

Push through the door to trigger a quick cutscene: Max slips into the yacht's movie screening room **(13)** and spies a trio of hijackers tearing open the cabin walls with a crowbar. What are they looking for? As Max says, "Something on the boat had attracted the sharks."

When you regain control, Max crouches in cover behind a theater chair. If you have Bullet Time in your gauge, use it to tag all three with headshots. A fourth gunman appears from behind the bar on the left. Make him your final victim. Examine the wall that the hijackers were tearing open. Then proceed through the master stateroom beyond and continue out into the windowed corridor.

DISCARDED NEWSPAPER

In the cabin with the torn-up wall, examine the newspaper on the round table near the pried wall.

PRIED WALL

Defeat the four enemies tearing up a wall on the second deck and examine the wall they were destroying.

EXPLORE THE MAIN FLOOR STATEROOMS.

Explore the next stateroom down the hall—Daphne Bernstein's room—to find some painkillers in the bathroom. Exit to the corridor again and approach the next stateroom door **(14)** with your gun aimed at it—when you push the door open, a hijacker is waiting behind the bed. Gun him down! Two more hijackers camp in the bathroom **(15)**—one who hops into the doorway to attack and another hiding out of sight back by the toilet.

DAPHNE'S PASSPORT

Just after leaving the pried-wall cabin, enter the first cabin on the right in the hallway. Find Daphne's passport on the desk in the back of the first of two connecting rooms.

DAPHNE'S JEWELRY BOX

After leaving the pried-wall cabin, enter the second cabin (third door) on the right in the hallway. Three enemies are in this cabin: one in the bedroom where the jewelry box sits on a shelf and two enemies in the bathroom. Kill the enemies and then examine the box.

Return to the corridor. Proceed to the stairs where you can dispatch three more fatigue-clad gunmen boarding the yacht out on its bow **(16)**.

MISSION: UPPER DECKS

CLEAR THE UPPER DECKS.

Move to the next stairs and start clearing the five gunmen from the top deck **(17)**, the area with the main bar and hot tub where the chapter opened. Use the lower deck and stairs as cover and as a retreat if needed. Two armed kidnappers are posted at the windows and doors of the bar **(18)**, and some rush onto the deck to fight. When the final kill camera tells you the area is clear, head inside.

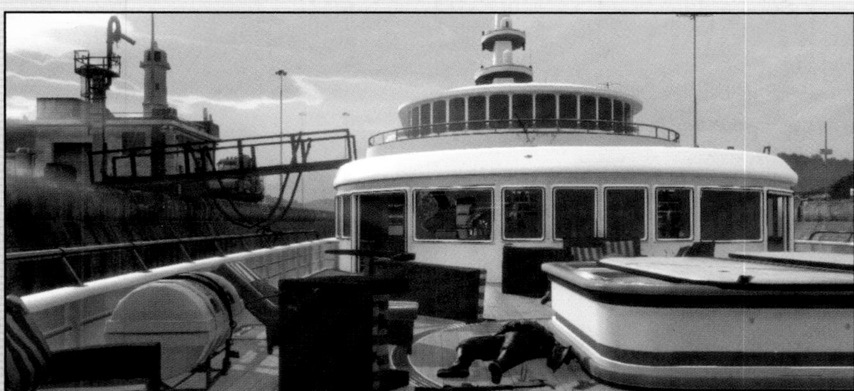

Find painkillers on a coffee table in the room beyond **(19)**, next to the boxes of cigars. Proceed through the half-open door onto the deck walkway. As you move along the gunwale rail **(20)**, soldiers open fire from atop the canal lock on the shore. Pick them off, including one who pulls up in a pickup truck as you move down the walkway. Conserve your ammo and try for as many headshots as possible. Another tough battle lies ahead. If you shoot the truck repeatedly, it will explode, killing three of the soldiers.

When the shore is cleared, enter the lounge **(21)** at the far end of the walkway. Remember, you can play the piano! Grab two bottles of painkillers from the nearby table. Then exit astern onto the open deck and climb the stairs to the yacht's helipad area **(22)** where a helicopter is just taking off.

CLEAR THE HELIPAD AND BRIDGE.

Several uniformed gunmen guard the helipad deck, including one behind a bar in the corner. This is a tough fight, so it's a good place to use Bullet Time for headshots that in turn let you refill the gauge. Pick up a dropped FAL or SPAS-15 and prepare for the next fight. When the area seems clear, be cautious—when you approach it, the automatic door slides open that leads into the ship's high-tech bridge area, **(23)** and more gunmen emerge. Three more A.U.P. goons are posted inside, behind a second sliding door to the helm.

When you finally clear the bridge, don't go all the way forward to the helm **(24)** yet. First, grab the painkillers sitting on one of the navigation consoles. Then shoot at the captain's portrait hanging on the wall to reveal a safe with a golden gun part inside.

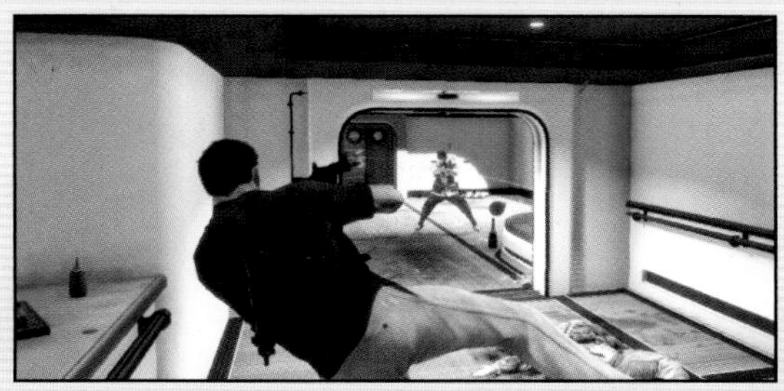

PART 1/3 GOLDEN AK-47

In the room just before you reach the wheelhouse, which triggers the next stage of attack on land, shoot the picture from the wall on the left to reveal a secret safe. Shoot the safe to open it. The gun part is inside the wall safe.

REUNITE WITH PASSOS.

When you climb the steps into the helm, you trigger a cutscene. Max spots Passos and Marcelo loading a pickup truck onshore, and he hops off the boat to join them. The hijackers have gunned down a few unfortunate passengers, but Daphne, her yacht's crew, and most of her guests are missing. Marcelo displays a remarkable lack of concern about Daphne's fate, but Passos agrees to join Max in the search for the remaining passengers.

PANAMA CANAL

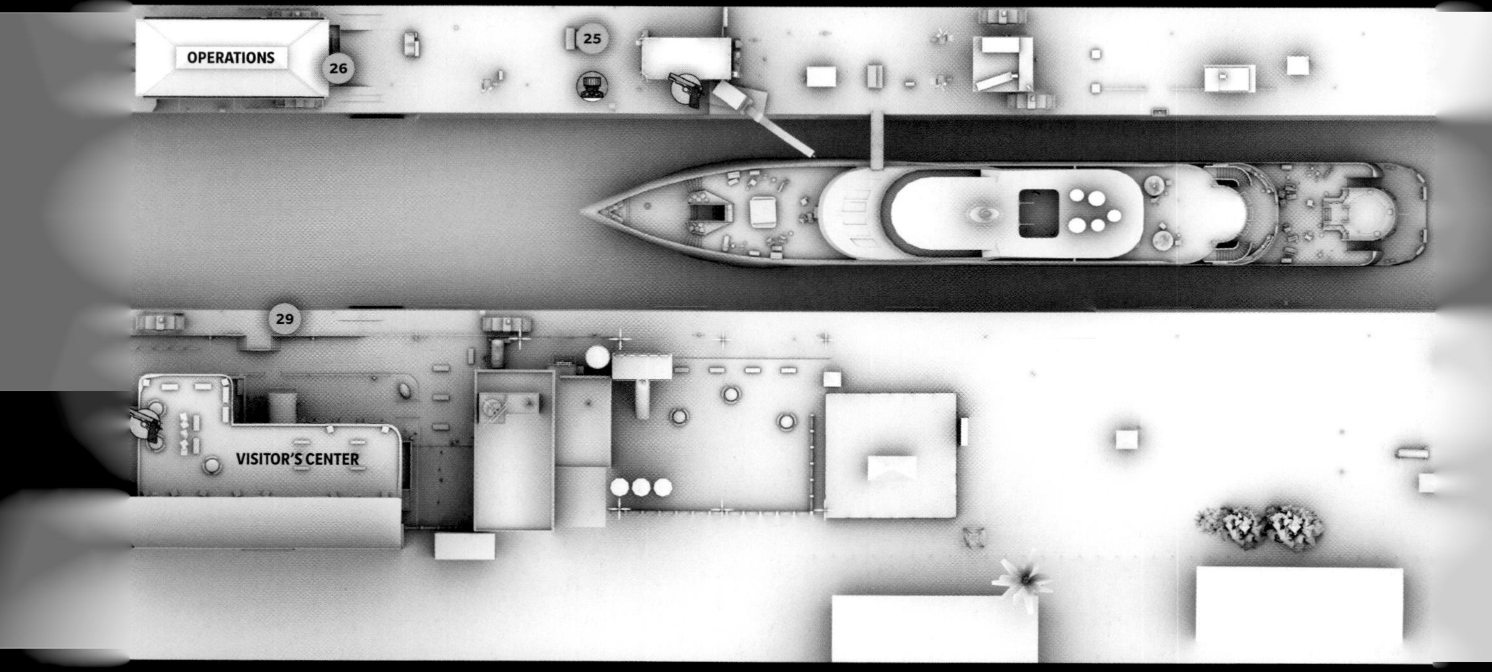

OPERATIONS BUILDING

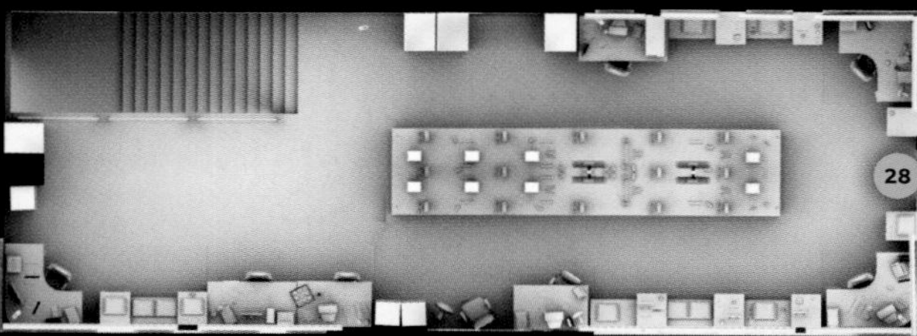

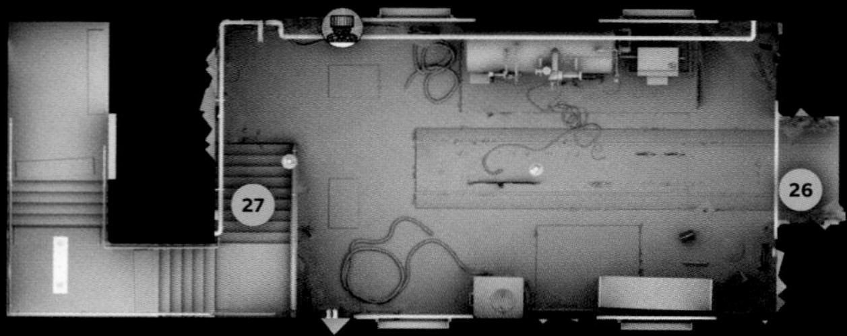

MISSION

FIGHT YOUR WAY INTO THE OPERATIONS BUILDING.

Max and Passos approach the lock's Operations Building where paramilitary gunmen are zip-lining across the canal to the Visitor's Center. When the scene ends, you crouch in cover **(25)** facing the building. Passos points out a nice weapon in the nearby pickup truck—an MPK with a red dot scope. (You'll also find Painkillers and an ammo case for all weapons.) Use the second weapon to pick off the first wave of gunmen on the balconies. When they're eliminated, Passos pushes forward to the next cover as more gunmen emerge, including shooters on either side of the arched doorway. When the coast is finally clear, Max follows Passos down the tracks to the building's railcar entrance **(26)**.

W WEAPONS NONE | PAINKILLERS 

GET TO THE CONTROL OFFICE.

From cover just outside the entrance, pick off the two gunmen who descend the stairs **(27)** on the other side of the garage. Now you can explore the area, switch out weapons, return to the ammo case in the pickup truck to restock, and find the painkillers in the medicine cabinet inside the garage.

PART 2/3 GOLDEN AK-47

After leaving the yacht and after clearing the enemies around the tower, head to the opposite side of the building that you started the tower battle at to find this gun part.

Climb the stairs to the control office ("Oficina de Control"). Two more soldiers open fire when you arrive, so dispatch them and proceed to the exit door **(28)** across the room.

ZIP-LINE ACROSS THE CANAL.

Reaching the doorway triggers a cutscene—Max emerges onto the balcony just in time to see the last uniformed thug begin his zip-line descent. Max jumps aboard! When control returns, use the automatic Bullet Time to decimate the paramilitary forces lined up outside the Visitor's Center across the canal.

VISITOR CENTER

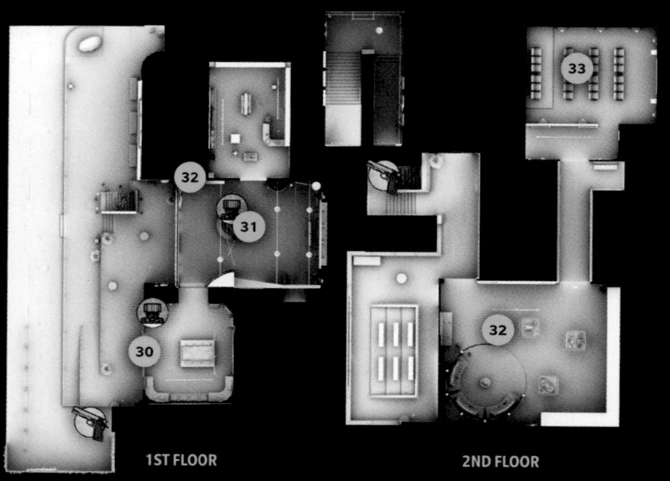

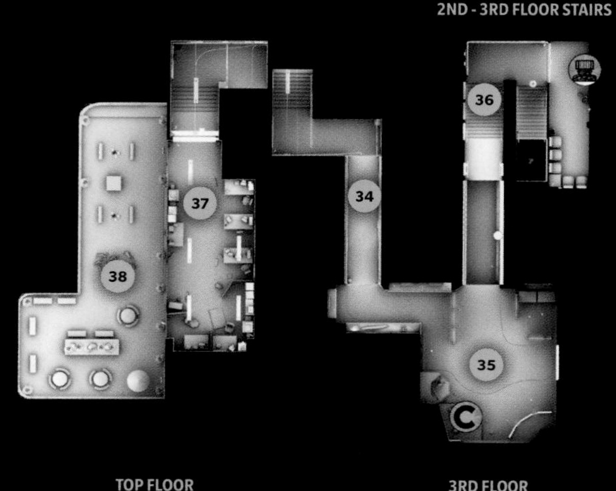

NEW WEAPONS NONE | PAINKILLERS 

MISSION

CLEAR OUT THE GROUND FLOOR.

When the zip-line ride ends, Max drops into cover just outside the center's main entrance **(29)**. Patiently pick off all of the shooters in the doors and through the windows of the ground floor. When the final kill camera plays, enter the information room on the right **(30)** to find some painkillers on the corner desk.

PART 3/3 GOLDEN SUPER SPORT

This gun part is located outside the operation center. After zip-lining across the channel and eliminating the immediate threat, find this gun part in a corner, on the right side of the building, beside the wheelchair ramps.

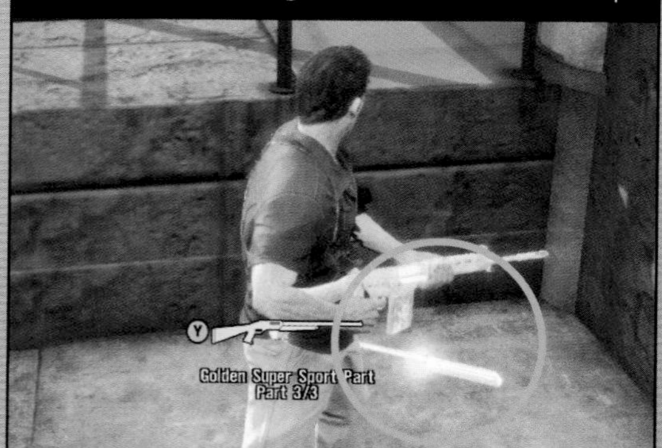

Move into the main lobby where you see a barred gate closing off access to the main exhibitions hall. Go behind the circular reception desk **(31)** where you can find more painkillers. Approach the desk console and press the "Open security door" control indicated onscreen. You see the gate swing open **(32)**. Head through the gate into the stairwell and defeat the enemy coming around the first corner.

CLEAR OUT THE SECOND FLOOR.

Climb the staircase with your gun ready as you near the top. The second floor features another room full of exhibits **(32)** and a small theater **(33)**. Shoot the paramilitary squad in the first hallway, clear the exhibit room of enemies covering behind glass exhibit cases, and fight down the next hallway. At the far end, turn left to reach the staircase. (You won't find anything in the theater to the right.)

PART 3/3
GOLDEN AK-47
Just before you reach the second-floor exhibition room via the exterior walkway, explore the exterior staircase to the right. The last Golden AK-47 part in on the first landing.

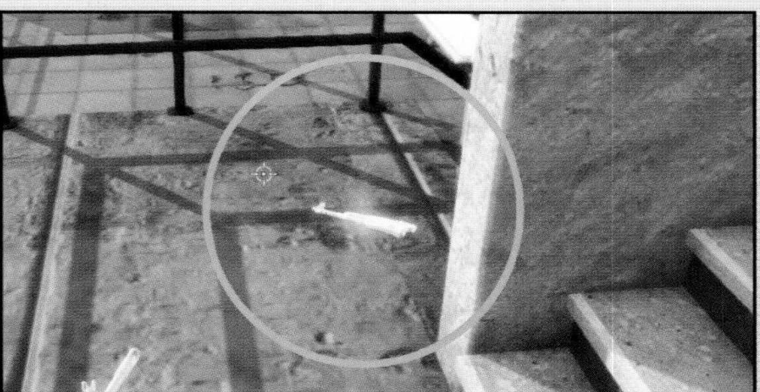

VISITOR CENTER DISPLAY

After clearing the enemies in the area, examine this display on the last exhibition floor before you reach the office with the blood trail. The trail leads to the slaughter balcony at the end of the mission.

CLEAR OUT THE THIRD FLOOR.

Climb upstairs with your weapon ready again as more soldiers try to halt your relentless advance. On the landing between floors, turn right to find painkillers in a medicine cabinet outside the bathrooms. Then continue upstairs to the next floor, which features a museum. When you reach the top of the stairs, shoot the soldier up ahead then sprint down the corridor **(34)** as other shooters fire at you from a walkway through the windows on your left. Try using a running sideways ShootDodge to fire through the windows if you have difficulty here. In the museum **(35)**, veer to the left and dispatch the walkway gunmen who shot at you. Now you can explore the museum and examine the surveyor's exhibit.

CLIMB TO THE TOP FLOOR.

Go down the walkway and climb the stairs **(36)** to the top floor **(37)**. Your arrival triggers a grim cinematic: Max finds the missing passengers and crew outside on the rooftop patio **(38)**. When Passos arrives, his only response is: "I didn't think it would be like this."

XII THE GREAT AMERICAN SAVIOR OF THE POOR

THE IMPERIAL PALACE HOTEL, SÃO PAULO
5:30 PM, TUESDAY

As the flashback ends, Detective Da Silva enlightens Max further, shining a light on some dark truths behind Branco family dynamics. Then the cop drops off Max outside the creepy, run-down wreck of the Imperial Palace Hotel. Max slips through a broken-out window into the hotel's basement.

Quick work with an empty "Nada" water bottle and some duct tape adds a crude silencer to the barrel of Max's PT92 pistol. Then he moves across the basement toward an ill-lit hallway...

BASEMENT

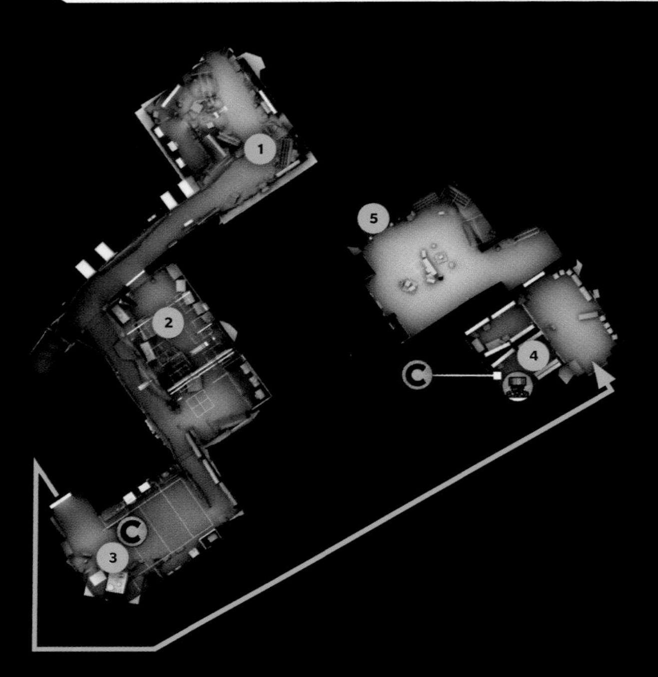

NEW WEAPONS

NONE

PAINKILLERS 

MISSION

EXPLORE THE BASEMENT AREA.

You take control in the dark, debris-strewn depths of the hotel basement **(1)**. Walk to the right, toward the lighted hallway. The first room on your left is the run-down remains of a laundry facility **(2)** filled with broken, industrial-sized washers. Move through the room and exit via the hole in the far wall.

Turn left and take a few steps to trigger a disturbing scene—Max spies a pair of Crachá Preto thugs tossing bloody garbage bags and sealed body bags into a blazing incinerator **(3)**. After the scene, enter the incinerator room and examine the closest gurney.

GURNEY

In the beginning of the mission, examine the gurneys in the incinerator room.

Push through the next door into a storage area. You can find some painkillers in the first enclosure on the left **(4)**. You can also examine an ammunition crate etched with the name "Unidade de Forcas Especiais"—another connection between Colonel Becker's UFE and the Crachá Preto.

AMMO CRATE

Through the doors of the incinerator room, you come to a hallway with a couple cages to the left. Enter the first cage to find painkillers and the UFE ammo crate. Examine it.

Move through the next door to trigger another scene: Max watches the two Crachá Preto militiamen board a freight elevator **(5)**. After they disappear upward, he follows their lead and rides up to the hotel's second floor.

MISSION

FIGHT THROUGH THE SECOND FLOOR.

Exit the freight elevator **(6)** and take cover at the first doorway—you hear voices in the next room. It's the same two guys from the incinerator room. Lean around and pick off the two men in the large hotel suite **(7)** plus two more who rush in if they hear a noise. To avoid the backup fight, shoot one of the first two in the head with the silencer and quickly use the earned Bullet Time to shoot the second gunman in the head. Pick up a dropped MD-97L assault rifle, then hustle to the connecting door to the next suite **(8)**. If the backup fight occurs, you can pick up a Bull revolver after the four Crachá Preto troops are dead.

PART 1/3 GOLDEN RPG

This gun part is in the bathroom in the same room where you catch up to the two men from the incinerator.

Exit the suite and follow the corridor through one wall hole into a small, shattered storeroom then stop at the next hole **(9)**. Start shooting through the hole at the multiple Crachá Preto attackers who open fire from the next two rooms up ahead.

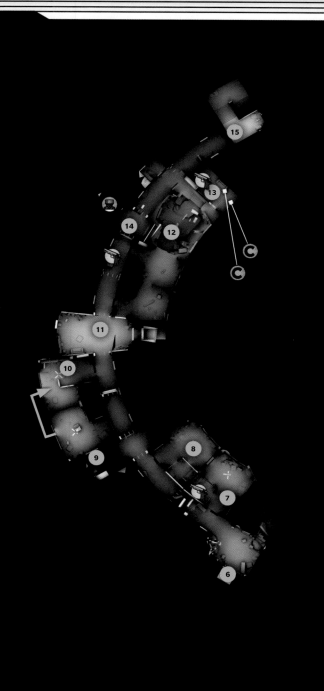

NEW WEAPONS

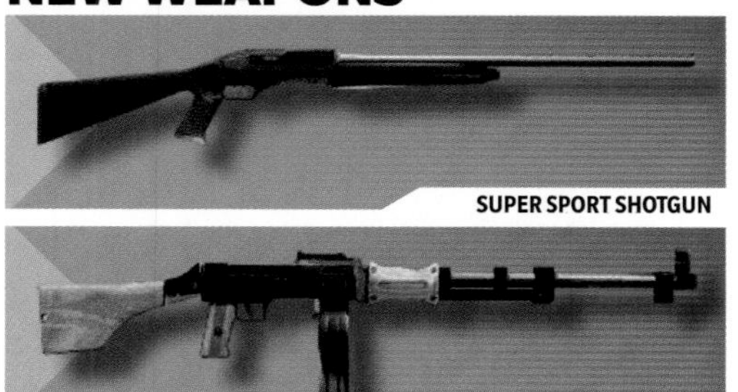

SUPER SPORT SHOTGUN

RPD LIGHT MACHINEGUN

PAINKILLERS

To reach the second room, you must exit onto the balcony and get to the big sliding doors leading back inside. Target the explosive gas canister **(10)** (circled in the screenshot) near the second room's left wall to take out the new gunmen rushing in from the hall.

Move out into the hall and press the flashing button on the wall to open the metal security gate. Push through the gate into a central sitting room **(11)** with an old sofa and purplish-red wall coverings where more gunmen rush at you. Clear out the room, the corridor, and the two large suites beyond.

Watch for your victims to drop a new weapon here, the light but brutish Super Sport shotgun. It's a solid mid-range weapon with a nice spread and good punch. Clearing the area brings you to the brink of a large section of collapsed flooring **(12)**.

PART 1/3 GOLDEN FMP G3S

If you stand facing the room with the collapsed floor (before crossing it), a hallway is visible to your left. This gun part is just inside the hallway, on the floor, beside a room-service cart.

CLEAR OUT THE COLLAPSED FLOOR AREA.

Crachá Preto gunmen open fire from the far side of the gap. Once you eliminate the first wave, drop down into the collapsed section; more gunmen appear up above. Dispatch them and climb up the crumpled floor section that serves as a ramp.

Explore the corridors and rooms around the collapse. Foes in this area drop another powerful new weapon: the RPD light machine gun. Find the room **(13)** with a sofa and a photocopy you can examine—it's an ID card for Raul Passos. When you exit this room, be prepared to gun down a single gunman in the next hallway.

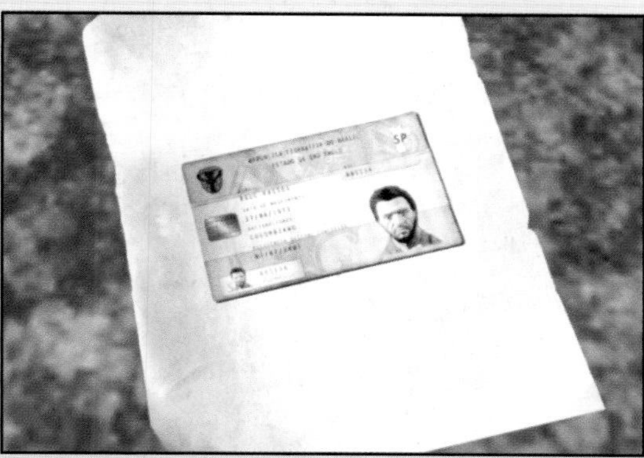

PASSOS' ID CARD

Find this photocopy of Passos' ID card on the floor inside the room that is just opposite the room with the collapsed floor. It could be under a small table since the table can move during the battle. Max learns that Passos is actually Colombian.

WALL PHOTOS

Find this wall of photos in the room just on the other side of the collapsed floor. Also inside this room: Passos' ID card clue.

BAD GUN

Look for the RPD light machine gun on the hotel's second floor. It can tear right through attackers.

Three more soldiers are posted at the end of the hall that leads to the blue stairwell doors **(15),** but nail another explosive gas canister directly behind them for three quick kills. (The explosion also blasts open the doors.)

Before going through the doors to use the stairs, turn and go to the opposite end of the corridor **(14)** to find another RPD that you can scavenge for rounds or wield if you haven't found one of these brutal LMGs yet. The storeroom near this RPD contains painkillers. Return to the stairs and climb up to the third floor.

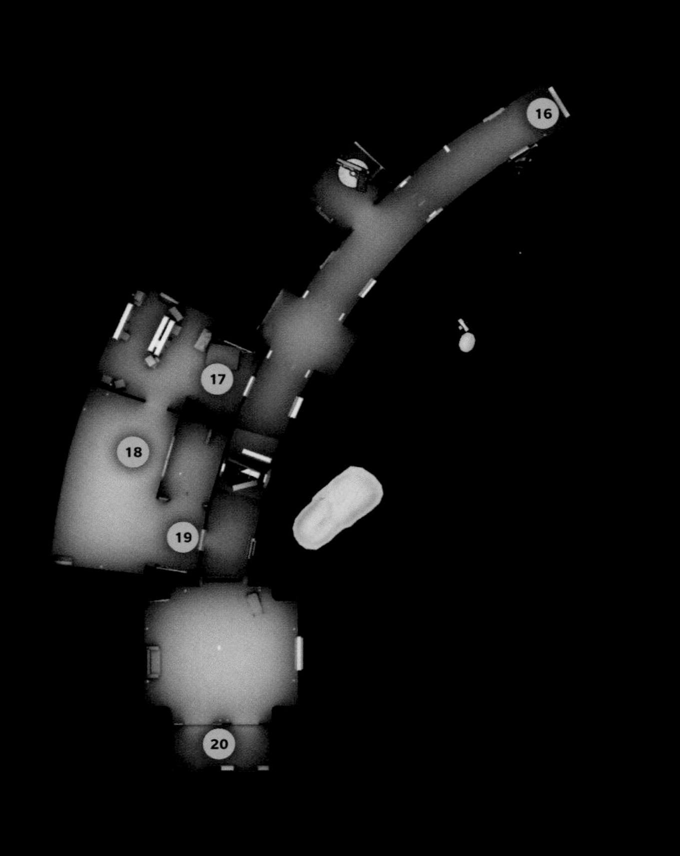

NEW WEAPONS

NONE

PAINKILLERS

MISSION

EXPLORE THE THIRD FLOOR.

PART 2/3

GOLDEN RPG

After climbing the stairs to the floor above the level with the collapsed floor, you push through some doors and reach a long empty hallway. Find the hole in the right wall that leads into a crumbled bathroom. This gun part is on the floor near the tub.

Exit the stairwell **(16)** and move down the hallway to the door that's slightly ajar on the right. Note the massive lock installed on the outside. Approach the door to trigger a long series of cutscenes: Max ducks into a storeroom **(17)** and finds more evidence of a major UFE presence here in this Crachá Preto stronghold. He grabs incriminating papers for Detective Da Silva to review later.

Then, Max kicks open a padlocked security door. Inside the next room **(18),** he finds a handful of abducted favela residents... including the Comando Sombra boss himself. The captives are beaten, bloody, disoriented, and in shock. Max sends them on their way, including Serrano.

The scene continues—Max shoots open the next door **(19)** and finds an elevator shaft **(20)**. The cars are inactive, but he finds an emergency ladder inside the shaft and climbs it to the next floor above.

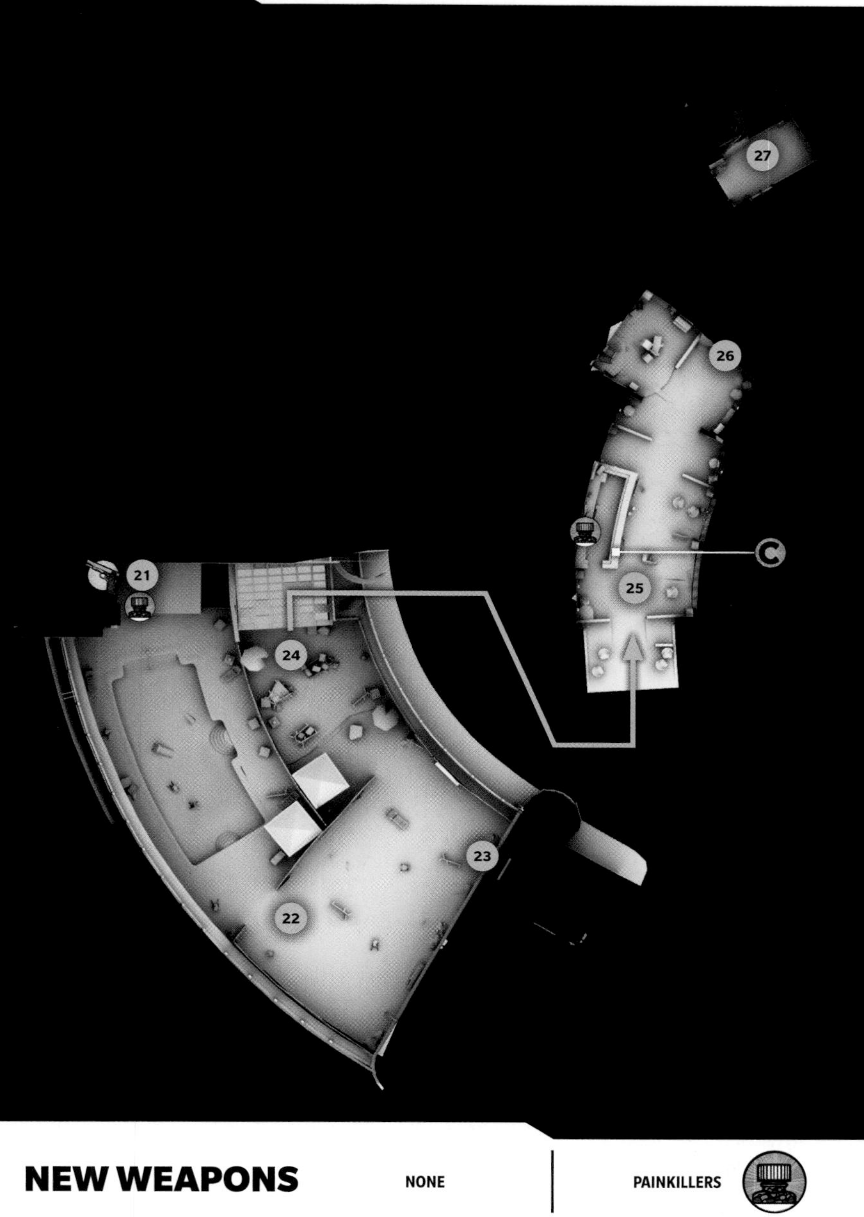

After you eliminate the first trio, more gunmen emerge from the tennis court **(22)** beyond the far end of the pool. Take cover behind the lobby desk and pick them off. Step outside and move past the pool. When you reach the tennis court, aim at the door **(23)** at the opposite corner—three more gunmen burst onto the court from there.

PART 2/3 GOLDEN FMP G3S

This gun part can be found behind the counter in the rooftop pool house.

NEW WEAPONS NONE | PAINKILLERS

MISSION

CLEAR THE OUTDOOR POOL AND COURT AREA.

Max emerges into the lobby **(21)** of what used to be the hotel's recreation area. Beyond the windows and glass doors ahead you see an empty swimming pool and three armed thugs. Max takes cover behind a cart that has two bottles of painkillers on it, so be sure to snag those. Then open fire on the Crachá Preto using the the SPAS-15 that's leaning against the cart.

Take cover at the end of the court's fence and lean around to target shooters on the outdoor deck **(24)** with more emerging from the restaurant/lounge beyond. Be patient because these foes are plentiful and use cover well.

NEWSPAPER ARTICLE

Once you clear the lounge beyond the pool, find this newspaper on the bar countertop. This is the room just before the organ donor operating room. You learn Victor Branco is winning the election from the sympathy votes.

EXPLORE THE HOTEL LOUNGE.

Clear the restaurant/lounge **(25)** and find the painkillers behind the bar. Examine the newspaper atop the bar—the headline roughly translates to "Victor Branco demonstrates force in the face of tragedy." Take a crack at playing the piano on the stage before you move on. (If you've been playing the game's pianos all along, Max should be getting pretty good at his theme song by now.)

DISCOVER THE OPERATING ROOM.

When you approach the exit door **(26)** next to the stage, you trigger a long cutscene: Max enters the kitchen behind the restaurant/ lounge. It's been converted into something completely different. The refrigerated storage is filled with coolers labeled with names of body parts: "Heart," "Liver Tissue," "Kidney." And a manic fellow in surgery scrubs is hurriedly tossing bloody chunks into bins. When Serrano shows up, Max is content to leave the "surgeon" to his karmic fate. Max ends up in a small connecting corridor **(27)**.

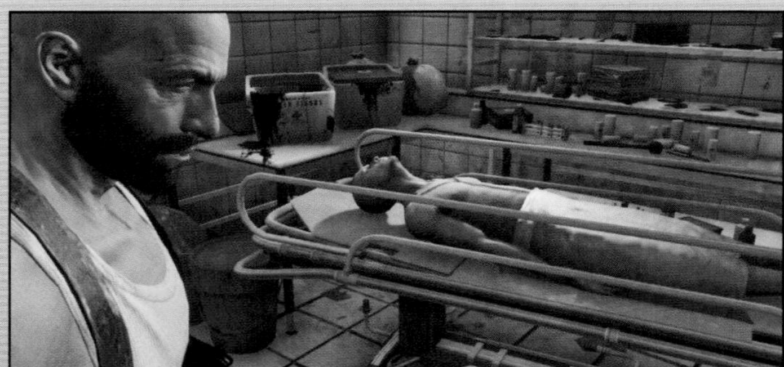

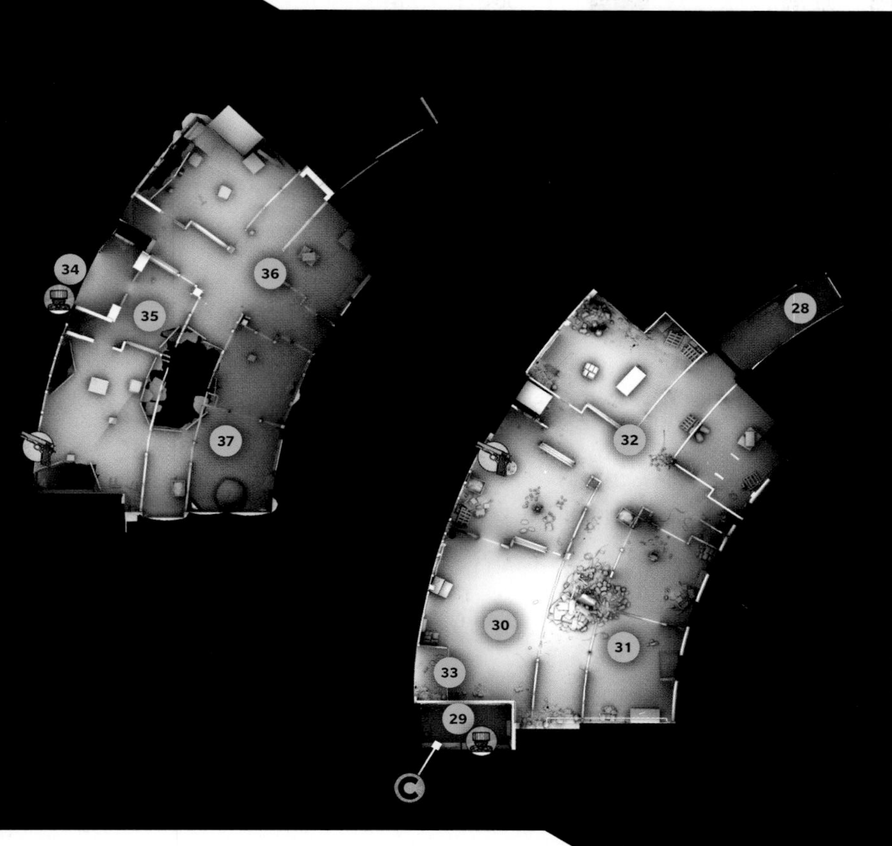

NEW WEAPONS NONE | PAINKILLERS

PART 3/3 GOLDEN FMP G3S

This gun part is located behind a chair on the right side of the first room where you plant three bombs on support columns.

MISSION

EXPLORE THE DEMOLITION AREA.

Push through the next doors into a curving hallway **(28)** that leads into a dilapidated open area with crumbling support columns, some of which are marked for demolition.

Move all the way across the area to the equipment closet **(29)** to trigger a scene: Max finds boxes full of C4 explosive on the shelves inside. He fills a duffel bag with charges and exits the closet. Then he approaches the nearest red support column **(30)** and plants a C4 charge on it.

PLANT C4 ON RED COLUMNS.

When control returns, your task is to plant a C4 charge on each of the remaining red support columns marked for demolition ("Para Demolição")—two more in this fourth- floor area *and* three on the floor above. But before you do that, turn around and go back inside the equipment closet to grab the painkillers. Examine the receipt sitting on the shelf to the far right, then grab the RPD light machine gun leaning on the shelf to the far left.

DONATION RECEIPT

Find this receipt on the shelf in the back corner of the weapons and explosives storage room on the first floor of the destructible support columns. This receipt shows Victor paying Neves $400,000.

Exit the closet and veer right to approach the next red column **(31)**. Press the "Plant explosive" button indicated onscreen; Max places a C4 charge on the column. Find the other red column across the room **(32)** and repeat the process. (You can do these in any order.)

When you plant the second charge, you hear Max comment on the situation during the cutscene, then "more of the rats come out of their holes"—a heavily armed Crachá Preto squad unlocks the security gate **(33)** from upstairs (near the equipment closet) and fans out across the floor.

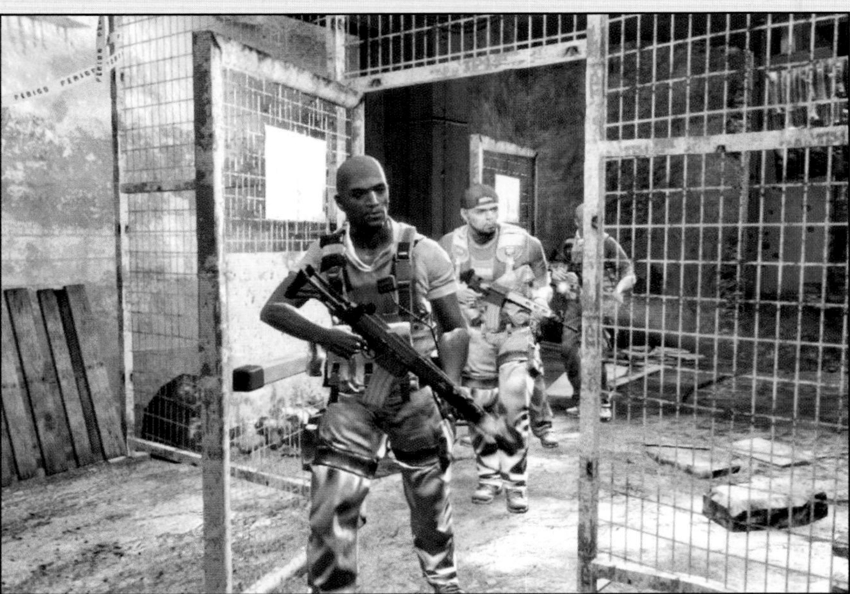

CLEAR THE FOURTH-FLOOR DEMOLITION AREA.

You start out in good cover behind a low wall section, and you have excellent firepower if you grabbed the RPD from the equipment closet. Be patient and hold your fire until you can see the group clearly through the beam obstructions. Enter Bullet Time and aim for as many heads as you can in one attack.

Once you clear the room, move through the newly opened gate **(33)**. Climb the rickety wooden ramp that runs up to the next floor.

NAIL THE SNIPERS AND GUNMEN.

When you reach the small fifth-floor balcony at the top of the wooden ramp, two snipers open fire at Max from a building across the way. Max jumps into cover behind a railing **(34)** and picks up the M82A1 sniper rifle with scope that just happens to be sitting there. Note that a bottle of painkillers and an ammo case with ammo refills for all weapons sit on the balcony, as well.

Use the scoped rifle to pick off the two snipers first. Three more gunmen open fire from the same building. You can get a bead on their positions by tracking the red targeting lasers. Don't linger too long when targeting them through your scope—remember, they have accurate scoped rifles too, and you're visible to them when you're aiming. If you spend too much time getting them in your sights, you'll get sniped. Use Bullet Time each time you pop up from cover to snipe a sniper.

After you nail the two snipers, take out the other three gunmen. When you've eliminated all five total shooters from the building opposite yours, replace the sniper rifle with the RPD again and use the ammo case to restock.

CLEAR THE FIFTH-FLOOR DEMOLITION AREA.

This next fight is a dangerous one. Push through the yellow security gate with the "Perigo"("Danger") sign and start gunning down the Crachá Preto soldiers wandering amongst the columns and walls.

But be ready—*before* you can clear the room, a separate squad of three gunmen sneaks up to the security gate behind you from the lower floor! If you have enough Bullet Time saved up, use it here to drop all three in one firing burst. Otherwise, sprint across the room and take cover behind a pillar.

PART 3/3

GOLDEN RPG

After clearing the enemies from the second floor of destructible columns, find the final RPG part on an exterior ledge that is adjacent to the floor entrance.

PLANT EXPLOSIVES ON THE RED COLUMNS.

After you clear out the entire death squad, proceed to each one of the three red columns marked for demolition ("Para Demolição") and plant C4 charges as you did down on the fourth floor **(35, 36, 37)**. After placing the first charge, four more death squad gunmen attack from the hallway at the end of the floor. Once you eliminate them, no more foes appear in this area. But before you place the last charge, you might want to return to the ammo case out on the balcony to restock ammo for all weapons.

HOTEL ROOF

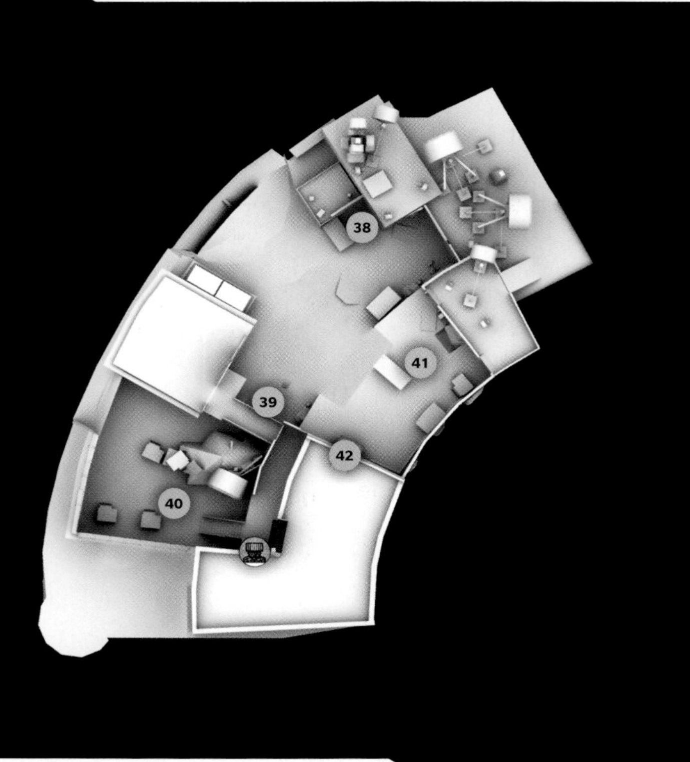

NEW WEAPONS

NONE

PAINKILLERS 

MISSION

CLEAR THE ROOFTOP.

Placing the final charge triggers a long cinematic sequence—holding up the detonator, Max emerges onto the hotel's rooftop where a full platoon of the vigilante militia is deployed. The Crachá Preto leader, Álvaro Neves, has arrived via helicopter and engages in a barbed exchange with Max. When Max has had enough, he detonates the C4 charges.

The chapter's remaining gunfights can be tricky because the C4 has destabilized the building. Regular tremors cause Max to lose his balance and also affect your targeting reticle, causing it to sway around the screen. You start out in cover behind an air-conditioning unit **(38)**. Start picking off the right-wing soldiers. If ever there was a good place for Bullet Time, this is it. When you clear the first area, a fiery explosion tears apart a rooftop structure.

After the smoke clears, rush forward past the burning debris and gun down the militiaman at the gate **(39)**. Rush through the gate and veer through the opening to your right.

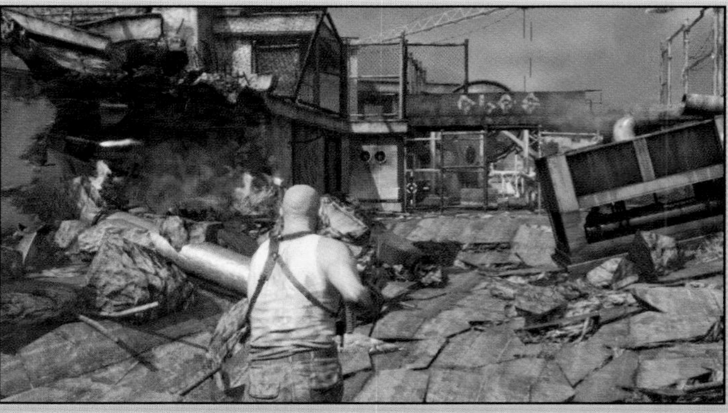

Careful! More gunmen are waiting just around the next corner **(40)**. When you approach and shoot them, another explosion is triggered. This blast tears open the gate at the top of the staircase ahead. The enemy posted there drops a powerful LMG .30 machinegun.

Climb the stairs, go through the gate, and turn right to find a tiny closet with a medicine cabinet loaded with painkillers. Then follow the walkway through another gate. Gun down a lone Crachá Preto soldier and run toward the exit door across the roof. Unfortunately, another explosion destroys the exit structure, trapping Max on the roof.

DISPATCH THE MACHINE GUNNER.

Even more unfortunate, three more gunmen appear atop the roof structure behind you. But when you dispatch them, a heavily armored machine gunner wielding a big LMG .30 suddenly pops up. Drop into cover. Don't rise when the gunner is firing unless you can activate Bullet Time. Aim for the gunner's head, but be ready to duck.

WATCH THE CHAPTER-ENDING MOVIES.

When the machine gunner finally falls, watch as an explosion knocks Max to the roof. Neves gets the drop on Max and appears ready to end his little crusade...until Raul Passos makes a surprise appearance.

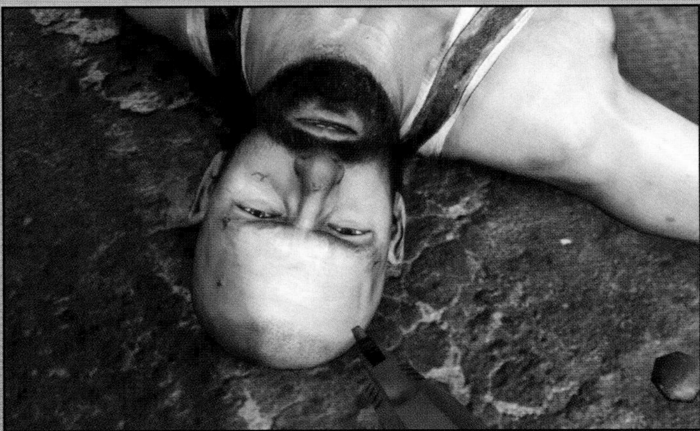

XIII A FAT BALD DUDE WITH A BAD TEMPE

55TH BATTALION OF THE CITY POLICE SPECIAL FORCES UNIT

8:48PM, WEDNESDAY

The chapter opens with a long sequence of cinematic scenes. First, Max says his goodbyes to Passos and Giovanna, and confers with Detective Da Silva on a "creative" plan to reach the UFE commander, Colonel Becker.

Then Max makes a truly bold first move—he walks into UFE's downtown police headquarters and surrenders. After simply handing over his weapon, he asks to speak with Colonel Becker. UFE guards handcuff and haul Max through the precinct holding cells to an interrogation room.

Da Silva has promised Max "a ten o'clock showcase," so Max has to endure a half hour of enhanced interrogation techniques until the clock ticks to ten. Fortunately, the UFE make the mistake of uncuffing their seemingly submissive prisoner before they try to beat some answers out of him.

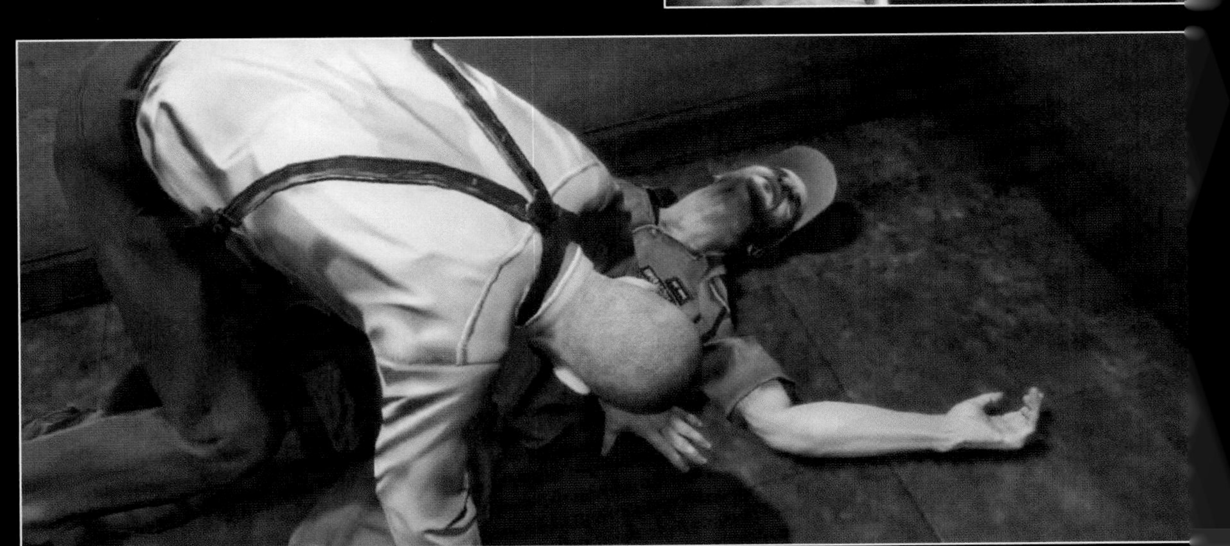

HOLDING CELLS

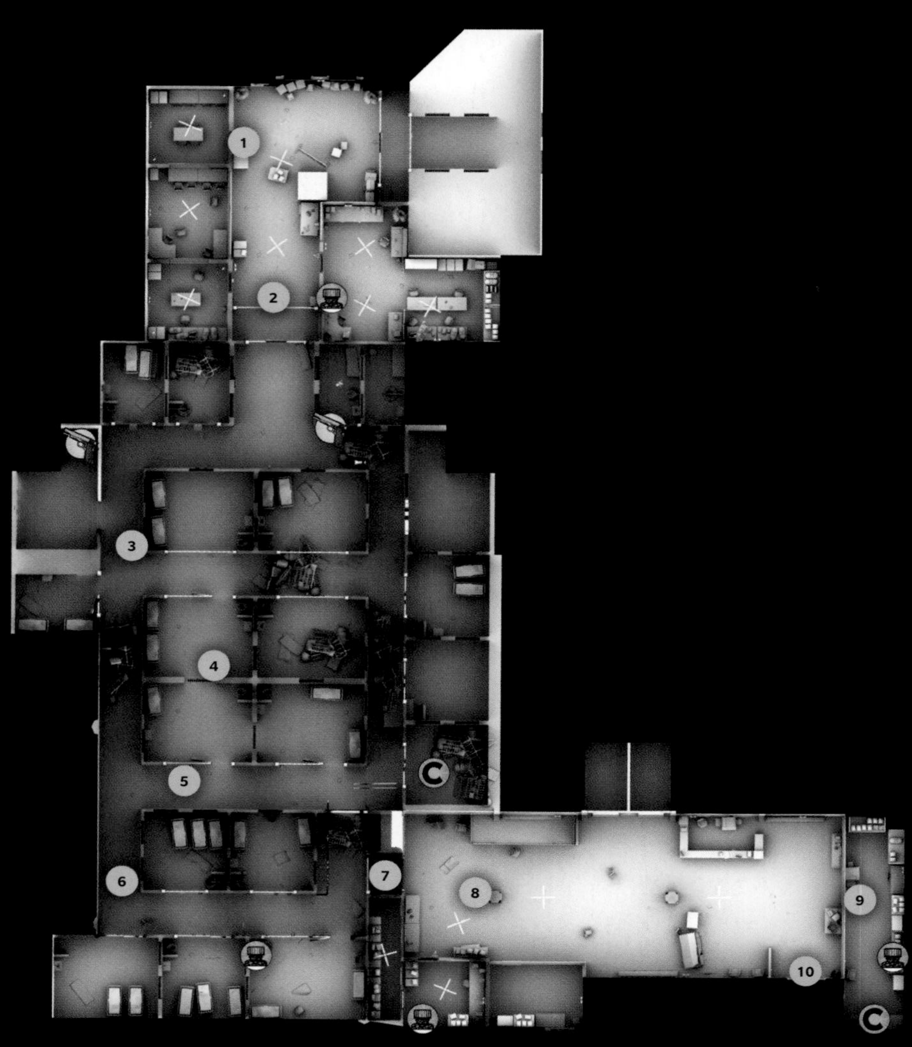

NEW WEAPONS

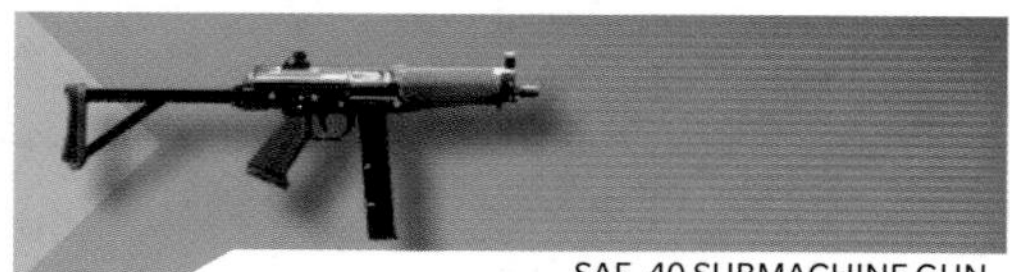
SAF .40 SUBMACHINE GUN

PAINKILLERS

MISSION

ESCAPE THE INTERROGATION AREA.

Max starts out armed with a 1911 pistol as he hides behind a locker **(1)** just outside his interrogation room. Many UFE guards in this level are heavily armored. Aim for heads as much as possible or you'll waste a lot of ammo. Lean around and pick off the first cop in the hall, then pick up the new weapon he drops—an SAF .40 submachine gun. Move to the doorway ahead and dispatch the two cops in the main room. Search the room to find painkillers before approaching the metal gate **(2)**.

This triggers a cutscene—Max ducks back into the office as a mob of armed favela residents making a jailbreak emerges from the holding cell area. They gun down arriving UFE guards just outside the room. As the prisoners fight past him and continue around the corner, Max assumes this distraction is the promised "showcase" of Detective Da Silva.

CLEAR OUT THE HOLDING CELLS.

When you regain control, Max stands at the open metal gate. Move through the holding cells until you hear voices and halt at the corner of the "A" corridor **(3)**, taking cover. Lean around the corner and gun down the two UFE cops forcing two prisoners to kneel at gunpoint.

PART 1/3 GOLDEN MPK

After breaking out of the interrogation room in the beginning of the chapter, turn left at the end of the first cellblock hallway to find this gun part on the tray outside the first cell.

The prison rebellion has blocked off hallways, forcing you to cut through holding cells. Go down the hall to the "B" corridor and move through Cell B1 to the doorway **(4)**. Take cover under the Comando Sombra graffiti. Lean around and nail two more UFE police in the corridor **(5)** beyond the next cell. Go pick up a dropped M4 Super 90 shotgun then move to cover at the corner of the next corridor **(6)**. Again, lean around and blast the approaching UFE cops.

PART 1/3 GOLDEN LAW

This gun part is located in the showers on the right, just feet away from the first two guards you must defeat in the cellblock hallway.

Now Max comments that it's "time to leave this palace." But don't approach the exit gate **(7)** until you've found the painkillers stashed in the nearby cell and have discovered the hidden Clue.

TOURIST

After clearing the prison cell hallways and before leaving, head back to the previous prison cells until you find the tourist inside one of the cells. Talk to him to obtain the clue and then exit the cell area.

CLEAR THE EXCHANGE HALL.

Push through the exit gate to trigger a cutscene: Max peeks into the prisoner exchange hall to see a wild gunfight between escaping favela gangsters and UFE cops hiding behind their desks. The prisoners are definitely getting the worst of it.

When control returns, Max stands in cover behind a pillar **(8)**. Gun down the full squad of UFE that rushes aggressively at your position. Watch out for attackers who try to flank you by using an office doorway to your right. (Ironically, it's under a sign that reads "Silencio Por Favor"—"Silence Please.") One last cop stays put in the windows of the back office at the far end of the hall. Root him out!

After the final kill camera tells you the coast is clear, find the painkillers in the small corner office. Proceed to the back office **(9)** to find more painkillers on a desk. Examine the laptop (circled) at the far end to see Monday's arrest log: the Nova Esperança "arrests" are definitely off the books. Then approach the flashing button (also circled) and press the "Open security door" button indicated onscreen. The door just outside the office window **(10)** opens for you. It leads outside to the precinct parking lot.

PRISON LOG

A laptop is located on a tall desk in the room where you find the security door button that grants access to the exterior—where an armored car is attacking prisoners. Examine the laptop to see the prison log.

PRECINCT PARKING LOT

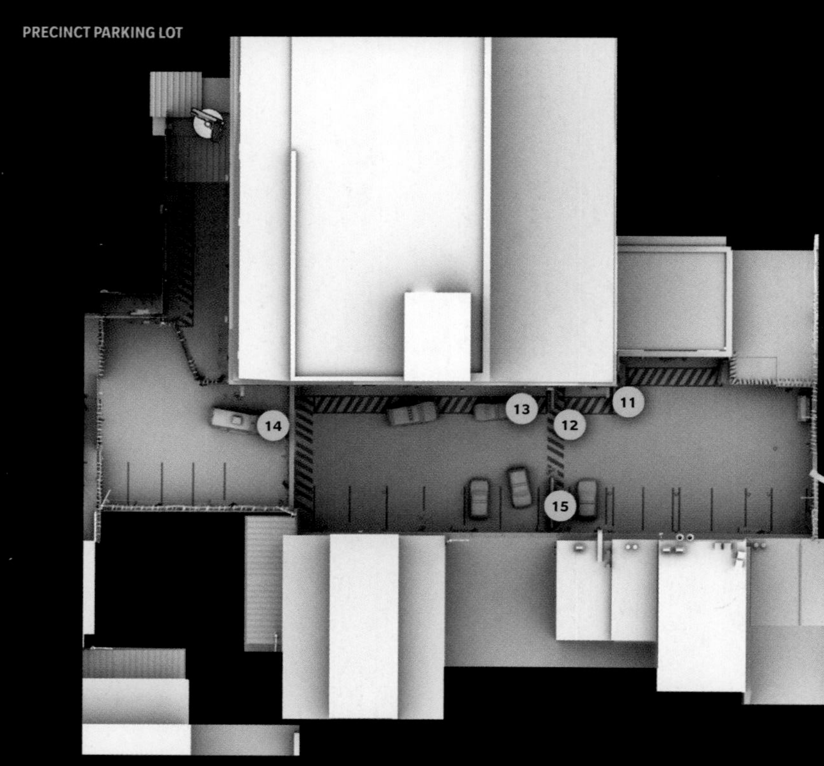

NEW WEAPONS

LAW (LIGHT ANTI-TANK WEAPON)

PAINKILLERS

MISSION

DESTROY THE APC WITH THE LAW.

Approaching the security door triggers a cutscene: Max sees a favela crew exchanging gunfire with a hulking UFE armored personnel carrier (APC) with a thundering .50 caliber machine gun mounted on its roof. One of the gangsters launches a LAW rocket at the beast, but his untrained shot veers wildly off-course. The APC guns down the poor gangsters and Max moves into cover behind a concrete divider **(11)**.

This is a particularly fun challenge. The APC's gun is so powerful that it shatters the concrete of your hiding place! And you cannot damage the APC with standard bullets. But four LAW rocket launchers are available to you—one dropped by the fallen gangster **(12)**, another leaning against the rear bumper of the first squad car **(13)** on the right, a third on the ground just a couple of feet behind it, and one more leaning against the first concrete divider on the left side of the parking lot, not far from an ammo case **(15)**. Each LAW is loaded with a single rocket.

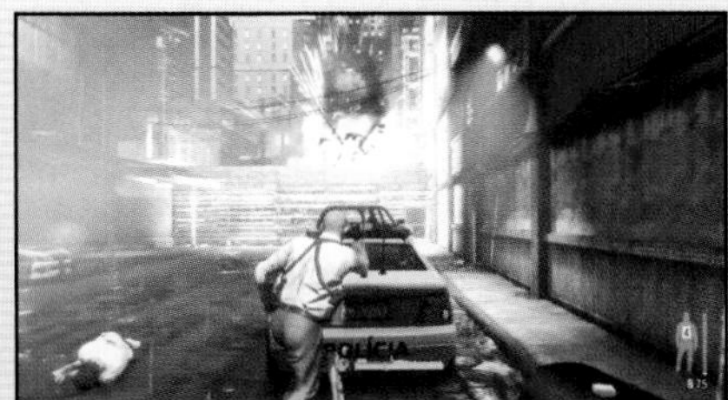

Here's where Bullet Time is a thing of beauty (once the APC's attacks fill your meter). Wait until the APC gun **(14)** stops firing briefly, trigger Bullet Time, then sprint out to the LAW on the ground by the fallen gangster. Pick it up on the roll. When you pop back up, aim at the APC until the targeting reticle turns red and fire. Then, just to be safe, dive behind the first squad car on the right.

If your rocket destroys the APC, congratulations! If you miss, then you're in cover behind the police car with access to another pair of LAW launchers. You can grab one, wait until the APC's machine gun pauses again, and then pop up and fire.

PART 2/3 GOLDEN LAW

This gun part is located next to a dumpster in the underground parking area below the armored truck that you must blow up with an RPG.

CLEAR OUT THE PARKING LOT COPS.

Note that there's also a Grenade Launcher on the ground next to that ammo case behind the concrete divider **(15)** on the left side of the parking lot. Once the APC is destroyed, hostile UFE cops start emerging from an underground section of the lot **(16)**, located beneath the overpass where you found the APC. Launch any remaining LAW rockets at them, then switch to the Grenade Launcher and lob explosives. If you are comfortable using the 1911 pistol, then it's worth saving the grenade launcher until later.

Once the area has been secured, leave the underground lot via the red doors **(17)**, but approach them warily. An escaping prisoner will push them open, but then get shot down by a pursuing UFE guard. Dispatch the guard, climb the staircase to the next doorway, and head into an exterior alley. Gun down two more UFE cops huddled over a fallen prisoner, and shoot a third cop in the entry just to the left. Go through the doors into an entry corridor **(18)** that leads to the precinct house gym.

PART 1/3 GOLDEN G6 COMMANDO

After destroying the armored truck, enter the double doors, climb the stairs, and defeat the guards in the next alley. At the opposite end of this alley is a short wall. The gun part is behind the short wall.

GYM/CAFETERIA ATRIUM

NEW WEAPONS

NONE

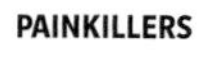

MISSION

CLEAR THE POLICE GYM.

Enter the gym locker room **(19)** and find painkillers in the tenth locker on the left wall, plus more in the fifth locker on the right wall. Take cover at the open doorway and lean around to pick off UFE cops in the gym **(20)**. After you drop the first crew, hustle to the center pillar for cover and gun down the reinforcements that rush up the far hallway **(21)**. A well-placed grenade from the launcher will make quick work of the UFE troops.

When the room is secured, go down the hall and find painkillers in the women's restroom ("Sanitário Feminino") on the right, and a Golden Weapon Part in the men's restroom ("Sanitário Masculino") on the left. Then exit via the red doors into the precinct cafeteria.

PART 2/3 GOLDEN MPK

After destroying the armored truck and re-entering the police station, you will reach a gym. The gun part is on the men's bathroom shower floor.

CLEAR THE KITCHEN/DINING AREAS.

Immediately swivel left and nail the cop in the kitchen ("Cozinha") **(22)**. Then slide up against the opposite wall and lean around the corner to dispatch several UFE through the windows of the administration office **(23)**.

PART 2/3 GOLDEN G6 COMMANDO

This gun part is located in a small cubbyhole under the food service counter in the kitchen.

Enter the administration office to find a note on the desk against the wall—a promissory note for $1.2 million to Armando Becker from Dr. Fischer, the surgeon you met back in the Imperial Palace Hotel. As Max puts it, "Becker's blood money." Indeed, Becker was earning millions for delivering his favela organ donors to the good doctor.

PROMISSORY NOTE

Located on a desk inside the administration room, which is near the cafe and kitchen. It shows evidence of the blood money coming from Dr. Arthur Fischer, the organ doctor, and being paid to Becker.

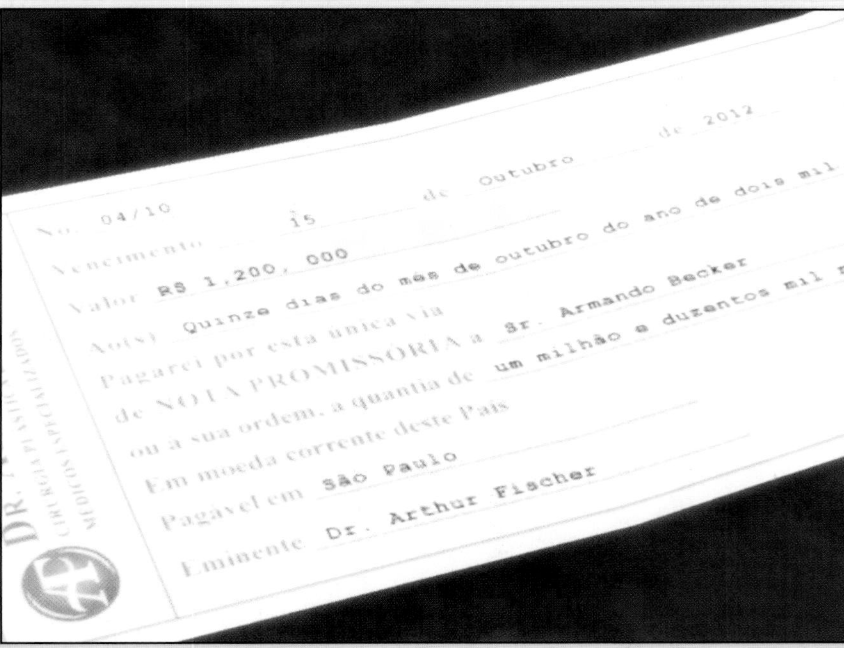

Nº 04/10 — Vencimento 15 de Outubro de 2012
Valor R$ 1.200.000
Ao(s) Quinze dias do mês de outubro do ano de dois mil
Pagarei por esta única via
de NOTA PROMISSÓRIA a Sr. Armando Becker
ou à sua ordem, a quantia de um milhão e duzentos mil
Em moeda corrente deste País
Pagável em São Paulo
Eminente Dr. Arthur Fischer

When you're finished exploring, exit via the red doors with the emergency light flashing above it **(24)**. Be sharp as you leave—the next area is well guarded.

FIGHT THROUGH THE ATRIUM TO THE CONTROL ROOM.

This is the building's central atrium, a large open area. Immediately open fire on the UFE gunmen directly across the space in the security control room **(25)**. Use the big pillars for cover. When the guards are dispatched, find the painkillers in the notary's office (under the "Cartorios S.I.G." sign). Then enter the control room to trigger a quick cutscene.

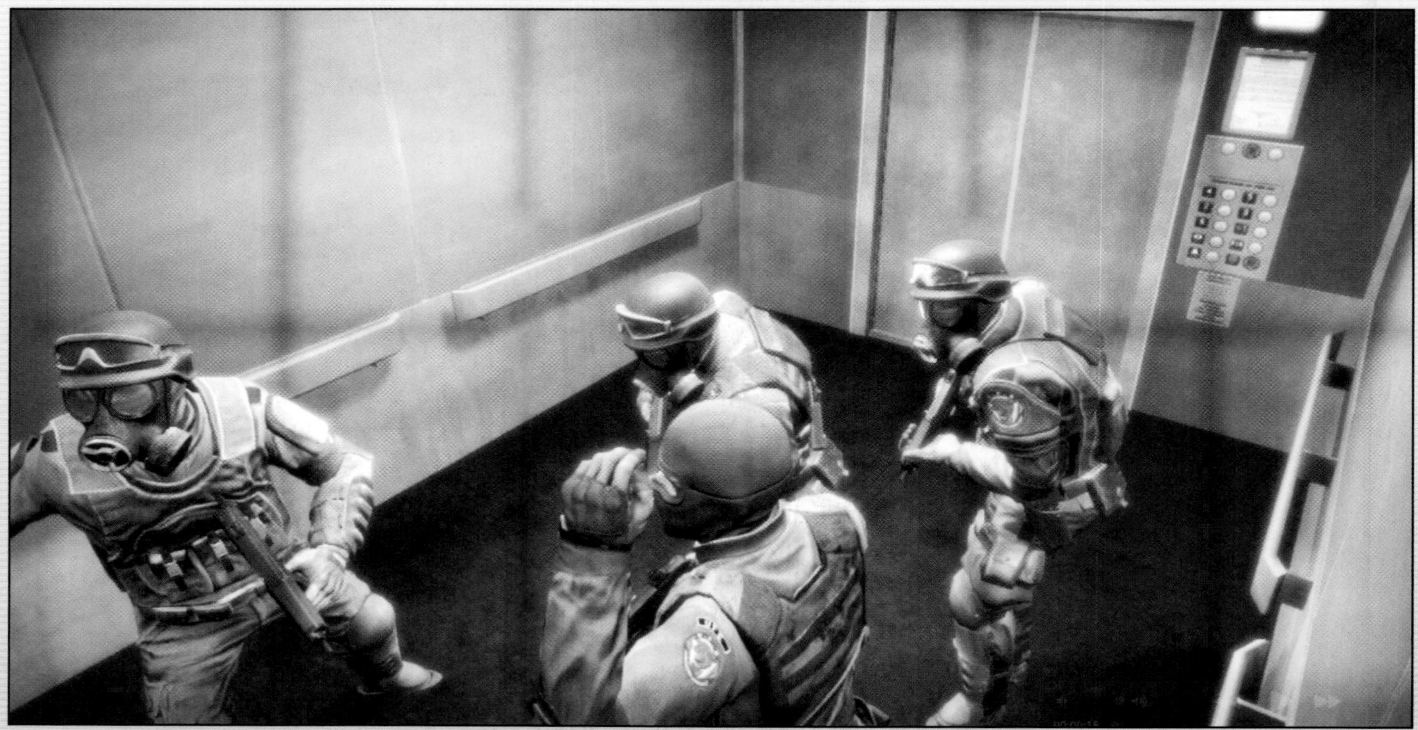

PART 3/3 GOLDEN G6 COMMANDO

This gun part is on the floor of the notary's office adjoining the atrium.

PART 3/3 GOLDEN MPK

This gun part is on the table, under the screen at the end of the large briefing room adjoining the atrium.

Max checks the live video feed from the security monitors and sees prisoners giving their captors a good fight. But a big UFE squad of cops wearing gas masks is approaching via elevator **(26)**. Clearly, they plan a tear-gas assault. Moments later they arrive on the opposite side of the atrium.

FEND OFF THE TEAR-GAS ASSAULT!

This can be a difficult fight. Immediately open fire in Bullet Time and hit as many targets as you can before the tear-gas canister explodes and reduces your visibility. When the remaining attackers disappear in the gassy haze, rely on your aiming reticle to locate targets—whenever it turns red, fire!

Don't stay exposed too long looking for targets or you'll get gunned down. Pop up from cover in the window or doorway, do a quick aiming sweep, fire when the reticle turns red, then pull back into cover. These UFE have SAF .40 submachine guns with green targeting lasers. So take cover if one of the laser beams is drawing a bead on you. Also, be ready for several cops to make aggressive rushes at the control-room door. Use melee attacks on those brave enough to rush you and then get back to cover quickly. If you still have the grenade launcher from the APC fight, now is a great time to use it.

When you finally clear this difficult room, Max observes: "If the heat was rising, it means I was getting closer to the source." Plunder weapons and ammo from the fallen UFE then board the elevator **(26)** and use the "Press 5th floor button" control indicated onscreen. Max starts riding upward... but the car jams on the 2nd floor and he must force the doors open to escape the elevator shaft.

MISSION

CLEAR THE ADMINISTRATIVE OFFICES.

You regain control right outside the elevator **(27)**. Take out the UFE shooter who slides out behind the reception desk, then go through the door directly ahead into a box-filled storage room **(28)**. Grab the painkillers on the desk, then exit and push through the doors to the right of the reception desk.

You emerge into an open administrative area **(29)** with cubicles in the center and glass-walled offices and conference rooms on the outside. Gunmen immediately open fire from across the room. Duck into cover behind a cubicle and clear the central area first. Then look for cops posted in the offices around the outside of the area. Some rush in to fight, others stay put—so be ready for anything.

Once it seems you've cleared the offices, stay sharp—one last heavily armored UFE guard bursts into the room wielding an LMG .30 machinegun. When you take him out, Max utters one of our favorite lines: "I killed more cops than cholesterol, and still no sign of Becker." Search the area: you can examine a paper file in one office **(30)** that suggests the UFE had tipped off the AUP—the right-wing paramilitary death squad in Panama—about the money shipment that led to the assault on Daphne Bernstein's yacht.

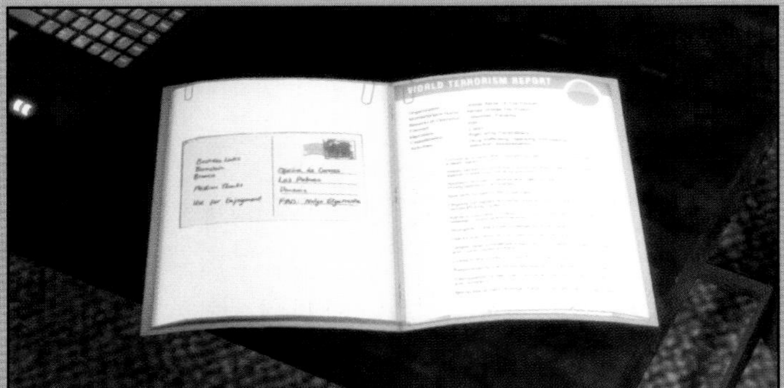

NEW WEAPONS NONE | PAINKILLERS

You also find painkillers and a laptop with an e-file on Detective Da Silva in another office **(31)**. It appears that Max's cop friend is clean. When you're finished searching, approach the doors under the flashing emergency light **(32)**. This triggers a quick scene: Max loots a UFE corpse for a key card that unlocks the door.

POLITICAL FOLDER

After the major fifth-floor battle ends, explore the offices around the central cubical grid. A folder is inside the middle office, along the right wall, on the edge of a desk. Examine it. You learn that the Brazilian cops tipped the AUP about the money.

E-FILE ON DA SILVA

Examine the laptop in the office in the back left corner of the large fifth-floor office battle area. This is just before the slide show room.

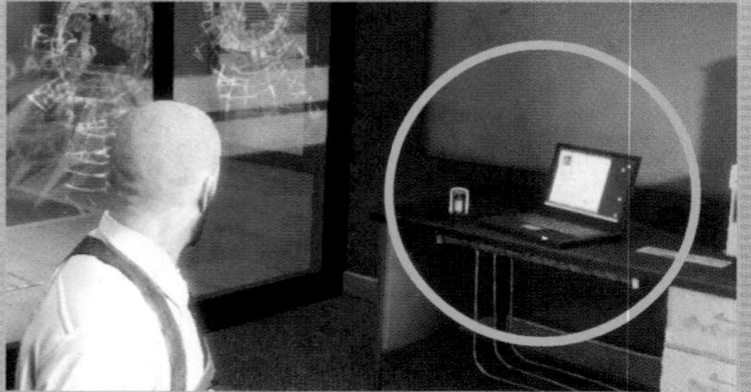

EXPLORE THE BRIEFING ROOM.

The next room is the police briefing room. Approach the open laptop on the podium **(33)** and press the "Play briefing" button indicated onscreen. You learn a lot of key information about the bigger chessboard on which Max seems to be such a lowly pawn. When the slide show ends, exit the room via the doors next to the screen.

SLIDE SHOW

A briefing room with a lit projector is just beyond the fifth-floor office battle. Step onto the small stage and activate the slide show on the podium. There are multiple slides. Watch them all.

CLEAR OUT THE EVIDENCE ROOM.

The next room **(34)** is a small check-in lobby for the big evidence room beyond **(35)**. Push through the entry doors and start eliminating the UFE cops deployed amongst the evidence stacks. When you reach the far end of the room, be prepared for one last gunman who rushes at you as the security gate retracts.

When you finally clear the evidence room, Max points out that he already has all the evidence he needs... and of course, he's right. You won't find anything of interest in the room, although you can switch out guns in the weapons locker **(36)**. Exit the room via the red door to the stairwell **(37)**.

ESCAPE THE GASSED STAIRWELL!

Entering the stairwell triggers a quick cutscene: A tear-gas grenade rolls down the stairs at the first landing. Hurry upstairs past the next floor and shoot at the square grate on the wall above the next landing **(38)**. Approach it to trigger another scene: Max pulls himself into the now-open vent, crawls along the ventilation duct... and falls through into the precinct's IT (Information Technology) room!

MISSION

FIND THE VIDEO EVIDENCE IN IT.

When control returns, Max is sprawled on the floor **(39)** of the IT room facing a surprised UFE guard. Quickly dispatch the guard as he turns, then get up and walk around the component stack. Approach the desk with monitors to trigger a scene: Max finds a disk with the missing surveillance video from the Branco security system. He pops it into the drive and watches the perpetrator at work—Bachmeyer, the same UFE lieutenant Max saw in the favela making the handshake deal with the Crácha Preto for human donors. Now Max has a new reason to hunt down Becker and his corrupt inner circle.

Exit the IT room via the only door. Follow the hallway past the check-in desk to a glass door etched with the city police logo ("Polícia da Cidade"). This leads into the police forensics lab **(40)**.

CLEAR THE FORENSICS LAB.

Suddenly, UFE cops zip-line in through the windows and throw down smoke grenades! Stay covered at the end of the first counter and aim for heads in Bullet Time. Several UFE cops are also found prowling amongst the test tubes and beakers of the lab. Terminate their scientific interest with headshots. When the lab is secured, go directly to the exit door **(41)**.

Opening the door triggers a scene: Max comes face to face with Bachmeyer. The standoff ends with the UFE lieutenant's retreat, and Max bursts through the next door in pursuit.

WEAPONS NONE | PAINKILLERS  

SURVIVE THE "KILL ROOM" GAUNTLET.

But as Max enters the next room, you find that Bachmeyer has lured you into a trap. This long locker room **(42)** is lined with windows that face across the alley to a parallel balcony where a row of UFE marksmen open fire. Max responds with a classic Max Payne move: he dives onto a rolling cart and rides it the length of the room in Bullet Time. You don't have any movement control: just aim and shoot. Concentrate on getting at least one bullet in each sniper to take them out. They're heavily armored but, in this challenge, one bullet each will do them in. Eliminate as many UFE marksmen as possible before the cart stops and Max hops off.

When you regain full control, finish off any remaining shooters on the opposite balcony. Note that an ammo case with refills for all weapons sits on the bench against the lockers along the back wall.

CLEAR THE PRECINCT ARSENAL.

Once the UFE marksmen across the way are eliminated, you hear a buzz and the entry gate next to the arsenal checkout window swings open **(43)**. (You must eliminate *all* balcony marksmen to trigger this gate opening.) As you move through the open gate, an UFE gunman rushes you from the next gate. Gun him down and grab the painkillers from a medicine cabinet next to the interior entrance.

More UFE cops open fire from the aisles and stacks of the arsenal itself. Take them out and proceed into the arsenal's main room to find all kinds of weapons and ammo.

OPEN THE SECURITY DOOR.

Around the corner to the right, you find an alcove **(44)** with two important items. First, grab the flak vest hanging in the locker. It gives Max added protection against UFE bullets. Just to the right, you find a desk with a flashing button. Approach it and press the "Open security doors" button indicated onscreen. The exit door swings open **(45)**.

FLAK VEST

Examine and wear the flak vest found in the armory near the firing-range door switch.

Go through the newly opened door into the prep room for the precinct's firing range. Grab the painkillers from the cabinet by the next set of doors, and then continue into the tactical training area.

GET THROUGH THE TACTICAL TRAINING COURSE.

A maze-like tactical training course winds through the next room **(46)**. But instead of dealing with wooden silhouette targets, Max gets his "training" from live UFE commandos scattered throughout the course. Just follow the green arrows painted on floors and walls. Move from cover to cover and watch for enemy shooters posted both high and low, lurking around every corner.

Look for an ammo case **(47)** for restocking ammo along the way. When you finally reach the staircase at the end **(48)**, watch for one last UFE gunman, and look for the painkillers in the cabinet next to the exit door. Then step through the door into the firing range.

CLEAR THE FIRING RANGE.

Just past the entry door, take cover behind the tall pile of sandbags on the left **(49)**. This cover is far superior to the breakable wooden slats elsewhere in the range, where another big UFE squad is deployed. Stay behind the sandbags for the duration of the fight for best chances of survival.

Once the final kill camera displays the demise of the last UFE fighter in the range, you can explore and pick up ammo and weapons. But when you reach the far end, Max faces a rare moral choice—a UFE policeman **(50)** puts down his weapon and surrenders, raising his hands. You can spare him, shoot him, or just give him a swift melee kick into unconsciousness.

PART 3/3 GOLDEN LAW

The final LAW part is located behind the sandbags you use for cover in the firing-range shootout.

Around the corner in the utility room **(51)**, one last hostile UFE gunman stands in your way. Dispatch him and find the cabinet stocked with painkillers next to the twin sinks. Then exit the area via the far door and climb the stairs beyond to the top floor.

TOP FLOORS COMMAND CENTER/ BECKER'S OFFICE

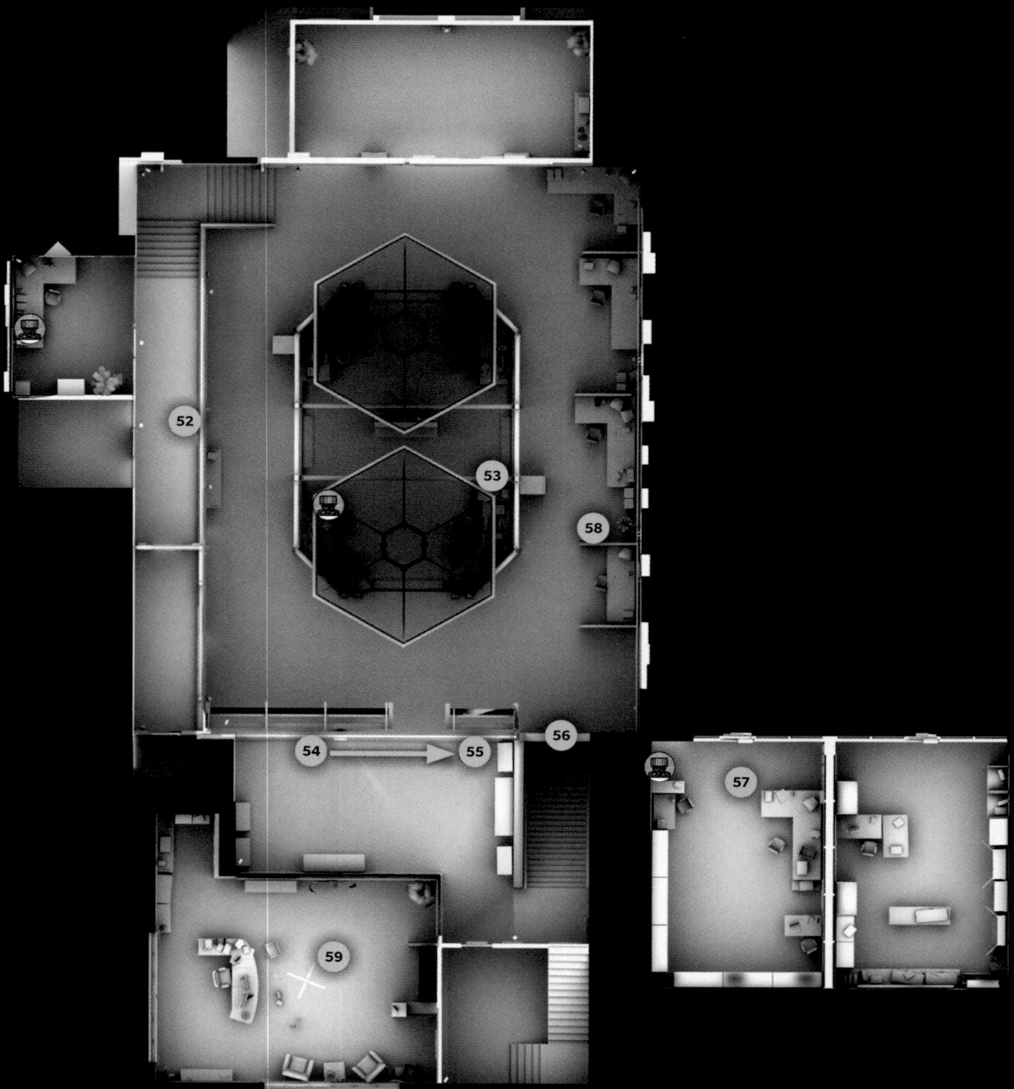

NEW WEAPONS NONE | PAINKILLERS 

MISSION

CLEAR THE COMMAND CENTER.

Approaching the door at the top of the staircase triggers a cutscene: Max hears voices and spies Bachmeyer with another grim-looking squad of UFE. The UFE lieutenant spots Max and orders his troops to the attack.

When control returns, you crouch on an upper walkway **(52)** overlooking the high-tech work bays of the UFE command center. Two UFE gunmen start charging up the stairs just ahead. You can slip into the office to your left for cover (and to find some painkillers) or just nail them quickly with a diving ShootDodge. More UFE cops pour into the space downstairs as you proceed down the stairs. Return to the high vantage point of the walkway for clean shots at targets below.

When the area is cleared, a short cutscene plays: After Max heads downstairs, Bachmeyer appears at the upstairs railing across the room. Once again, the UFE lieutenant confronts Max but then drops below the railing and opens fire.

KILL BACHMEYER.

When control returns, Max is in cover downstairs **(53)** as more UFE minions pour into the area and Bachmeyer shoots down from the railing above **(54)**. You can't hit Bachmeyer directly—he ducks into cover too quickly—so focus on his officers first. If you get low on health, a painkillers bottle sits on a filing cabinet at the next workstation. When you finally dispatch the wave of cops on the ground floor, turn your attention back to Bachmeyer.

Again, Bachmeyer is too quick to target directly, even using Bullet Time. However, you *can* target the lights on the ceiling directly above him (circled in our screenshot). When that section of ceiling collapses, Bachmeyer rushes across the balcony to the left **(55)** and begins firing again.

As he does so, another UFE crew bursts through the security gate to the stairwell on the left **(56)**—they relock it behind them. Eliminate them, then search the offices to the right of the stairs, where you're out of Bachmeyer's line of sight. (He keeps firing wildly anyway.) One of the rooms **(57)** has painkillers in a medicine cabinet.

Now move to a spot along the left wall **(58)** where you can target the ceiling above Bachmeyer's new position. Keep shooting at it until a big fan housing falls onto Bachmeyer and flushes him out—he finally stands up. Activate Bullet Time and nail him quickly!

When Bachmeyer finally falls off the balcony, the chapter-ending cinematic sequence begins. Max grabs the dead lieutenant's passkey to Colonel Becker's office upstairs and swipes open the security gate. In the office **(59),** he finally gets his hands on Becker's slimy, amoral neck... but the big boss gets the drop on him. Max nearly manages a reversal, but Becker's taser gun affords the bad guys an escape. Another locked security door ends Max's pursuit, but he knows where rich guys always go to escape the nasty messes they make: their private jets.

XIV ONE CARD LEFT TO PLAY

PIRATININGA AIRPORT
2:07 PM, THURSDAY

Detective Da Silva drops off Max outside Terminal 2 at São Paulo's Piratininga Airport. He tells Max to search the main terminal while he checks for the Branco jet in the hangar. Max dodges past airport security and UFE commandos onto the baggage conveyor. He rides the belt to the Terminal 2 baggage processing area.

BAGGAGE PROCESSING AREA

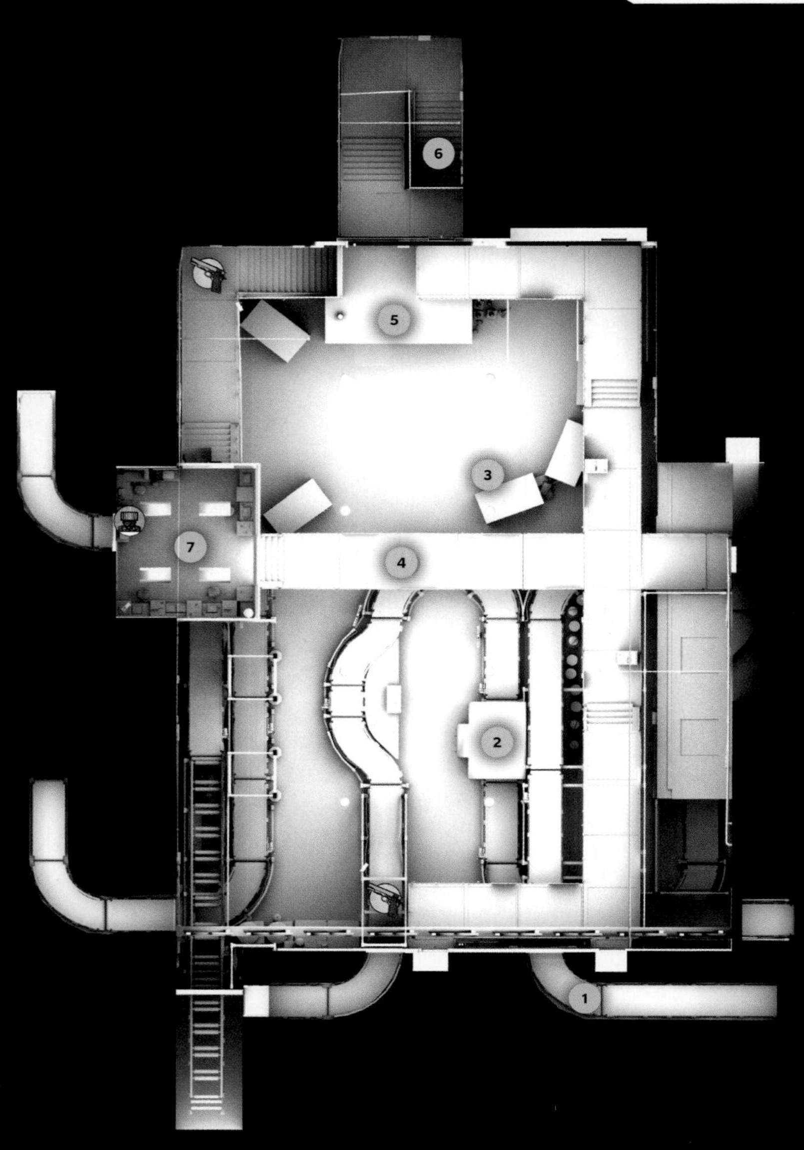

NEW WEAPONS NONE | PAINKILLERS 

MISSION

CLEAR OUT THE BAGGAGE AREA.

This area is teeming with UFE special forces posted high and low. Ride the conveyor belt around the first curve **(1)**—you see baggage handlers fleeing across a raised catwalk above you. Open fire at gunmen who pop up behind the baggage carts **(3)** at the far end of the room. Move inside the baggage scanner **(2)** or drop down beside it as cover against shooters up on the catwalk **(4)**.

Once you clear the floor and catwalk, watch for guards emerging from the ground floor office **(5)**. One guard remains in the room until the end of the battle. The glass is bulletproof so you must lure him out or go in shooting. Dispatch him, enter the office, and climb the back stairs **(6)**.

As you reach the top, watch for attackers down the left catwalk. Then a big squad of UFE cops emerges from the upstairs office **(7)** and advances. Wipe them out and enter the office to find painkillers in an open locker plus a back-door exit. After finding the two Golden Gun Parts in the baggage area, approach the exit doors to trigger a cutscene: Max pushes through and locks the doors behind him to cut off any pursuit.

PART 1/3 GOLDEN ROTARY GRENADE LAUNCHER

This Golden Gun Part is located on top of a conveyor cage along the left wall as you begin the mission in the baggage sorting room. You can see it as you cross the catwalk to the control room, and you can reach it by following the catwalks to the front of the room and by hopping over the railing.

PART 2/3 GOLDEN ROTARY GRENADE LAUNCHER

Before you leave the baggage sorting room through the doorway in the control room, head through the unlocked door on the right and find the Golden Gun Part along the catwalk in the corner.

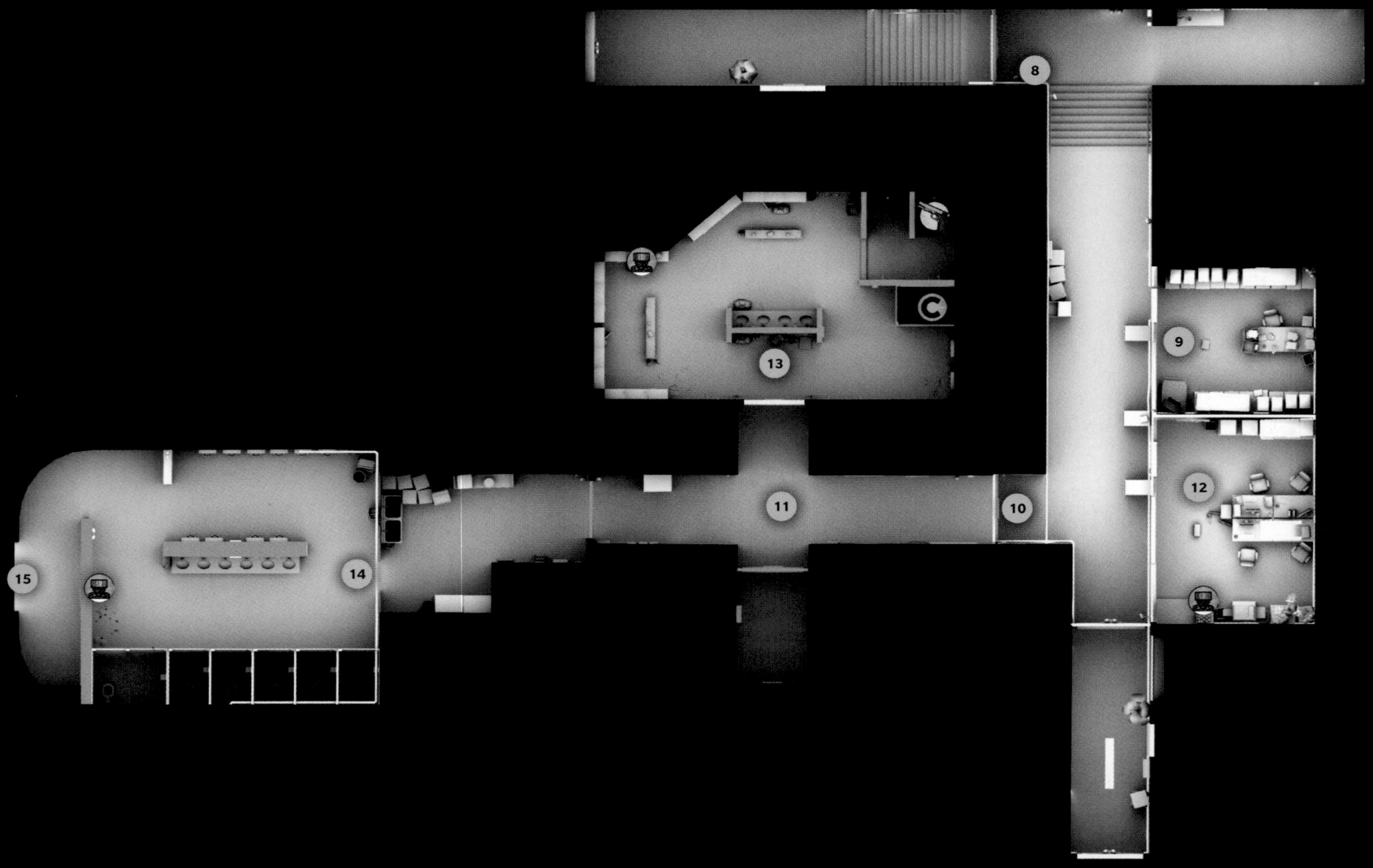

NEW WEAPONS NONE

PAINKILLERS 

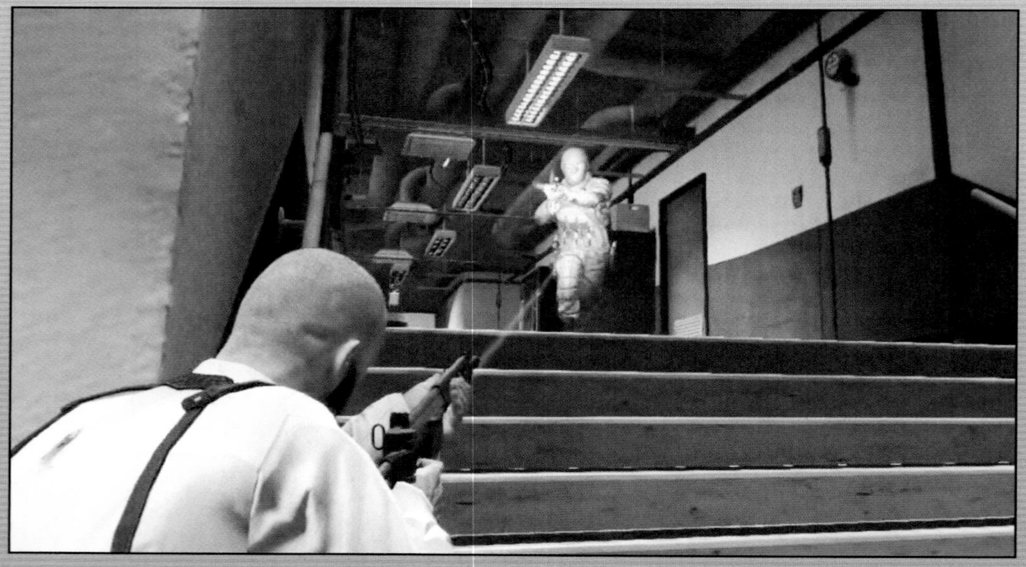

MISSION

CLEAR OUT THE BACK OFFICE AREA.

When you regain control, Max waits in cover at the bottom of a staircase **(8)** leading up to a small airport office corridor. Gun down the UFE cop at the top of the stairs, then wait for a second cop to emerge from the door at the far end of the corridor and nail him too. A third gunman appears just around the right corner of the connecting hallway **(10)**. Use Bullet Time to take him out or use the hallway cabinets for cover.

You can explore the first office on the left **(9)**, but you won't find anything of interest. Move to cover at the corner of the hall and battle two more UFE who jump into the hall from both sides up ahead **(11)**. When both fall dead, the area is clear.

FIND THE DEPARTURE GATES.

Turn and explore the second office **(12)** to find some painkillers. Max calls it the "back office" and says Becker and Victor Branco are likely on their way to the departure lounge. Exit and follow the corridor to the first right at **(11)** that leads into the employee locker room **(13)**. Find the painkillers in an open locker to the left of the entry doors. Return to the main corridor.

EX-COP (ANDERS)

You can find Anders for the last time in the locker room reached just before the airport terminals. This is the same room where you find the last Golden Grenade Launcher part in a shower stall. Anders is located in the toilet stall beside the shower. He only appears if you found him the other two times in previous chapters.

Proceed through a utility room into the customer restroom **(14)** via the service door. As you approach, Max points out that the route is leading you toward the main terminal. Find two more bottles of painkillers in a restroom cabinet. Leave via the front entrance **(15)** to trigger a cutscene.

PART 3/3 GOLDEN ROTARY GRENADE LAUNCHER

A locker is on the right side of the final hallway before you reach the airport departure gates. Find this Golden Gun Part in the shower stall. You can also find Anders in the nearby toilet stall if you've found all of his previous locations.

DEPARTURE CONCOURSE

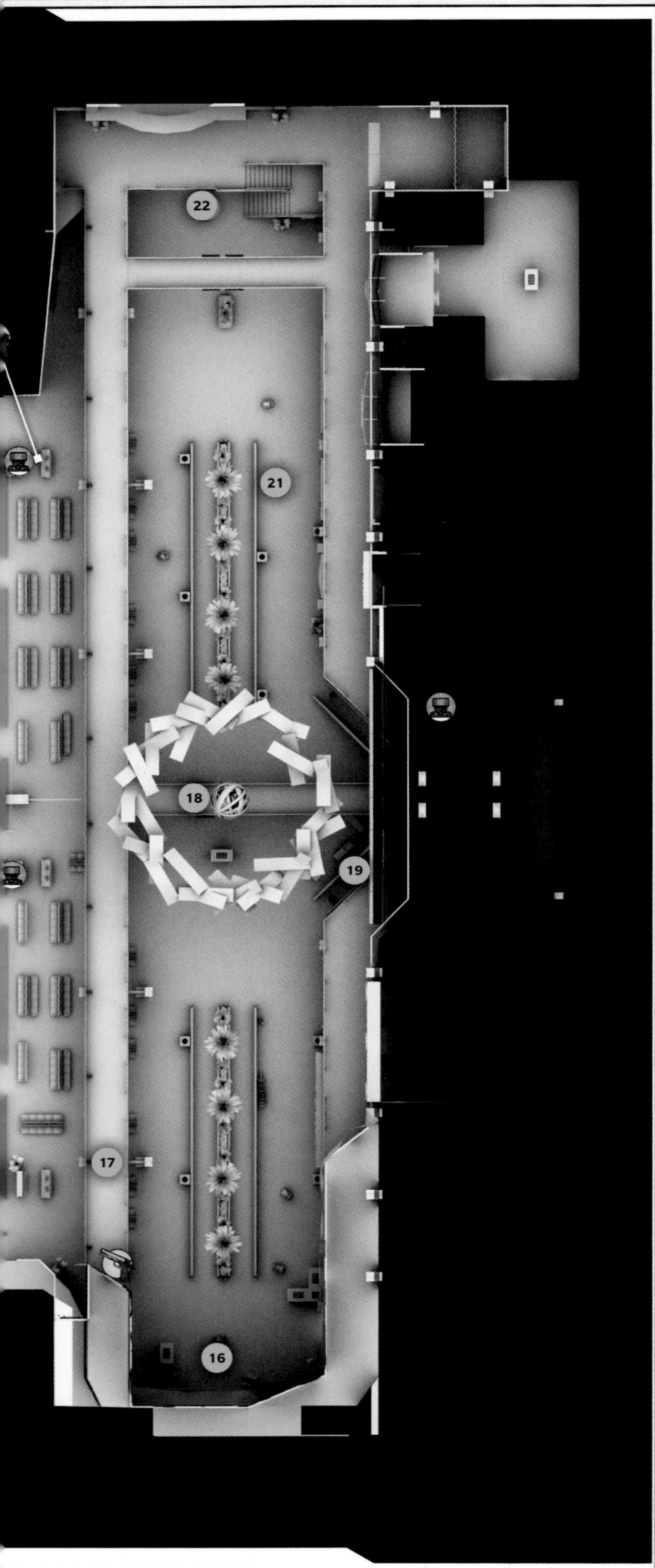

MISSION

CLEAR THE FIRST HALF OF THE DEPARTURES CONCOURSE.

Max emerges into a concourse where the main terminal's departure gates are located. The area is swarming with UFE units, and airport security is evacuating all passengers from the concourse. Get ready for a pitched battle against Becker's army across this huge interior space.

After Max hustles into cover behind a small baggage-filled cart **(16)**, control returns to you. UFE troops advance rapidly up both sides of the moving walkways directly in front of you as well as along the raised walkway **(17)** above you on the left. With so many targets making a simultaneous rush, Bullet Time is your best bet for survival. Consider moving to better cover as well.

NEW WEAPONS

NONE

PAINKILLERS 

Advance from pillar to pillar up the concourse to the midway point marked by a row of sliding partition doors. Find the painkillers sitting on a gate podium just to the left of the midway partition. Eliminate a pair of shooters on the raised walkway **(18)** under the globe sculpture, and then climb the escalator on the far right **(19)** to reach the upper level. Look for more painkillers in a medicine cabinet on the wall near the top of the escalator.

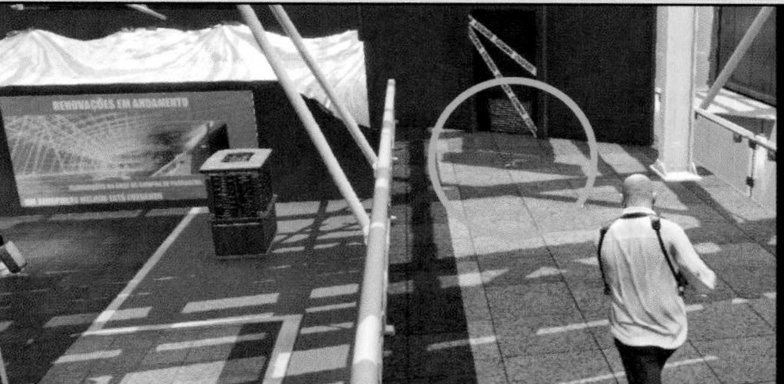

PART 1/3 GOLDEN RPD

This Golden Gun Part is located on the top left balcony of the first passenger waiting area of the airport. Take the escalator up to reach it.

CLEAR THE SECOND HALF OF THE DEPARTURES CONCOURSE.

From the high vantage of the center walkway **(18)**, pick off as many UFE as you can down in the second half of the concourse **(20)** beyond the partition doors. Look for more shooters on both sides of the upper level too. Work from one side to the other.

Just when it seems you've secured the concourse, three last UFE gunmen raise the security gate and rush through to attack, including one commando (circled) who starts tossing grenades from the far end of the concourse **(21)**. Shoot any thrown grenades in the air if you can then target the grenadier. Once he's eliminated, dispatch the other two gunmen.

PART 2/3 GOLDEN RPD

This Golden Gun Part is located in the second waiting area of the airport and behind the last passenger help desk on the left. Look for Gate 17.

When the final kill camera shows you the area is finally clear, search the fallen gunmen for ammo and weapon pickups and find the painkillers sitting on one of the gate podiums on the ground floor. Then approach the flashing button **(21)** next to the lowered gate. Press the "Open gate" button indicated onscreen to raise the gate.

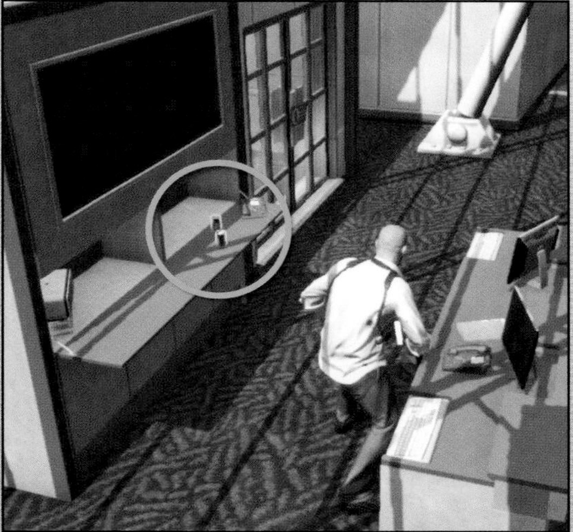

TRAM STATION/CONTROL OFFICE

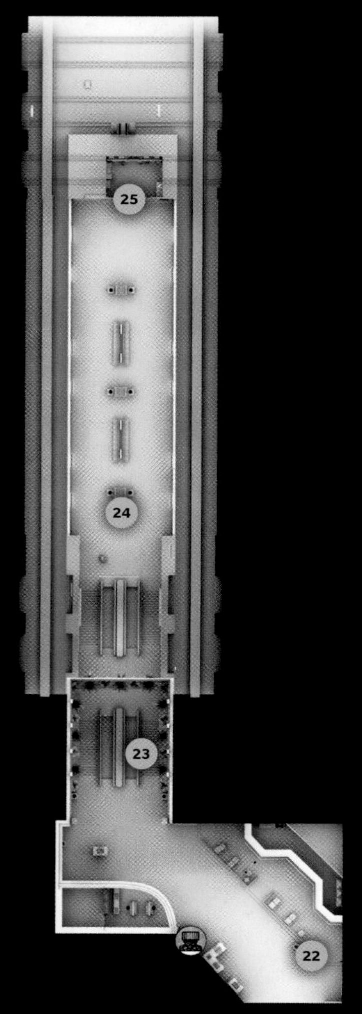

NEW WEAPONS NONE | PAINKILLERS

MISSION

FIGHT TO THE TRAM BOARDING STATION.

As Max runs through the rising gate, more UFE guards arrive via the bank of escalators ahead. One of them hits an alarm button for the tram station. Max drops into cover behind a concrete trash bin **(22)**. Once you terminate this first wave of cops, another squad of UFE rushes up the escalators to attack. After you dispatch this second wave, find the medicine cabinet with painkillers just left of the Palavra Final store. Then approach the escalators **(23)** that run down to the tram boarding station.

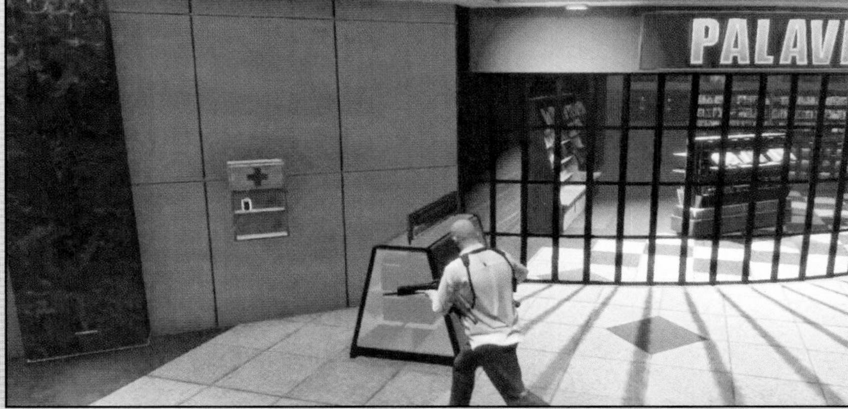

Two more UFE open fire from the next landing below. Dispatch them and descend to the tram station. As you arrive, a tram pulls from the platform on the left. Take cover behind the first pillar **(24)**. Suddenly, the lights go out as the tram system's power is shut down. More cops deploy further down the station platform, including one behind the very next pillar and several emerging from the control room at the far end **(25)**.

RESTORE POWER TOTHE TRAM SYSTEM.

Fight your way toward the control room. When the area is secured, enter the control room and grab the painkillers from the medicine cabinet and the Mini-30 assault rifle from the floor.

Then approach the flashing button **(26)** and press the "Restore power" control indicated onscreen to power up the trams again.

Now hurry to the office window and take cover—as you do, a tram arrives on the tracks to the right and unloads a UFE strike team. And while you engage that crew, another tram arrives on the left track and disgorges a second UFE team! Stay in cover. Use Bullet Time to pick off targets two or three at a time. Watch out for one last gunman who pops out of the nearest car on the left. When he goes down, the area is safe.

Search all of the fallen UFE for ammo and weapons before you board the tram...because stepping through any open tram door triggers a cutscene that takes you out of the station for good.

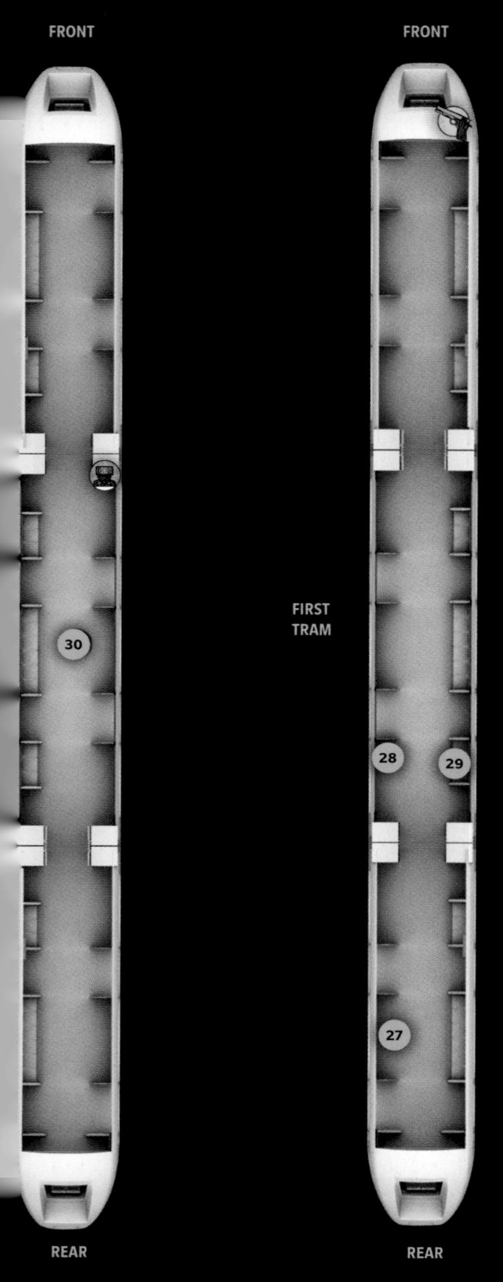

MISSION

CLEAR THE RIVAL TRAM.

When you enter the tram, Max thinks he's getting a breather until the tram arrives at the next terminal station...but no such luck. A second tram filled with UFE goons pulls up beside him, and the tram ride turns into a wild rolling firefight. You start out in the rear of the first tram **(27)**. Move from window to window picking off enemy shooters in the second tram.

Note that the first tram holds a Mini-30 assault rifle **(28)** and, directly across the aisle, an ammo case **(29)** that gives you refills for all weapons. The tram ride doesn't end unless all UFE are down in the second tram, so keep shooting until the rival tram is wiped clean.

CLEAR YOUR TRAM.

When the last UFE rider falls on the first tram, a cinematic plays: Max watches a UFE chopper drop a team of seven hardcore commandos wearing gas masks onto the roof. You can bet that tear gas is in their arsenal. When control returns, open fire right into the billowing gas as the commandos rush up the length of the first tram.

When the last commando falls, watch the cutscene as Max switches trams in spectacular fashion.

WEAPONS

NONE

PAINKILLERS 

CLEAR YOUR NEW TRAM.

Max ends up prone on the second tram's floor **(30)** when control returns to you. From the floor, quickly take out the remaining UFE. When the tram is cleared, stand up and grab three precious bottles of painkillers from a small compartment right in front of you.

PART 3/3 GOLDEN RPD

This Golden Gun Part is in the back of the last train car you ride. Do not step off the train until you get this part or you will miss your opportunity to collect the final part.

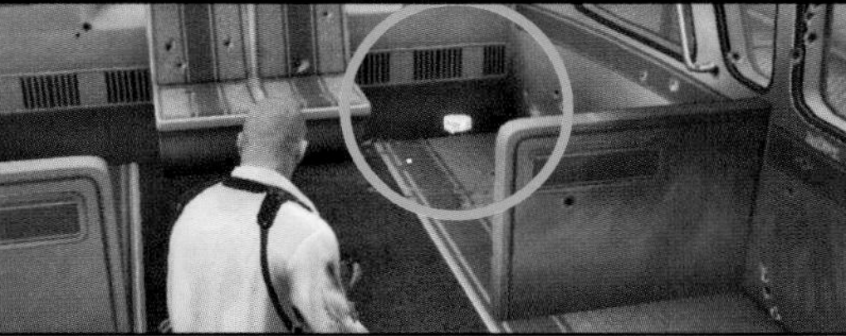

The tram's arrival at the station triggers a long cutscene as Max dodges Becker's UFE army on his way to the Branco's corporate jet hangar.

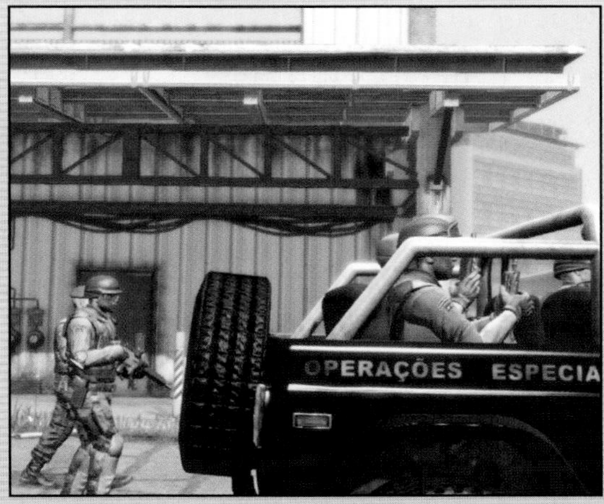

FÁBRICAS BRANCO HANGAR

NEW WEAPONS NONE

PAINKILLERS 

MISSION

DEFEAT BECKER'S MEN.

Max spots Colonel Becker ushering Victor Branco aboard the corporate jet and he steps out of hiding in a brazen challenge. The UFE troops spread out to attack. Becker seizes a heavy police shield and Grenade Launcher and takes up a position on the platform atop an aircraft boarding staircase.

As you regain control behind a baggage cart **(31)**, Becker immediately fires a grenade from his perch **(32)**. Shoot it quickly! After this first shot, Becker fires grenades only at rather lengthy intervals while you're still fighting his UFE minions. Any direct grenade hit on Max in the open results in instant death. If you stay in cover behind the baggage carts, most of Becker's grenades detonate on the other side and do not automatically kill Max... although they do inflict some minor health damage, and also make Max fall back before automatically returning to cover. However, two direct grenade hits on any cart knocks off the baggage, at which point that cart becomes ineffective as cover.

Start by eliminating the shooter in the Branco jet's open hatch **(33)**—he has the best shooting angle at you. Then start targeting the other attackers and use headshots to boost your Bullet Time meter.

This is a *very* tough fight. It's best to stay close to the spot where you start—the cover is good and you have an ammo case nearby. But be aware that enemies will be rushing you from different directions. Reinforcements eventually arrive in vehicles—first two jeeps, then a squad car—and may flank you. So be ready to adjust your position to find better cover.

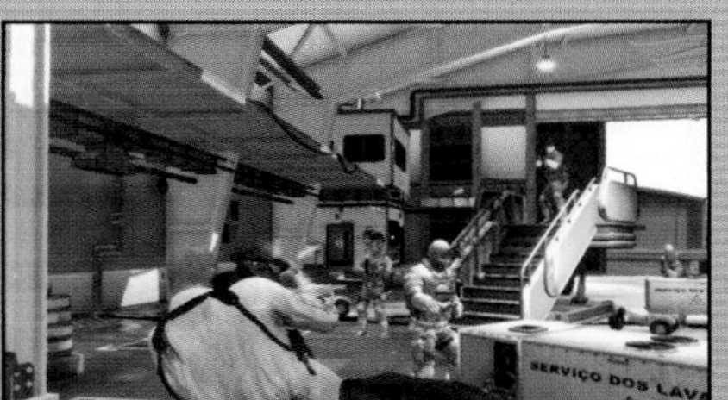

DEFEAT BECKER.

When you get down to the last minion alive other than Becker, the Branco jet starts to pull out of the hangar onto the tarmac. Nail that last UFE commando to trigger a brief cutscene: Max sprints up the second aircraft staircase and makes a stunning ShootDodge dive toward Becker just as the UFE commander fires his Grenade Launcher. Nail the RPG round immediately to detonate it near Becker.

And this brings you back full circle to the beginning... the beginning of the game, that is. Max stands over his mutilated victim with another moral choice to make. Execute the poor bastard? Or leave him in his grisly misery? If you just walk away, you earn the Achievement named "You Push a Man Too Far."

MISSION

BLAST YOUR WAY TO THE BRANCO JET.

Detective Da Silva picks up Max and the chase is on. A full convoy of UFE vehicles deploys to stop you from reaching the Branco jet. But you have a Grenade Launcher, unlimited ammo, and a pretty good driver in Da Silva. All you have to do is lob grenades out ahead of your vehicle at various UFE units including a nasty helicopter that will hound you the entire route if you don't hammer it out of the sky.

Remember that your Grenade Launcher is heaving heavy projectiles that travel in an arc, not a straight line like a bullet. Lead your targets by aiming slightly above them; the farther away they are, the higher you should aim. And the more UFE units you manage to destroy, the less damage you take. Your goal is to survive the gauntlet so you can get on the jet's tail before it accelerates to takeoff speed.

TAKE OUT THE BRANCO JET.

Once you get past the last line of UFE vehicles, the only target left is the Branco jet. Lob your grenades out in front of the craft so it taxis right over the detonations. Your primary target is the two tail engines, but a direct hit on either wing can deal considerable damage to the jet. Just two or three solid blasts can disable the plane, but lobbing projectiles at a moving target is not easy.

WATCH THE CLIMAX & DENOUEMENT.

When you finally disable the Branco jet, you've won. Max gets a face-to-face meeting with the beneficiary of all the mayhem, and a chance to set things right... or at least, less wrong. We won't spoil the ending, so enjoy!

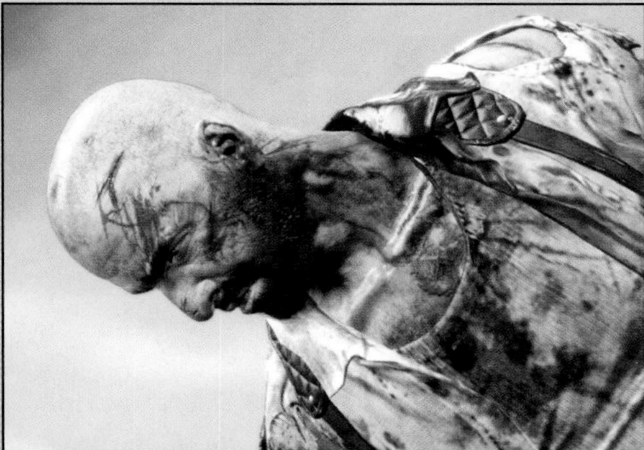

CLUES

A list of Clues and Golden Gun Parts appears on the right side of the screen when you enter the in-game pause menu. The Clues in this *Collectibles* category are grayed out, so you really don't know what you are looking for, but you do know how many items are available. During gameplay, you're prompted to examine a Clue when you are close enough to interact with it. After you've examined a Clue, the name and a checkmark appear in the collectibles pause menu. These 65 Clues give you insight on your situation and the developing mystery. In this section of the guide you can find a detailed location description and a revealing screen shot of the location of every Clue in the game.

CHAPTER I: SOMETHING ROTTEN IN THE AIR

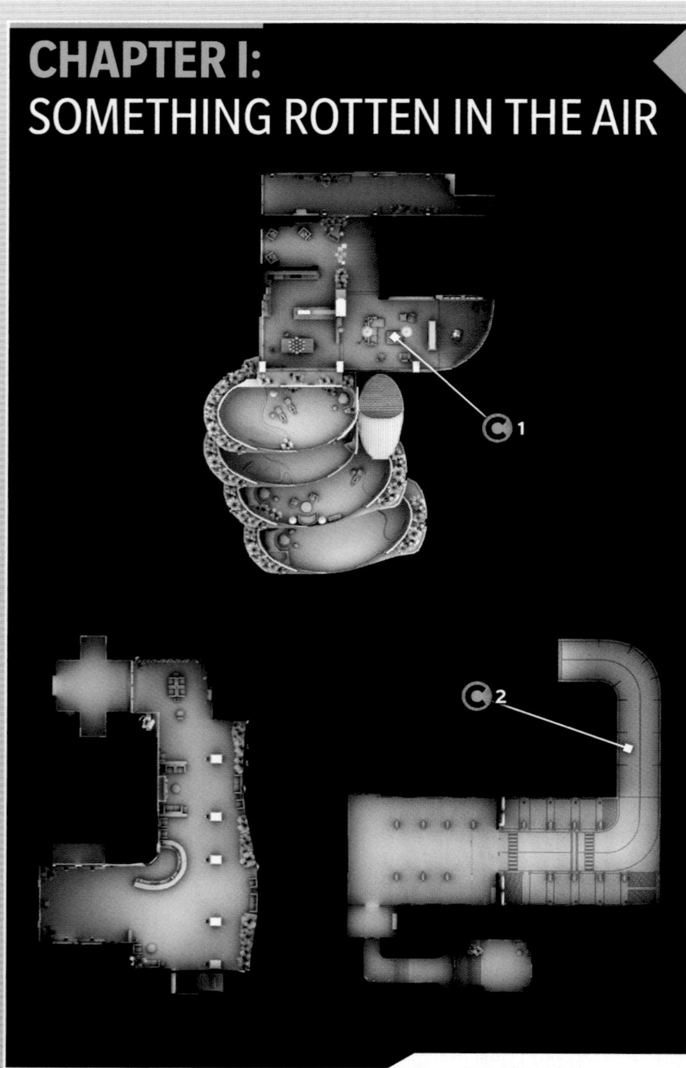

CLUE INTERACTION

Sometimes you may find a clue but cannot interact with it. This is because you must clear the enemy threat in the area. Once you have defeated all the enemies in the area, return to the clue and try again.

1 CELEBRITY MAGAZINE

This magazine is next to a bottle of painkillers located on the large coffee table in the middle of the penthouse living room.

2 DROPPED PHOTO

Located on the sloped drive between parking garage levels.

CHAPTER II: NOTHING BUT THE SECOND BEST

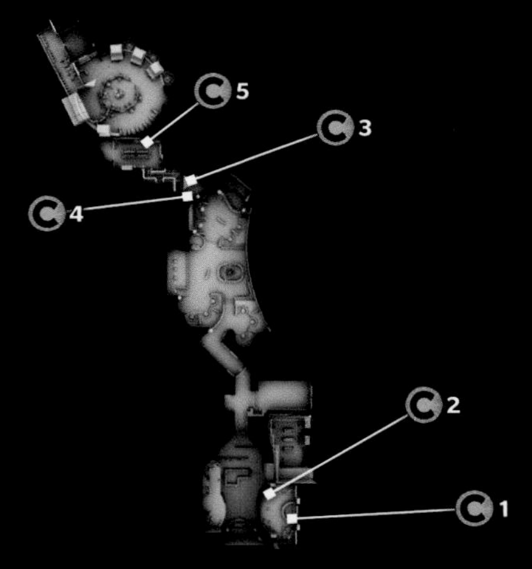

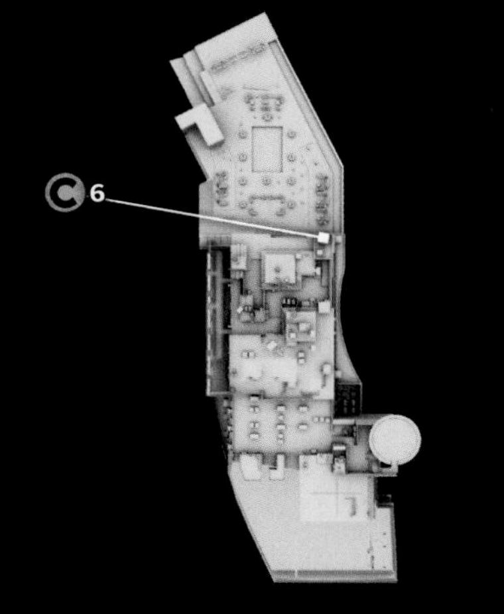

1 NIGHTCLUB FLYER

Located on the front edge of the bar, in the VIP room. The Golden Mini-30 part 1/3 is behind the same bar.

2 DEAD SOCCER STAR

His body is located on the floor of the VIP room when you return after jumping through the window to the dance floor during the aerial shooting challenge. Claudio lies dead in front of the seat that Marcelo desired.

3 TORN DRESS PIECE

After leaving the DJ bar area that you reached through the neon hallway, you push through some double doors and reach a bathroom area. Two clues are in this area. The most obvious is Fabiana's *Torn Fabric* piece on the edge of the counter near the kitchen doorway. The other is the guy in the middle bathroom stall...

4 EX-COP (ANDERS)

In the same bathroom area where you find Fabiana's *Torn Dress Piece*, push open the middle bathroom stall door on the left to meet the ex-cop, Anders Detling from North Dakota.

5 PORTUGUESE NEWSPAPER

Located on the edge of the counter on the right side of the kitchen. Clear the room then read the paper about Victor Branco's political career.

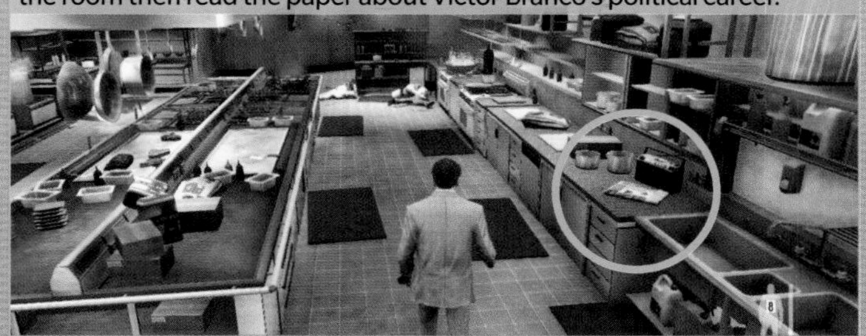

6 GIOVANNA'S NECKLACE

Located on the third landing as you head down the stairwell leading away from the rooftop.

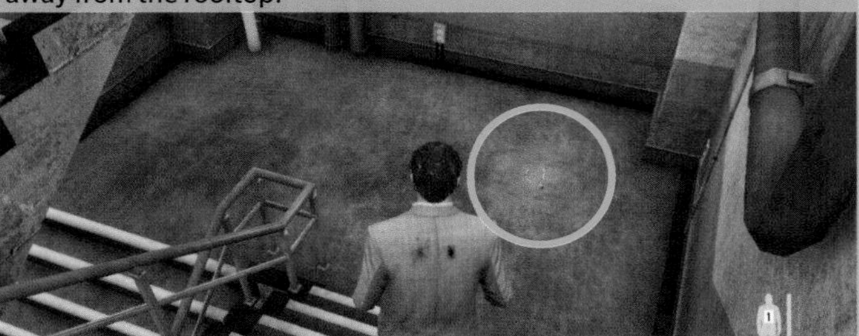

CHAPTER III: JUST ANOTHER DAY AT THE OFFICE

 1 PICTURE OF VICTOR

Examine the large framed picture of Victor on the wall of the office, beside the medical room, where Passos patches up Max.

 2 BLOOD STAINED DOOR

Just as you leave the soccer and medical room area, Passos waits beside the elevator for you to push some buttons. The Blood Stained Door is adjacent to the elevator.

 3 BLOOD STAINED HALLWAY

After leaving the gift shop, Passos and Max have to run past the sniper in the stands and then clear a concessions hallway. After the battle, examine the bloody handprint on the column on the right wall.

 4 SOCCER STAR MEMORIAL

Claudio's memorial is located at the end of the VIP lounge where Max battles a large group of paramilitary soldiers.

CHAPTER IV:
SOMETHING ROTTEN IN THE AIR

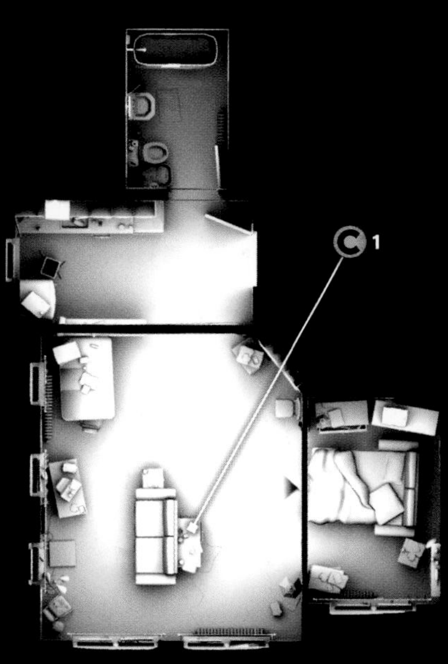

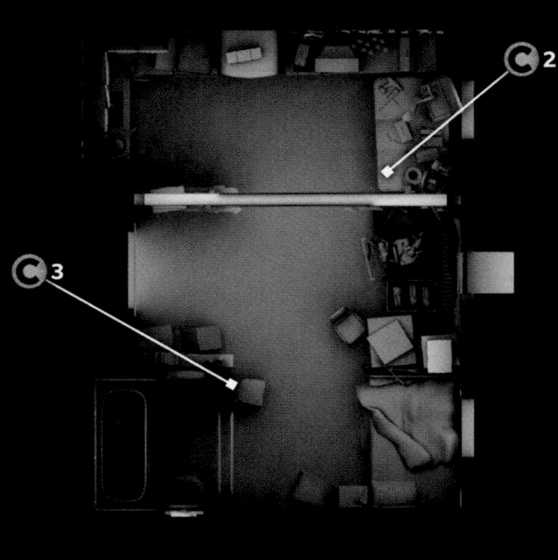

1 MAX'S NYPD BADGE

Find Max's NYPD badge in his apartment, on the edge of the table, behind his living room couch.

2 BREWER'S JOURNAL

Mr. Brewer is Max's crazy hygiene-fanatic-human-bomb neighbor who blows himself up at the end of the second hallway. Enter the apartment from which he came and find the manifesto on the edge of his bomb-making table and next to a bottle of painkillers.

3 NEWSPAPER CLIPPINGS

Numerous newspaper clippings are stuck to the wall in Mr. Brewer's apartment near the doorway. Examine these.

CHAPTER V: ALIVE IF NOT EXACTLY WELL

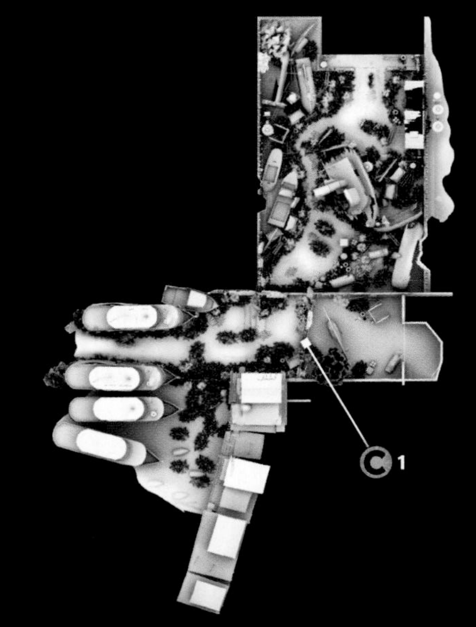

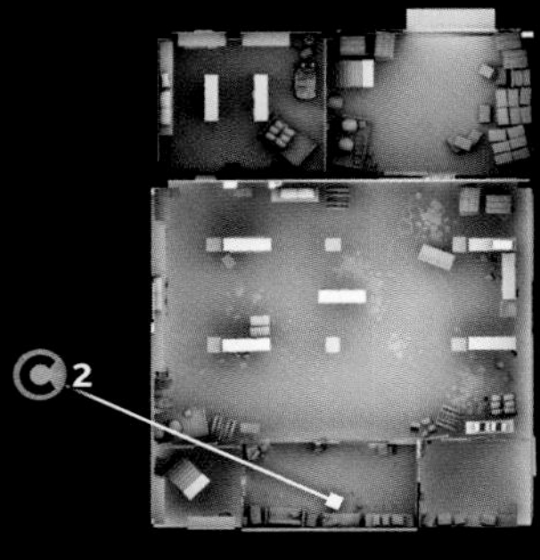

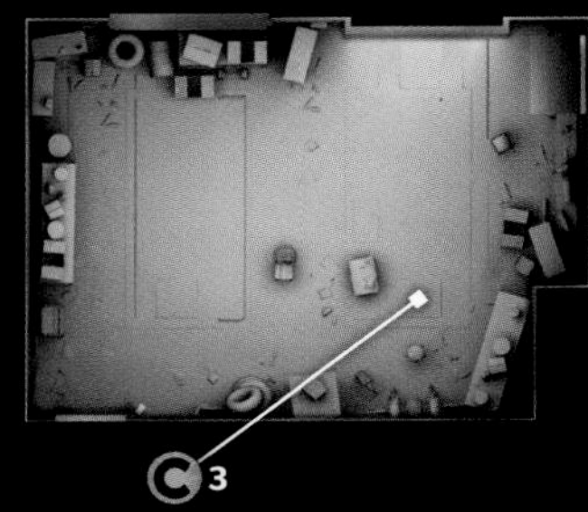

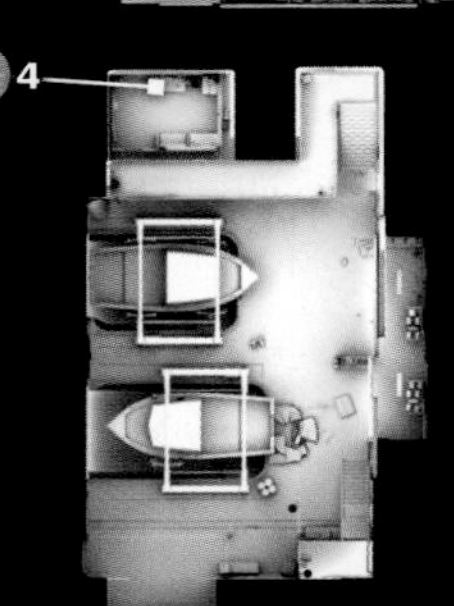

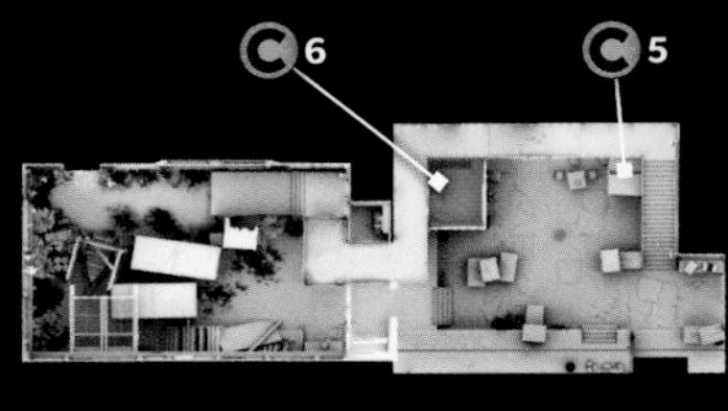

1 PARKED HELICOPTER

Located at the beginning of the mission. At the end of the first area, before you leap over the worn concrete wall, walk up to the fence and examine the nearby helicopter.

 2 RANSOM NOTE

In the first warehouse—where you take cover by an office window to prepare for a shootout—the ransom note is on the same desk where the kidnap video is playing on the small monitor.

 3 VIDEO CAMERA

When you reach the warehouse where Fabiana was being held captive, examine the video camera on the tripod. This is reached just before the boathouse shootout.

 4 BRANCO FAMILY PHOTO

You must enter the small office inside the first boathouse to open the garage door. Inside this little office is a photo on the edge of the table. Examine it.

 5 BOATHOUSE NEWSPAPER

A small shack is inside the second boathouse, below the catwalk, in a corner across from the first-floor office. The newspaper is on the floor of this shack.

 6 NIGHTCLUB FLOOR PLANS

A small first-floor office is inside the second boathouse and across from the shack where you find the boathouse newspaper. The blueprints of the nightclub are on the edge of a table inside the office.

CHAPTER VI: A DAME, A DORK, AND A DRUNK

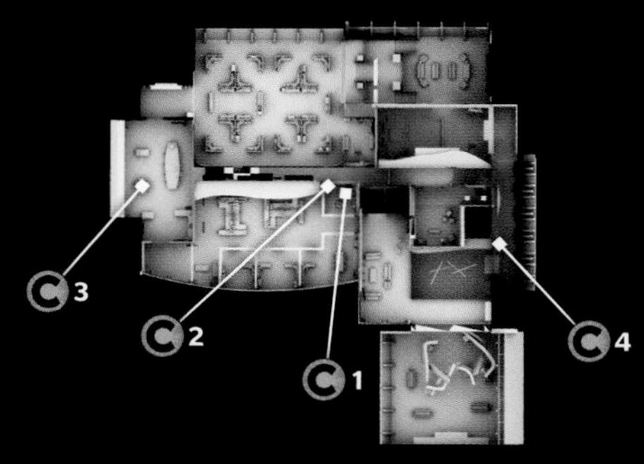

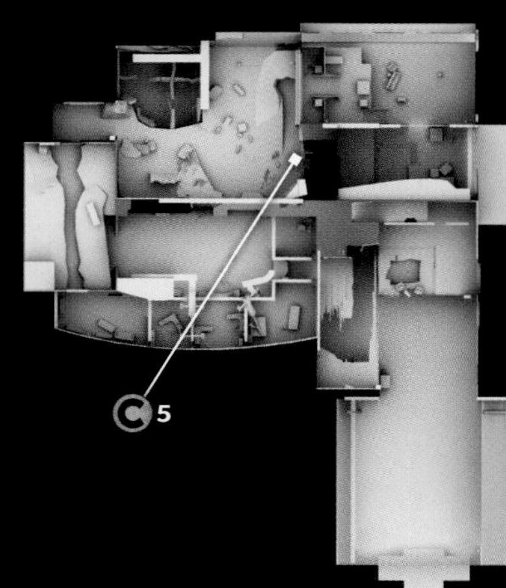

1 FILE ON FABIANA

The folder is on Victor Branco's desk inside his office. This is the first office on the right side of the first room you battle inside.

2 RODRIGO'S EMAIL

After the first office shootout, turn back and enter Victor Branco's glass-wall office and examine his computer on the filing cabinet beside his desk. The email shows that Victor is looking for campaign contributions since Rodrigo holds the purse strings rather tight.

3 ARCHITECTURAL MODELS

Examine the model in the middle of the second office battle scene.

4 SCHOOL PICTURE

Located on the hallway wall, just beyond the bathroom with the painkillers, and before the lobby where you battle the well-armed soldiers.

5 DEAD IT GUY

After disarming the enemy in the beginning of the office fire, examine your friendly IT guy's body.

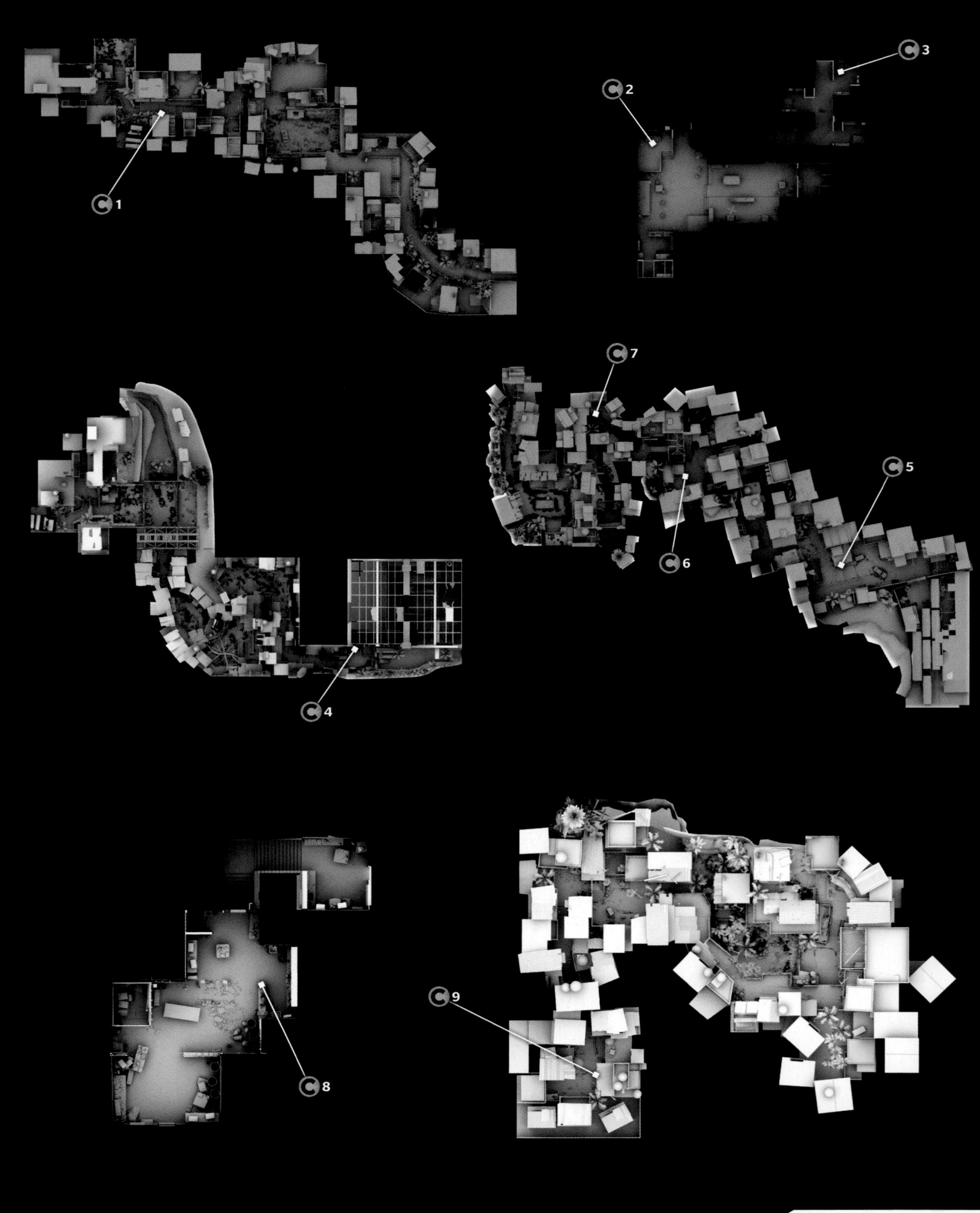
1
2
3
7
5
6
4
9
8

1 EX-COP (ANDERS)

Speak with Anders through an open window on the left just before you reach the strip club. Anjos do Morro (Angels of the Hill) is the charity business with which Giovanna works. You discover this when you find her flyer later.

2 PHOTO OF SERRANO

After the initial shootout with the thugs in the strip club (including one guy in the connecting hallway), return to the couch where you started and find Serrano's photo on the floor near the couch.

3 TOURIST

In the last "bedroom" on the right before the exit, you can find a young American man hiding under the bed. Approach the bed and speak with the coward who's in the wrong place at the wrong time.

4 LOWER GANG SPRAY TAG

Examine the gang tag on the wall and to the left of the padlocked door to the party warehouse.

5 MIDDLE GANG SPRAY TAG

After leaving the party warehouse and entering the new gang territory, you will see a hooded gang member patrolling the rooftop in a cinematic. Examine the gang tag below the balcony he was patrolling. If you fire your weapon in this area, the gang member will re-enter the balcony and attack.

6 SHRINE TO CLAUDIO

When you reach the middle gang territory, and after spotting the flare-shooting thug, you can find this shrine in a clearing near a wooden staircase.

7 FLYER FOR GIOVANNA

Find Giovanna's Anjos do Morro charity flyer on the ground and to the right of the graffiti-laden doorway. You must push through this doorway to enter the ramshackle apartment in mid-favela.

8 BAG OF OXIDADO

The Oxidado is in the drug house that Max eventually blows up. The drug is in the first room that you clear. Examine these drugs on the kitchen counter.

9 UPPER GANG SPRAY TAG

Moments after blowing up the Oxidado drug lab, you start in a new area facing this gang tag. Examine the Comando Sombra gang tag.

CHAPTER VIII: NO REPRIEVEMENT GONNA BE FOUND OTHERWISE

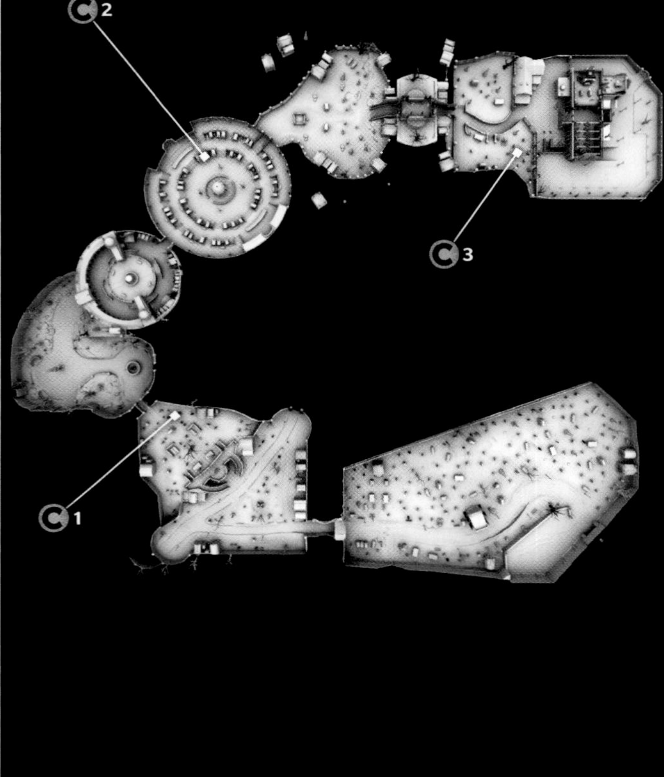

1 VALERIE'S TOMBSTONE

After defeating the mobsters in the upper cemetery area behind the grenade-launching mobster on the balcony, find Detective Valerie Winterson's tombstone on the right side and before approaching Passos at the gate ahead. Max is the reason she is buried here. (Play *Max Payne 2* to learn why.)

2 NICOLE MAUSOLEUM

Nicole Horne's mausoleum is located in the same rotunda where you saved Passos from the guy holding a gun to his head. This mausoleum is in the lower area—the most inner circular walkway. Nicole is the one who ordered the hit on Max's wife.

3 VINNIE'S TOMBSTONE

After beating the goons with a shovel, move forward in the same graveyard. Just beyond an angel tombstone, you'll find Vincent Gognitti's tomb. It's easy to spot since it is much darker than the others in the area.

CHAPTER IX:
I DIDN'T THINK MY DAY COULD GET MUCH WORSE BUT...

1 DEAD GANG MEMBERS

Examine the body leaning against the wall in the first apartment you pass through in this chapter. Afterward, Max comments about São Paulo's finest and the Comando Sombra.

2 DEAD UFE MEMBERS

The dead UFE member is located around the corner from where you see a resident shot in an alley. This is just after the big alley shootout with the armored UFE and just before the old lady's house. Kill the two remaining UFE members around the corner then examine the body.

3 DEAD RESIDENTS

After the old lady's house and the helicopter shooting challenge, you reach a spot where three UFE members are harassing a resident and end up killing him. Once the gun battle is over, examine the resident's body.

CHAPTER X: IT'S DRIVE OR SHOOT SISTER

1

2

 1 OFFICE NEWSPAPER

Examine the newspaper on the countertop inside the fueling station office. This is the second battle area in the mission. Max is front-page news.

 2 AD CAMPAIGN POSTER

When you leave Giovanna near the office bathroom to clear the floor above, and once you head down the next set of stairs, one more soldier attacks from a security room. A Camila Machado ad campaign poster is located in the hallway in-between. Examine it.

CHAPTER XI: SUN TAN OIL, STALE MARGARITAS AND GREED

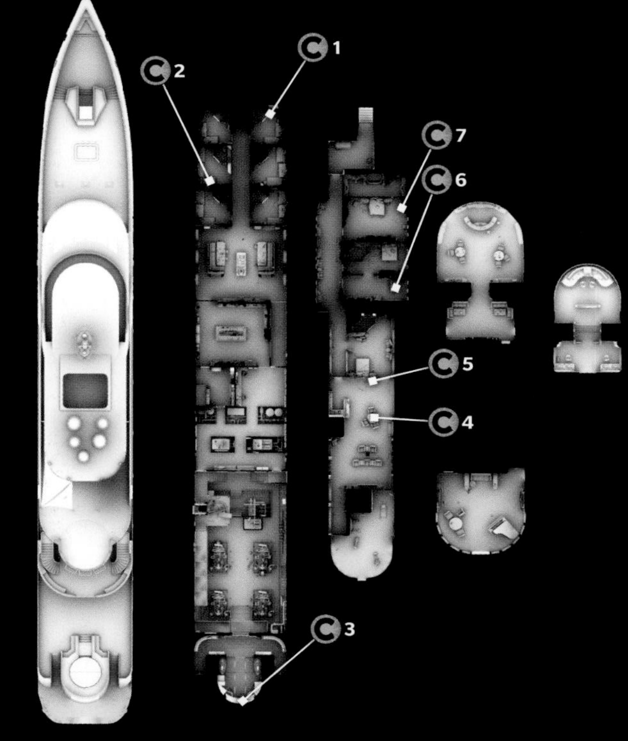

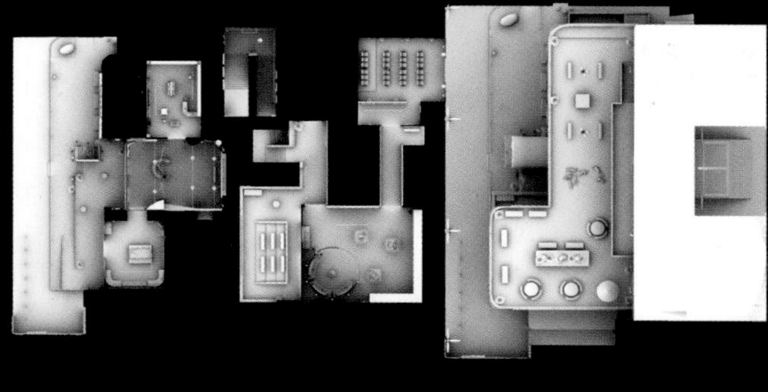

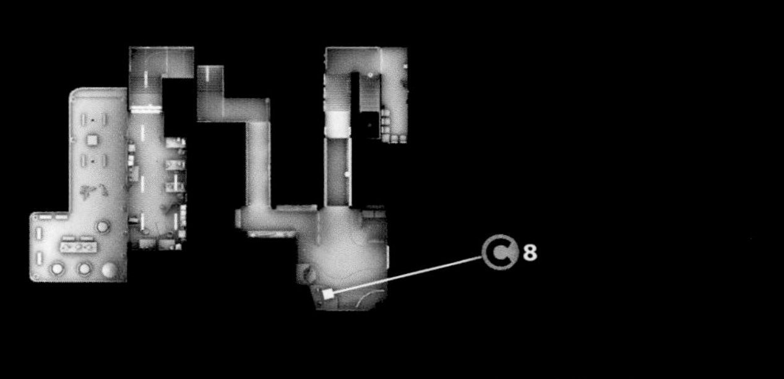

1 NOTES ON MAX

Clear the hallway and kitchen of enemies in the beginning of the level. Then explore the cabin directly across the hallway from Max's room to find this note on Max in Marcelo's room.

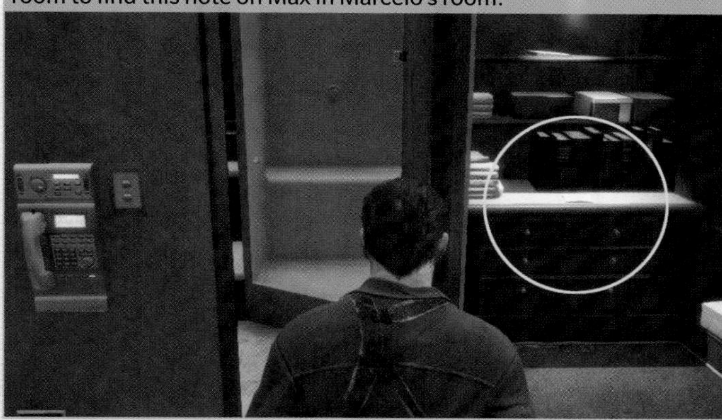

2 PASSOS' BED

From the beginning of the level, enter Passos' room, which is the second cabin on the right (first one after Max's cabin), and examine Passos' bed.

3 BLOOD TRAIL

When exiting the first floor stern of the ship through the showers and scuba supply room, you can find a blood stain on the floor as the back door opens.

4 DISCARDED NEWSPAPER

In the cabin with the torn-up wall, examine the newspaper on the round table near the pried wall.

5 PRIED WALL

Defeat the four enemies tearing up a wall on the second deck and then examine the wall they were destroying.

6 DAPHNE'S PASSPORT

Just after leaving the pried-wall cabin, enter the first cabin on the right in the hallway. Find Daphne's passport on the floor behind the desk in the back of the first of two connecting rooms.

7 DAPHNE'S JEWELRY BOX

After leaving the pried-wall cabin, enter the second cabin (third door) on the right in the hallway. Three enemies are in this cabin: one in the bedroom where the jewelry box sits on a shelf and two enemies in the bathroom. Kill the enemies and then examine the box.

8 VISITOR CENTER DISPLAY

Examine this display on the last exhibition floor before you reach the office with the blood trail. The trail leads to the slaughter balcony at the end of the mission.

CHAPTER XII: THE GREAT AMERICAN SAVIOR OF THE POOR

1 GURNEY

In the beginning of the mission, examine the gurneys in the incinerator room.

2 AMMO CRATE

Through the doors of the incinerator room, you come to a hallway with a couple cages to the left. Enter the first cage to find painkillers and the UFE ammo crate. Examine it.

3 PASSOS' ID CARD

Find this photocopy of Passos' ID card on the floor inside the room that is just opposite the room with the collapsed floor. It could be under a small table since the table can move during the battle. Max learns that Passos is actually Colombian.

4 WALL PHOTOS

Find this wall of photos in the room just on the other side of the collapsed floor. Also inside this room: a Golden RPG part and Passos' ID Card clue.

5 NEWSPAPER ARTICLE

Once you clear the lounge beyond the pool, find this newspaper on the bar countertop. This is the room just before the organ donor operating room. You learn Victor Branco is winning the election from the sympathy votes.

6 DONATION RECEIPT

Find this receipt on the shelf in the back corner of the weapons and explosives storage room on the first floor of the destructible support columns. This receipt shows Victor paying Neves $400,000.

CHAPTER XIII: A FAT BALD DUDE WITH A BAD TEMPER

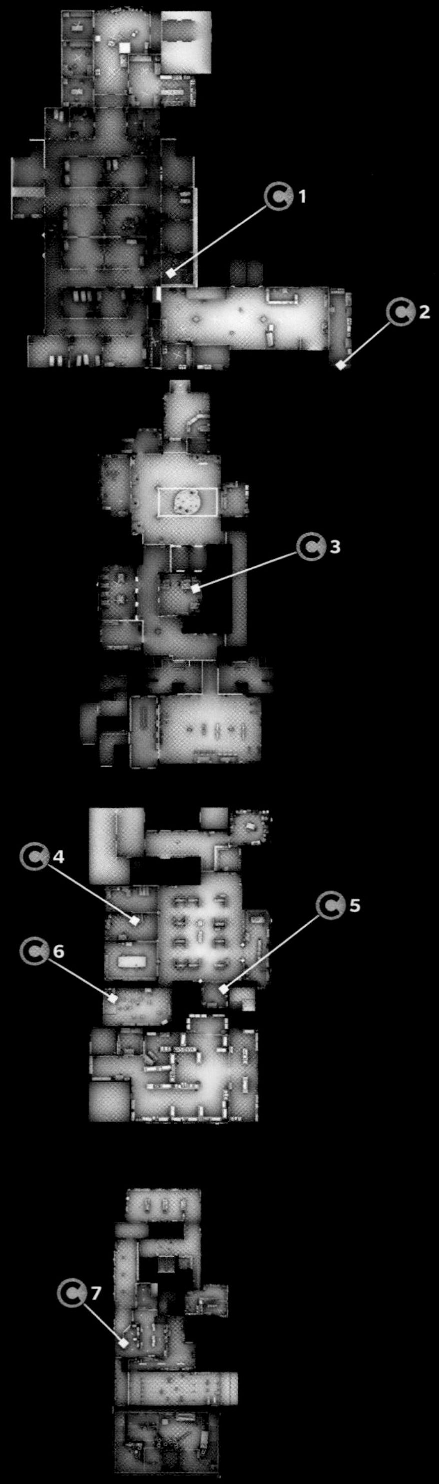

1
2
3
4
5
6
7

1 TOURIST

After defeating all the enemies in the jail cell area, do not exit; instead backtrack through the cell hallways a little ways following the sound of the tourist's pleas for help. You'll find him in near a dead-end hallway. Max is not surprised to find he ended up in jail.

2 PRISON LOG

A laptop is located on a tall desk in the room where you find the security door button that grants access to the exterior—where an armored car is attacking prisoners. Examine the laptop see the prison log.

3 PROMISSORY NOTE

Located on a desk inside the administration room, which is near the cafe and kitchen. It shows evidence of the blood money coming from Dr. Arthur Fischer, the organ doctor, and being paid to Becker.

4 POLITICAL FOLDER

After the major fifth-floor battle ends, explore the offices around the central cubical grid. A paper folder is inside the middle office, along the right wall, on the edge of a desk. Examine it. You learn that the Brazilian cops tipped the AUP about the money.

5 E-FILE ON DA SILVA

Examine the laptop in the office in the back left corner of the large fifth-floor office battle area. This is just before the slide show room.

6 SLIDE SHOW

A briefing room with a lit projector is just beyond the fifth-floor office battle. Step onto the small stage and activate the slide show on the podium. There are multiple slides. Watch them all to receive credit for finding this cule.

7 FLAK VEST

Examine and wear the flak vest found in the armory near the firing-range door switch.

CHAPTER XIV: ONE CARD LEFT TO PLAY

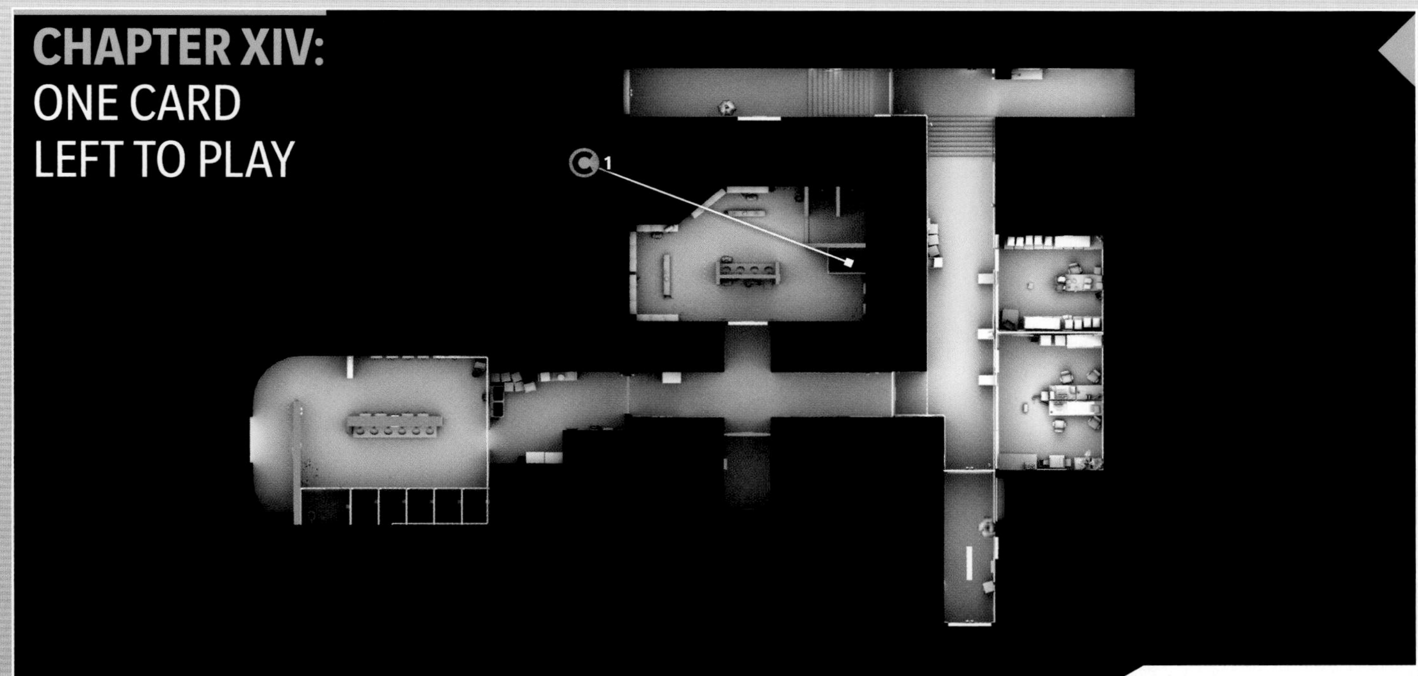

1 EX-COP (ANDERS)

You can find Anders for the last time in the locker room, just before the airport terminals. This is the same room where you find the last Golden Grenade Launcher part in a shower stall. Anders is in the toilet stall beside the shower. He appears here only if you found him the other two times in previous chapters.

GOLDEN GUNS

There are 84 Golden Gun Parts in *Max Payne 3*. You can collect Clues in either Story or Arcade modes, but Golden Gun parts can be found only in single player Story mode. Collecting all three parts creates a beautiful gold version of the weapon the next time you use it. Golden Guns also add performance enhancements. You can turn off this Golden Gun effect in the Settings menu if you wish.

MULTIPLAYER GOLD TINT

Collecting all three Golden Gun Parts for a weapon also unlocks a gold plating option in its multiplayer counterpart. You can find this cosmetic enhancement in the Arsenal Attachment menu for the weapons you've unlocked.

CHAPTER I: SOMETHING ROTTEN IN THE AIR

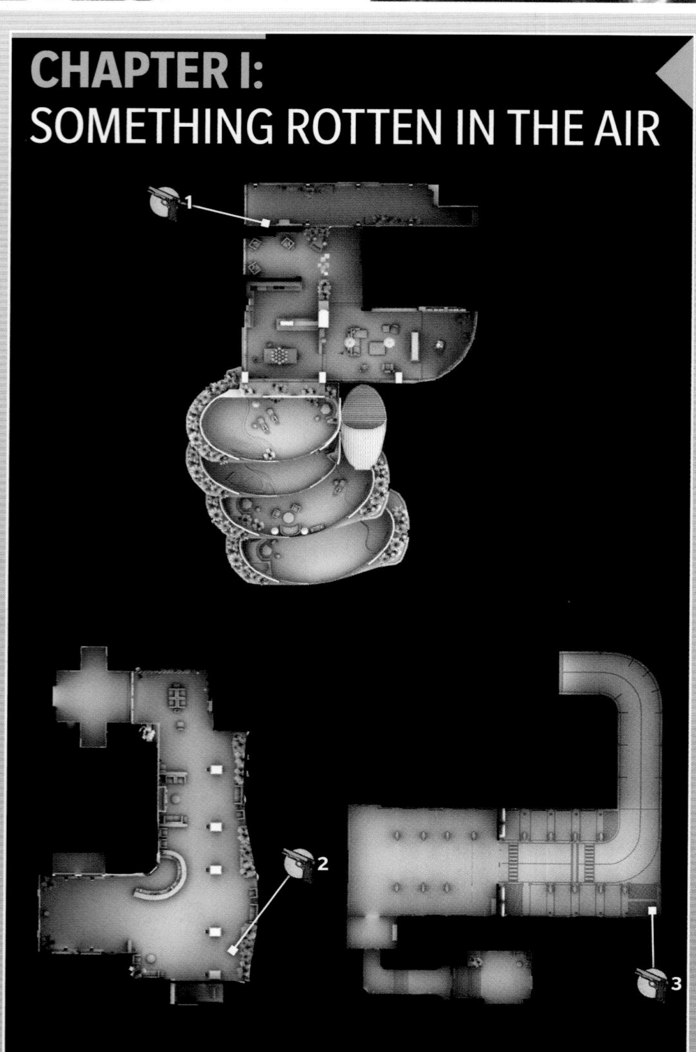

1 GOLDEN PT92 PART 1/3

This gun part is located at the end of the first hallway where you begin the game. After shooting the first enemy and then completing the ShootDodge training, head to the forward left corner of the hallway and pick up the first gun part.

2 GOLDEN PT92 PART 2/3

When you reach the next floor via elevator, you face more bad guys and more basic training. Once the enemies are dead, turn around and retrieve this gun part from in front of the first wooden planter in the room.

3 GOLDEN PT92 PART 3/3

This part is located in the parking lot in parking bay B01. This is just through the roll-up door triggered with a switch and in the forward right corner.

CHAPTER II: NOTHING BUT THE SECOND BEST

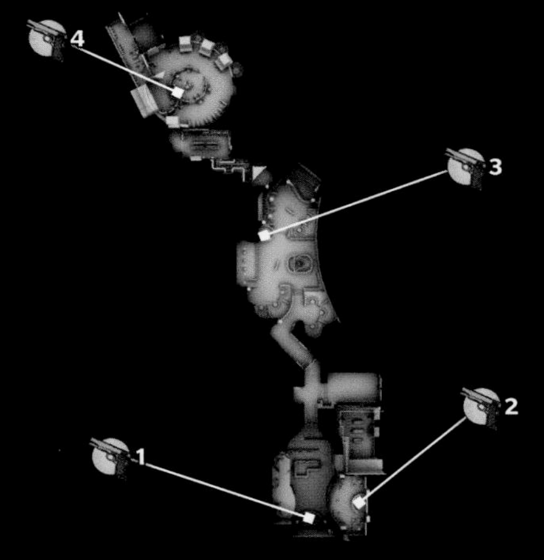

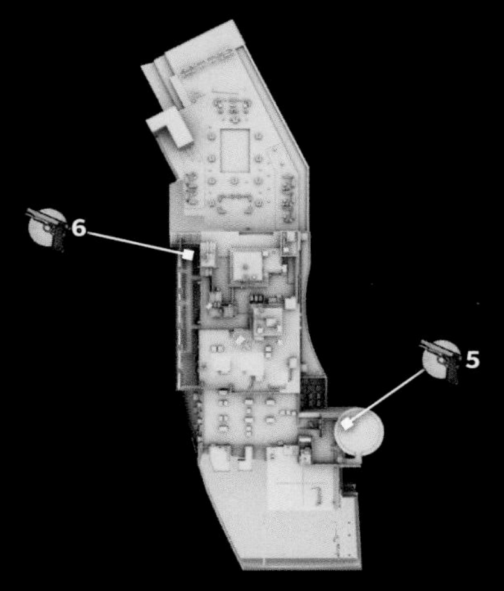

1 GOLDEN .38 REVOLVER PART 1/3

You can find this gun part on the floor of the DJ booth in the first dance floor area where you begin the chapter. Get it on your way back to the VIP lounge after checking the barricaded exit.

2 GOLDEN MINI-30 PART 1/3

After returning to the VIP room (where you jumped through the window just minutes before), find this gun part on the floor behind the bar.

3 GOLDEN .38 REVOLVER PART 2/3

You can find this gun part on the floor in the DJ booth in the purple lounge (just beyond the neon hallway). Follow the stairs on the left side of the room across a balcony seating area through a door and into the DJ booth/balcony. You can also find painkillers here.

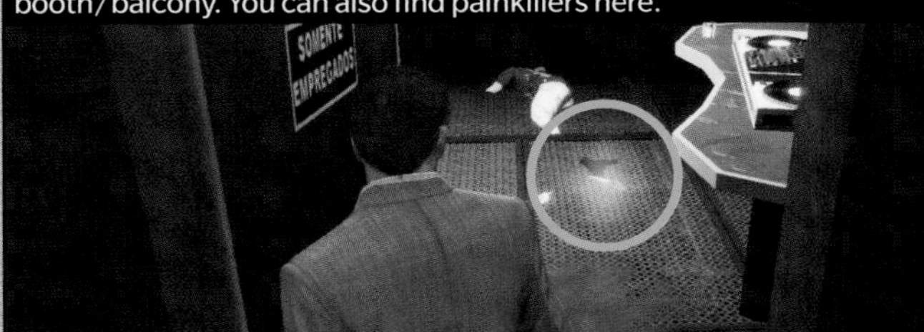

4 GOLDEN MINI-30 PART 2/3

Find this gun part in the circular restaurant seating area. The part is on the counter between booth seats.

5 GOLDEN MINI-30 PART 3/3

This gun part is in the glass-enclosed lounge beneath the helipad. Head down the stairs from the helipad, then turn right and push through the unlocked double doors. The part is on the floor to the left, near a couch.

6 GOLDEN .38 REVOLVER PART 3/3

The final part to the revolver is on the neon BOITATA billboard catwalk. It's at the far end where Giovanna turned around while you were sniping from the helicopter.

CHAPTER III: JUST ANOTHER DAY AT THE OFFICE

1 GOLDEN M10 PART 1/3

You can discover this gun part on the floor near a camera in the media room, which can safely be explored after defeating the attackers that storm the media room after the failed interrogation.

2 GOLDEN M82A1 PART 1/3

This gun part is on a low shelf, on the left side of the room as you enter the gift shop. Turn around when you gain control of Max while covering behind the sales counter during the gunfight.

3 GOLDEN M10 PART 2/3

When you leave the control room to enter the stands and try to catch the guy with the moneybag, continue down to the lowest level of the stands and find this gun part in the lowest left corner.

4 GOLDEN M10 PART 3/3

This part is located on the chair in the front row of the VIP lounge just before the soccer star memorial.

5 GOLDEN M82A1 PART 2/3

When you exit the top floor of the stadium and look down on the enemies from the top row of bleachers, follow the stairs directly in front of you down to the bottom. Then turn left around the wall to find this gun part. This wall is also great to use as cover from the remaining enemies in the area.

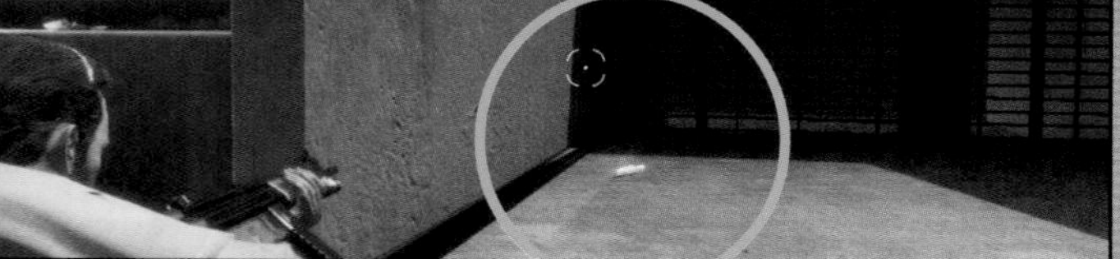

6 GOLDEN M82A1 PART 3/3

Immediately after the sniping challenge, find this gun part behind a short column at the far right end of the top row of bleachers.

1
3
2
4
7
5
6
9
8

1 GOLDEN 1911 PART 1/3
After clearing the first area of enemies, turn around and find this gun in the front right corner of the bar near the locked entrance.

2 GOLDEN 1911 PART 2/3
Clear the bar and the billiards room, head upstairs, and find this gun part at the end of the upstairs hallway.

3 GOLDEN 1911 PART 3/3
After eliminating the goons in the parking lot and before following Passos into the alleyway, return to the bottom of the stairs and find this weapon part beside the stairs.

4 GOLDEN M500 PART 1/3
This gun part is located inside Max's apartment on the floor between the window and the couch.

5 GOLDEN SAF 40 CAL PART 1/3
After watching Mr. Brewer blow himself up, find this gun part on what's left of the burned apartment floor then head up the stairs to the rooftop.

6 GOLDEN M500 PART 2/3
Clear the initial rooftop of danger, then double back and find this gun part behind the stairs enclosure through which you accessed the roof.

7 GOLDEN SAF 40 CAL PART 2/3
After the falling water tower Bullet Time challenge, traverse the rooftops to the left instead of following Passos to the right. On the last rooftop (the one with the fence), find this gun part in the right corner, beside a bird coop.

8 GOLDEN M500 PART 3/3
After battling goons on the initial floor of the abandoned apartment building, head up the stairs to survive another ambush. The gun part is outside and at the end of the scaffold. Get to it before you approach Passos on the fire escape or you'll miss the opportunity.

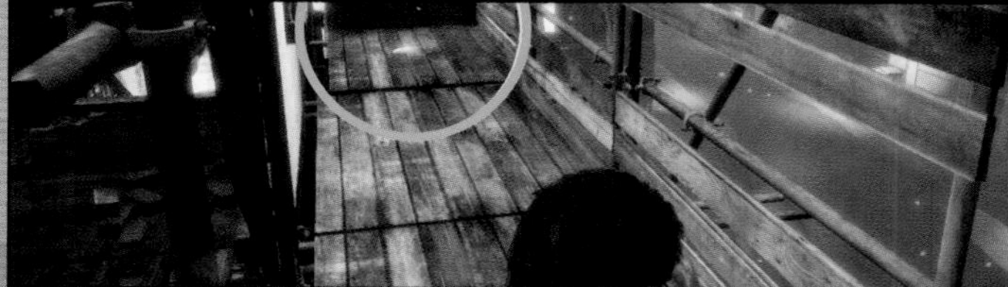

9 GOLDEN SAF 40 CAL PART 3/3
After defeating the enemies in the chop shop, find this gun part on the desk of the shop's long office.

CHAPTER V: ALIVE IF NOT EXACTLY WELL

1 GOLDEN MICRO 9MM PART 1/3

Open the roll-up door to exit the first warehouse and shoot the enemies in the shipping container and the enemies to your right. Once the area is clear, climb the shipping containers on the right to find this gun part on top.

2 GOLDEN MICRO 9MM PART 2/3

Exit the warehouse where Fabiana was being held and look in the nook between the building on the right and the fence.

3 GOLDEN MICRO 9MM PART 3/3

After the boathouse leaping shootout challenge and clearing all the enemies within, head to the second floor and find this gun part at the end of the winding catwalk.

4 GOLDEN LMG .30 PART 1/3

Explore the area through the back doors of the second boathouse to find this gun part inside the trash-filled shipping container.

5 GOLDEN LMG .30 PART 2/3

This gun part is located in the shack beside the docks control booth. You reach this just after opening the sliding gate.

6 GOLDEN LMG .30 PART 3/3

On the opposite side of the first control shack you reach on the piers (near the scoped FAL). You must work your along the pier pathway to reach the back side of the shack; a fence blocks access from the first side.

CHAPTER VI:
A DAME, A DORK, AND A DRUNK

1 MD-97L PART 1/3

On floor of the office with a glass wall, across from Victor Branco's. This is the first battle area of the mission.

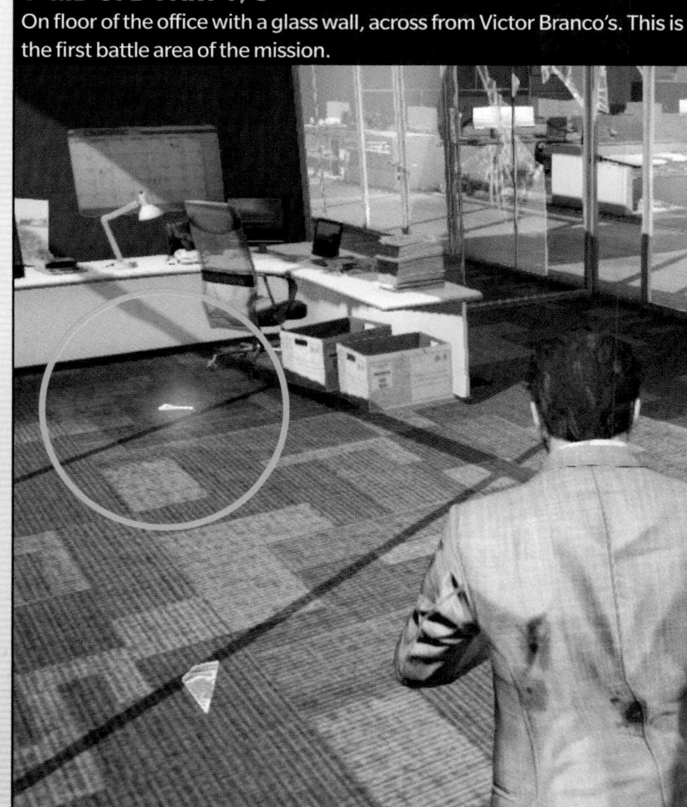

2 MD-97L PART 2/3

Immediately after shouting up to Rodrigo Branco on the balcony above the waterfall courtyard, turn around and find this gun part on the small bridge near the waterfall.

3 MD-97L PART 3/3

After completing the difficult battle in the lobby, smash the architectural model display case on the right side of the room (near the reception desk) and take this gun part from inside.

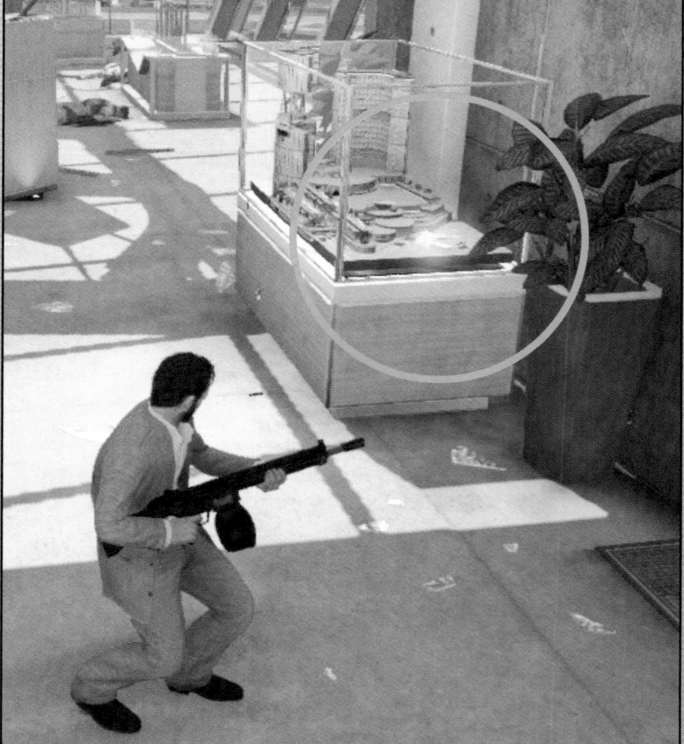

CHAPTER VII: A HANGOVER SENT DIRECT FROM MOTHER NATURE

1 GOLDEN SAWN-OFF PART 1/3

In the strip club bathroom, on the floor in the middle stall.

2 GOLDEN SAWN-OFF PART 2/3

After sniping the enemies inside the party warehouse from the middle level room, exit the room through the next door and find this part on the ground in the nook on the left before you head downstairs.

3 GOLDEN SPAS-15 PART 1/3

Behind a pile of rubble consisting mostly of metal oil drums on the second level as you are leaving the party warehouse. Look back into the room from the hallway exit while shooting the remaining enemies in the building to see this hidden item.

4 GOLDEN SPAS-15 PART 2/3

When you reach the middle of the Favela, a cinematic introduces the new gang. Before you exit this area through the back-right alleyway, find this gun part behind a stack of wood on the right side of the building with the middle favela gang tag.

5 GOLDEN SPAS-15 PART 3/3

Just beyond the four consecutive flights of stairs, a hooded gang member is seen on an adjacent rooftop holding up the flare with which he'll announce your presence. Shoot him, drop off this staircase, and head to the dead-end on the right. Turn back and look at the base of the stair structure to find the gun part.

6 GOLDEN SAWN-OFF PART 3/3

This gun part is in the Molotov battle area. Once you deal with the enemy, approach the gate to the left of the exit stairs. Be careful: someone will shoot at you from farther ahead. Eliminate those enemies through the gate and then pick up this gun part near the gate.

CHAPTER VIII: NO REPRIEVEMENT GONNA BE FOUND OTHERWISE

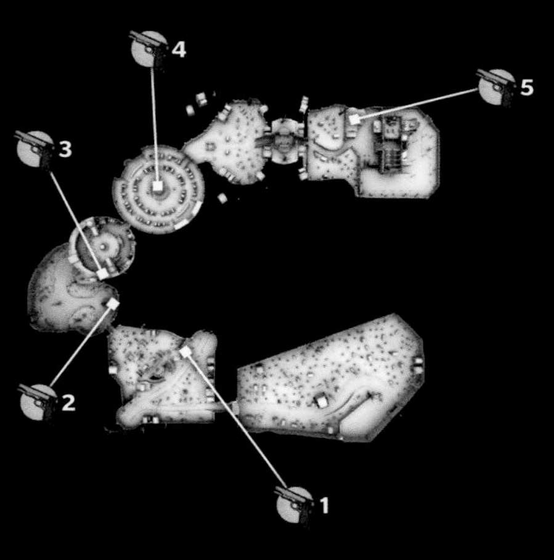

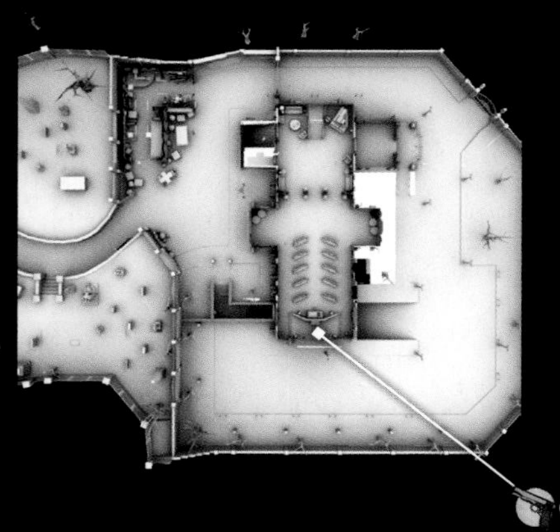

1 GOLDEN AUTO 9MM PART 1/3

This gun part is found before the two-stair hill just after you shoot the van gate crasher. There are two small mausoleums to the right of the first set of stairs on the right (below the grenade launching mobster). The weapon part is on the ground before the second mausoleum.

2 GOLDEN 608 BULL PART 1/3

This part is adjacent to the collection of parked vehicles where Passos leaves you. The gun part is on the ground behind the circular planter.

3 GOLDEN AUTO 9MM PART 2/3

This gun part is on a shelf in the dead end to the right as you enter the rotunda. If you've crossed over the fountain platform, you've gone too far. Be sure to clear the area of enemies before attempting recovery.

4 GOLDEN 608 BULL PART 2/3

"You Max Payne?" This gun part is beside the sarcophagus and behind the goon holding a gun to Passos' head.

5 GOLDEN AUTO 9MM PART 3/3

On the small bathroom floor in the marble shed near the morgue. You reach this just after leaving the graveyard from your shovel-wielding escape.

6 GOLDEN 608 BULL PART 3/3

Find this gun part on the floor behind the pulpit inside the church. Pick it up after you clear the enemies from the first floor but before you head to the second floor to take out the balcony gunman.

CHAPTER IX: I DIDN'T THINK MY DAY COULD GET MUCH WORSE BUT...

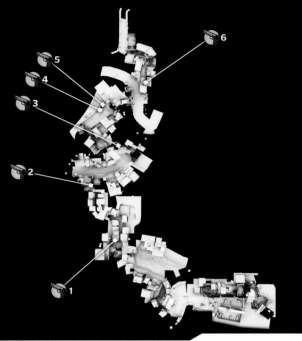

1 GOLDEN DE .50 PART 1/3

This gun part is in the lower doorway dugout found during the large alley firefight with the armored gunmen on your return to Fevala.

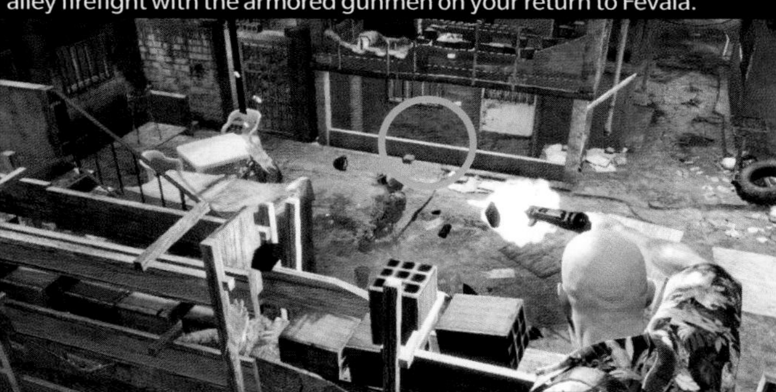

2 GOLDEN M972 PART 1/3

This weapon part is in the old lady's apartment. She runs and hides in a backroom when she spots you. The gun part is on her bathroom shower floor. Take the Painkillers in her medicine cabinet as well.

3 GOLDEN M972 PART 2/3

This gun part is at the bottom of the third consecutive set of stairs you reach after you fall through a ceiling after the helicopter shooting challenge.

4 GOLDEN DE .50 PART 2/3

Check the heavy vegetative corner along the metal gate just after seeing the round-up scene. Keep the camera positioned around your feet and you will find this gun part in the corner thick with bushes and overgrowth.

5 GOLDEN M972 PART 3/3

Just as the round-up cinematic ends, you find yourself in a heavily vegetated yard. On the other side of the forward left corner wall is a nook near a gate where you can find this gun part.

6 GOLDEN DE .50 PART 3/3

The last gun part in this chapter is found in the area where you battle the last group of soldiers on a walkway bridge. Push through an unlocked gate near the jump that leads into a barred porch. This is where you will discover the last gun part.

CHAPTER X: IT'S DRIVE OR SHOOT SISTER

1 GOLDEN FAL ART 1/3

This gun part is located in the bus graveyard where you begin the chapter. It is on the floor of the half-bus with the chopped rooftop.

2 GOLDEN M4 SUPER 90 PART 1/3

After defeating the enemies in the paint garage where you completed the hoist aerial shooting challenge, you can find this gun part on the floor of the paint storage room.

3 GOLDEN M4 SUPER 90 PART 2/3

After clearing the paint garage of enemies, find this gun part on a corner workbench on the opposite side of the room from the stairs Giovanna lowers.

4 GOLDEN FAL PART 2/3

This gun part is located inside the bus in the garage reached after leaving the paint garage.

5 GOLDEN M4 SUPER 90 PART 3/3

This gun part is located in the second floor of the office where a battle with many guards occurs. Find this gun part on the desk in the corner office on the right as you come up the stairs.

6 GOLDEN FAL PART 3/3

Find this gun part behind the desk in the office at the bottom of the stairs. It's in the same room with the security door button.

CHAPTER XI: SUN TAN OIL, STALE MARGARITAS, AND GREED

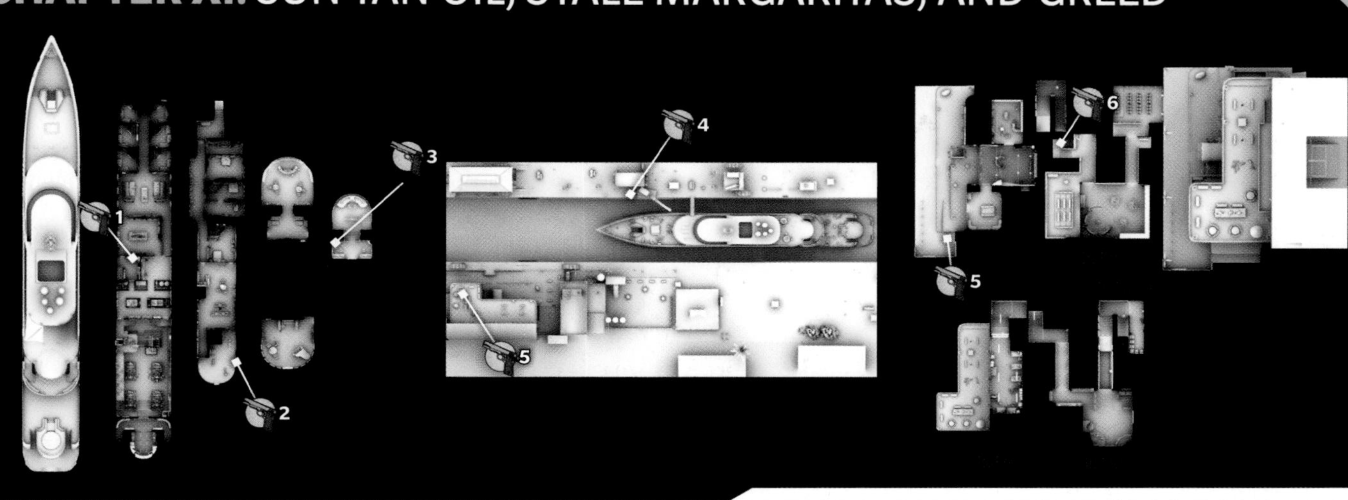

1 GOLDEN SUPER SPORT PART 1/3

From your cabin, pass through the dining area and enter the kitchen through the door on the right. Once inside the kitchen, keep heading forward through the doorway with the plastic strips. Then turn and look down into the left corner to find this gun part.

2 GOLDEN SUPER SPORT PART 2/3

After surviving the engine room explosion, head outside to the back of the ship. After defeating the enemies on the upper deck and before reentering the ship via the fitness room, find this gun part hidden at the dead-end walkway on the right side of the ship's fitness room.

3 GOLDEN AK-47 PART 1/3

In the room just before you reach the wheelhouse, which triggers the next stage of attack on land, shoot the picture from the wall on the left to reveal a secret safe. Shoot the safe to open it. The gun part is inside the wall safe.

4 GOLDEN AK-47 PART 2/3

After leaving the yacht and after clearing the enemies around the tower, head to the opposite side of the building at which you started the tower battle to find this gun part.

5 GOLDEN SUPER SPORT PART 3/3

This gun part is located outside the operation center. After zip-lining across the channel and eliminating the immediate threat, find this gun part in a corner, on the right side of the building, beside the wheelchair ramps.

6 GOLDEN AK-47 PART 3/3

Just before you reach the second-floor exhibition room via the exterior walkway, explore the exterior staircase to the right. The last Golden AK-47 part in on the first landing.

CHAPTER XII: THE GREAT AMERICAN SAVIOR OF THE POOR

1 GOLDEN RPG PART 1/3

This gun part is in the bathroom in the same room where you catch up to the two men from the incinerator.

2 GOLDEN FMP G3S PART 1/3

If you stand facing the room with the collapsed floor (before crossing it), a hallway is visible to your left. This gun part is just inside the hallway, on the floor, beside a room-service cart.

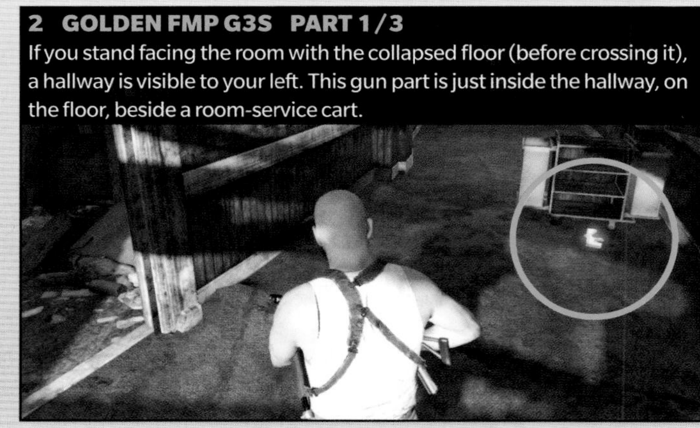

3 GOLDEN RPG PART 2/3

After climbing the stairs to the level with the collapsed floor, push through some doors to reach a long empty hallway. Find the hole in the right wall that leads into a crumbled bathroom. This gun part is on the floor near the tub.

4 GOLDEN FMP G3S PART 2/3

This gun part can be found behind the counter in the rooftop pool house.

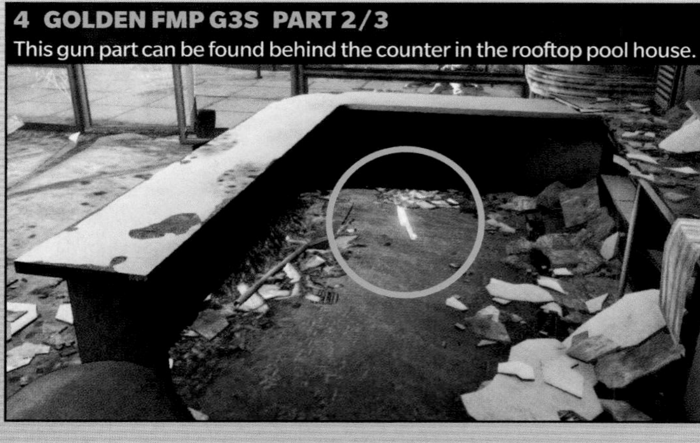

5 GOLDEN FMP G3S PART 3/3

This gun part is located behind a chair on the right side of the first room where you plant three bombs on support columns.

6 GOLDEN RPG PART 3/3

After clearing the enemies from the second floor of destructible columns, find the final RPG part on an exterior ledge that is adjacent to the floor entrance.

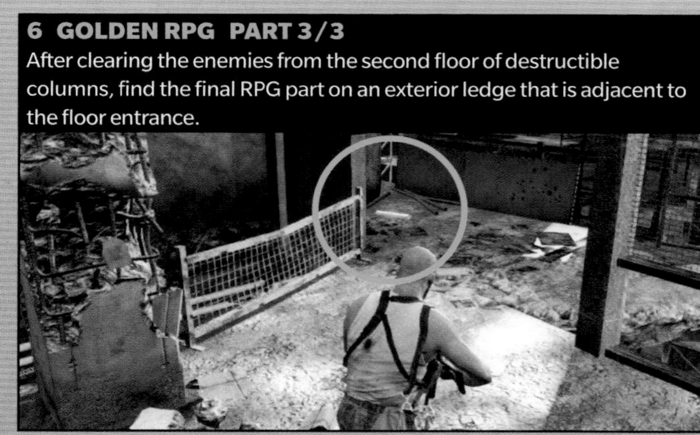

CHAPTER XIII: A FAT BALD DUDE WITH A BAD TEMPER

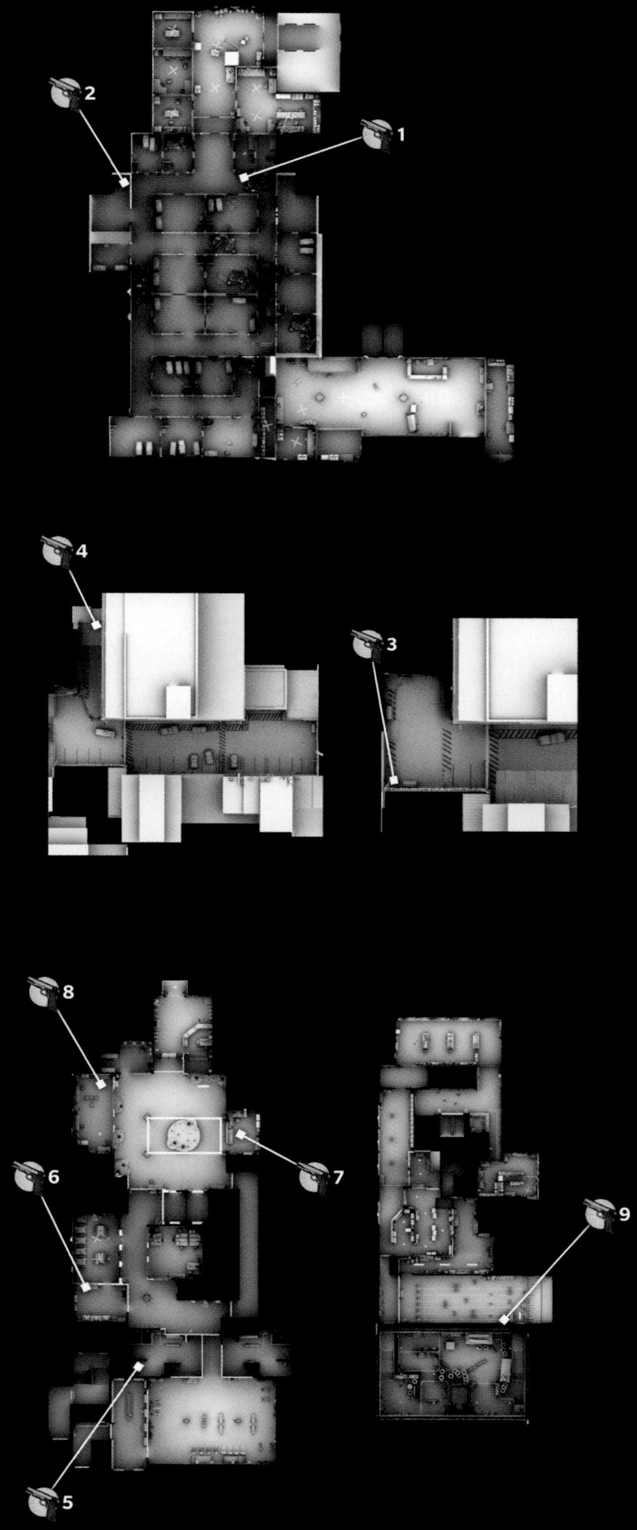

1 GOLDEN MPK PART 1/3

After breaking out of the interrogation room in the beginning of the chapter, turn left at the end of the first cellblock hallway to find this gun part on the tray outside the first cell.

2 GOLDEN LAW PART 1/3

This gun part is located in the showers on the right, just feet away from the first two guards you must defeat in the cellblock hallway.

3 GOLDEN LAW PART 2/3

This gun part is located next to a dumpster in the underground parking area below the armored truck that you must blow up with an RPG.

4 GOLDEN G6 COMMANDO PART 1/3

After destroying the armored truck, enter the double doors, climb the stairs, and defeat the guards in the next alley. At the opposite end of this alley is a short wall. The gun part is behind the short wall.

5 GOLDEN MPK PART 2/3

After destroying the armored truck and reentering the police station, you will reach a gym. The gun part is on the men's bathroom shower floor.

6 GOLDEN G6 COMMANDO PART 2/3

This gun part is located in a small cubbyhole under the meal counter in the kitchen.

7 GOLDEN G6 COMMANDO PART 3/3

On the floor of the S.I.G. office with the printers in the same area as the control room where you battle the UFE guards that storm out of the elevators.

8 GOLDEN MPK PART 3/3

In the briefing room on a table under a projection screen. This long room is adjacent to the control room where you battle the UFE guards that storm out of the elevators.

9 GOLDEN LAW PART 3/3

The final LAW part is located behind the sandbags you use for cover in the firing-range shootout.

CHAPTER XIV: ONE CARD LEFT TO PLAY

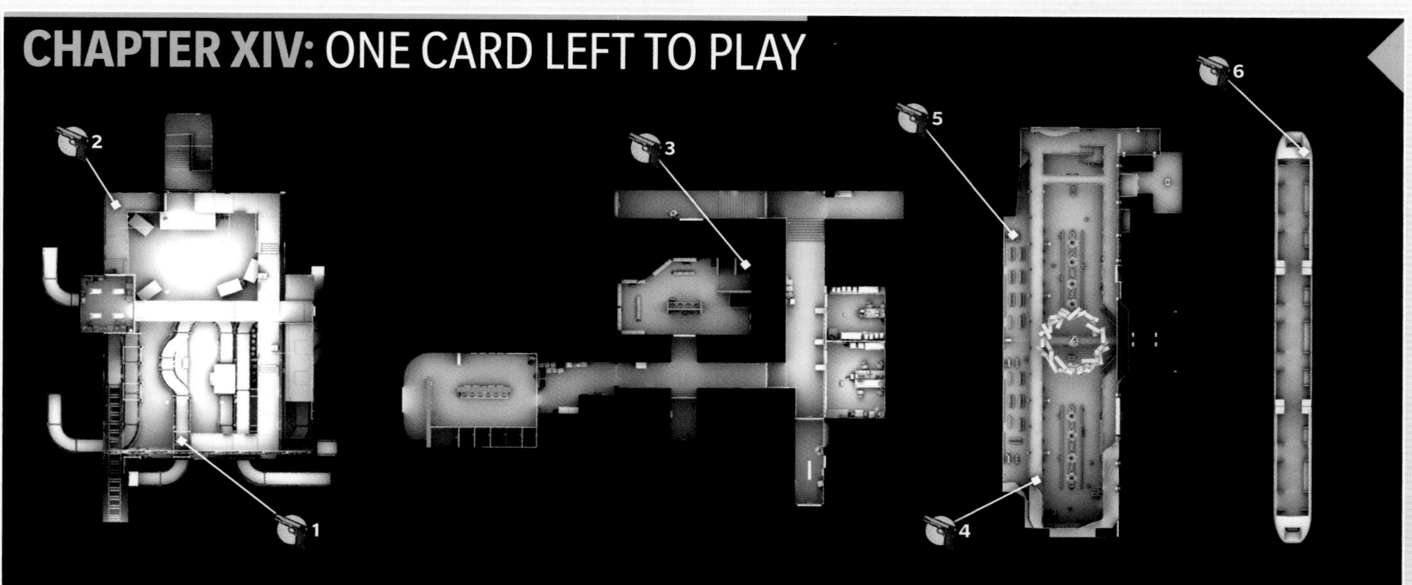

1 GOLDEN ROTARY GRENADE LAUNCHER PART 1/3

On top of a conveyor cage along the left wall as you begin the mission in the baggage sorting room. You can see it as you cross the catwalk to the control room. Get it by following the catwalks to the front of the room and hopping over the railing.

2 GOLDEN ROTARY GRENADE LAUNCHER PART 2/3

Before you leave the baggage sorting room via the doorway in the control room, head through the unlocked door on the right and find the this part along the catwalk in the corner.

3 GOLDEN ROTARY GRENADE LAUNCHER PART 3/3

A locker is on the right side of the final hallway before you reach the airport departure gates. This gun part is in the shower. You can also find Anders in the nearby toilet stall if you've already found all of his previous locations.

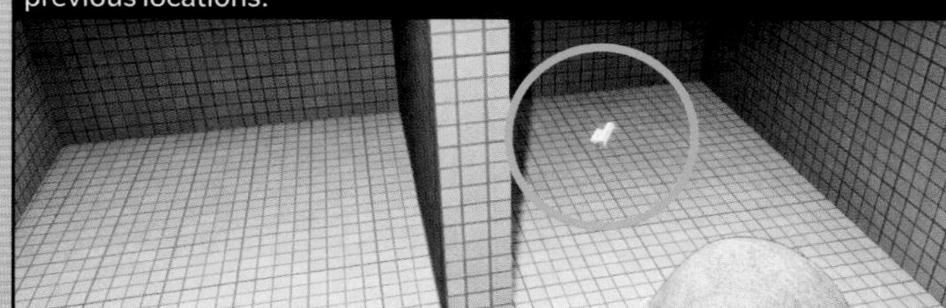

4 GOLDEN RPD PART 1/3

This gun part is located on the top left balcony of the first passenger waiting area of the airport. Take the escalator up to reach it.

5 GOLDEN RPD PART 2/3

This gun part is located in the second waiting area of the airport and behind the last passenger help desk on the left. Look for Gate 17.

6 GOLDEN RPD PART 3/3

This gun part is in the back of the last train car you ride. Do not step off the train until you get this part or you will miss your opportunity to collect the final part.

UNLOCKABLES

STORY MODE UNLOCKABLES

If you are looking for Story mode Clues and Golden Gun Parts, see the Collectibles section of the guide.

SINGLE PLAYER ACHIEVEMENTS & TROPHIES

	DISPLAY NAME	DESCRIPTION	XBOX VALUE	PS3 VALUE
	Feel The Payne	Story Complete [MEDIUM]	30	Bronze
	Serious Payne	Story Complete [HARD]	50	Silver
	Maximum Payne	Story Complete [OLD SCHOOL]	80	Gold
	Payne In The Ass	Story Complete [HARDCORE]	20	Bronze
	Part I Complete	Complete Part I Of The Story	20	Bronze
	Part II Complete	Complete Part II Of The Story	20	Bronze
	Part III Complete	Complete Part III Of The Story	20	Bronze
	A New York Minute	Finish In A New York Minute	60	Gold
	The Shadows Rushed Me	Unlock And Complete New York Minute Hardcore	50	Silver
	Out The Window	Get 6 Kills While Diving Through The VIP Window [FREE AIM]	10	Bronze
	The One Eyed Man Is King	Cover Passos With Perfect Aim	10	Bronze
	Something Wicked This Way Comes	Get 7 Kills While Jumping From The Rickety Boat [FREE AIM]	10	Bronze
	That Old Familiar Feeling	Clear The Hallway Of Lasers	10	Bronze
	Amidst The Wreckage	Destroy All The Models In The Boardroom	5	Bronze
	So Much For Being Subtle	Get 9 Kills While Being Pulled By A Chain [FREE AIM]	10	Bronze
	The Only Choice Given	Get 8 Kills While Dangling From A Chain [FREE AIM]	10	Bronze
	Trouble Had Come To Me	Clear Everyone On The Bus Ride	15	Bronze

DISPLAY NAME	DESCRIPTION	XBOX VALUE	PS3 VALUE
Along For The Ride	Trigger A Bullet Cam On The Zipline [FREE AIM]	10	Bronze
Sometimes You Get Lucky	Get A Headshot During The Rooftop Tremors	5	Bronze
It Was Chaos And Luck	Get 6 Kills While Riding The Push Cart [FREE AIM]	10	Bronze
The Road-Kill Behind Me	Total Everything On The Runway	10	Bronze
You Push A Man Too Far (Secret Achievement)	Don't Shoot The Dis-Armed Man	5	Bronze
The Fear Of Losing It	Survive A Level Without Painkillers	20	Bronze
It's Fear That Gives Men Wings	10 Bullet Time Kills In A Row	20	Bronze
You Might Hurt Someone With That	Shoot 10 Airborne Grenades	20	Bronze
One Bullet At A Time	100 Headshots	20	Bronze
You Play, You Pay, You Bastard	100 Kills With Melee	20	Bronze
With Practiced Bravado	100 Kills During ShootDodge	20	Bronze
Colder Than The Devil's Heart	Kill 30 Enemies In 2 Minutes	15	Bronze
A Few Hundred Bullets Back	Use Every Weapon In The Game	20	Bronze
Past The Point Of No Return	Take 100 Painkillers	10	Bronze
An Echo Of The Past	Find All Exploration Items	35	Bronze
You Sure Know How To Pick A Place	Discover All Tourist Locations (Anders & Dave Clue locations)	10	Bronze
A License To Kill	Collect All Golden Guns	40	Silver
All Of The Above	Finish All Grinds	100	Gold

SINGLE PLAYER GRINDS

The Grinds menu, where you can see each Grind possible and what level has been reached with each Grind, can be found on the Story menu. The Story menu is accessed from the Main menu.

GOLDEN GUN GRINDS

One Grind is available for each weapon in the game, and it is awarded when you collect all three Golden Gun Parts for one weapon. Instead of listing each weapon here, we have lumped them all into one category (the first entry in the list). For help finding all the Golden Gun Parts, see the Collectibles section in this guide.

NAME	DETAILS	BRONZE	SILVER	GOLD	PLATINUM
GOLDEN GUNS	Collect all 3 Gold Gun Parts for every weapon	N/A	N/A	N/A	N/A
Bloodbath	Kill 1000 enemies	200	500	1000	2500
Head Master	Get 500 headshots	100	250	500	1000
Arms Dealer	Shoot 100 enemies in the arm or hand	25	50	100	250
Leg Payne	Shoot 100 enemies in the leg or foot	25	50	100	250
Below The Belt	Shoot 100 enemies in the groin	25	50	100	250
Dodge Brawl	Kill 500 enemies during ShootDodge	100	250	500	1000
Artful Dodger	ShootDodge for 20 minutes total	5	10	20	50
Take Your Time	Kill 500 enemies during Bullet Time	100	250	500	1000
Bullet River	Shoot 10,000 rounds	1000	2500	10,000	25,000
Take A Load Off	Shoot 100 enemies while prone	25	50	100	250
Slow Dive	Perform an 8 second ShootDodge	5	6	7	8

	NAME	DETAILS	BRONZE	SILVER	GOLD	PLATINUM
	Cam Lover	Watch 100 bullet cams	25	50	100	200
	Wreckage	Blow up 100 vehicles	25	50	100	200
	Double Damage	Kill 750 enemies while dual wielding	150	300	750	1500
	Blow Out	Kill 100 enemies with explosions	25	50	100	250
	Guesswork	Kill 100 enemies with blind fire	25	50	100	250
	The Turtle	Kill 500 enemies from cover	100	250	500	1500
	Back From The Dead	Win 100 Last Man Standings	25	50	100	250
	Fire Works	Shoot 100 explosives out of the air	25	50	100	250
	Scrapper	Melee 100 enemies	25	50	100	250
	Pharmacist	Use 500 painkillers	50	100	500	1000
	Fall Guys	Cause 100 enemies to topple over railings	25	50	100	250
	Keep it Simple	Kill 100 enemies with hand guns	100	250	500	1000
	Shotgun Dues	Kill 100 enemies with shotguns	100	250	500	1000
	Rapid Fire	Kill 100 enemies with sub-machine guns	100	250	500	1000
	If it Ain't Broke	Kill 100 enemies with rifles	100	250	500	1000
	Eagle Eye	Kill 100 enemies with sniper rifles	100	250	500	1000
	The Lounger	Kill 100 enemies while lying on your back	100	250	500	1000

MULTIPLAYER UNLOCKABLES

MULTIPLAYER ACHIEVEMENTS & TROPHIES

	NAME	DESCRIPTION	XBOX VALUE	PS3 VALUE
	Full Monty	Complete One Of Each Game Mode Including All Gang Wars	10	Bronze
	Payne Bringer	Kill 100 Other Players	30	Silver
	Max Payne Invitational	You Invited Someone To Play	5	Bronze
	Man Of Many Weapons	Unlock All Weapons	25	Bronze
	Man Of Many Faces	Unlock All Faction Characters	25	Bronze
	Deathmatch Challenge	Winner In Any Public Deathmatch	20	Bronze
	Grave Robber	Looted A Body	5	Bronze
	The Gambler	Won A Wager	15	Bronze
	Sweep	Flawless Team Gang Wars Victory	10	Bronze
	Training Complete	Achieve Level Rank 50	25	Silver
	Dearest Of All My Friends	Kill Someone On Your Friends List	10	Bronze

MULTIPLAYER GRINDS

Grinds are multiplayer challenges that earn you extra XP and cash when completed. Grinds are automatically tracked, and you can view your progress, completed grinds, and awards through the Grinds menu.

This first list, Training Grinds, illustrates game modes and features that are unlocked in multiplayer mode by completing Grinds. To unlock Payne Killer and Gang Wars, for example, you must make 100 Multiplayer kills.

TRAINING GRINDS

GRIND	TASK	AWARD
Standard playlists Unlock	100 Enemy Kills	XP: 200 / unlocks standard playlists: Large DM, Large Team DM, Large Gang Wars, and Payne Killer.
Advanced playlists Unlock	500 Enemy Kills	XP: 200 / unlocks advanced playlists: Small Last Man Standing games
Hardcore playlists Unlock	5000 Enemy Kills	XP: 200 / unlocks hardcore playlists: Hardcore DM, Hardcore Team DM, and Hardcore Gang Wars.
Freak Out	Activate a Burst	XP: 250
Get Your Hands Dirty	Get a Melee Kill	XP: 250
First Of Many	Get 3 Headshots	XP: 250
To The Victor The Spoils	Loot a Body	XP: 250
Flexible Killer	Kill with the 4 preset loadouts	XP: 250
Raise The Stakes	Earn $2000	Unlocks: Wagers

WEAPON GRINDS

GRIND	TASK	AWARD
Good Arm	5 Frag Grenade Multikills	XP: 200
Fire in the Hole	50 Frag Grenade Kills	XP: 200
Tools of the Trade	25 Kills with .38 Revolver	XP: 200
Dead Reckoning	10 Headshots with .38 Revolver	XP: 100
Tools of the Trade	50 Kills with 1911	XP: 200
Dead Reckoning	10 Headshots with 1911	XP: 100
Tools of the Trade	50 Kills with DE .50	XP: 200
Dead Reckoning	10 Headshots with DE .50	XP: 100
Tools of the Trade	50 Kills with PT921	XP: 200
Dead Reckoning	10 Headshots with PT921	XP: 100
Tools of the Trade	50 Kills with 608 Bull	XP: 200
Dead Reckoning	10 Headshots with 608 Bull	XP: 100
Tools of the Trade	50 Kills with MD-97L	XP: 200
Dead Reckoning	10 Headshots with MD-97L	XP: 100
Tools of the Trade	50 Kills with AK-47	XP: 200
Dead Reckoning	10 Headshots with AK-47	XP: 100
Tools of the Trade	50 Kills with FAL	XP: 200
Dead Reckoning	10 Headshots with FAL	XP: 100
Tools of the Trade	50 Kills with G6 Commando	XP: 200
Dead Reckoning	10 Headshots with G6 Commando	XP: 100
Tools of the Trade	50 Kills with Mini-30	XP: 200
Dead Reckoning	10 Headshots with Mini-30	XP: 100

GRIND	TASK	AWARD
Tools of the Trade	50 Kills with RPG	XP: 200
Dead Reckoning	10 Headshots with RPG	XP: 100
Tools of the Trade	50 Kills with Rotary Grenade Launcher	XP: 200
Dead Reckoning	10 Headshots with Rotary Grenade Launcher	XP: 100
Tools of the Trade	50 Kills with M4 Super 90	XP: 200
Dead Reckoning	10 Headshots with M4 Super 90	XP: 100
Tools of the Trade	50 Kills with Sawn Off	XP: 200
Dead Reckoning	10 Headshots with Sawn Off	XP: 100
Tools of the Trade	50 Kills with M500	XP: 200
Dead Reckoning	10 Headshots with M500	XP: 100
Tools of the Trade	50 Kills with SPAS-15	XP: 200
Dead Reckoning	10 Headshots with SPAS-15	XP: 100
Tools of the Trade	50 Kills with Super Sport	XP: 200
Dead Reckoning	10 Headshots with Super Sport	XP: 100
Tools of the Trade	50 Kills with LMG .30 cal	XP: 200
Dead Reckoning	10 Headshots with LMG .30 cal	XP: 100
Tools of the Trade	50 Kills with RPD	XP: 200
Dead Reckoning	10 Headshots with RPD	XP: 100
Tools of the Trade	50 Kills with SAF .40 cal	XP: 200
Dead Reckoning	10 Headshots with SAF .40 cal	XP: 100
Tools of the Trade	50 Kills with M10	XP: 200

GRIND	TASK	AWARD
Dead Reckoning	10 Headshots with M10	XP: 200
Tools of the Trade	50 Kills with MPK	XP: 100
Dead Reckoning	10 Headshots with MPK	XP: 200
Tools of the Trade	50 Kills with M972	XP: 100
Dead Reckoning	10 Headshots with M972	XP: 200
Tools of the Trade	50 Kills with Micro 9MM	XP: 100
Dead Reckoning	10 Headshots with Micro 9MM	XP: 200
Tools of the Trade	50 Kills with AUTO 9MM	XP: 200
Dead Reckoning	10 Headshots with AUTO 9MM	XP: 100

GRIND	TASK	AWARD
Tools of the Trade	50 Kills with M82A1	XP: 200
Dead Reckoning	10 Headshots with M82A1	XP: 100
Tools of the Trade	50 Kills with FMP G3S	XP: 200
Dead Reckoning	10 Headshots with FMP G3S	XP: 100
Live And Let Diode	50 Laser Sight Kills	XP: 200
On The QT	50 Suppressor Kills	XP: 200
Total Recoil	50 Compensator Kills	XP: 200
In The Spotlight	50 Flashlight Kills	XP: 200
One More Round	50 Extended Mag Kills	XP: 200

ACTION GRINDS

GRIND	TASK	AWARD
Rise From Your Grave	5 Health Recovers Without Dying	XP: 50
The Longest Yard	5 ShootDodges Over 10 Meters	XP: 150
Safety Deposit	5000 Cash Earned	XP: 250
Ill Gotten Gains	5000 Cash From Looting	XP: 100
Gun Runner	Sprinted for 26 Miles	XP: 1000
Vulture Culture	25 Lootings Done	XP: 250

GRIND	TASK	AWARD
Pain Relief	10 Painkillers From Looting	XP: 150
Welcome to the Real World	10 ShootDodges	XP: 150
High Roller	25 Rolls	XP: 150
Habit Forming	10 Painkillers Used	XP: 150

ITEM GRINDS

GRIND	TASK	AWARD
Meta Vendetta	25 Tracking Device Vendetta Kills	XP: 100
Marathon Man	Travel 26 Miles With Sneakers	XP: 1000
Tagging The Turf	10 Spray Can Turf Captures	XP: 50
Pouching Tiger	25 Ammo Pouch Last Stand Kills	XP: 50
Shot In The Arms	10 Autoinjector Kills In Enemy Burst Bubble	XP: 50
Balaclava Backlash	10 Balaclava Kills From Behind	XP: 50
Sticky Bomb	25 Sticky Tape Grenade Kills	XP: 50
Satisfaction Guaranteed	25 Manufacturers Guarantee Kills In Enemy Double Dealer	XP: 50
Best Of The Vest	10 Light Body Armor Kills	XP: 50

GRIND	TASK	AWARD
Tough Nut	25 Medium Body Armor Kills	XP: 50
Heavy Hitter	25 Heavy Body Armor Kills	XP: 50
Camo Killer	25 Urban Camo Kills	XP: 50
Eavesdropper	25 Listening Device Kills	XP: 50
Static Attack	25 Walkie-Talkie Kills	XP: 50
Empty Threat	25 Hollow Point Kills	XP: 50
Diplomatic Immunity	25 ID Card Kills	XP: 50
Busted	25 Most Valuable Player Kills With Bounty Orders	XP: 50
Multitool Multitude	25 Enhanced Operations	XP: 50

BURST GRINDS

GRIND	TASK	AWARD
Adrenaline Junkie	500 Adrenaline Earned	XP: 50
Back In The Game	25 Last Stand Recovers	XP: 100
Pound Of Flesh	1000 Big Dog Health Added	XP: 50
Slow Cooked	5 Bullet Times Used	XP: 25
Slo-Mo Killer	10 Kills In Bullet Time	XP: 50
Back From The Brink	10 Kills In Last Stand	XP: 50
Blue On Blue	5 Sneaky Used	XP: 25
Covert Killer	10 Kills In Sneaky	XP: 50
Tooled Up	5 Trigger Happy Used	XP: 25
Big Bang	10 Kills In Trigger Happy	XP: 50
Trust No-One	5 Paranoia Used	XP: 25
Red Dead	10 Kills In Paranoia	XP: 50

GRIND	TASK	AWARD
Healthy Bonus	25 Big Dog Used	XP: 100
Voyeuristic Intention	5 Intuition Used	XP: 25
Veiled Threat	5 Grounded Used	XP: 25
Take Me To Your Dealer	5 Weapon Dealer Used	XP: 25
Death Dealer	10 Kills Using Weapon Dealer	XP: 50
Big Hearted	5 Fresh Blood Used	XP: 25
Even The Field	5 Double Dealer Used	XP: 25
Double Death Dealer	10 Kills Using Double Dealer	XP: 50
Adrenaline Drain	5 Burst Bubble Used	XP: 25
1 Small Beginnings	5 Level 1 Bursts Triggered	XP: 25
2 Building It Up	5 Level 2 Bursts Triggered	XP: 25
3 As Good As It Gets	5 level 3 Bursts Triggered	XP: 25

MODE GRINDS

GRIND	TASK	AWARD
Full House	All Game Modes Played	XP: 1000
Mover And Shaker	All Gang Wars Game Modes Played	XP: 1000
Leader Of The Pack	All Gang Wars Game Modes Won	XP: 1000
On The Podium	10 Deathmatch Games Won Top 3	XP: 100
Lucky Day	5 Deathmatch Games Won Without Dying	XP: 50
Playing It Safe	5 Team Deathmatch Games Won Without Dying	XP: 50
Best Of The Best	5 TDM Wins Top Player	XP: 50
Bring The Payne	10 Kills As Max or Passos	XP: 50
All Aboard The Payne Train	5 PK Games Dominated by Max or Passos	XP: 100
Top Notch	5 Deathmatch Games Won	XP: 100
Team Player	5 Team Deathmatch Games Won	XP: 100

GRIND	TASK	AWARD
Taking The Turf	10 Turfs Captured	XP: 100
Storm The Castle	10 Siege Checkpoints Captured	XP: 250
Checkpoint Charlie	10 Transit Checkpoints Captured	XP: 100
Take The Payne	5 Payne Killer Games Won	XP: 100
A Lifetime Of Payne	One Hour As Max or Passos in Payne Killer	XP: 1000
Blown Away	25 Bombs Planted	XP: 250
Cut The Wire	25 Bombs Diffused	XP: 250
Total Pro	10 Assassinations Targets Killed	XP: 100
The Bodyguard	25 Assassinations Targets Defended	XP: 250
Max Tax	25 Max Or Passos' Looted	XP: 50
A Payne In The Passos	5 Max or Passos Kills	XP: 50

KILL GRINDS

GRIND	TASK	AWARD
Butcher	25 Kill Streak	XP: 150
Master Butcher	25 Kill Streak	XP: 150
King Butcher	25 Kill Streak	XP: 150
All Rounder	1 Kill With Each Weapon	XP: 1000
Party Pooper	50 Bursts Denied	XP: 250
Killing Machine	100 Enemy Kills	XP: 50

GRIND	TASK	AWARD
Bullet In The Head	25 Headshot Kills	XP: 100
Low Rider	50 Crouching Kills	XP: 50
Shooting Up	50 Kills While Prone	XP: 50
Airborne Killer	50 Shoot Dodging Kills	XP: 50
Fast and Loose	50 Kills While Free Aiming	XP: 50
In The Crosshairs	50 Kills While Aiming Down Sights	XP: 50

GRIND	TASK	AWARD
Hide And Seek	50 Kills While In Cover	XP: 50
Slo Mo Mo Fo	50 Shoot Dodgers Killed	XP: 50
Team Effort	500 Assists	XP: 100
Retaliation Across The Nation	50 Vendettas Won	XP: 250
Best friends Forever	50 Teammates Saved (health recovery)	XP: 250
Knockout Blow	25 Melee Kills	XP: 50

GRIND	TASK	AWARD
Blindsided	25 Melee Kills In Back	XP: 50
No Place To Hide	50 Kills While Victim Crouching	XP: 50
Spot On	1000 Kills While Victim Aiming Down Sights	XP: 50
Dishonorable Discharge	100 Kills From Behind	XP: 50
Best Served Cold	50 Nemesis Kills	XP: 250
They Never Learn	50 Vendettas Defended	XP: 250

HARDCORE GRINDS

GRIND	TASK	AWARD
Legal High	5 Painkillers Used Without Dying	XP: 1000
Hardcore Butcher	25 Kill Steak	XP: 1000
Salt Of The Earth	10 Games Finished Without A Teamkill	XP: 150
A Butcher Among Butchers	25 Kill Streak Without A Teamkill	XP: 1000

GRIND	TASK	AWARD
Annihilation Machine	100 Enemy Kills	XP: 50
Hard Boiled	5 Games Won	XP: 100
Old Habits Die Hard	5 Painkillers Used	XP: 100
Bring To The Block	10 Headshot	XP: 150

MULTIPLAYER AWARDS

MULTIPLAYER XP AWARDS

GENERAL XP AWARDS	XP AMOUNT
Kill (all kill awards are added to this)	25
Headshot	25
Assist	5-25
Teammate Save	15
Gang Member Save	25
Nemesis	10
Upstart	10
Sudden Death Kill	10
Corpse Loot	5
Trickshot: Falling Kill	15
Trickshot: Melee Kill	10
Trickshot: ShootDodge Kill	10
Trickshot: Lucky Bullet	5
Trickshot: Death from Above	15
Kill When Dead	10
Vendetta Win	20
Vendetta Survived	10
First Kill in Round	20
Win the Round	10
Burst Performed Level 1	10
Burst Performed Level 2	20
Burst Performed Level 3	30
Streak Denied	10 (per level of streak denied)
Feud Kill (Crew Feud)	10
Feud Won (Crew Feud)	20
Team Balanced	20
Team Revenge (Gang)	20
Team Revenge	10
Reviving a Teammate	20
Reviving a Gang Member	25

DEATHMATCH	XP AMOUNT
First Place	60
Second Place	45
Third Place	30
Fourth Place	20
Other Places	10

PAYNE KILLER	XP AMOUNT
First Place	300
Second Place	250
Third Place	200
Fourth Place	175
Other Places	150
Deathmatch Payne Killer: Shooting Combo on Max or Passos	1 (scales by damage)

DEATHMATCH LAST MAN STANDING	XP AMOUNT
First Place	100
Second Place	80
Third Place	70
Fourth Place	60
Other Places	50

TEAM DEATHMATCH	XP AMOUNT
First Place	30
Second Place	20
Third Place	10
Other Places	5

GANG WARS	XP AMOUNT
Takedown: Kill as Target	20
Takedown: Kill Target	30
Takedown: Kill Near Target (Gang)	10
Takedown: Kill Near Target	10
Short Fuse: Planted a Bomb that Detonated	30
Short Fuse: Defused a Bomb	20
Short Fuse: Defused Just in Time	10
Short Fuse: Plant a Bomb	10
Short Fuse: Kill Planter	10
Short Fuse: Kill Diffuser	10
Delivery: Intercepted an Enemy Item	10
Delivery: Delivered Item	20
Delivery: Item Pickup	10
Delivery: First Item Pickup	10
Delivery: Kill Carrier	10
Delivery: Kill Near Carrier	5
Delivery: Kill Near Carrier (Gang)	20
Delivery: Kill as Carrier	20
Grab: Delivered Item	20

GANG WARS	XP AMOUNT
Grab: Item Pickup	10
Grab: Kill Enemy Carrier	10
Grab: Kill Near Carrier (Gang)	20
Grab: Kill Near Carrier	5
Grab: Kill as Carrier	20
Siege: Be the Last Survivor	25
Siege: Capture a Territory	20
Siege: Kill the Last Survivor	20
Last Stand: Victor	20
Last Stand: Winning Kill	20
Last Stand: Kill While Last Man	20
Last Stand: Last Man on Team	10
Team DM: Sudden Death Winning Kill	20
Team DM: Last Kill for Winners	20
Total Turf/Turf Grab: First into Turf	10
Total Turf/Turf Grab: Captured Turf	20
Total Turf/Turf Grab: Defended Turf	10
Transit: Captured Point	20

MULTIPLAYER CASH AWARDS

GENERAL REWARDS	CASH AMOUNT	MODIFIERS
Wagers	150-500	Item: Badge of Honor (+25%)
Looting: Regular Cash	10/25/50/75	Item: Badge of Honor (+25%)
Looting: Extra Cash	200/250/300	Item: Badge of Honor (+25%)
Paranoia: Killed Target	50	Item: Badge of Honor (+25%)
Item Bounty Orders: Kill Target	5 (on all kills)	Item: Badge of Honor (+25%)
Kill Streak: 3 Kills	25	Item: Badge of Honor (+25%) (Not available in Deathmatch Payne Killer)
Kill Streak: 5 Kills	50	Item: Badge of Honor (+25%) (Not available in Deathmatch Payne Killer)
Kill Streak: 10 Kills	100	Item: Badge of Honor (+25%) (Not available in Deathmatch Payne Killer)
Kill Streak: 20 Kills	200	Item: Badge of Honor (+25%) (Not available in Deathmatch Payne Killer)
Kill Streak: 50 Kills	10000	Item: Badge of Honor (+25%) (Not available in Deathmatch Payne Killer)

DEATHMATCH	AMOUNT	MODIFIERS
Payne Killer: Loot Max or Passos' Corpse	250	Item: Badge of Honor (+25%)
GANG WARS MODE SPECIFIC	AMOUNT	MODIFIERS
Short Fuse: Bomb Defused	75	Item: Badge of Honor (+25%)
Short Fuse: Bomb Planted	75	Item: Badge of Honor (+25%)
Takedown: Target Survived	200	Item: Badge of Honor (+25%)
Takedown: Killed Target	200	Item: Badge of Honor (+25%)
Grab: Item Delivered	25	Item: Badge of Honor (+25%)
Grab: Item Picked Up	25	
Delivery: Drop Off Used	20	Item: Badge of Honor (+25%)
Delivery: Intercepted Enemy Item	10	Item: Badge of Honor (+25%)
Delivery: Picked Up Item	10	
Team Deathmatch: Winning Team	75	Item: Badge of Honor (+25%)
Team Last Man Standing: Surviving Players on Winning Team	150	Item: Badge of Honor (+25%)

MULTIPLAYER ADRENALINE AWARDS

GENERAL ADRENALINE AWARDS	AMOUNT
Hit an enemy	0.80%
Assist	11.20%
Kill	22.40%
Level 1 Streak Denied	11.11%
Level 2 Streak Denied	22.22%
Level 3 Streak Denied	33.33%
Loot a small amount of adrenaline	33.33%
Loot a large amount of adrenaline	100.00%
Win a vendetta	20.00%
Survive a vendetta	10.00%
DEATHMATCH MODE SPECIFIC	AMOUNT

GENERAL ADRENALINE AWARDS	AMOUNT
DM Payne Killer: Become Max or Passos	100%
GANG WARS MODE SPECIFIC	AMOUNT
Takedown: Kill Target	10%
Takedown: survive as assassin	10%
Short Fuse: Defuse	20%
Short Fuse: Plant	20%
Delivery: Drop Off	10%
Grab: Drop Off	10%
Total Turf / Turf Grab: Captured Territory	10%
Transit: Captured "Territory"	10%

MULTIPLAYER RANK UNLOCKABLES

This list illustrates everything that is unlocked in multiplayer as you increase your Rank. There are 50 levels of Rank to achieve. Increasing Rank unlocks Cash, Titles, Weapons, Items, Bursts, Loadout slots, weight-carrying bonuses, and Outfits.

RANK	XP REQ	CASH	TITLE	WEAPONS	ITEMS	BURSTS & LEVELS	LOADOUT	GAME FEATURES	AVATAR UNLOCKS
1	0	—	Soldado	PT92	Light Body Armor	Big Dog	Weight 12	Avatar customization	Comando Sombra faction + outfit 1
—	—	—	—	M500	—	Intuition 1	—	—	—
—	—	—	—	.38 Revolver	—	Trigger Happy	—	—	—
—	—	—	—	M10	—	—	—	—	—
—	—	—	—	MPK	—	—	—	—	—
2	1000	200	—	Flashbang	—	Big Dog 2	Weight +1	—	De Marcos faction + outfit 1
—	—	—	—	—	—	Intuition 2	—	—	—
—	—	—	—	—	—	Trigger Happy 2	—	—	—
3	2300	300	—	—	—	Big Dog 3	—	—	UFE faction + outfit 1
—	—	—	—	—	—	Intuition 3	—	—	
—	—	—	—	—	—	Trigger Happy 3	—	—	—
4	3700	400	Cabo	1911	Ammunition Pouch	—	Slots-3	—	—
—	—	—	—	SAF .40	Manufacturer's Guarantee	—	—	—	—
—	—	—	—	M972	Walkie Talkie	—	—	—	—
—	—	—	—	FAL	Field Bandages	—	—	—	—
—	—	—	—	AK-47	Sneakers	—	—	—	—
—	—	—	—	Mini-30	Sutures	—	—	—	—
—	—	—	—	M4 Super 90	ID card	—	—	—	—
—	—	—	—	RPD	Helmet	—	—	—	—
—	—	—	—	Tin Can	Balaclava	—	—	—	—
—	—	—	—	Grenade	Lockbox	—	—	—	—

RANK	XP REQ	CASH	TITLE	WEAPONS	ITEMS	BURSTS & LEVELS	LOADOUT	GAME FEATURES	AVATAR UNLOCKS
—	—	—	—	—	Bounty Orders	—	—	—	—
—	—	—	—	—	Gas Mask	—	—	—	—
—	—	—	—	—	Military goggles	—	—	—	—
—	—	—	—	—	Medical Supplies	—	—	—	—
—	—	—	—	—	Urban Camo	—	—	—	—
—	—	—	—	—	Autoinjector	—	—	—	—
5	5500	500	—	—	—	—	Weight +1	—	Tropa Z faction + outfit 1
6	9700	600	—	—	—	Bullet Time	—	—	Punchinellos faction + outfit 1
7	14400	700	3º Sargento	—	—	Paranoia	—	—	Cracha Preto faction + outfit 1
8	19700	800	—	—	—	Sneaky	—	—	Comando Sombra Lookout outfit
9	25500	900	—	—	—	Paranoia 2	—	—	De Marco Night Out outfit
10	31800	1500	2º Sargento	—	—	—	—	—	Tropa Z Football outfit
11	38600	1600	—	—	—	Bullet Time 2	—	—	UFE Combat Support outfit
12	45800	1700	—	—	—	—	Weight +1	—	Punchinello Associate outfit
13	53500	1800	1º Sargento	—	—	Paranoia 3	—	—	Cracha Preto ex-military outfit
14	61700	1900	—	—	—	Grounded	—	—	—
15	70300	2000	—	—	—	—	—	—	Comando Sombra Dealer outfit
16	79400	2100	Sub-Tenente	—	—	Intuition 2	New loadout allowed	—	—
17	88900	2200	—	—	—	—	—	—	De Marco Biker outfit
18	98800	2300	—	—	—	Bullet Time 3	—	—	—
19	109100	2400	Cadete	—	—	—	Weight +1	—	Tropa Z DJ Outfit
—	—	—	—	—	—	Grounded 2	—	—	—
20	119900	3000	—	608 Bull	Vampire Fangs	—	—	—	—
—	—	—	—	SPAS-15	Multi-Tool	—	—	—	—
—	—	—	—	FMP G3S	Spray Can	—	—	—	—
—	—	—	—	MD-97L	Tracking Device	—	—	—	—
—	—	—	—	AUTO 9MM	Smart Phone	—	—	—	—
—	—	—	—	RPG	Booby trap	—	—	—	—
—	—	—	—	Smoke Grenade		—	—	—	—
—	—	—	—	Tear Gas Grenade	Quick Holster	—	—	—	—
—	—	—	—	—	Med Body Armor	—	—	—	—

RANK	XP REQ	CASH	TITLE	WEAPONS	ITEMS	BURSTS & LEVELS	LOADOUT	GAME FEATURES	AVATAR UNLOCKS
21	131100	3100	—	—	—	—	—	—	UFE Urban Combat outfit
22	142700	3200	Aspirante	—	—	Sneaky	—	—	—
23	154700	3300	—	—	—	—	—	—	Punchinello Consigliere outfit
—	—	—	—	—	—	Intuition 3	—	—	—
24	167100	3400	—	—	—	—	Weight +1	—	—
25	179900	3500	—	—	—	—	Loadout slot + 1	—	Cracha Preto Moonlighting Detectivce outfit
—	—	—	—	—	—	Sneaky 2	—	—	—
26	193100	3600	3º Tenente	—	—	—	—	—	—
27	206600	3700	—	—	—	Fresh Blood	—	—	Comando Sombra Favela General outfit
28	220500	3800	—	—	—	—	—	—	—
29	234800	3900	—	—	—	Grounded 3	—	—	De Marco Mob Meet outfit
30	249500	4500	2º Tenente	—	—	Fresh Blood 2	Weight +1	—	—
31	264500	4600	—	—	—	—	—	—	UFE Special Operations outfit
32	279900	4700	—	—	—	Weapon Dealer	—	—	—
33	295700	4800	—	—	—	—	—	—	Punchinello Capo outfit
34	311800	4900	—	—	—	Sneaky 3	Loadout slot + 1	—	—
35	328300	5000	1º Tenente	—	—	Fresh Blood 3	Weight +1	—	Tropa Z Coolest Kid in the Favela outfit
36	345200	5100	—	—	—	—	—	—	—
37	362400	5200	—	—	—	Burst Bubble	—	—	Cracha Preto Union Rep
38	380000	5300	—	—	—	—	—	—	—
39	397900	5400	—	—	—	Weapon Dealer 2	—	—	—
—	—	—	—	—	—	—	Weight +1	—	—
40	416200	6000	Capitão	Super Sport	Heavy Body Armor	—	—	—	—
—	—	—	—	MICRO 9MM	Sticky tape	—	—	—	—
—	—	—	—	DE .50	Brass Knuckles	—	—	—	—
—	—	—	—	G6 Commando	Hollowpoint Rounds	—	—	—	—
—	—	—	—	Grenade Launcher	Pacemaker	—	—	—	—
—	—	—	—	LMG	Pocket Watch	—	—	—	—
—	—	—	—	M82A1	Gorilla mask	—	—	—	—
—	—	—	—	Sawn Off	—	—	—	—	—
41	434800	6100	—	—	—	Burst Bubble 2	—	—	Comando Sombra Leader

RANK	XP REQ	CASH	TITLE	WEAPONS	ITEMS	BURSTS & LEVELS	LOADOUT	GAME FEATURES	AVATAR UNLOCKS
42	453800	6200	—	—	—	Weapon Double Dealer	—	—	Tropa Z Leader
43	473100	6300	—	—	—	Weapon Dealer 3	—	—	UFE Leader
44	492700	6400	—	—	—	—	Weight +1	—	—
45	512700	6500	Major	—	—	Weapon Double Dealer 2	—	—	Cracha Preto Leader
46	533000	6600	—	—	—	Burst Bubble 3	—	—	DM Leader
47	553600	6700	—	—	—	—	New loadout allowed	—	—
48	574600	6800	—	—	—	Weapon Double Dealer 3	—	—	Punch Leader
49	595900	6900	—	—	—	—	Weight +1	—	—
50	619500	7000	Coronel	—	Badge of Honor	—	—	DM Max	Max Heads
—	—	—	—	—	—	—	—	UFE Max	—
—	—	—	—	—	—	—	—	Tropa Z Max	—
—	—	—	—	—	—	—	—	Comando Sombra Max	—
—	—	—	—	—	—	—	—	Cracha Preto Max	—
—	—	—	—	—	—	—	—	Punch Max	—

MULTIPLAYER WEAPON LEVELS & ATTACHEMENTS

Racking up kills and completing Grinds levels up your equipped weapon and unlocks new features for that weapon and its attachments.

WEAPON	LEVEL 2	LEVEL 3	LEVEL 4	LEVEL 5	LEVEL 6	LEVEL 7	LEVEL 8	LEVEL 9	LEVEL 10
.38 Revolver	Compensator	Dual Wield	Gas Block	$500	$600	Barrel Urpgrade	$800	$900	$1000
PT92	Laser Sight	Suppressor	Extended Mag	Compensator	Dual Wield	Gas Block	Gas System Kit	Mag Guide	$1000
1911	Laser Sight	Suppressor	Extended Mag	Dual Wield	Compensator	Gas Block	Gas System Kit	Mag Guide	$1000
DE .50	Red Dot	$300	Gas System Kit	$500	Mag Guide	$700	Gas Block	Dual Wield	$1000
Auto 9mm	Laser Sight	Gas Block	Extended Mag	Gas System Kit	Dual Wield	Barrel Urpgrade	$800	Mag Guide	$1000
608 Bull	Laser Sight	$300	Compensator	$500	$600	$700	Dual Wield	$900	$1000
M10	Laser Sight	Compensator	Suppressor	Extended Mag	Dual Wield	Gas Block	Barrel Urpgrade	Gas System Kit	$1000
MPK	Laser Sight	Gas Block	Extended Mag	Mag Guide	Gas System Kit	Suppressor	Barrel Urpgrade	$900	$1000
M972	$200	Extended Mag	$400	Barrel Urpgrade	Dual Wield	Gas Block	Gas System Kit	Mag Guide	$1000
Micro 9mm	Compensator	Extended Mag	Laser Sight	Suppressor	Gas Block	Gas System Kit	Mag Guide	Dual Wield	$1000
M500	Laser Sight	Red Dot	Gas Block	Gas System Kit	Barrel Urpgrade	$700	$800	$900	$1000
M4 Super 90	Laser Sight	Barrel Urpgrade	Gas Block	Gas System Kit	$600	$700	$800	$900	$1000
Super Sport	Laser Sight	Gas System Kit	Barrel Urpgrade	Red Dot	Gas Block	$700	$800	$900	$1000
Sawn Off	$200	$300	$400	Dual Wield	$600	$700	$800	$900	$1000
SPAS-15	Laser Sight	Gas System Kit	Red Dot	Gas Block	$600	Barrel Urpgrade	$800	$900	$1000
AK-47	Laser Sight	Suppressor	Barrel Urpgrade	Extended Mag	Gas Block	Gas System Kit	Mag Guide	$900	$1000
MD-97L	Laser Sight	Compensator	Extended Mag	Red Dot	Barrel Urpgrade	Gas Block	Gas System Kit	Mag Guide	$1000

WEAPON	LEVEL 2	LEVEL 3	LEVEL 4	LEVEL 5	LEVEL 6	LEVEL 7	LEVEL 8	LEVEL 9	LEVEL 10
FAL	Laser Sight	Compensator	Extended Mag	Red Dot	Barrel Uprgade	Gas Block	Gas System Kit	Mag Guide	$1000
G6 Commando	Laser Sight	Compensator	Gas Block	Barrel Uprgade	Gas System Kit	Mag Guide	$800	$900	$1000
SAF .40	Laser Sight	Gas System Kit	Suppressor	Gas Block	Compensator	Barrel Uprgade	Mag Guide	$900	$1000
Mini-30	Suppressor	Extended Mag	Compensator	Scope	Gas Block	Gas System Kit	Mag Guide	Barrel Uprgade	$1000
M82A1	Compensator	Extended Mag	Gas Block	Gas System Kit	Mag Guide	Barrel Uprgade	$800	$900	$1000
FMP G3S	Extended Mag	Gas Block	Gas System Kit	Mag Guide	Barrel Uprgade	$700	$800	$900	$1000
LMG .30	Gas System Kit	$300	Gas Block	$500	Barrel Uprgade	$700	Mag Guide	$900	$1000
RPD	Gas Block	$300	Gas System Kit	$500	Barrel Uprgade	$700	Mag Guide	$900	$1000
RPG	$200	$300	$400	$500	$600	$700	$800	$900	$1000
Grenade Launcher	$200	$300	$400	$500	$600	$700	$800	$900	$1000
LAW	$200	$300	$400	$500	$600	$700	$800	$900	$1000

ARCADE MODE UNLOCKABLES

MULTIPLAYER AVATAR UNLOCKS

These are awarded if the player gets Platinum in any of the Arcade Modes.

CHARACTER	NOTES
Comando Sombra	Open from start.
De Marcos	Unlocked at Rank 2.
UFE	Unlocked at Rank 3.
Tropa Z	Unlocked at Rank 5.
Punchinellos	Unlocked at Rank 6.
Crachá Preto	Unlocked at Rank 7.
Tropical Max	Unlocked at Legend level 1.
Bodyguard Max	Unlocked at Legend level 2.
Smart Casual Max	Unlocked at Legend level 3.
Bad Day Max	Unlocked at Legend level 4.
Down To Business Max	Unlocked at Legend level 5.
Victor	Unlocked by attaining platinum ranking in Chapter I score attack and New York Minute.
Fabiana	Unlocked by attaining platinum ranking in Chapter II score attack and New York Minute.
Claudio	Unlocked by attaining platinum ranking in Chapter III score attack and New York Minute.
Rudy	Unlocked by attaining platinum ranking in Chapter IV Part II score attack and New York Minute.
New York Bar Girl	Unlocked by attaining platinum ranking in Chapter IV Part I score attack and New York Minute.
Docks Passos	Unlocked by attaining platinum ranking in Chapter V Part II score attack and New York Minute.
Helicopter Pilot Passos	Unlocked by attaining platinum ranking in Chapter V Part I score attack and New York Minute.
IT Guy	Unlocked by attaining platinum ranking in Chapter VI Part I score attack and New York Minute.

CHARACTER	NOTES
Bodyguard Passos	Unlocked by attaining platinum ranking in Chapter VI Part II score attack and New York Minute.
Stripclub Barman	Unlocked by attaining platinum ranking in Chapter VII score attack and New York Minute.
New York Passos	Unlocked by attaining platinum ranking in Chapter VIII score attack and New York Minute.
Milo	Unlocked by attaining platinum ranking in Chapter IX score attack and New York Minute.
Giovanna	Unlocked by attaining platinum ranking in Chapter X score attack and New York Minute.
Marcelo	Unlocked by attaining platinum ranking in Chapter XI score attack and New York Minute.
Dr Arthur Fischer	Unlocked by attaining platinum ranking in Chapter XII score attack and New York Minute.
Rodrigo	Unlocked by attaining platinum ranking in Chapter XIII score attack and New York Minute.
Bachmeyer	Unlocked by attaining platinum ranking in Chapter XIV score attack and New York Minute.
Booze and Pills Max	Unlocked by beating New York Minute Hardcore.
Max Payne Advanced (16 bit) (SINGLE PLAYER ONLY)	Beat the game in old school mode.
Black and White Max Payne 1 (SINGLE PLAYER ONLY)	Attain platinum ranking in New York Minute and Completing New York Minute Hardcore.
Black and White Max Payne 2 (SINGLE PLAYER ONLY)	Attain platinum ranking in New York Minute and Completing New York Minute Hardcore.

ARCADE XP REWARDS

SCORE ATTACK & NEW YORK MINUTE

CHAPTER I: ROOFTOP PARTY; CHAPTER VI: OFFICE; CHAPTER IX: FAVELA 2

MEDAL	XP REWARD
BRONZE	100
SILVER	250
GOLD	500
PLATINUM	750

CHAPTER II: NIGHTCLUB; CHAPTER III: STADIUM; CHAPTER IV: NY BAR/APT; CHAPTER V: THE DOCKS; CHAPTERT VII: FAVELA 1

MEDAL	XP REWARD
BRONZE	250
SILVER	500
GOLD	750
PLATINUM	1000

CHAPTER VIII: CEMTERY; CHAPTER X: BUS DEPOT

MEDAL	XP REWARD
BRONZE	500
SILVER	750
GOLD	1000
PLATINUM	1250

CHAPTER XI: PANAMA; CHAPTER XII: HOTEL; CHAPTER XIII: UFE POLICE PRECINCT; CHAPTER XIV: FINALE

MEDAL	XP REWARD
BRONZE	750
SILVER	1000
GOLD	1250
PLATINUM	1500

MAX PAYNE 3 CHEATS

UNLIMITED AMMO

Collect all golden gun pieces to unlock unlimited ammo.

UNLIMITED BULLET TIME

Get gold medals on every score attack level to unlock unlimited Bullet Time.

ONE HIT KILL

Finish game on hardcore to unlock One Hit Kill.

BULLET CAM ON EVERY KILL

Find every clue to unlock Bullet Cam On Every Kill.

UNLIMITED PAYNE KILLERS

Finish game on hard to unlock Unlimited Payne Killers.

MULTIPLAYER

Max Payne 3 offers an innovative new way to experience combat online. In addition to an assortment of competitive and cooperative game modes like Deathmatch and Payne Killer, *Max Payne 3* multiplayer introduces an original, narrative-driven team mode called Gang Wars, where the outcome of each match determines the story and game types for five consecutive rounds.

In multiplayer, you will level up to unlock new weapons, attachments, items, customizable Avatar features, and a range of special abilities called Bursts.

BASICS 254
ARSENAL 257
MODES & STRATEGIES 268
MAPS 269
DEATHMATCH 272
PAYNE KILLER 274
GANG WARS 276

MULTIPLAYER BASICS

XP & LEVELING UP

It wouldn't be a modern multiplayer mode without XP. In *Max Payne 3*, you earn XP by getting kills, looting, saving teammates, completing objectives, Grinds, Vendettas, using Bursts, and playing matches to name a few. Earning XP increases your Rank and doing this unlocks weapons, attachments, titles, Bursts, Avatars, loadout weight limits, playlist game types, and other game features. Level 50 is the maximum Rank you can achieve. From there, you can choose to go *Legend*...

WEAPON LEVELING SYSTEM

Racking up kills and completing Grinds levels up your equipped weapon. Leveling up your weapons unlocks new features for that weapon and its attachments. There are 10 levels to reach for each weapon. Attachments are added to your weapon in the Loadout menu and only once you've set the weapon to a position on your loadout. Your weapon level is displayed on the loadout menu when a weapon is selected along with a Kill/Death ratio and Accuracy stats. Find a complete list of weapon unlocks per level in the Multiplayer Unlockables section in this guide.

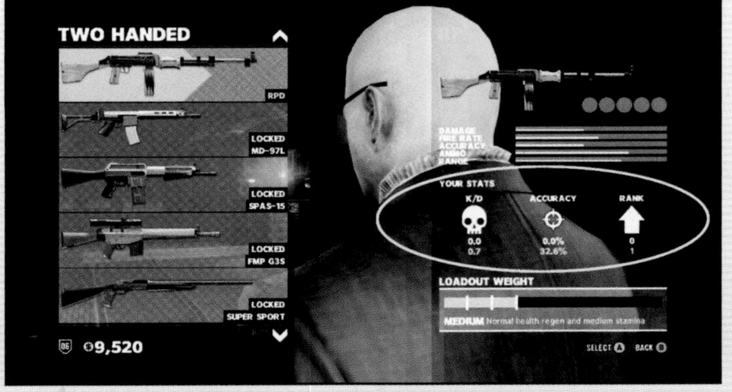

BECOME A LEGEND

50 If you choose to become a Legend at level 50, you trade in your Rank, weapons, and cash for a new shield icon, a new selectable title, and a cash multiplier. To do this, enter the multiplayer main menu and find the Legend option tucked between Private Match and Arsenal. Enter this menu and confirm your decision on the next screen. At Legend level 1, you unlock the Badge of Honor gear item that increases cash earned by an additional 20% with every level. You can reach level 50 ten times and receive a new Legend status each time. Here are the badges you will receive at each *Legend* level.

Level	Badge	Reward
Legend Level 1		**Tropical Max**
Legend Level 2	SEGURANÇA	**Bodyguard Max**
Legend Level 3		**Smart Casual Max**
Legend Level 4	Casey	**Bad Day Max**
Legend Level 5	FABRICAS BRANCO	**Down to Business Max**

RANK UNLOCKABLES

Look for the multiplayer awards list in the Unlockables section of this guide to see how much XP, Cash, and Adrenaline is earned by performing certain actions. You can also find a master list of everything unlocked at each Rank level.

LOOTING

Hold B on Xbox 360 (Circle on PlayStation 3) while standing over the dead enemies to loot their bodies for cash, extra adrenaline, or painkillers.

WAGERS

Unlock Wagers after completing the Grind "Raise The Stakes" by earning $2000 in multiplayer games. Once unlocked and while in Gang Wars intermissions, you have a chance to wager on match-specific criteria. Press X on the Xbox 360 (or Square on the PlayStation 3 controller) to access Wagers. A particular wager is presented and you must choose one player from a list of teammates or opponents that you believe will win the bet for you. For instance, which listed gamer will get the first kill.

COMPLETE LIST OF ALL POSSIBLE WAGERS

COMMON WAGERS

- First Kill
- First Death
- First Melee Kill
- First Headshot Kill
- First Adrenaline Fill
- First to Trigger a Burst
- First Vendetta Won
- First Corpse Loot
- Fewest Deaths
- Best Kill Streak
- Last Kill
- Most Accurate
- Most Assists
- Most Headshots
- Most Vendettas Defended
- Most Vendettas Won
- Most Melee Kills
- Most Time Alive
- Most Kills
- Most Deaths
- Most Money Looted
- Most Bodies Looted
- Most Kills From Behind
- Most Kills When Prone
- Most Cash Earned
- Most Distance Traveled
- Most Bullets Fired

BOMB-SPECIFIC WAGERS

- First Bomb Plant
- First Bomb Defused
- First Planter Killed
- First Diffuser Killed

DELIVERY

- First Drop Off
- First Package Stolen
- Most Packages Stolen

TURF-BASED

- First Capturer Kill
- Most Capture Points
- Most Skilled Capturer (Total Turf only)

ASSASSINATION

- First Assassination Target Defended

MISCELLANEOUS

- Who Will Be The Last Man Standing

VENDETTA

A Vendetta option appears on the screen during respawn if a particular player is repeatedly killing you during a multiplayer session. Before you respawn or accept a respawn to speed things up, select the X on the Xbox 360 or the Square on the PlayStation 3 to place a Vendetta on your nemesis. Doing so places this icon on your nemesis' name. Unfinished Vendettas carry over between rounds and are available in all play modes. If you successfully kill that target before he or she kills you, then you have settled the Vendetta and earn extra XP. Your nemesis can defend the vendetta and earn extra XP if he kills you before you kill him.

TRACKING DEVICE

The *Tracking Device* gear item may throw your weight into territory you are not comfortable with, but this item is priceless if you have a score to settle with a nemesis. Equipping this item reveals the location of your Vendetta on the minimap.

ARSENAL

The Multiplayer Arsenal menu consists of Loadouts, Avatars, and Titles. All of these options are covered in this section of the guide. The Arsenal is your hub for multiplayer customization. Access the Arsenal through the multiplayer menu to create and equip custom loadouts, unlock and purchase new weapons, customize your Avatar's appearance and add titles to your name.

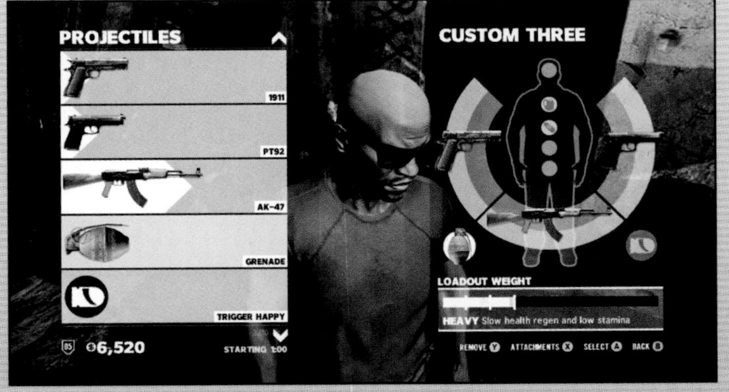

LOADOUT

The loadout section provides four preset loadouts that suit various play styles. They are: Soldier, Snitch, Dealer, Lookout. The following are the initial Preset Loadout details. More weapons and items are added as you level up and purchase more weapons.

PRESET LOADOUTS

LOADOUT	SINGLE-HANDED WEAPONS	TWO-HANDED WEAPON	ITEMS	PROJECTILE	BURST	WEIGHT
SOLDIER	PT92 & .38 Revolver	AK-47	Light Body Armor	Grenade	Trigger Happy	Medium (normal health regen and medium stamina)
SNITCH	M10 & PT92		Sneakers	Grenade	Intuition	Light (fast health regen and high stamina)
DEALER	PT92	M500	Ammunition Pouch	Grenade	Big Dog	Medium (normal health regen and medium stamina)
LOOKOUT	.38 Revolver	Mini-30	Sutures	Flash Grenade	Trigger Happy	Medium (normal health regen and medium stamina)

Leveling up to level 4 unlocks customizable loadout slots to create your own loadouts with weapons, items, projectiles, and Bursts that you have unlocked.

All loadout items to fill these loadout slots are unlocked by leveling up and purchased with the cash you have earned. Use LB and RB on the Xbox 360 (L1 and R1 on PlayStation 3) to scroll through your weapons, items, projectiles and Bursts menus.

Weapons and items all have various effects on your mobility, speed, and health regeneration. Be sure to keep an eye on your loadout weight when customizing your player. Remember that as you level up weapons and rank you unlock attachments for your weapons.

Creating a custom loadout is all about personal preference and equipping items and weapons that enhance your fighting style and strengths. When creating custom loadouts, consider the different game play modes. You may want to read the coverage of the different scenarios in Gang Wars and consider including items that speed turf captures and bomb planting and diffusing. Study the Bursts and tailor a loadout specifically for a particular scenario.

AVATARS

Modify a custom Avatar for each faction in multiplayer. Your Avatar can be customized with numerous cosmetic alterations to the outfit and physical appearance. The look of your multiplayer Avatar is persistent over all gang matches in multiplayer.

You can customize the following features: Heads, Hair, Hats, Glasses, Torso, Accessories, Hands, Tattoos, Legs, Shoes, Head Armor, Body Armor. Many options are available within each of these categories. Explore and have fun creating an endless number of unique characters. Visit the Multiplayer Unlockables section of this guide to find Avatar unlockables by Rank level.

FACTION	UNLOCKED
Comando Sombra	From Start
De Marcos	Rank 2
UFE	Rank 3
Tropa Z	Rank 5
Punchinellos	Rank 6
Crachá Preto	Rank 7
Tropical Max	Legend Level 1
Bodyguard Max	Legend Level 2
Smart Casual Max	Legend Level 3
Bad Day Max	Legend Level 4
Down To Business Max	Legend Level 5
Bad Day Becker	"You Push a Man Too Far" Achievement

TITLES

New titles are unlocked by reaching higher ranks or completing Grinds. Choose a title for your Avatar that really shows off your cred. Visit our multiplayer unlockables section of this guide to find title unlockables by Rank level.

BURSTS

Bursts are special abilities that you can assign during loadout and activate during gameplay that give you, and sometimes your entire team, a specific advantage. Bursts are tied to the multiplayer adrenaline meter. You earn adrenaline as you would earn Bullet Time in the single-player Story mode: by registering hits, kills, or looting.

For a full list of Adrenaline awards, see our Adrenaline Awards List in our Multiplayer Unlockables section of this guide.

Each Burst has three levels that are activated depending on how much adrenaline you have.

EQUIPPING BURSTS

- Bursts are unlocked through ranking up.
- The Burst title and the rank required to unlock it is displayed when highlighted in the Arsenal.
- Bursts are then purchased and equipped in the Arsenal menu. Purchased Bursts are white and black while unlocked but un-purchased icons are grey and black.
- You can only equip a single Burst per loadout.
- Trigger Happy is the default Burst.
- Each Burst can be upgraded twice (three level max)
- Burst upgrades are unlocked through leveling up or by completing challenges—upgrades are not purchased.

THE BURST METER

The Burst and Adrenaline meters are one and the same. XP awards and kills cause the meter to fill. There are multipliers (bonus adrenaline) on kills and other XP awards like Bullet Time awards in single-player Story mode.

The Burst meter is split into thirds. It fills from the bottom up; once it is full, no more Burst can be earned. When you die and respawn, you keep any completed thirds on the meter and lose any incomplete ones.

Each successive Burst meter third is harder to charge than the last. The same number of kills gives a lower increase in Burst. This effect is gradual, but it does keep you from haphazardly spending your Bursts. Make them count!

If you only have a level 1 upgrade, then all three segments can fill, but only one segment is used at a time as you activate a Burst.

ACTIVATING A BURST

- A level 1 Burst can be activated when the first Burst meter segment is filled.
- A level 2 Burst can be activated when the second Burst meter segment is filled.
- A level 3 Burst can be activated when the third Burst meter segment is filled.

An icon appears over the Burst meter when a Burst level is ready. The text and icon indicate the Burst level available. This also reappears to remind you when you respawn. You activate a Burst by clicking down on the Right Control Stick (Xbox 360) or by clicking down on the R3 button (PlayStation).

BURST LIST

The following is a list of the bursts and what they do.

Burst	Icon	Description	Levels
BIG DOG		Health boosts for you and your team.	Level 1: Boosts your health and health of teammates who are within 5 meters of you. Level 2: Health boost affects all visible teammates in line of sight. Level 3: Health boost affects all teammates.
INTUITION		Locates your enemy to give you an edge.	Level 1: Launches spotter flares above the enemy team. Level 2: Hearing increased—all enemies spotted by teammates appear as silhouettes. Level 3: All enemies appear as silhouettes to your entire team.
TRIGGER HAPPY		More firepower.	Level 1: Grants 1 magazine of armor-piercing, white tracer ammunition for 20 seconds. Level 2: Spawns an LMG .30 and DE .50 and increases accuracy. Level 3: Spawns a Grenade Launcher with extra ammo.
BULLET TIME		Slows time.	Level 1: Adrenaline sharpens your reflexes for 2.5 seconds. Level 2: Increases the duration of the effect to 4 seconds. Level 3: Increases the duration of the effect to 6 seconds.
PARANOIA	?	Your opponents won't know whom to trust. Enemies equipped with ID Card gear items are immune to these effects.	Level 1: Members of the enemy team see each other as enemies. Their gamertag blips appear red to them. Level 2: Enables Bounty plus friendly fire for one member of the enemy team for 30 seconds. Level 3: Enables Bounty plus friendly fire for the entire enemy team for 30 seconds.
SNEAKY		Disguise your gamertag. Appear as friendly to enemies. Enemies equipped with ID Card gear items are immune to these effects.	Level 1: Your name appears as friendly to enemies for 10 seconds. Level 2: Your name appears as friendly to enemies for 30 seconds. Level 3: Effect lasts until death.
GROUNDED		Hide from the enemies' minimap.	Level 1: You disappear from any enemy player's minimap and HUD instantly for 10 seconds—counters all intuition Bursts. Level 2: Your team disappears from the map for 20 seconds. Level 3: Scrambles the enemy map and shows false information. Lasts 20 seconds—counters all intuition Bursts.
FRESH BLOOD		Power up your team's next 6 respawns.	Level 1: You and 5 of your teammates gain 20% bonus health for the next 6 spawns. Level 2: You and your teammates gain 30% bonus health and a .5 Adrenaline segment for the next 6 spawns. Level 3: You and your teammates gain 50% bonus health and 1 adrenaline segment for the next 6 spawns.
WEAPON DEALER		Special deals to make your weapon more powerful.	Level 1: Your team does not consume ammunition for 10 seconds. Level 2: Increases the duration of the effect to 20 seconds. Level 3: Also grants incendiary ammunition for the full duration.
BURST BUBBLE		Block your enemies' Bursts while powering yours. Enemies equipped with the Autoinjector gear item are immune to these effects.	Level 1: Stops enemies from gaining Adrenaline or using Bursts for 20 seconds. Level 2: Increases team Adrenaline by 16.5% and decreases enemies' Adrenaline as much as 16.5%. Level 3: Doubles the amount of Adrenaline added to your team and removed from enemies.
WEAPON DOUBLE-DEALER		Gives your enemies dodgy weapons. Enemies equipped with a Manufacturer's Guarantee are not affected by this Burst.	Level 1: Enemies drop their extra grenades to the ground, primed. Level 2: Enemies lose their backup magazines and ammunition. Level 3: All enemy grenades drop their pins.

ITEMS

You can equip and carry up to five items at a time, giving your player persistent passive abilities while equipped. Keep in mind that items all have weight: the more you use, the heavier and slower your Avatar will become. Weight affects health regen and stamina as well.

HEAD ITEMS

Head items range from protection from general attacks and projectiles to helping you identify booby-traps and earn Adrenaline.

HELMET

Lowers damage taken to the head by 50%. This is the heaviest head item.

GAS MASK

Protect yourself from tear gas. This is a light head item.

MILITARY GOGGLES

Protect yourself from flash grenades and identify booby- trapped corpses. This is a lighter head item than the Helmet and the Gas Mask.

BALACLAVA

Earn extra adrenaline for non-melee kills from behind. This is the lightest of head items.

CHEST ITEMS

These items make you harder to put down in battle, but the heavier ones will slow you down a bit and slow your health regen.

LIGHT BODY ARMOR

Light Body Armor reduces ballistic damage to the front of the torso by 15%. The helmet reduces ballistic damage to the head by 50%. Out of the four chest items, this is the second-lightest.

URBAN CAMO

Urban Camo makes your gamer tag darker in color; it also appears for only a short duration when spotted by an enemy.

MEDIUM BODY ARMOR

Medium Body Armor reduces ballistic damage to the torso by 25% at the front and 10% at the back. This is heavier than the Light Body Armor, making it the second-heaviest chest item.

HEAVY BODY ARMOR

Heavy Body Armor reduces ballistic damage to the torso by 33% at the front and 25% at the back. This is the heaviest chest item available.

GEAR ITEMS

Gear items are all rather light items with very similar weight. But monitor the Loadout Weight gauge: a few items are twice as heavy as the rest.

AMMUNITION POUCH

Carried and max ammo increased by 50% and provides unlimited ammo when in Last Stand.

LOCKBOX

You do not lose your painkillers when you die.

BOUNTY ORDERS

Earn extra cash for killing the highest enemy player on the scoreboard.

ID CARDS

Distribute ID cards to your team, preventing effects that might confuse team affiliation. Prevents effects from the following Bursts: *Paranoia* and *Sneaky*.

FIELD BANDAGES

Your health replenishes at a faster rate.

SNEAKERS

Reduces the noise you make while moving, making it more difficult for enemies to detect you.

AUTOINJECTOR

Injects you with extra Adrenaline for kills and prevents loss of Adrenaline from enemy effects. This counteracts the effects from enemies equipped with *Burst Bubble*.

MULTI-TOOL

This is one of the heavier gear items. It decreases the time needed to use objective items. For instance, this would speed up the time to plant or defuse a bomb.

TRACKING DEVICE

Your Vendetta target is always visible on your map. This is one of the heavier gear items. Watch your weight gauge when equipping.

STICKY TAPE

Your grenades stick where they land.

PACEMAKER

Automatically use Adrenaline to enter Bullet Time when in Last Stand.

BADGE OF HONOR

This item is unlocked at Legend level 1. Badge of Honor increases the amount of cash earned in multiplayer by 25%.

MANUFACTURER'S GUARANTEE

Protects your weapons from any effects that might damage them. Protects against the Weapon Double Dealer Burst.

SUTURES

Reduces the time before your health starts to replenish after injury by 50%.

WALKIE TALKIE

Your map receives intel from teammates, showing the location of any enemies spotted by your team.

VAMPIRE FANGS

Gives you health for killing enemies.

SPRAY CAN

This is a great item to use for Gang Wars as you are often faced with the task of capturing turfs. This item allows you capture territories more quickly.

QUICK HOLSTER

You draw your weapon and reload more quickly.

HOLLOWPOINT ROUNDS

Severely damages targets you kill, increasing the time it takes them to respawn. This is a very good item to equip for the Gang Wars scenario *Turf Grab* as well as other turf- capturing scenarios.

POCKET WATCH

Enemy Bullet Time affects the holder as if it were friendly Bullet Time. Use this when you are playing opponents who overuse Bullet Time.

CREWS

Crews are an easy way for Social Club members to play *Max Payne 3* multiplayer with friends. Playing in a Crew yields extra XP in matches and improves your team-based skills.

Create, join, and manage Crews through the Social Club website—this is your hub for customizing and managing all aspects of your Crew, including the Crew name and emblem. You can also join and manage Crews through the in-game multiplayer menu. These crews will carry over into *Grand Theft Auto V*.

You can be a member of more than one Crew at a time. When joining a match that has a member of your Crew in it, you will automatically join their side. You can also invite gamers with whom you've recently played to join your Crew, or apply to join their Crew through the in-game Crews menu.

CREW FEUDS

Once a crew gets a number of uncontested kills on members from another crew, they trigger a Crew Feud that runs concurrent with whatever mode is being played. This is only visible to the members of the two crews who are pitted against each other. When a Crew Feud occurs a special Crew Feud meter will appear on screen and the members of the first crew to earn 10 kills against members of the opposing Crew will be awarded Bonus XP.

WEAPONS

SINGLE-HANDED WEAPONS

.38 REVOLVER

This standard handgun packs quite a wallop at close range. It's a very damaging weapon but the tradeoff is a lesser rate of fire and lesser accuracy, ammo capacity, and range.

PT92

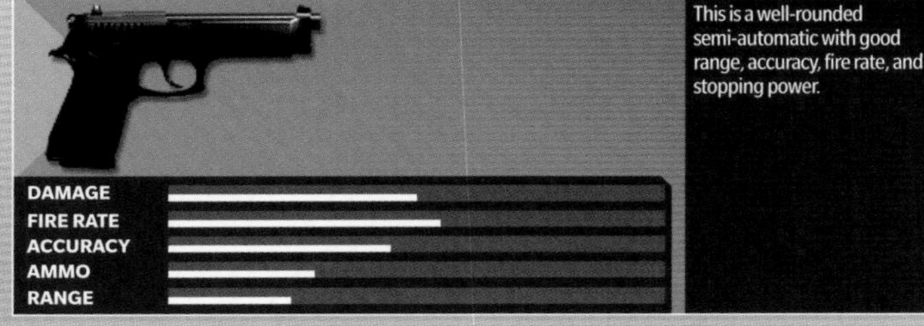

This is a well-rounded semi-automatic with good range, accuracy, fire rate, and stopping power.

M10

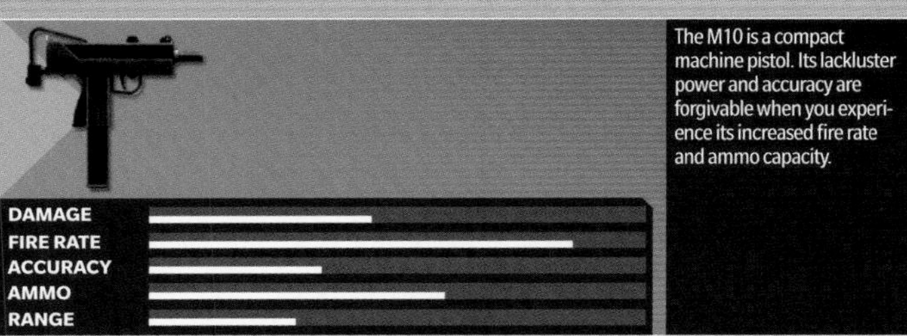

The M10 is a compact machine pistol. Its lackluster power and accuracy are forgivable when you experience its increased fire rate and ammo capacity.

1911

The M1911 pistol is a single-action, semi-auto handgun with .45 caliber rounds. It's very similar to the PT92 in stats, but has slightly better range.

M972

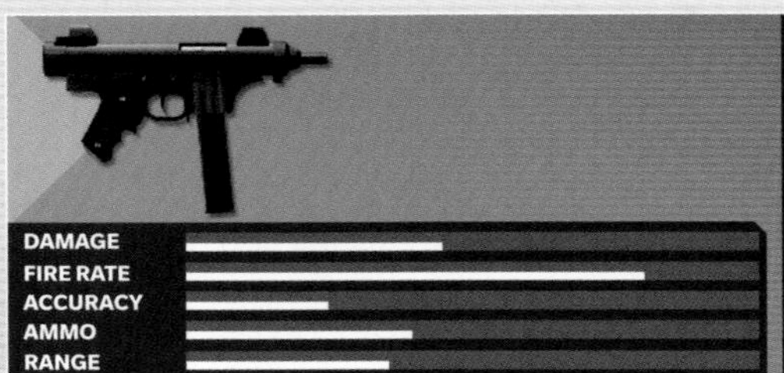

While the M10 has it beat on fire rate and accuracy, the M972 submachine gun has better range.

608 BULL

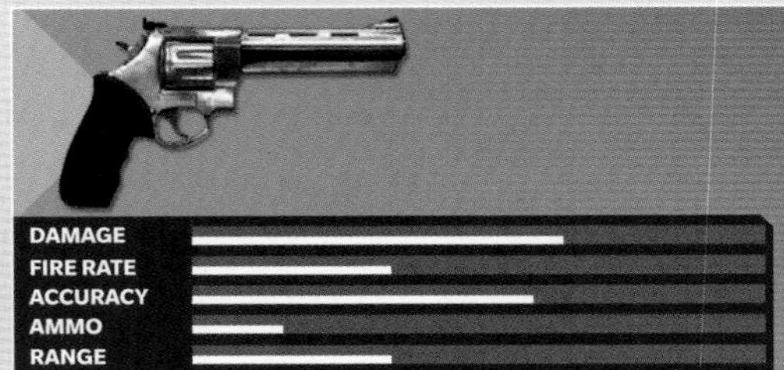

The 608 is a double-action revolver that chambers the .357 round. The long barrel gives it incredible accuracy and range. The rate of fire is low but is a good compromise for the other powerful features. Its damage is only surpassed by the .38 Revolver, but the Bull exceeds the .38 in all other stat categories.

AUTO 9MM

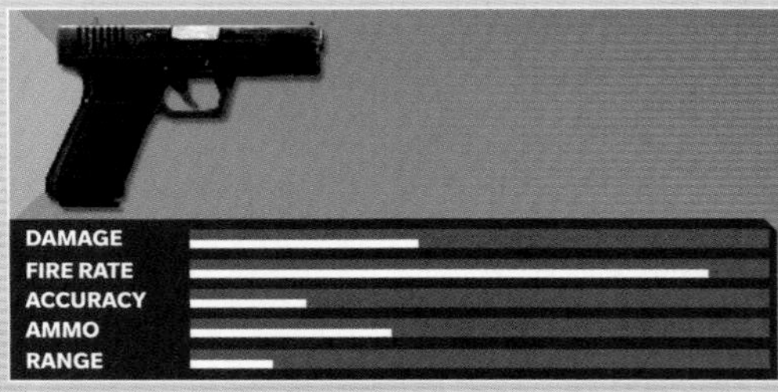

Using this fully auto pistol is like firing a little submachine gun. The rate of fire is equal to the M10 but its damage, accuracy, ammo capacity, and range are not as strong. However, it is extremely exhilarating to operate this weapon.

SAWN-OFF

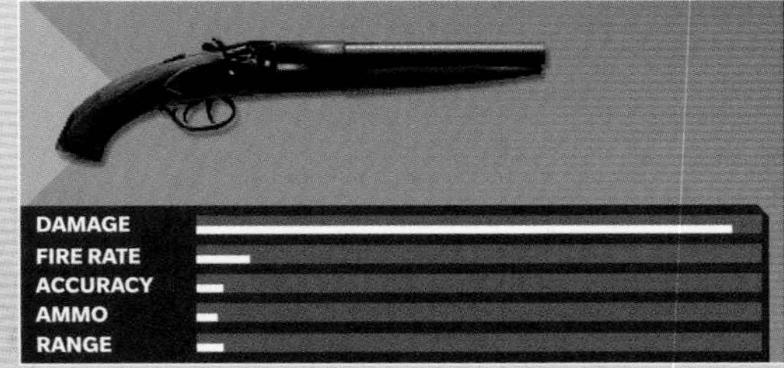

The Sawn-Off shotgun is extremely powerful when used as a close-range weapon—as it's intended to be used. The damage is only matched by the M500, sniper rifles, and the RPG. Holster the weapon when fighting mid to long range

MICRO 9MM

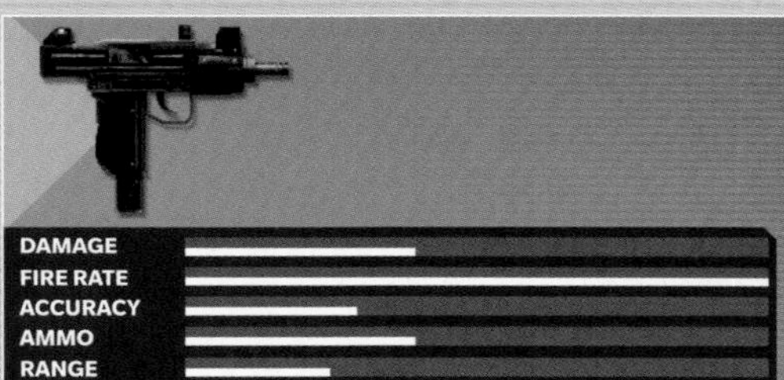

The Micro 9mm has the fastest rate of fire of all the weapons in the game. However, in comparison to other submachine guns, it has slightly less damage, range, and ammo capacity. It's more accurate than the M972 submachine gun, but the Micro 9mm is also much heavier.

DE .50

The DE is a gas-operated semi-automatic pistol with .50 caliber rounds that has an effective range of 50 meters. This is the third most powerful handgun in the arsenal and, like the 608 Bull, it has the best range. The DE's accuracy is fair and ammo capacity is average.

TWO-HANDED WEAPONS

AK-47

The AK-47 is a great weapon due to its ease of use and durability. Stat-wise, it's a little heavy. But it's a well-balanced weapon and a great choice to take into any battle.

MINI-30

The Mini-30 is a well-rounded weapon that exceeds all of the AK-47's stats except for ammo capacity. It also is a little lighter than the AK, so you can move faster or pack more items in multi-player mode.

MPK

This assault rifle was designed for short-range battle by special services. The weapon offers more damage and accuracy in a lighter frame than the AK-47 but carries fewer rounds. This weapon has a superb rate of fire.

M500

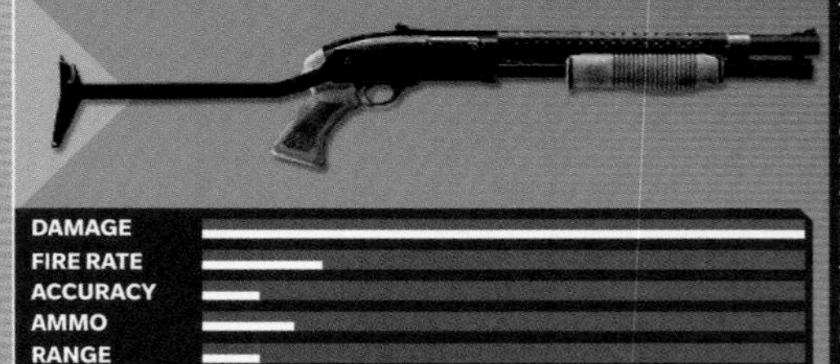

The M500 riot shotgun packs a monster punch at close range. The sniper rifle and the RPG are the only weapons that match its damage capabilities, neither of which are close- range weapons. It is more damaging but lighter than the M4 Super 90. The compromise is slightly less accuracy and slower rate of fire.

SAF .40

This submachine has a magazine that holds 30 9mm rounds. It's very similar to the MPK, however the SAF .40 does slightly more damage, has a much faster rate of fire, and holds more ammo per magazine.

FAL

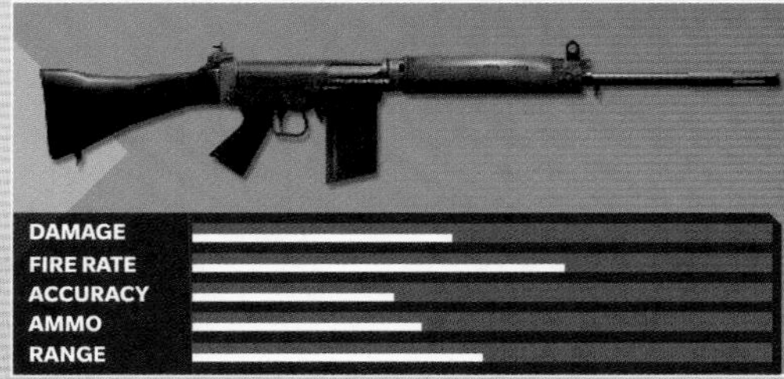

The FAL is a fine weapon, but the Mini-30 is lighter in weight and has it beat in most other stats. The FAL would be the next best choice.

MD-97L

This weapon is a compact, semi-automatic version of the FAL. Where the FAL has a little more damage, this weapon offers a faster rate of fire and is more accurate. The range is equal to the FAL, but the MD-97L is a little heavier to tote.

FMP G3S

This scoped rifle is not quite as damaging nor has the range and accuracy of the M82A1 sniper rifle. But it does have a faster fire rate and holds more ammo per magazine. This is an assault rifle with a scope and not a sniper rifle, so use it accordingly.

M4 SUPER 90

This combat shotgun weighs more than the M500, but the Super 90 makes up for it in all other stats except damage. It has better range, rate of fire, and ammo capacity—all slightly better than the M500.

RPD

The RPD is extremely damaging, but it will slow you down. It's one of the three heaviest weapons available. However, this is one of the best mid-range weapons in the game.

SPAS-15

This pump-action/semi-automatic combat shotgun is fed by a detachable box magazine holding 12-gauge 70mm rounds. It's heavier than the Super 90 and does less damage. Still, it more than makes up for this with a higher rate of fire. In the time it takes an opponent to fire one shot with the Super 90, you can deal twice the damage with two quick shots from the SPAS-15.

SUPER SPORT

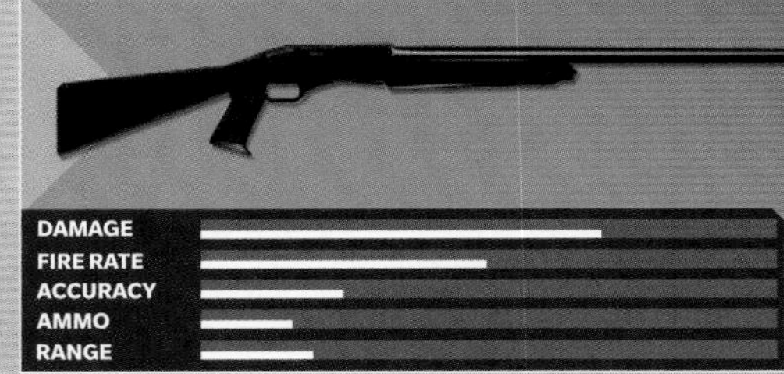

This semi-auto rifle does a lot of damage with a fast rate of fire. This is a very lethal weapon. It beats the SPAS-15 in all stats except damage, making it a great alternative shotgun choice.

G6 COMMANDO

This a well-rounded assault rifle has better damage and accuracy than the equally weighted MD-97L and holds more rounds per magazine. It is also more accurate and has a faster rate of fire than the slightly lighter and more damaging FAL. The AK-47, another mid-range weapon, has slightly more damage, but the Commando beats it in all other stats.

M82A1

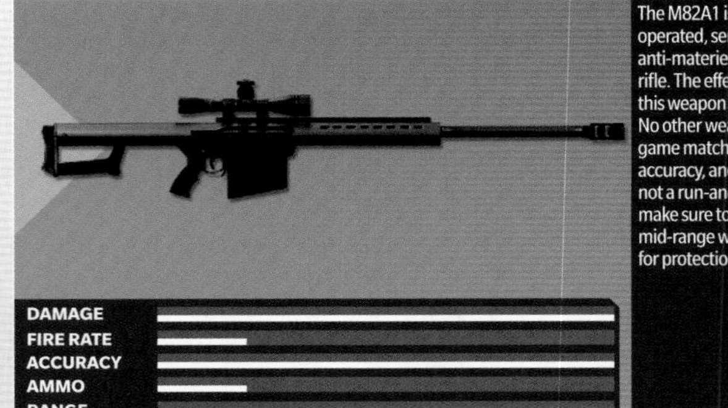

The M82A1 is a recoil-operated, semi-automatic anti-materiel scoped sniper rifle. The effective range of this weapon is 7.450 yards. No other weapon in the game matches its damage, accuracy, and range. This is not a run-and-gun weapon: make sure to have a decent mid-range weapon with you for protection as well.

LMG .30

This recoil-operated light machine gun (LMG) is an extremely heavy weapon and will slow your movement considerably. It is one of the three heaviest weapons available. Use cover tactics to play it safe. Use cover while hunting for enemies and use this weapon to tear your opponents to shreds. It has outstanding ammo capacity, range, fire rate, and accuracy.

ROTARY GRENADE LAUNCHER

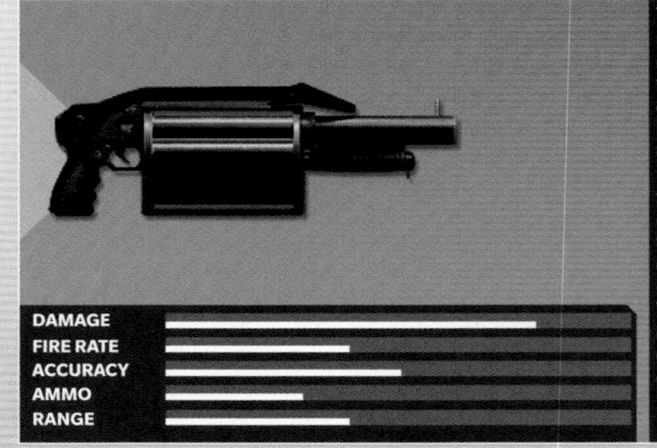

This shoulder-fired grenade launcher is not a very practical weapon and requires time to aim your shots in the correct arch to hit targets. It is a mid-range and very damaging weapon and is useful for targets that huddle together (i.e. enemies defending a base). Be sure to have a good mid-range option in your holster and use this for special occasions. This is one of the three heaviest weapons available and does a considerable amount of damage.

RPG

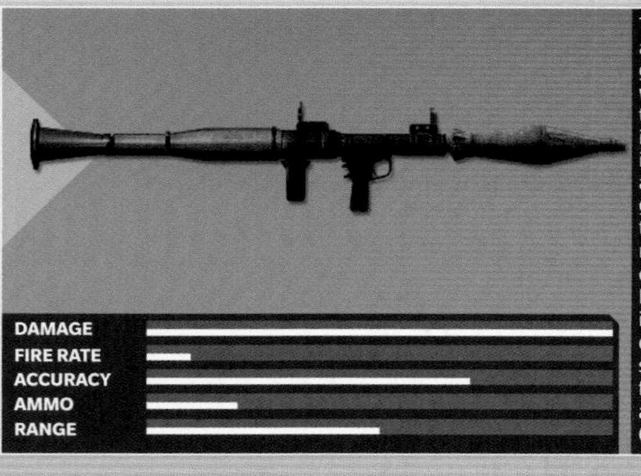

This is a shoulder-fired, anti-tank rocket-propelled grenade weapon. The warheads fired are affixed to a rocket motor, and flight is stabilized using fins. This is not as heavy as you would assume and lighter than the grenade launcher. Equipping this weapon will slow your movement as when you carry a heavy machine gun. It's one of the most damaging weapons as well as one of the slowest to reload. It is surprisingly accurate at the far reaches of medium range and more accurate than the Grenade Launcher.

LAW

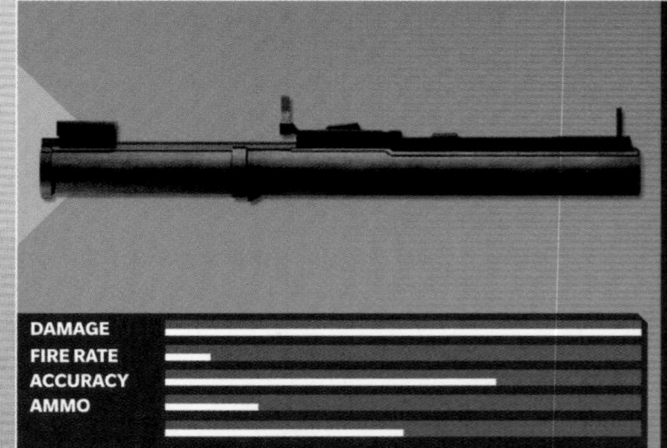

The Light Anti-Tank Weapon is a portable single shot anti-tank system that fires 66 mm unguided rockets. The warhead can inflict serious damage to heavy duty vehicles and structures.

MULTIPLAYER PROJECTILES

Select one of four different types of thrown weapons to equip: explosive, smoke, gas, and tin can. Projectiles can be quickly selected by holding the LB and then tapping the RB button the Xbox 360 or by holding the L1 and then tapping L2 on the PlayStation 3. You throw the projectile by aiming as you would with any weapon and then pressing the fire button to throw.

FLASH GRENADE

A Flash Bang is a non-lethal weapon designed to temporarily stun enemies by overpowering their senses with an intense flash of light and a loud blast of noise.

SMOKE GRENADE

Smoke Grenades create a thick cloud of smoke that can be used to mask movement and impair targeting.

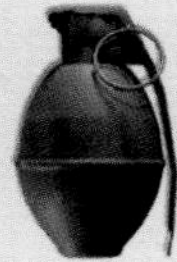

GRENADE

A Frag Grenade propels razor-sharp metal fragments upon exploding. These fragments will kill or injure anyone caught within six meters of the explosion.

TEAR GAS

Tear Gas Grenades release a cloud of toxic gas that debilitate, and then kill, anyone caught within the gas cloud.

TIN CAN

A low-tech noisemaker that creates a localized audio distraction for around 20 seconds.

MOLOTOV

A Molotov is a crude but effective incendiary that will ignite and explode on impact.

MULTIPLAYER MODES & STRATEGIES

You can choose to join one of many Playlists to compete with the entire online community or create a Private match where you can invite and play with your friends. Playlists use a matchmaking system that place you in matches with appropriate players based on your level, the types of matches you choose, and numerous other factors related to your personal ranking. If you have formed a persistent crew through the Rockstar Games Social Club, you will be placed in matches with your gang mates if they are online.

AUTOMATIC MAP SIZING

Maps are automatically tailored to fit the size of your teams or the number of players. Areas are opened or restricted dynamically to make each playing experience seem fresh and to keep it competitive and fun.

PLAYLISTS

Playlists are divided into Free Aim and Soft Lock aim modes.

GAME MODE	AIM MODE
Large Team Deathmatch	Soft Lock, Free Aim
Large Deathmatch	Soft Lock, Free Aim
Gang Wars	Soft Lock, Free Aim
Payne Killer	Soft Lock, Free Aim
Team Deathmatch	Soft Lock, Free Aim
Deathmatch	Soft Lock, Free Aim
Rookie Team Deathmatch	Soft Lock, Free Aim
Rookie Deathmatch	Soft Lock, Free Aim
Last Man Standing	Soft Lock, Free Aim
Hardcore Deathmatch	Free Aim
Hardcore Team Deathmatch	Free Aim
Hardcore Gang Wars	Free Aim

HARDCORE

In Hardcode modes, turf capturing and bomb planting and defusing are faster. The minimap only appears when the intuition Burst is active, Friendly Fire is on, and health regeneration is off.

MULTIPLAYER MAPS

BUS DEPOT

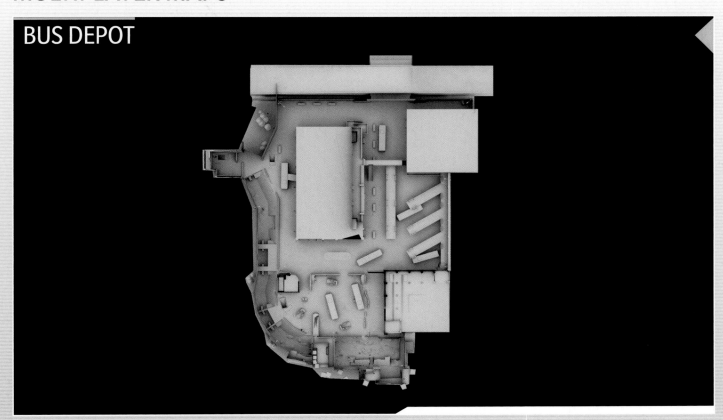

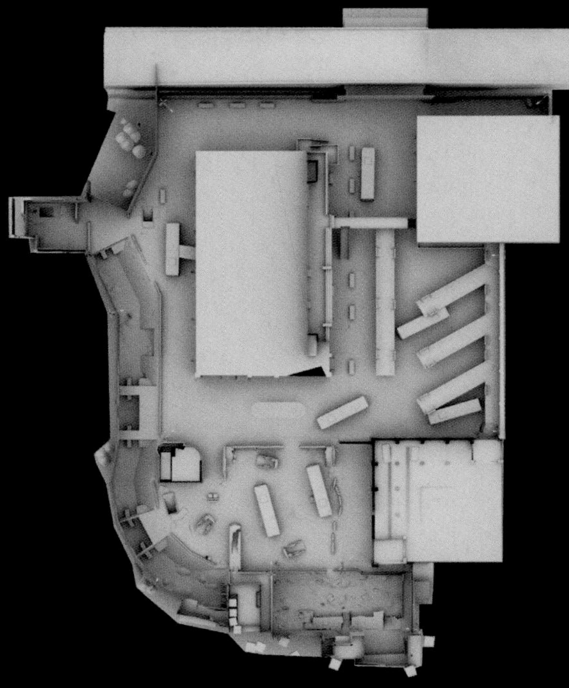

THE FAVELA

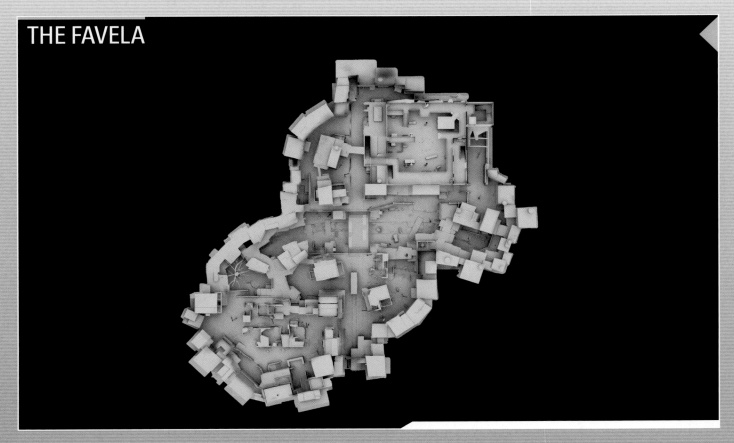

THE DOCKS

HOBOKEN ALLEYS

OFFICE

DEATHMATCH

ROOKIE MODES

Deathmatch and Team Deathmatch modes reserved for players new to *Max Payne* Multiplayer. Up to 8 players.

DEATHMATCH

It's every gangster for himself. Kill everyone as often as possible. Up to 8 players.

TEAM DEATHMATCH

Work with your team to take down your rivals. The gang with the most kills wins. Up to 8 players.

LARGE DEATHMATCH

Take down your enemies on a large-scale Deathmatch on a large map. This mode allows up to 16 players and is always played on a full-sized map.

LARGE TEAM DEATHMATCH

A Team Deathmatch with larger teams on a larger map. This mode allows up to 16 players and is always played on a full-sized map.

DEATHMATCH TIPS

- Your Bullet Time will also help allies.
- ShootDodge and roll will break any aim locks on you.
- Become Legend or complete Single Player challenges to unlock Story characters to use in Deathmatch.
- ShootDodge and roll will break any aim locks on you.
- Rank up to unlock Faction characters and customize them for Team Deathmatch and Gang Wars.
- Compete with friends and players for Payne Thresholds.
- In Hardcore mode, Turf capturing and Bomb planting and defusing is faster.
- Gain the high ground and your team will have the advantage.
- In Hardcore mode, you earn more XP.
- Kill 100 enemies to unlock Standard playlists.
- Kill 500 enemies to unlock Last Man Standing playlists.
- Kill 5000 enemies to unlock Hardcore playlists.
- Use tear gas on your own turf to prevent the enemy from capturing them back.
- Loot the enemies you have killed to rub some salt in that wound.
- Collect the Golden Guns in Single Player to unlock the Gold Tint Attachment.
- Put your vendetta targets back in their place with a melee strike for that extra sting.
- Kill an enemy with Vampire Fangs to regain some lost health in the battle.
- Add Extended Magazines to your Auto 9mm to keep up the firepower for longer!
- While crouched, you can go prone to lower your profile.
- Burst fire your automatic weapons for increased accuracy.
- Attachments can buff your weapons Damage, Accuracy, Ammo, and Range.
- The right mix of bursts will give your team the edge.
- Earn weapon attachments by ranking up your weapon.

PAYNE KILLER

ACCOMPLISHMENT	POINTS
Kill as Max or Passos	10
Assist teammate as Max or Passos	15
Become Max or Passos	20 (+2 Painkillers)
Shot combos on Max or Passos	1-10
Team Kills Max or Passos	10
Melee attack on Max or Passos	5-6

This mode allows up to 8 players and is a blend of cooperative and competitive play. The first player to make a kill will become Max Payne and the second killer becomes Raul Passos. It's kind of a vampire-ish move, but you could kill a buddy of yours so he becomes Passos if you are Max. Those two players must work together and fight to stay alive while earning as many points as possible. The remaining players must try to take down Max and Passos. Any player that kills one of the two marked targets will become whichever character they kill and then fight to stay alive for as long as possible.

MAX TAX

Looting Max's or Passos' corpse earns you $250! It also completes the Max Tax Grind.

The match starts with 10 minutes on the clock. The white score on the left of the clock is yours whether you are Max, or Passos, or not. The red number to the right of the clock is the highest scoring opponent's score.

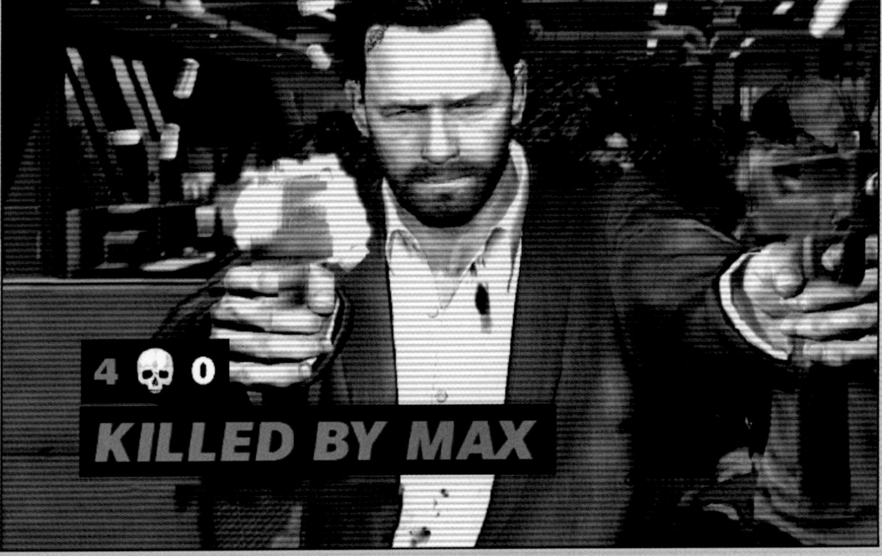

Max and Passos are very difficult to kill. Not only do they react to bullets as if they wear heavy armor but they also have painkillers and can loot corpses for more. Even a single melee attack will not take out Max or Passos like it would any other *normal* opponent. Needless to say, the Max and Passos team is usually the team with the most points. So the goal is to be on the winning team and stay there.

Everyone is in it to win it for themselves, so organizing a team to take out Max and Passos doesn't usually happen. However, when the gauntlet is passed to another player, it's usually from those large battles where multiple opponents are attacking Max or Passos. Ganging up on the tough duo is the best way to take one of them down. In a mass attack situation when Max or Passos goes down, the player that inflicted the most damage becomes Max or Passos.

If you are Max or Passos, you must work together to maintain your position. Stay together as much as possible to prevent mass attacks that threaten your lives. The game encourages this type of strategy: you make more points saving your teammate than you do just making a normal kill. Your teammate appears as a white dot on the map. Keep an eye on it. Don't travel so close together that a grenade attack could take you both out, but watch each other's backs to prevent ambushes. As Max or Passos, you are equipped with the Bullet Time Burst: use it. The team with the most points when the time is up is the winner—which is usually Max and Passos.

GANG WARS

Gang Wars takes key events from the single-player story and uses them as jump-off points for multiplayer matches with shifting objectives all linked by a shared story thread. Complete multiple objectives with your gang. Each objective forms part of a larger branching story arc that will change dynamically based on the outcome in each round. In this section, we cover in great detail all the scenarios possible in a round of Gang Wars.

DESCRIPTION: *All-out warfare as the gangs battle for supremacy. The team with the most kills wins.*

Tips & Details

A four-minute time limit is set and you must destroy as many enemies in that time limit as possible. No time is added to the clock in this scenario. The team with the most lives remaining when time is up wins the round. And of course, a team that eliminates all the enemies is also victorious.

The score is displayed at the top of the screen beside the game clock. Your team score appears in white and your opponents are red. When points are added to the score, the person who earned the kill is credited beside the score along with the number enemies killed in one attack.

Basic tactics for this style of game dictate that if you are in the lead, your team can hunker down into good cover positions with exposed angles covered by other teammates and allow the losing team to come hunting for you—and you know they will, because they need the points.

If you are on a team that is behind in points, then you must work together as a team to find the other team's weak link. Don't run willy-nilly all over the map, making yourself an easy target. Use cover and hunt smart. Talk to your team and devise a plan to expose the enemy's weakness and exploit it for multiple points. Find the high ground and use it to your advantage. If the enemy has taken it, take it from them.

DESCRIPTION: *The chosen target has only one life to fight to the death.*

Map Icons

 The target, when uncovered.

 The number of kills before the target is uncovered.

Tips & Details

This is a manhunt. The video of a player is shown for a few moments at the beginning of this scenario. This player is your mark. Kill the designated target. Uncover the target by killing his defenders (teammates).

When the challenge begins, a number of red player icons appear next to the three-minute time limit clock. These are the number of enemy kills you must make before the target becomes marked—a red reticle marks the target player on the minimap. Also, at the start of the challenge, the player's gametag is displayed under the clock, revealing that he/she is the target. If you identify the target by simply reading his/her gamertag or just by recognizing the character shown in the beginning of the challenge, you don't have to match the number of kills shown near the clock to reveal the mark. Instead, just shoot the mark. Shooting the mark uncovers the mark for the rest of the team and negates the need to shoot the number of kills displayed near the clock needed to reveal the mark. Revealing the mark through either process places the red reticle icon over the mark's character and displays it on the minimap as well.

The defending team often sticks together to protect the mark. Using grenades is often a good way to break up the group and reveal the true target. Cutting off the mark's escape routes and surrounding the mark is a very good tactic when playing as the attacking team. Finding the higher ground is always a good strategy for both offense and defense.

SHORT FUSE

DESCRIPTION: *One gang must destroy one of two locations.*

Map Icons

 A bombsite to attack.

 A bombsite to protect until it explodes.

 The number of bombing attempts remaining.

Plant bomb icon.

Defend a bombsite icon.

The four-minute clock display with bombs remaining and bombsite conditions.

Tips & Details

As the offensive team, you have four minutes to plant a bomb at one of two bombsites and to prevent the enemy from defusing the bomb. This icon will have the number 1 or 2 inside, indicating the areas to plant bombs. These icons appear in the environment and on the minimap to guide you to the site.

You have four attempts to plant the bomb. This bomb count is displayed in white on the friendly side of the clock. When you plant a bomb, one bomb is subtracted from your total. Two red numbers representing the bombsites without planted bombs are on the opponent's side of the clock. When a bomb is placed, one of those numbers will turn white to indicate which bombsite location has a planted bomb.

To plant a bomb, approach the site and press and hold the button indicated inside the red circle. Hold the button until the white gauge around the icon fills completely. When the bomb is set, the red plant icon turns into a white icon with the bombsite number inside (site 1 or 2). As soon as you plant the bomb, the white fill gauge circling the plant icon begins to drain. You have one minute until the bomb explodes. This time is displayed on the master clock at the top of the screen as well. If your team can successfully defend the bombsite until the gauge empties, then you will successfully blow up the site and win the game.

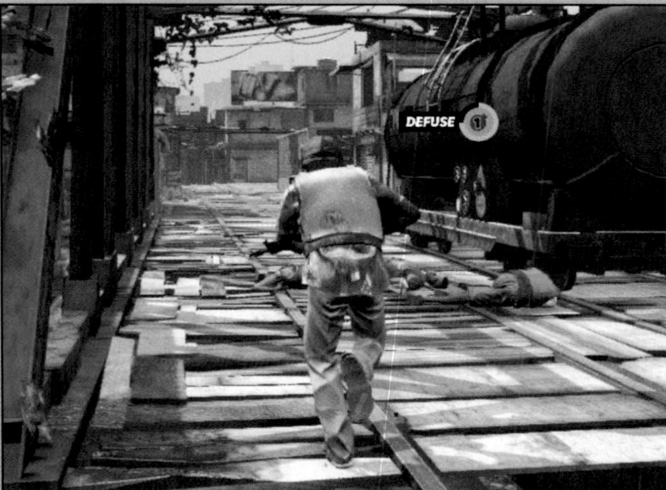

As the defensive team, you must attempt to defuse the bomb in a similar manner as it was planted in order to stop the bomb timer. If you are successful, the master clock resumes the amount of time that was remaining before the bomb was set—minus the set bomb countdown time. Also, with time pressing, the bomb planting team loses another bomb and must desperately fight to plant another. You do not need to detonate both sites: just destroy one site to win the challenge.

EQUIP MULTI-TOOL

Multi-Tool decreases the amount of time needed to plant and defuse bombs.

DESCRIPTION: *Both gangs must compete to collect and deliver their team's items to a single drop-off point.*

Map Icons

 A bag.

 A drop-off point.

 A teammate carrying a bag.

 An enemy carrying a bag.

Tips & Details

POINT SYSTEM

ACCOMPLISHMENT	POINTS
Kill	1
Interception	5
Drop-off	10

Score by delivering bags from your staring area to the drop-offs and by killing enemies or intercepting enemy bags. The team with the highest score wins.

Only two bags appear on the map at one time. One bag appears at your starting position. This is true for the opposing team as well. As soon as the game starts, grab the bag (indicated in-game and on minimap as a green bag icon) and run. If a teammate beats you to it, protect him along his route to the drop-off point instead of hunting down another bag. You must work together to win.

Whenever you are running with a bag or protecting a teammate with a bag, always be on the lookout for an enemy carrying a bag. An enemy carrying a bag is marked on the minimap with the same icon floating over his gamertag. You can help your team tremendously by delivering bags and by stopping the delivery of enemy bags. If you can do both at the same time, then you will be a very valuable teammate.

If you drop an enemy carrying a bag, don't waste your time looting his body. Instead, pick up the bag and you'll get an instant 5 bonus points for an interception! Picking up a bag and looting the body are two different button assignments, which makes it easier when the bag is so close to a dead body. Having one player on your team focus solely on interceptions is a very good tactic.

When you are holding a bag, the drop-off icon appears on the minimap and appears in the environment to help you locate it quickly. The shortest route to the drop-off point is not always the best one. Stay out of open areas. Take alternate routes that provide more cover to keep away from enemies. Drop the bag in the yellow marker using the same button used to pick up the bag.

GRAB

Both gangs fight over two bags to get to their drop-off point.

Map Icons

 A bag.

 A drop-off point.

 A teammate carrying a bag.

 An enemy carrying a bag.

Tips & Details

POINT SYSTEM

ACCOMPLISHMENT	POINTS
Kill	1
Drop-off	10

Score points by grabbing bags from around the map and returning them to your drop-off. Highest score wins. This challenge is very similar to the *Delivery* scenario and all the same tips apply here. The only differences between *Grab* and *Delivery* are that the *Grab* bags are not near your starting position and there are no interception points. Once you take down an enemy bag carrier, you must pick up the bag and drop it in your drop-off location.

Grab forces teams to battle for fewer bags that aren't necessarily close to your starting position or your drop-off location. Only two bags appear on the map at one time (just as in *Delivery*). *Grab* is a more intense and violent challenge than *Delivery*.

Whenever you are running with a bag or protecting a teammate with one, always be on the lookout for an enemy doing the same thing. An enemy carrying a bag is marked on the minimap with the same icon floating over his gamertag. You can help your team tremendously by delivering bags and halting the delivery of enemy bags. If you can do both tasks simultaneously, you're a valuable teammate, indeed!

DESCRIPTION: *Gangs battle for an important piece of turf.*

Map Icons

 The turf to claim.

 The turf owned by your team. Protect it.

 The turf owned by the enemy. Capture it.

Capturing turf.

The turf owned by your team being captured by the enemy.

 The Score bar.

Tips & Details

Take and hold the turf to score points. The first team to fill their score bar wins. You have thirty seconds at the beginning of the challenge before scoring can start. This gives you time to rush to the turf, marked with this icon.

Only one turf location is in the challenge, and both teams will be fighting hard to occupy it the longest. Stand in the turf marker until the defend icon appears. Having multiple teammates capturing the turf speeds the filling of the capture icon. Once you are in defend mode, the score bar fills. This is going to take some serious team effort for success. Once you enter defend mode, all teammates must work together to cover every enemy attack angle possible to hold your ground as long as you can.

It's always a good idea to have one defender in a high and distant position that has a good line of sight on the turf. Since most players gravitate to the turf, having a high, distant vantage point to take out opponents moving toward the turf is priceless.

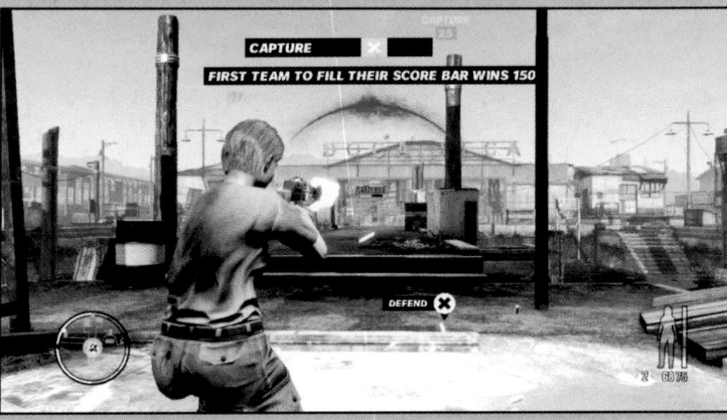

When you need to clear opponents from the turf, remember the previous tip and be cautious on your approach. Grenades are very useful in this challenge. An opponent is usually on or near the marker when they are defending. A well-placed grenade will clear the area.

EQUIP HOLLOWPOINT ROUNDS

The gear item Hollowpoint Rounds severely damages opponents when you kill them and increases the time it takes for them to respawn. This is exactly what you need to turn this kind of battle in your favor.

Also, while the capture icon does fill more quickly if you have multiple teammates in the turf marker at once, this also leaves more teammate vulnerable to attacks and one grenade could take out multiple teammates. Then you could lose ground and have to rush back to the location after respawning only to find that the enemy has taken the turf. This scenario can be avoided if one teammate captures and both the capturing player and the teammate(s) defend. Only support a teammate in the turf marker to capture it more quickly if you are certain that your defenses are strong.

DESCRIPTION: *Gangs fight to control multiple territories.*

Map Icons

 A turf owned by your team. Protect it.

 Unclaimed turf.

 A turf owned by the enemy. Capture it.

 Capturing turf.

 The turf owned by your team being captured by the enemy.

Score bar and turf ownership numbers.

Tips & Details

In Total Turf, you must take and hold the sections of turf to score points. The first team to fill their score bar wins. This challenge is very similar to *Turf Grab* but instead of one turf location there are several. As with *Turf Grab*, the first 30 seconds of the challenge ticks away without the possibility of scoring. However, don't let this stop you from rushing to the nearest turf, capturing it, and defending it.

There are three turf locations, so your tactics differ from *Turf Grab*. Here, your team is spread thin, capturing and defending multiple turf locations. To win, your team only needs to concentrate on holding two of three locations. Let the enemy have one turf location if your team is confident it can successfully hold two. If your team holds two turfs, there's no way the enemy can beat you with only one turf contributing to their score bar.

Monitor the score bar at the top of the screen. It also indicates which of the three turf locations your team has claimed or lost. White numbers are the turfs you are currently defending and the red numbers are those you must capture from the enemy. These colored numbers also appear on the minimap. Blinking numbers indicate enemy activity on that turf.

DESCRIPTION: *Each gang member has only one life to fight to the death.*

Map Icons

Clock and team lives remaining.

Tips & Details

Last Man is a team deathmatch challenge, but each player only has a single life. The last team standing wins. The challenge starts with four minutes on the clock. The amount of one-life players on each team is indicated on the gauge on either side of the clock at the top of the screen. If the clock runs out of time and lives still remain on both teams, then you enter "Sudden Death" and the game continues until one player remains and wins.

There are a few different strategies that work well to make your team victorious. You can stick together as a team and hunt cautiously together to eliminate the opponents. This way you have more guns on one opponent at one time. If you use this strategy, make sure when you move together that you are not bunched up so much that a grenade attack could take out your entire team.

Another strategy would be to stick together as a team—keeping a safe grenade-blast distance away from each other—and lock down an area that can be used as a fortress. Teammates should cover all access points. Your team is as strong as its weakest link.

Another tactic would be quite the opposite approach. Forget your team and wander off to a good location far from the war and hunker down and wait for the final opponent(s) to find you. If you have a good location where you can see enemies coming from a distance or have the height advantage, then you'll have the upper hand.

DESCRIPTION: *With their back to the wall, one gang must hold on to three territories, one after the other.*

Map Icons

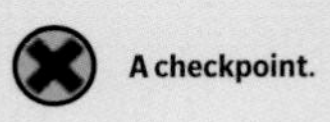 A checkpoint.	3:40 1 2 3 Clock and offender checkpoint gauge.	3 2 1 3:59 Clock and defender checkpoint gauge.

Tips & Details

There are three checkpoints to capture and your team must either take them all or defend opponents from taking them. Checkpoints cannot be lost once captured. The challenge begins with four minutes on the clock. 40 seconds are added to the clock when a turf is captured. Checkpoints are only active one at a time. When one is captured, then the next becomes accessible. All fighting will be concentrated on one little area on the map at a time. As the offensive team, if you do not capture the three checkpoints before the clock runs out, your team loses.

If you are on the defending team, try everything to delay the opponents from taking the first turf checkpoint during the initial time allotted. If all else fails, you need to at least keep the enemies from capturing the last checkpoint.

It doesn't take much of a slip in your defense to allow an opponent to get in the checkpoint and overtake it. It only takes 10 seconds to capture a checkpoint, and that is without any special items in your loadout that speed up captures. Defenders should use loadouts that include grenades, grenade launchers, or rocket launchers. Firing these at occupied checkpoints will clear them out in an instant.a

PASSAGE

DESCRIPTION: *One gang tries to take five checkpoints to escape and win while the opposing team tries to stop them and defend their checkpoints from being overtaken. Checkpoints cannot be lost once taken.*

Tips & Details

Checkpoints spawn on the map one at a time. The checkpoint location icon on the minimap (as well as one floating in the environment) appears as a red circle with a black X inside accompanied by the caption CAPTURE. The checkpoints eventually line the escape route. So once you've captured a checkpoint, it is secured and cannot be recaptured. Once it's secured, the next capture checkpoint appears farther along the route.

A time limit is involved to make it more difficult or to keep it fair (depending on what side you are on). You have four minutes to complete your challenge, be it taking or defending. The timer stops when a capture is in progress. When a checkpoint is taken, a little time is added to the clock. A checkpoint gauge is next to the clock at the top of the screen. This displays which checkpoints have been taken and which have not.

If you are on the team trying to take the checkpoints, then the checkpoint numbers are on the right side of the clock. The timer stops when a capture is in progress. When a checkpoint is taken, the number associated with that checkpoint turns from red to white and the gametag of the player who took the checkpoint appears briefly in place of the "Capture" label.

If you are on the team trying to defend the checkpoints, then the checkpoint gauge is on the left side of the clock and the color scheme is reversed.

To secure a checkpoint, stand in the red glowing area that marks the spot and remain there until the circular capture icon fills completely with the white fill gauge. The more comrades you have in the capture marker, the faster you can capture it. Also, using the Spray Can item speeds your own capture ability.

A good team tactic, which is also dependent on your team size, is to have a couple players actually doing the capturing while the others cover all angles around the marker to fight off opponents who are trying to stop you. Lying prone in the checkpoint area makes you a harder target to see and hit if the checkpoint is up higher on another level (like a higher level on a building). Cover areas are rarely inside the capture marker, so it is a dangerous place to be.

The last checkpoint is typically the hardest to take and the most violent because everyone is completely focused on the one location and not out scouting for sneaky opponents. Grenades are handy for clearing defenders from the area and are equally effective for taking out those trying to capture the checkpoint. Since you know an opponent must be in the marker to take it, a grenade on the mark will surely stop them.

DESCRIPTION: *A Showdown-style game mode, but each team has limited lives.*

Tips & Details

This is a team deathmatch-style game. However, each team has limited lives, based on wins in previous rounds. The number of lives the entire team shares is displayed on the top of the screen beside the game clock. There is a five-minute time limit.

Survivor is always played as the last round in Gang Wars to determine the winner of the series. The points (lives) given at the beginning of the challenge are based on how your team has done in the previous Gang Wars challenges. Your team gets two points for every previous game won. If teams are tied, then the number of points will be equal. This is designed to give credit where it is due: to the team that is doing well.

Your points are displayed in white and the enemies are red. Basic deathmatch tactics apply here. If you are losing, then you need to desperately but cautiously hunt down the enemy to swing the points in your favor. If you are a strong player, then step up for the team and take out as many enemies as possible. If you know you are a weaker player than others on your team, do them a favor and hunker down in cover and watch intently for opponents sneaking up on you.

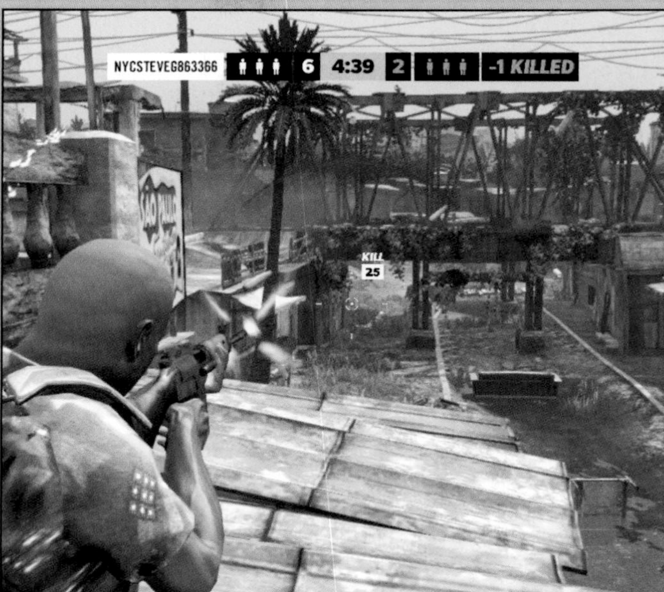

If you are on the winning team, you can hold down a fortress and cover all access points and wait for the losing team to arrive and try to claim some kill points. Pick them off as they leave cover. The team with the most points when the clock runs out is the winner.

SHOWDOWN

DESCRIPTION: *The gangs battle to the death, their strength dependent on the previous rounds.*

Tips & Details

Showdown is not too much different than Survivor. It's a team deathmatch that will decide the winner of the match. The starting points are based on wins in previous rounds. Showdown will always be played in the final round of Gang Wars.

The team in the lead of the total Gang War progress is given more points (kills) on the scoreboard. This handicaps the losing team, but rightly so: it shouldn't be easy for them to win after the all the great accomplishments of the winning team. So the game could start off 3-9 or 6-3, depending on what team you're on.

Five minutes are on the clock. Make good use of your time. If you are a winning team, then hunkering down in a good defensive position is smart. Have your teammates cover all attack angles, but don't bunch up together so closely that a grenade could do you all in.

If you are on the losing team, you must hunt to get your points. Work together as a team to find the weakest links in the winning team and exploit them. Use as much cover as possible as you find your targets. Do not run out in the open area—all maps have at least one.

ROCKSTAR GAMES PRESENTS

MAX PAYNE 3

SIGNATURE SERIES GUIDE

By Tim Bogenn & Rick Barba

DK/BradyGames, a division of Penguin Group (USA) Inc.
800 East 96th Street, 3rd Floor
Indianapolis, IN 46240

ISBN 13 EAN: 978-0-7440-1381-8

Printing Code: The rightmost double-digit number is the year of the book's printing; the rightmost single-digit number is the number of the book's printing. For example, 12-1 shows that the first printing of the book occurred in 2012.

15 14 13 12 4 3 2 1

Printed in the USA.

BRADYGAMES STAFF

Publisher
Mike Degler

Editor-In-Chief
H. Leigh Davis

Licensing Manager
Christian Sumner

Marketing Director
Katie Hemlock

Operations Manager
Stacey Beheler

CREDITS

Senior Development Editor
David B. Bartley

Translations
Chris Hausermann

Book Designer
Dan Caparo

Production Designer
Tracy Wehmeyer

ACKNOWLEDGEMENTS

We'd like to thank Sam and Dan Houser, Jennifer Kolbe, and everyone at Rockstar Games for their outstanding support on this project—especially Ramon Stokes, Josh Moskovitz, Mark Adamson, Gene Overton, and Josh Needleman. Thanks also to the multiplayer team—Lloyd Thompson, Mike Hong, James Dima, Curtis Reyes, Steve Guillaume, Justin Scott, Neil McCaffrey, and Mike Nathan—your collective time and talents have helped make this guide great.